American-Russian Relations in the Far East

THE MACMILLAN COMPANY
NEW YORK • BOSTON • CHICAGO
DALLAS • ATLANTA • SAN FRANCISCO

MACMILLAN AND CO., LIMITED
LONDON • BOMBAY • CALCUTTA
MADRAS • MELBOURNE

THE MACMILLAN COMPANY
OF CANADA, LIMITED
TORONTO

AMERICAN-RUSSIAN RELATIONS
IN THE FAR EAST

By *PAULINE TOMPKINS*, PH.D.

Lecturer in Political Science, Wellesley College

THE MACMILLAN COMPANY: NEW YORK 1949

FOR MEMA

Whose vision, love, and understanding

will journey with me always, lighting the way

CONTENTS

Acknowledgments   ix
Introduction   xi

PART ONE
I.   The Tradition of Friendship   3
II.   Rivalry in Asia: The First Stage   16
III. Japanese Interlude   30

PART TWO
IV.   Prelude to Intervention: The Long Debate   47
V.   Intervention in Siberia: I   87
VI.   Intervention in Siberia: II   119
VII. Diplomacy by Protest   142
VIII. Diplomacy by Conference   162
IX.   Washington Aftermath   181
X.   Rivalry in Asia: The Second Stage   189
XI.   America and the Sino-Soviet Dispute   220
XII. The Manchurian "Incident" and American Recognition of Russia   247

PART THREE
XIII. The Fruits of Recognition   267
XIV. The Fruits of War   287
XV.   The Fruits of Anarchy   336

Appendices   340
Bibliography   398
Index   415

MAPS

Siberia During the Allied Intervention   88

American and Soviet Interests in Eastern Asia: 1949   309

ACKNOWLEDGMENTS

The author is indebted to many persons and institutions for assistance at different stages in the writing of this book.

The greatest debt is owed Miss Ruth W. Russell, who was associated with the work from its inception, and who read and criticized the entire manuscript, making valuable and constructive suggestions at each step of its progress. Whatever merit the book possesses is due in no small measure to her encouragement, patience, and quiet inspiration.

Grateful acknowledgment is made to Dr. Robert B. Stewart, Dean of the Fletcher School of Law and Diplomacy, for his unfailing interest in the project and his many kindnesses to the author. Gratitude is expressed also to the following Fletcher School professors: Dr. Frank Nowak, who acted as advisor during the period of research and original drafting, and who read and criticized the major portion of the work, and Drs. Ruhl J. Bartlett and G. Nye Steiger, who made helpful criticisms of the manuscript.

To Professor Norman J. Padelford, of the Department of Economics and Social Science, Massachusetts Institute of Technology, appreciation is expressed for time granted the author in which to pursue her research and writing, and for suggestions regarding maps. The maps were drawn by Mr. Olmstead Peet.

Part of the research in primary source materials was carried on in Washington. In this connection thanks are extended to Dr. G. Bernard Noble, Chief, Division of Historical Policy Research, Department of State, for granting access to the archives of the Department covering the period 1914–1932; to Mrs. Natalie Summers, Consultant in the Division of State Department Archives, for her suggestions, and for her first-hand descriptions of diplomatic personnel and conditions in Petrograd in 1917; and especially to Mrs. Arline V. B. Pratt, formerly of the Division of Historical Policy Research, whose unusual kindness and helpfulness greatly facilitated the author's work.

Acknowledgment is also made to Dr. St. George L. Sioussat, Chief, Division of Manuscripts, Library of Congress, for permission to use the private papers of the following men: Ray Stannard Baker, Tasker H. Bliss, William Jennings Bryan, Robert Lansing, Breckinridge Long, William Boyce Thompson, and Henry White; to Dr. Thomas P. Martin, Assistant Chief, for his many suggestions regarding the manuscript materials; and to the staff of the Division, for its unfailing courtesy and understanding assistance.

The author wishes to thank Mrs. Woodrow Wilson for granting access to the private papers of Woodrow Wilson.

Appreciation is due the authors and publishers who kindly gave permission to quote from other works.

The research was subsidized in part by the Margaret Yardley Fellowship, 1946–1947, awarded by the New Jersey State Federation of Women's Clubs. Warm thanks are gladly extended to that organization for its generous assistance.

Finally, mention should be made of the cooperation of the staff and personnel of the Widener Memorial Library and the Wellesley College Library.

The author assumes full responsibility for all opinions and interpretations, as well as for possible errors and omissions.

PAULINE TOMPKINS

Wellesley College
Wellesley, Massachusetts
29 March 1949

INTRODUCTION

It is a tragic thing to witness the atrophy of peace. The tragedy, immense in itself at any time, is overwhelming in this day and generation. For this is a fateful century in which a myriad forces have reached their culminations: man has pounded the distance from space and the hours from time; science has shrunk the room of earth, drawing a discordant globe to the uncomfortable nearness of the front parlor; the "backward" peoples and the "progressive," the "exploiting" nations and the "exploited," together with every variant of culture, creed, and color exist in a proximity which is explosive. Amongst the babel of tongues few speak alike or think alike, and although the peoples now dwell under one roof, there are worlds between them.

It will be many decades before History unravels the intricate tapestry of the twentieth century. Yet this much do we know already: this is a century of transition. The logic of scientific, political, and economic development demand the creation of a unified world. Simultaneously the blind undertow of tradition balks at evolution, and sanctifies yesterday's status quo. The world has swallowed itself, but assimilation lags.

There have been other eras of transition: the successive growth of political units from the family and clan and tribe to the emergence of the nation state; the development of economic society from the nomadic farmer, the feudal serf, and the early mercantilist to the complex economic organization spawned from the Industrial Revolution. Characteristic of every step in political and economic evolution has been a widening radius of interdependence among peoples; equally characteristic has been the resistance of "the average man," innately conservative, and of those groups to whom the enlarged society meant the relinquishing of power—economic, political, or both. Consequently, the era of transition is historically a restive, fractious era, productive of ill will and violence, but from it man has evolved a potentially better sociopolitical order.

Apart from its genetic relation to former periods of change, the twentieth century is unique in the crises confronting it. In the first place the relatively homogeneous society incorporated in each earlier stage of political and economic evolution has no counterpart today. On the contrary, the tremendous social, psychological, cultural, and religious differences among earth's inhabitants make the concept of a united world ludicrous to the generality of men, and immensely complicate its achievement. At the same time, the disproportionate advance of science has rendered obsolete any kind of world except one that is united. The dilemma is terrifying. Prior to this generation, and faced with a similar problem on a lesser scale, man could postpone his decision by retiring to the as-yet unaffected hinterland or, if he chose to obstruct the tide of change, his world could absorb the impact of conflict. Today the hinterland has vanished, and obstruction is tantamount to annihilation.

The twentieth century is, therefore, a century with an ultimatum: unite or perish. There is no middle course. We have been told this so frequently, by so many, that the frightening impact of the words has lost its power to alarm. Today both peoples and nations seem peculiarly unreceptive to the ultimatum. Instead, a trend is crystallizing in the conduct of American diplomacy which seeks, curiously, to unite a nationalistic with a global—an internationalist—foreign policy. No better illustration could be found of the utter confusion of purpose characterizing this "time of troubles." For on the one hand we have joined, and were instrumental in establishing, an international organization dedicated to the goal of world peace and cooperation. On the other hand, we have embarked upon a balance of power policy, whose highest goal is neither peace nor unity, but the preservation of the sovereign nation-state.

In the space of the past few years the concept of "equilibrium," or balanced power, has been voiced often enough to have insinuated itself quite naturally into our political thinking. It has been made to sound so reasonable, so practical, so logical, that we have accepted it with few hesitations. The fact that there is no such thing as a "balance" of power, as no one of the contestants is satisfied until it has a preponderance of strength on its side; that historically the policy has emptied itself in struggle, as one group of nations seeks to prevent power from accumulating in the hands of a rival group; that the system perpetuates anarchy and enthrones war as the final arbiter of disputes among nations—these facts have been brushed aside by advocates of the policy. In their place, they list an armory of reasons for espousing the doctrine. In the face of objections to the theory, raised by a determined minority, they reply that, like it or not, there is no alternative. And they add, wistfully perhaps, that the balance of power can guarantee American security in the years ahead.

This book was not written primarily to contradict that assertion. Nor was it written mainly to criticize the balance of power theory. Undertaken initially in fulfillment of a requirement for the degree of Doctor of Philosophy, it aspired to explore a field in diplomatic history which had been notably barren of research. It was intended to provide a hitherto unwritten chapter in the chronicle of American-Russian relations. As the research progressed, however, it became apparent that a thesis was emerging which quite transcended the author's original purpose. That thesis did not motivate, but rather grew out of the study, for the story of American-Russian diplomacy in the Far East is a history in microcosm of world politics within the ordered anarchy of the balance of power. As such, it is history with a compelling lesson, and history with a stinging indictment.

The pages which follow, therefore, contain an oblique attack on the doctrine of balanced power, the more damning because it emerges as a by-product of the central theme. In the opinion of the author, the balance of power theory is essentially spurious and misleading. It is parading before the nations under false pretenses, with glib promises of peace which lie totally beyond its competence. The sooner it is exposed, ridiculed, and rejected, the greater will be our final chance to construct a durable world order.

There may be historians, political scientists, and laymen who will draw different lessons from the story of American-Russian relations, and who will challenge the philosophy which runs as a thread throughout the succeeding chapters. Their criticisms, however, serve only to justify this book, which is not merely descriptive of an historical record, but equally of a deep personal conviction. For in these desperate, turbulent, confusing times we would nearly all agree that those with earnest convictions—the product of long thought and careful study—have a solemn and an urgent duty to proclaim them.

PART ONE

CHAPTER I

The Tradition of Friendship

I am confident that Russia (while her present monarch lives) is the most cordially friendly to us of any power on earth, will go furthest to serve us, and is most worthy of conciliation.

Thus wrote Thomas Jefferson of Tsar Alexander I.

The mutual esteem of democrat and autocrat, revealed in their lengthy correspondence in the early nineteenth century, contributed substantially to one of the most quixotic myths ever to claim the fancy of the American people: the myth of traditional American-Russian friendship. Between 1800 and 1870 a series of events provided sufficient mortar to cement the tradition in a façade so imposing that it continues to haunt us even in these days of querulous relations. But because the tradition rests on myth, and because in turn the myth is the product of wishful thinking rather than of objective reporting, the story of American-Russian amity is basically superficial. This is not to impugn the motives of either nation, or to deny the eras of "good feeling" which avowedly have existed. Instead, it is to suggest that friendship among sovereign states is ordinarily a by-product of practical politics; it tends to be essentially self-interested, therefore frequently transitory.

Generalizations are dangerous, yet one can observe in the history of international relations certain conditions for friendship which have recurred so faithfully that it is safe to make note of them here. On the negative side, nations incline toward amity when vast distances effectively isolate them except for routine commercial and diplomatic contacts, or when power-differentials (a first-class versus a second- or a third-class power) render conflict superfluous.

degree. The river-portage system of the Valdai Hills region in northwest Russia and the economic requirements of the fur trade largely accounted for Russia's expansion eastward. In the west and south the absence of natural boundaries and the desire for warm-water ports also spurred the Russian drive, but in both these areas the government of the Tsars was confronted with the determined opposition of European states. Nevertheless, until the end of the last century Russian foreign policy was essentially European— a part of the world in which the American Republic professed no political interest.

Divided by far spaces and absorbed in the problems and crises of two separate continents, the United States and Russia had early established a negative basis for mutual tolerance. These factors contributed to and helped to explain the seemingly incongruous friendship between President Jefferson and Tsar Alexander I. The warm interest expressed by the Tsar in the American democratic experiment was patently ludicrous. But the United States was not located on the Polish border; nor did the young country aspire to a role in international politics. It is questionable, however, whether the lively correspondence between the two heads of state would have thrived on this fare alone; the affirmative stimulus was supplied by joint antipathy to a third power, Great Britain.

As early as 1807 Jefferson put his finger on a major key to Russian-American friendship when he stated:

> Our nation being, like his [Alexander's], habitually neutral, our interests as to neutral rights . . . agree. And whenever conferences for peace shall take place, we are assured of a friend in him. In [questions] of neutral rights he will be with . . . every other power in the world, except England.

It was chiefly concern over neutral rights which turned the United States toward Europe and hastened the establishment of diplomatic relations between Russia and America in 1809. During the preceding quarter-century, when the new Republic was consolidating its independence, a mood of isolationism had taken hold and no effort had been made to secure Russian recognition. The effect of the Napoleonic Wars on American trade momentarily broke the magic of isolation, however, and in the pursuit of American interests Jefferson found a "friend" in Alexander.

In 1807, as a result of the Tsar's alliance with Napoleon following the Treaty of Tilsit, Russia and England were at war, and the British interdiction of Russian trade forced Alexander to look to America for commercial aid. André Daschkoff was appointed consul general at Philadelphia, and in 1809 John Quincy Adams was confirmed as the first American envoy to Russia.

If any doubt remained as to the underlying motive for American-Russian friendship it was resolved in a statement by the Russian Foreign Minister to Mr. Adams. Although opinion in Russia tended to favor England over America because of the tradition of commerce between the two states, he pointed out that

the English exclusive maritime pretensions and views of usurpation upon the rights of other nations made it essential to Russia that some great commercial state should be supported as her rival. The United States were such a state and the highest interest of Russia was to support and favor them, since by their relative situation the two powers could never be in any manner dangerous to each other.[1]

In less than a decade these words were put to their initial test. Following the conclusion of the Congress of Vienna in 1815 American interests were visibly threatened for the first time by Russian policy. Fortunately for the tradition of friendship, however, the threat failed to materialize.

The immediate issue to provoke American anxiety was the question of European intervention in Spain's rebellious South American colonies; the potential instrument of intervention was the Tsar's ill-famed Holy Alliance, consisting of Austria, Prussia, and Russia (the British having rejected an invitation to membership). Although still confessing to liberal theories Alexander was now consumed with a passion for "legitimacy." This not only implied a policy of nonrecognition of governments established through revolution, but translated into the actual history of the post-Vienna

[1] J. C. Hildt, *Early Diplomatic Negotiations of the United States with Russia* (Johns Hopkins University Studies in Historical and Political Science, Vol. 24; Baltimore: Johns Hopkins Press, 1906), p. 46.

years spelled foreign intervention as a means of restoring over-thrown monarchies.

It was more than a chimerical impulse of the enigmatic Tsar which accounted for his sedulous efforts to bring the "illegitimate" government of the United States into the Holy Alliance. Had he been successful Alexander envisaged a Russo-American entente which would have tied the two countries closely together and have made the Republic an integral part of the balance of power in Europe. As early as the summer of 1816, therefore, the American Chargé in St. Petersburg was sounded out with the purpose of detecting the views of his government. Six months later American Minister Pinckney was accorded treatment on an equality with diplomats of ambassadorial rank at the royal ball, and the Tsar was fervent in expressions of regard for the United States. In the spring of 1819 Pierre de Poletica was appointed Russian Minister in Washington. There he carried on extensive conversations with Secretary of State Adams with the dual objective of winning the Americans to the alliance and preventing them from pursuing a policy toward the South American colonies antagonistic to the European powers.

Opinion in the United States was hardly susceptible to Russian blandishments, however. Considerations of sentiment and self-interest alike precluded participation in European schemes which could only have redounded to the benefit of political reaction. Momentarily rebuffed by the failure of Poletica's mission, Alexander soon resorted to a new expedient for the achievement of the same end. In the past the American Government had sought unsuccessfully to negotiate a commercial treaty with Russia; now such a treaty was willingly offered by the Emperor. Adams shied away, however. Sensing the political motives which had dictated the Russian policy change, he concluded that for any commercial benefits received from the Tsar, a political equivalent would be exacted.

Although Russia advanced no plans for military aid to Spain in quelling the revolts in the Spanish colonies, the question of policy was discussed on two occasions at councils of European ministers, knowledge of which caused great concern in the United States. But in the latter part of 1819 Washington received assurances that the Tsar had dropped the project, and his former aversion to American recognition of the Latin states receded. Three years later the Russian Minister in Washington was notified that Russia would not intervene or lend support to Spain. The elasticity of a nation's foreign policy was thus demonstrated. The uncompromising foe of republicanism, Alexander nevertheless restricted his principles of intervention to Europe and regarded with outward calm the successful revolutions in the New World. Great Britain once again provided the explanation. Fearing a rapprochement between the Anglo-American powers on the basis of their common interest in the fate of the Spanish possessions, the Tsar determined not to risk alienating the United States over a problem so far removed from the European Continent and of such relatively minor importance to Russia.

Despite numerous reassurances, however, doubts persisted in America, and the French invasion of Spain following the popular uprising in that country produced an extreme state of nerves. Because of the continuing belief that the Holy Alliance was on the verge of forcible intervention in South America, Adams reported that President Monroe was alarmed "far beyond anything that I could have conceived possible."

A second issue between Russia and the United States increased the latter's anxiety at this time; together with the apprehension aroused by the Latin American situation, it accounted for several strongly worded statements to the Russian Minister and, in December 1823, for the enunciation of the Monroe Doctrine. In 1821 the Tsar had renewed the charter of the Russian-American Company for a twenty-year period and simultaneously had issued a ukase claiming the Pacific coast of America as far south as fifty-one degrees north latitude. All foreign vessels were warned not to proceed within one hundred Italian miles of the shore. In his protests to Baron Tuyll, Secretary Adams declared that by Russia's own admission in 1799 her boundary extended only as far south as the fifty-fifth parallel. Moreover, the American Secretary could not accept the closed-sea doctrine proclaimed by Alexander, the Pacific shores being four thousand miles apart at the fifty-first parallel. After further remonstrances the Tsar modified his position and the dispute was temporarily settled by the conclusion, in 1824, of a "Convention as to the Pacific Ocean and Northwest Coast of North America."

The Convention of 1824 was the first formal agreement entered into by Russia and the United States. It was followed in eight years by a Treaty of Commerce and Navigation. Thereafter for approximately two decades the American and Russian governments had few contacts. Relations were correspondingly "good," contributing in a negative fashion to the tradition of friendship. During these years, however, both states were occupied with problems which, while having no relation to each other, ultimately contributed a further link in the pattern of Russo-American amity. In the endless cycle of Russian foreign policy the Turkish question had again come to the fore and with it Tsarist penetration in the Near East. On the other side of the Atlantic, American statesmen were beginning the long debate which culminated in the Civil War. In each instance British action, or the threat implied in such action, served to promote American-Russian relations.

The beginning of the Crimean War in 1854 caused new fear in the United States, part of which stemmed from the American status of neutrality. This particular problem was settled satisfactorily through English recognition of the neutral principles enunciated by the United States. The British action was apparently made in an effort to forestall the possible entry of America into the war on the side of Russia. Nevertheless, London remained suspect in American eyes, largely through fear of an Anglo-French entente and subsequent intervention in the Western Hemisphere should Russia be defeated in the Crimean War. It was this apprehension, rather than any disinterested sentiment of friendship for Russia, which motivated Congressional petitions requesting the President to tender his good offices in an effort to end the war.[2]

With the outbreak of civil strife in America a few years later, Russia sided with the Union for much the same reasons that had

[2] B. P. Thomas, *Russo-American Relations, 1815–1867* (Johns Hopkins University Studies in Historical and Political Science, Vol. 48, No. 2; Baltimore: Johns Hopkins Press, 1936), pp. 115–116.

dictated American sympathy for Russia in its struggle against Britain and France. Throughout the nineteenth century the Tsarist Government had consistently supported the United States with the object of creating thereby a naval power which would offset Great Britain. The Civil War was accordingly regarded with the greatest dismay in St. Petersburg. In the early stages of the conflict top Russian officials alternated in expressing their sympathy for Lincoln's government and their fear of Anglo-French interference on behalf of the Confederate States. Early in 1861, before the actual commencement of hostilities, the Russian Minister in Washington lamented that England was "about to experience a stroke of fortune rare in the history of nations." And Baron Brunow, Russian Ambassador to Great Britain, commented:

> The English government . . . desires the separation of North America into two republics, which will watch each other jealously and counterbalance one the other. Then England, on terms of peace and commerce with both, would have nothing to fear from either; for she would dominate them, restraining them by their rival ambitions.[3]

It is difficult to compute the extent to which the Russian position, publicly stated, affected European interventionist and recognition schemes; however, the adamant stand of the Tsar was a factor in weakening the Anglo-French desire to interfere, and eventually the plans were dropped.

Russian sympathy for the Union cause appeared to reach its height in September 1863 when two Russian naval squadrons put in at San Francisco and New York with alleged "sealed instructions" to aid the North in case of French-British intervention. The reaction of the Lincoln Administration and the public was one of gratitude, as unquestioning as it was unqualified. The prevailing feeling for Russia was aptly couched in the words of Secretary Seward three months later: "In regard to Russia, the case is a plain one. She has our friendship, in every case, in preference to any other European power, simply because she always wishes us well, and leaves us to conduct our affairs as we think best." Not until 1915, when Professor Frank Golder published the results of his

[3] *Ibid.*, pp. 127–128.

examination of Tsarist archives, was the real motive behind the visit of the Russian fleet made known.[4] Paralleling the Civil War in America was a revolt in Russian Poland, and Alexander II, fearful lest Anglo-French protests against his repressive measures eventuate in war, had ordered his fleet to American ports to escape potential blockade by the British navy. Further proof of the purely Russian motives behind the fleet's visit is found in a communication from Foreign Minister Gorchakov to Admiral Popov, commanding officer of the ships stationed at San Francisco, in the winter of 1863–1864. In reply to the admiral's suggestions for protecting the west coast city in the event of an attack by Confederate ships, Gorchakov stated that he expected the Russian officer to maintain strict neutrality in all contingencies.

In 1867 the Russian Government sold Alaska to the United States for $7,200,000, and since then numerous theories have been advanced to account for the transfer. That Russian officials were contemplating the sale as early as ten years prior to its consummation indicates a variety of motives behind the project. The Russian-American Company, which had exploited the Alaskan coast commercially for several decades, entered on a period of decline subsequent to 1840 which made the territory increasingly undesirable financially. In 1857 both Stoeckl, the Russian Minister to the United States, and the Grand Duke Constantine, Alexander's brother, began exerting pressure on Gorchakov to negotiate a sale. Constantine stressed the financial angle, while Stoeckl viewed the continuing Russian possession of Alaska as a dangerous source of friction between the Tsar's Government and the United States. Moreover, in his eyes the Crimean War had amply proved the military weakness of Russia's hold on Alaska. Britain, fearing a possible sale of the territory to the United States at that time, had agreed to its neutralization throughout the war, but there was no guarantee that its neutrality would be respected in any future Anglo-Russian conflict. It would be far better, Stoeckl concluded, to sell Alaska to the American Government than to risk its loss to Britain.

[4] See Frank A. Golder, "The Russian Fleet and the Civil War," *American Historical Review*, Vol. XX, pp. 801–812.

Sentiment for the purchase had been voiced spasmodically in America for several years prior to 1867, finding some supporters in the Congress; but it was Secretary Seward who provided the driving power and who, together with Stoeckl, rushed the sale in that year. "Seward's folly" was ascribed by many contemporaries to the government's desire to pay off the debt of gratitude owed Russia because of her sympathy during the Civil War. While this feeling did not motivate the State Department, it did help to dispose the American people favorably toward the Alaska purchase, and in so doing facilitated treaty ratification. Seward's own motives were less altruistic. A farsighted expansionist, he had prophesied America's role as a Pacific power as early as 1846. Keenly interested in the Asiatic trade of the United States, he viewed Alaska as a natural naval outpost which would serve to protect American Far Eastern interests.

In short, Seward purchased Alaska as a long-term investment which would one day produce dividends of a military, political, and economic character. Conversely, Russia sold the territory primarily as a means of ridding herself of a financial and military burden. Throughout the entire proceedings the kindling power of Great Britain exerted only a minor influence on the final sale, and the tradition of American-Russian friendship was simply an accessory to the fact—albeit a most helpful one.

It was from fabric as fortuitous and coincidental as this that the pattern of American-Russian amity was cut, but while it is possible to assert that a genuine, if somewhat naïve, affection persisted for a period of years,[5] it is equally true that the foundations of this friendliness were extremely shallow. Indeed, the high-water mark of good relations between the two powers was reached during the American Civil War and at the time of the Alaska purchase; thereafter several factors contributed to a gradual decline in the tradition of friendship.

The ideological discrepancy between autocratic and democratic

[5] An example of the popular esteem for Russia was seen in the congratulatory resolution of the American Congress on the occasion of the Tsar's narrow escape from an attempted assassination. This was accompanied by the mission to Russia of the Assistant Secretary of the Navy, Gustavus Fox, in August and September, 1866.

government was one of these; but this, in turn, achieved importance only as increasing contacts between America and Russia were productive of friction. The harsh treatment accorded to Russian Jews and the uncompromising refusal of the Tsar's Government to grant visas to naturalized American Jews aroused deep resentment in the United States and resulted in the abrogation by Congress, in 1911, of the Commercial Treaty of 1832.[6] The Jewish pogroms were matched in this period by a further manifestation of Russian autocracy, namely the ruthless measures of the infamous Russian secret police, adopted in answer to the growing popular demand for liberal reforms.

While such instances served to create an intense emotional antipathy toward Russia, they were buttressed and abetted by two events of signal importance which led, in the early 1900's, to a striking reorientation in the historic relations of the two states. First, in the closing years of the nineteenth century Russia and America turned their energies toward Asia, where their respective interests conflicted sharply for the first time. Simultaneously, the major premise on which American-Russian friendship had rested—common hostility to Great Britain—was in process of dissolution as the Anglo-American powers cautiously launched a policy of rapprochement. Despite the Anglo-Russian entente of 1907 and the suspicion with which the Far Eastern powers (including Britain) regarded American maneuvers in Asia during these years, the fundamental policies which had for centuries pitted Russia and England against each other made their entente a tenuous one, while Anglo-American joint interests increased apace. Thus the decade of the nineties was an auspicious one. Marking the end of one century and the begin-

---

[6] 62d Congress, 2d Session, House Committee on Foreign Affairs, Report No. 179, *The Abrogation of the Russian Treaty*, 1911. The demand for abrogation was based on Article I which stated, in part: "The inhabitants of their respective States shall mutually have liberty to enter the ports, places, and rivers of the territories of each party, wherever foreign commerce is permitted. They shall be at liberty to sojourn and reside in all parts whatsoever of said territories, in order to attend to their affairs, and they shall enjoy . . . the same security and protection as natives of the country . . ." W. M. Malloy, *Treaties, Conventions, International Acts, Protocols and Agreements Between the United States of America and Other Powers* (Washington: G.P.O., 1910), Vol. II, pp. 1514–1519.

ning of another it witnessed the conclusion of the first act in the Russian-American drama. The conditions for friendship existing between 1800 and 1870 had vanished, and without them the tradition of friendship was meaningless.

When the curtain lifted again on American-Russian relations, the setting was one of rivalry, and the scene, the Far East.

CHAPTER II

Rivalry in Asia:
The First Stage

For approximately one hundred years following the defeat of Napoleon, Europe was spared a general war. The Congress of Vienna, in laying the ghost of French ambitions, ushered in a new era, the significance of which extended far beyond the European Continent. The age of modern imperialism was at hand. Released from total absorption in Europe's politics, the powers— first England and France, to be followed by Russia and Germany— launched forth on a period of expansion which dominated much of the nineteenth century, created new tensions and rivalries, and reached its apogee in 1914.

An immediate result of this new era was the forceful opening of China and Japan respectively to the pillage and the promise of the West. Between 1840 and 1895 China, with its great sprawling land mass of more than four million square miles and an estimated population of close to five hundred million, became the victim of systematic foreign aggression. Unable to wrench itself free from the centuries-old influence of its ancient culture and loath to adjust to the new conditions posed by the intrusion of the West, China was saved from utter disintegration less by its own efforts than by the debilitating rivalries of the states which plundered it.

Alone among the Western powers the United States held aloof both from physical pressure on China and from the annexation of Chinese territory. Ideologically averse to a policy of imperialism and foreign commitments, unwilling to expend its energies in competition with more powerful imperialist states, the American Government sought to protect its economic and commercial interests in China by a formula which, first stated in 1844 as the most-favored-nation clause, evolved at the end of the century into the open-door doctrine. The effect of the American policy was to place Washington on the side of China in the latter's efforts to resist the spheres of influence encroachments of third powers or, if resistance were impractical, to assure the United States of the privileges of the open-door in the newest concession areas. In concrete terms this came increasingly to mean the automatic and even predictable opposition of America to whatever nation constituted the greatest threat to Chinese sovereignty at a given moment. Since the closing years of the nineteenth century this policy has involved the United States in sharp diplomatic conflict with Russia and in war with Japan.

In marked contrast to the stubborn resistance of China to modernization of its institutions, the Japanese Government adapted itself, albeit reluctantly and after a severe internal crisis, to the realities which confronted it subsequent to the visit of Commodore Perry in 1853. Although forced to submit to the superior power of the Western states for a number of years, Japanese statesmen were able, through astute diplomacy and imitation of the West, to pave the way for the recognition of Japan as a Pacific power before the end of the nineteenth century. No sooner had the diplomatic spadework to this end been achieved than the armies of Nippon made their claim to military equality with the West by launching a major war against China in 1894. Ostensibly waged over a protracted dispute concerning the status of Korea, the growing fear of Russia was also a factor in the Japanese decision. That this fear was justified was apparent when the imperialistic Treaty of Shimonoseki (1895) was challenged by the European nations under Russian leadership. In no position to defy the powers, Japan accordingly modified the terms of the treaty.

The Tsarist Government of Russia had penetrated to the shores of the north Pacific as early as 1637. Fifty years later, after a long struggle with the newly established Manchus for jurisdiction of the Amur River, Russia sued for peace. The Treaty of Nerchinsk in 1689 was the first treaty entered into by China with a European country, and its territorial terms were observed for over a century and a half. Under them, the land which later comprised Manchuria fell to China, Russia was forced to withdraw beyond the watershed of the Amur, and trans-frontier trade was provided for.

By the mid-nineteenth century eastward expansion again brought Russia and China into contact, this time with results more favorable to the Tsar. Taking advantage of China's internal weakness which stemmed from the enervating Taiping Rebellion and of a second war against England and France, Russia seized the territory north of the Amur River. This was recognized by China in the Treaty of Aigun in 1858. A fortnight later, when Britain and France concluded their peace settlements at Tientsin, the Russian envoy assumed the benign role of China's friend, urging the allies to moderate their demands. In 1860 Russia was repaid for her benevolence in the Treaty of Peking, which ceded the territory known as the Maritime Province to the Tsar. There in 1861 Vladivostok was founded. Superiority in arms and some adroit diplomacy had thus combined to make Russia a Far Eastern power.

Japan's manifest ambition for a similar role, as revealed in her war against China in 1894, was hardly calculated to appeal to the Tsar. On the other hand, the Russian-inspired protest of the European powers over the original Sino-Japanese peace treaty in no way assuaged either Japan's fear of Russia or her Asiatic aspirations.

The conclusion of the Sino-Japanese War heralded a distinct turning point in Far Eastern international relations. In the first place, the sudden victory of Japan precipitated a new cycle of European imperialism in China, resulting in a spheres-of-influence-spheres-of-interest policy in which the rival states amassed huge chunks of territory under the questionable pseudonym of "leases." Secondly, not only Japan but also England found its Asiatic designs challenged by Tsarist aggressiveness, a factor of some importance in the orientation of British policy toward Japan after 1895. And third, Russian foreign policy now centered on Asia for a full decade, with results that distinctly alienated American friendship and eventuated in the Russo-Japanese War of 1904–1905.

One of the positive factors motivating the Asiatic orientation of the Tsar's policy was the desire to continue the Trans-Siberian Railroad to the Pacific. In return for services rendered China in ameliorating the peace terms imposed by Japan in 1895 the Manchu Government agreed to the establishment of the Russo-Chinese

Bank, the charter of which was granted to the Committee of the Siberian Railroad. In answer to the Chinese insistence that the road be in the hands of a private company, the Chinese Eastern Railroad Corporation was formed and under the terms of the secret Li-Lobanov Treaty of 1896 China ceded to the corporation the strip of land along which the railway was to run and granted it full policing and other authority. Two years later Russia obtained from China a twenty-five-year lease on Port Arthur and Dalny (Dairen) and on the Liaotung peninsula north as far as Pitzewo and Polanpu.

The strategic position of Russia in relation to North China, and the projects for railroad construction through Chinese territory aroused the serious apprehensions of the Japanese, who were already deeply concerned over Russian advances in Korea. It had been assumed by Japan, following her victory over China, that her role of "protector and adviser" to Korea was assured. Moreover, under the Nishi-Rosen Agreement of 1898 both Russia and Japan had recognized Korean independence and the Tsar had acknowledged the predominance of Japan's economic rights in the peninsula. Russia soon violated the spirit of the convention, however, and this contributed to the further deterioration of relations between the two countries.

It was at this time that the United States, emerging victorious from war with Spain, became a more active participant in Pacific affairs through the annexation of the Philippine Islands, and thereby confronted the Tsar with another potential rival in the Far East. There was little danger prior to the First World War that this rivalry would produce military conflict between the former "friends"; for although America aspired briefly to an expansionist program, she was still encumbered with the millstones of traditional "isolationism" and "non-entanglement" and was no more willing during this period than in 1931 to wage war on China's behalf or in her own economic interest. Nevertheless, Russian statesmen were sufficiently foresighted to sense the importance of their new antagonist and to resent American intrusion, while Britain and Japan viewed the United States at least as a psychological ally in their resistance to Russian Far Eastern pretensions. In the suc-

ceeding years the American Government strove to uphold a balance of power in Asia by maintaining China's territorial integrity, a policy which precluded lasting commitments to any of the interested states and contributed notably to the recurrent diplomatic clashes which henceforth marked American-Russian (and later American-Japanese) relations.

The first evidence of Washington's intentions on China's behalf was the formal enunciation of the open-door doctrine in 1899 and 1900.[1] This was followed a few months later by American efforts to restrict Russian imperialism as a consequence of the Boxer uprising in China. Under the direction of War Minister Kuropatkin the Russian military clique had taken advantage of the Chinese anti-foreign revolt to seize southern Manchuria. But although the United States resented Tsarist activity it was unwilling to fortify its policy with weapons other than those of diplomacy. Furthermore, the apparent acceptance by America of the primacy of Russian interests in northern China greatly reduced the effectiveness even of diplomatic protests.[2]

On the other hand the Japanese Government, greatly strengthened by the conclusion of its alliance with Britain in 1902, prepared to enforce its Far Eastern program by whatever means circumstances should warrant. Indeed, the Anglo-Japanese Alliance was a major factor in the Sino-Russian treaty of April 1902, in which the Tsar recognized Chinese sovereignty over Manchuria and agreed to withdraw his forces within eighteen months. Failure by Russia to honor

[1] In the previous year the American Ambassadors in England, Germany, and Russia were instructed to request from each government a declaration, the essence of which was that (1) it would not interfere with any treaty ports located within a foreign sphere of interest, (2) only the Chinese Government would collect duties, (3) harbor dues and railroad charges of the interested power would be nondiscriminatory. Identic instructions were sent in November to the American Minister in Japan and to the Ambassadors in France and Italy.

[2] On May 1, 1902, Secretary Hay wrote to President Roosevelt: "We are not in any attitude of hostility towards Russia in Manchuria. On the contrary, we recognize her exceptional position in northern China. What we have been working for two years to accomplish . . . is that, no matter what happens eventually in northern China and Manchuria, the United States shall not be placed in any worse position than while the country was under the unquestioned domination of China."

this treaty produced a comment from Secretary Hay reflective of the apathy of American opinion at the time. In April 1903 he stated: "I take it for granted that Russia knows as we do that we will not fight over Manchuria, for the simple reason that we cannot . . . we could never get a treaty through the Senate, the object of which was to check Russian aggression." In contrast to this attitude Japanese disturbance was extreme and in the late summer and autumn of 1903 an effort was made on Tokyo's initiative to reach a *modus vivendi* which would recognize the respective rights of the two states in both Manchuria and Korea. The refusal of Nicholas to compromise, based on a heady imperialism and an unquestioning belief in the superiority of Tsarist armed might over that of Japan, in a very real sense invited the disaster which followed.

On February 8, 1904, two days after severing diplomatic relations and four days prior to a declaration of war, Japan attacked the Russian fleet off Port Arthur. In taking this decisive step the Japanese Government was motivated by several factors, including assurances of German neutrality, the existence of the alliance with Great Britain, the desire to strike before Russian strength was more firmly entrenched in Manchuria, and the attitude of the United States. According to German sources,[3] the American role in encouraging Japan ("although perhaps unwittingly") was of real significance; for despite diplomacy of a purely verbal and at times inconsistent quality, Washington's opposition to the Russian Manchurian program was stated frequently over a period of several years, and of this opposition Japan was well aware. Of more immediate bearing was the American assertion on January 12, 1904, that in case of war its policy would be benevolent toward Japan.

President Roosevelt's personal feelings were expressed following Japan's victory in the initial encounter with the Russian fleet. On February 10, 1904, the President wrote his son:

For several years Russia has behaved very badly in the Far East, her attitude toward all nations, including us, but especially toward Japan,

[3] The German sources are given in Edward H. Zabriskie, *American-Russian Rivalry in the Far East* (Philadelphia: University of Pennsylvania Press, 1946), p. 101n, as Alfred Vagts, *Deutschland und die Vereinigten Staaten in der Weltpolitik*, Vol. II, p. 1175, and *Die Grosse Politik*, Vol. XIX, p. 5945.

being grossly overbearing. We had no sufficient cause for war with her. Yet I was apprehensive lest if she at the outset whipped Japan on the sea she might assume a position well-nigh intolerable toward us. I thought Japan would probably whip her on the sea . . . and between ourselves . . . I was thoroughly well pleased with the Japanese victory, for Japan is playing our game.

"Our game" was, in essence, the balance of power. In President Roosevelt's planning the balance was to be restored by allowing Japan to pursue her interests in Korea (so long as American concessions were recognized), by approving a postwar position for Russia in Manchuria (albeit with American commercial rights guaranteed), and by trusting in a sufficiently long drawn-out war so that both powers would be exhausted at its conclusion. In such a contingency neither state would exercise a preponderance of influence in Asia; instead, each would continue to check the other, and American interests would benefit.

Throughout the conflict the pro-Japanese alignment of American sympathies was so obvious that the Russian press, reflecting Foreign Office opinion, frequently lashed out with indignation at what it labeled an American-instigated war. The unfriendliness which marked American-Russian contacts was heightened at this same time by the anti-Jewish activities of the Tsar's Government, which had evoked such horror and disgust in the United States. However, by the end of 1904 the emphasis in Washington began to shift somewhat. Tokyo, whose success had been applauded earlier, now threatened to replace Russian dominance on the Asiatic mainland. Therefore at the end of the war Roosevelt urged a policy of moderation on the victor; and throughout the negotiations at Portsmouth, American opinion, taking its cue from the President, inclined steadily toward Russia.

Although the Treaty of Portsmouth showed the effect of Roosevelt's personal diplomacy, subsequent history indicates that the potentialities, rather than the actualities, of the settlement were of greater significance, and in these Japan remained the principal gainer. Proceeding at once to consolidate her newly attained position Japan concluded the Komura Treaty with China in December 1905; together with the terms of Portsmouth this established the basis for Nippon's claims in Manchuria. Simultaneously Tokyo made rapid strides in its Korean program. A convention in November 1905 placed the Japanese in full charge of Korean foreign relations; the protests of the latter, based on Japan's extortionist methods, were of no avail and, in fact, the Western governments politely withdrew their representatives from Seoul. The policy of Japan reached its natural culmination in the annexation of Korea in 1910. The reaction of the powers, one of looking the other way, was based on earlier commitments which had acknowledged the primacy of Tokyo's interests.

Although the Manchurian concessions which had accrued to Japan had received the official sanction of the Roosevelt Administration, and although Washington had likewise acceded to Tokyo's role in Korea,[4] the United States was unprepared to accept Japanese hegemony on the Asiatic mainland. Consequently, after an initial period of appeasement the ever widening radius of Tokyo's incursions in Manchuria evoked strong displeasure in America. This in turn led to an estrangement in the hitherto cordial relations of the two countries while in no way altering Japan's ambitions. Moreover, Washington's protests, in the main, were unsupported by any of the European foreign offices.

Seen in perspective, American Far Eastern policy throughout this period can perhaps be most charitably described as youthful. Historically the United States had confined its interests in Asia to those of a predominantly commercial nature, and in the nineteenth century the twin principles of the open-door and the most-favored-nation had sufficed to protect the American position. By the close of the century, however, the tactics of the other China powers had become increasingly imperialistic and it was quixotic to assume that the purely rhetorical diplomacy of Washington could guarantee American trading rights in the Far East. Nor was this the case. Another nation besides the United States had stood to benefit by open-door diplomacy; indeed, the original idea was as much British as American. To the former, whose commercial deal-

---

[4] Through the Taft-Katsura exchange of notes in 1905 the United States had recognized Japanese predominance and eventual suzerainty over Korea, in return for which Japan renounced any aggressive aims in the Philippines.

ings with China exceeded all other countries, the concept of equal trading opportunity exerted more appeal than that of partitioning China (thereby restricting the radius of financial operations). British support of the open-door doctrine had been in reality the decisive factor in the grudging respect initially accorded it by the other powers, for behind Whitehall stood the strong arm of the British navy. After the turn of the century, however, Great Britain had become increasingly engrossed with problems in Europe and proportionately less effective as a guarantor of the open-door. But the United States, despite its imperialist excursion in the Philippines, had remained essentially continental-minded and pacifist; apparently failing to comprehend that the worn clichés and platitudes of paper diplomacy could not stand of themselves, Washington had continued to iterate them and, on their tender strength alone, had sought to keep one foot in the China door.

Through a policy of "balanced antagonisms" President Roosevelt had aspired to uphold American interests in Asia. Thus, when Russia had appeared as the greatest threat to those interests, the United States had thrown its support to Japan and had accepted at face value the latter's glib assurances with regard to the open-door. But Japan's startling victory over Russia had placed her on the threshold of empire, and it was sheer wishful thinking to suppose that the Japanese either would or could simply shut off the dynamics of imperialism when confronted with such stunning opportunities for expansion. Moreover, by an ironic twist the very mildness of the Portsmouth Treaty (added to Russian fear of further Japanese inroads in Manchuria)—instead of establishing Russia as a balance to Japan as President Roosevelt had hoped— made the Tsar willing to seek agreement with Tokyo as a means of protecting his own Far Eastern interests. In the end, therefore, Roosevelt's policy backfired. Not only was the balance of power after the Russo-Japanese War shortlived, but the antagonism of those two nations was increasingly directed not at each other, but at the United States. In this one fact may be found a major clue to American-Russian relations in the Far East from 1905 until the eve of the First World War, for instead of one Asiatic rival America was now faced with two, neither of which was willing to respect the open-door in China and, by the same token, American commercial interests in Eastern Asia.

Of exceeding importance to the Far Eastern pattern after the Russo-Japanese War was the mounting crisis in Europe. In proportion as the powers were forced to concentrate their energies on international problems nearer home Japan found its position in Asia progressively enhanced. Moreover, the Triple Entente temporarily relaxed the historic rivalry between Russia and England; this, plus the apparent willingness of Britain and France to give Japan free scope in Manchuria in order to divert Tokyo's attention from Anglo-French holdings in China proper and Southeast Asia, meant a virtual open season for the Russo-Japanese imperial combine. The one potential threat to their Asiatic schemes was the United States, but Washington could muster only the encrusted diplomatic harangues of earlier days for the protection and furtherance of its Far Eastern commercial interests. These served not to moderate, but to aggravate, the policies of both Japan and Russia.

In view of these drastically changed conditions, the American Government might theoretically have been expected to do one of three things: implement its China policy by force, encourage a third power (or powers) to reestablish the balance in Asia, withdraw its influence from the Asiatic mainland. But while developments after 1905 required a shift in American policy, nothing definite was forthcoming. The first and third alternatives were never entertained by the State Department; as for the second, the European nations were now unwilling to risk conflict in the Far East and China was still politically impotent. Consequently Washington pursued a zigzag policy which, while underscored throughout by references to the open-door and the territorial integrity of China, lacked the ballast of military might, and therefore vacillated in its application according to the exigencies of every new situation.

In 1907 American financial efforts, revolving around the plans of E. H. Harriman for a global transportation system, were countered when they sought to penetrate Manchuria by the first of a series of Russo-Japanese treaties. Ever since the Portsmouth settlement the two states had been exploring the bases for a mutually satisfactory agreement concerning Manchuria, and despite a few sidelong glances in the direction of a pro-American alignment the Tsar found an understanding with Japan desirable in the interests of his Far Eastern and European policy. The significance of the 1907 treaty lay in the secret document, in which Russia admitted Japanese claims to Korea and interests in southern Manchuria, while Japan recognized the Russian position in northern Manchuria and Outer Mongolia.

The continued efforts of an American business group to advance money to China for railroad construction and industrial development in Manchuria were again checked by Japan a year later through the Root-Takahira exchange of notes.[5] The consequent refusal of the State Department to assume any responsibility for the Harriman project resulted in its further postponement, and ultimately the plan collapsed.

Following the inauguration of the Taft Administration, Washington again assumed a more vigorous Far Eastern policy. For a short interval in the early autumn of 1909 it even appeared that a rapprochement with Russia was not impossible; new Japanese ultimata to China were disconcerting both to the Tsar's Government and to the American investment group, and the former expressed an interest in an entente with Washington as a means of restricting Japanese imperialism in Asia. However, the United States gave no indication of pursuing the somewhat nebulous Russian suggestion; conversely, it embarked on a course which further alienated both Russia and Japan and drove them into closer accord. Through the provocative Knox proposals for the neutralization of all railroads

[5] The mild Japanese suggestion that Tokyo and Washington reaffirm the open-door principle in China carried with it a double meaning for Tokyo. Although the two states referred to the open-door, the qualifying word "territorial" was omitted from the phrase "the integrity of China," and in pledging to maintain "the existing status quo" they apparently expanded its meaning to include the whole Pacific area, rather than China proper. According to Professor Willoughby this was the most unsatisfactory element in the Root-Takahira exchange, for the "existing status quo" in the Pacific "could easily be construed as an acceptance by the United States of claims of right implicit in various acts of Japan in Manchuria since the Portsmouth Treaty." Westel W. Willoughby, *Foreign Rights and Interests in China* (Baltimore: Johns Hopkins Press, 1927), Vol. I, p. 175.

in Manchuria the United States sought to promote American investments in China by implementing the open-door policy. The proposals were made in the form of alternative suggestions. The first would have provided for an international loan to China, thus enabling her to purchase the Russian and Japanese lines, which would then be managed by the lending powers. The second plan concerned the railroad between Chinchow and Aigun, proposed a joint British-American effort to finance and construct it, but included an invitation to other interested states to participate in the project.

The Knox plan was foredoomed by the very situation which had prompted it. American Far Eastern policy had historically depended on the support of other powers, but the Manchurian picture in particular, and European conditions in general, rendered such support extremely unlikely in 1909. Neither France nor England would consider cooperation with the State Department without Russo-Japanese approval, and this was manifestly absent. The inalterable opposition of Tokyo to any scheme which threatened its predominance in southern Manchuria and the deep suspicion within Russia of American motives accounted for the two powers' unequivocal rejection of the proposal, and expedited in 1910 the conclusion of the second Russo-Japanese treaty.[6] Any illusions concerning the open-door and the integrity of China were effectively dispelled by this agreement, which omitted all reference to them. By the terms of the published document the signatories bound themselves to uphold the status quo in Manchuria, which obviously meant their existent spheres and concessions in that province. The unpublished treaty provided for the increment of their rights in Manchuria and carefully delimited their respective zones of exploitation.

The Far Eastern policy of the United States, which had aided in promoting the Russo-Japanese accords of 1907 and 1910, was equally an abettor of the next secret treaty of 1912. On the heels of the collapse of the neutralization scheme the State Department

[6] Russia and Japan were moving toward this treaty well before the American proposals had been made, but the latter hastened its consummation and provided the principal target at which it was aimed. See the quotation from *Novoe Vremya* (*New Times*) of July 7, 1910, in Zabriskie, *op. cit.*, p. 170.

encouraged China to request an American loan which would facilitate Chinese currency reform and, more importantly, aid in the industrialization of Manchuria; but the inability of the United States to finance unilaterally the full sum of $50,000,000, the desire of the Wall Street bankers for associates and the simultaneous requests of France, Germany, and England to participate in the project resulted in making the loan an international one. Russia and Japan, after unremitting pressure, were admitted to the loan in June 1912; but their victory did not end there. Each made its entry contingent on the acceptance, by the original four members of the consortium, of conditions which were an open mockery of the open-door principle and effectively nullified whatever hope the American Government may have had of checking Russo-Japanese predominance in Manchuria. Japan excepted from the scope of the loan her "special rights and interests" in "south Manchuria and Inner Mongolia adjacent to south Manchuria," while Russia insisted that her participation should not "operate to the prejudice of the special rights and interests" she claimed "in the regions of northern Manchuria, Mongolia, and western China."

Less than a month later the ultimate reaction to what had originally been an American-instigated loan proposal was witnessed in the third Russo-Japanese treaty. In defining yet more explicitly the areas in Manchuria which each reserved for its exclusive control and in elaborating spheres of influence in Mongolia, Russia and Japan were effectively placing another block in their Chinese wall and another obstacle to American entry therein. The whole situation was not without irony, for in March 1913 President Wilson reversed the Taft policy by withdrawing support from the American financial group.[7] A month later, when the loan agreement was finally concluded, the United States was not represented.

Between 1800 and 1914 the United States had attained the stature of a world power. While this fact was of the highest significance in determining American foreign policy in the twentieth

[7] For the reasons impelling this shift in policy see *Papers Relating to the Foreign Relations of the United States* (Washington: G.P.O.), 1913, pp. 170–171; F. V. Field, *American Participation in the China Consortiums* (Chicago: University of Chicago Press, 1931), pp. 110–116.

century, it was of equal importance in explaining that policy prior to 1914. Lacking the political and diplomatic maturity of the European powers, physically removed from the festering centers of international rivalries and thus from the necessity of growing up quickly (as Japan had been forced to do), the American people and Government pursued policies in which idealism, opportunism, and luck mingled interchangeably. Thus until 1895 the general relations of the United States and Russia had been characterized by a friendly tolerance which was substantiated by distance and by a mutual antagonism to Great Britain. After 1895, however, the amity of the two powers began a descending spiral which reached its nadir shortly before the First World War. The Chinese Empire, drawing the nations of the West into its vortex, became a focal point of world intrigue and of American-Russian hostility at the turn of the century. The imperial ambitions of Russia, matched and eventually surpassed by those of Japan, were challenged by various American sorties which, under the dual banners of enlightened self-interest and the open-door principle, pricked, goaded, and irritated the Russo-Japanese bloc while in no wise swerving it from its purpose. By 1914 a series of diplomatic defeats had been sustained by the United States, and its role as an Asiatic power seemed less auspicious than at any time in its foreign career. Moreover, by 1914 the last vestiges of traditional American-Russian friendship had disappeared. Thereafter with few exceptions relations between the two states were determined by the more realistic compulsions of the balance of power. *2 8 7 9 9*

CHAPTER III

Japanese Interlude

The First World War presented the Japanese Empire with "the opportunity of a thousand years," an opportunity which was seized upon with alacrity by the astute politicians in Tokyo and which, in consequence, materially altered the very fundament of the power structure in eastern Asia. Although contributing least among all the major allies to ultimate victory, Japan harvested by far the most bounteous crop. The implications of these facts, both for the position of the United States in the Orient and for American relations with Russia, were far-reaching. The initial aloofness of the Wilson Administration from Asiatic problems, as evidenced in the American withdrawal from the six-power consortium in 1913, had now to be replaced by a deep concern over the dramatically changed situation in the Far East. The Western powers, increasingly absorbed with the European crisis prior to the war, had literally gone home to wage their battles in August 1914. Accordingly there was no nation other than the United States to preserve some sort of equilibrium in Asia as against the imperialistic ambitions of Japan. In assuming the role thus cast upon it, America automatically became the arch antagonist of the Japanese expansionists. Notwithstanding a temporary hiatus pursuant to the Washington Conference, the latent hostility between the two states dominated their relations until the attack on Pearl Harbor in December 1941, with its now historic sequel.

The acuteness of American-Japanese rivalry was seconded by the mutual suspicions of Petrograd and Tokyo. Regardless of the series of treaties between them (to be matched in 1916 by still another) even the Tsar realized that his empire in the East was subject during the war to the pleasure of Japan, and in the years following the Russian revolutions the avidity of the Japanese for a Siberian foothold was but poorly disguised.

It is in the light of their respective policies toward Japan (which, in turn, were determined by its newly predominant position) that one finds a major clue to American-Russian relations in the Far East after 1914. There were other factors involved, but the existence of Japan as a potential threat to the Far Eastern interests of both countries exerted an inevitable influence on their interrelations.

Between 1914 and 1917 Japan took five notable strides on the path to empire. The first was directed superficially to the fulfillment of obligations under the Anglo-Japanese Alliance. In mid-August 1914 an ultimatum was dispatched to the German Government containing a two-fold demand that German armed vessels be withdrawn from Asiatic waters and that the leased territory of Kiachow be delivered to Japan "with a view to eventual restoration of the same to China." On August 23, lacking a satisfactory response from Berlin, Japan declared war.

Even before the Japanese ultimatum, the United States, cognizant of the potential threat to the balance of power should Asia be embroiled in the war, had made a fruitless attempt to neutralize the Far East. However, Washington was unprepared to assume any positive responsibility for the safeguarding of China's interests, a fact which was made unequivocally plain in a cable to Minister Reinsch under date of November 4, 1914. While reiterating the sincerity of America's friendship for China, and the desire to promote "by peaceful methods" the welfare of the Chinese people, the State Department confessed: "it would be quixotic in the extreme to allow the question of China's territorial integrity to entangle the United States in international difficulties." [1]

Given the qualified verbal protests of the Wilson Government and the forced acquiescence of Japan's European Allies, it was not strange that Nippon's imperialists proceeded apace with their plans. To the Chinese request for enlightenment when Japanese forces had occupied the Kiachow-Tsinan Railroad, Tokyo made forthright response: "The aim of the Imperial Government is not only

[1] *Papers Relating to the Foreign Relations of the United States* (hereinafter cited as *For. Rel.*), 1914, Supplement, pp. 170–171.

the overthrow of the base possessed by the enemy, but also to cause the control and administration of this inseparable railroad to fall into our possession." And two months later Baron Kato, in answer to an interpellation on Sino-Japanese relations in the lower legislative house, denied the existence "of any agreement with any foreign nation by which Japan was bound to retrocede [Kaiochow] to China." [2]

Thus by 1915 Tokyo had made an impressive beginning in the policy which a later decade would fancifully describe as "the Greater East Asia Co-Prosperity Sphere." Participation in the war on the Allied side had yielded the plum of German concessions in China. To these Japan now determined to add further conquests, and accordingly the second step in the imperial timetable was taken. This consisted of the infamous Twenty-one Demands, first presented on January 18, 1915, and consummated in truncated form by the treaties of four months later.

On January 23 Paul Reinsch had advised Washington of the "long list of demands" and the secrecy surrounding their precise character, and in succeeding days he had expressed grave apprehension lest the open-door be unqualifiedly shut if Japan were left unopposed. The hesitation of both the State Department and President Wilson to act unilaterally in blocking Japan is apparent from the documents of the period. However, the self-interest of the United States demanded that some effort be made on China's behalf, and this was done initially in the Bryan note to Tokyo of March 13.[3] In the course of the preceding month the rough content of the Twenty-one Demands had reached Washington and knowledge of their nature hastened the decision to intervene diplomatically. In essence the Japanese demands, dealing with Shantung, South Manchuria and Eastern Inner Mongolia, Central

    [2] *Ibid.*, pp. 192, 206.
    [3] *For. Rel.*, 1915, pp. 105–111. This note developed from a letter to Wilson, dated February 22, in which Bryan elaborated at length his views on the Asiatic situation. In the letter appeared the following rather amazing statement: "I am not sure but that it would be worth while for China to agree to the cession of Manchuria to Japan if, by doing so, she could secure freedom as to the rest of the country . . ." *For. Rel*, The Lansing Papers, 1914–1920, Vol. II, pp. 405–407.

China, and a further group of miscellaneous items, far exceeded the crassest imperialism of the West by literally undermining the inner bases of Chinese sovereignty. Notwithstanding their character, Bryan's protest in March left much to be desired, concentrating on the last group and practically granting Tokyo a free hand in Shantung and in those very areas which had been the subject of the Russo-Japanese treaties before the war.

On May 11, after Washington had been rebuffed in its attempt to rally Japan's European Allies to a joint protest, the State Department dispatched a second note to Tokyo, shorter, clearer, and stronger than the first. Thus it was stated that the United States could not recognize "any agreement or undertaking" between Japan and China which impaired American treaty rights, China's political or territorial integrity, or the open-door policy. The influence of this note upon the form of the final treaties with China was considerable, although there is evidence pointing to diplomatic pressure by Great Britain, and the Chinese authorities themselves demonstrated unusual resistance in the series of conferences which preceded the ultimate settlement.

Nevertheless, without the positive and forceful backing of third powers, China's capacity to block foreign demands was as severely limited in the 1915 negotiations as in the past. And once again the political disunity within the vast reaches of the sub-continent provided a major clue to Japan's audacity and to China's acquiescence. For although the dynasty had been replaced in 1912 by a parliamentary government, the battle for the Republic had by no means been won. President Yuan Shih-kai had been intimately connected with the Manchus, and it was believed that he planned to overthrow the new government whenever opportunity presented. At the same time the determined leaders who, under the astute guidance of Dr. Sun Yat-sen, had carried through the Revolution of 1911, rested in uneasy opposition to Yuan. Possessing control of parliament, they had consistently thwarted every step of the President since the founding of the Republic, and their stronghold in Canton was a noted center of resistance to all monarchist sympathies. In May 1914 Yuan had promulgated a new constitution which further alienated the Canton party by literally sabotaging parliament and concentrating all power in the hands of the President. The widening rift between the conservative and liberal Chinese groups, added to a resurgence of warlordism, plagued China until 1927, and made the shaky Peking Government peculiarly susceptible to foreign pressure.

The failure of the American effort to evoke a joint protest over the Twenty-one Demands from Japan's Allies provided an interesting sidelight on Russo-Japanese relations at this time. In a cable to the Russian Ambassador in Tokyo on May 10, Foreign Minister Sazonov reported a conversation in which the American Ambassador asked him "to uphold the steps which the United States plans to take to convince the Japanese Government of the necessity of peace with China. I did not assent to this plan," Sazonov stated, "pointing to our treaty of alliance with Japan." [4] As is so often true in diplomatic correspondence, an ordinary statement of fact is productive of deeper significance when identified with the atmosphere pervading at the time of its origin. Thus it is at least doubtful whether the Tsar regarded with equanimity the implications to the Russian Far East inherent in Japan's demands on China, notwithstanding the "permission" he had extended to Tokyo in the treaties between the two countries. One may even suppose that Malevski, representing Russia in Japan, wrote with irony of receiving the thanks of Kato for his "moral support against American attempts at interference." [5] But the realities of the situation brooked no other procedure than the one Russia had followed. Alone the Tsar could do nothing to check Japan, and the history of American policy in the Far East offered no hope that Washington would back its diplomacy with any material strength. Moreover, Tsarist Russia was still sufficiently expansionist-minded to anticipate a return engagement in Asia at the conclusion of the European war, and the basic objections of the United States to such expansion, coupled with the need of guaranteeing Japanese good will, created insuperable obstacles to the American proposal of May 1915.

[4] Quoted in A. Whitney Griswold, *The Far Eastern Policy of the United States* (New York: Harcourt, Brace and Company, 1938), p. 194, note 1.
[5] *Ibid.*, p. 194, note 2.

In order to protect her growing empire Japan had adhered to the Declaration of London in October 1915, thus assuring participation on an equal basis with her Allies at a future peace conference. This was followed nine months later by the third step in Tokyo's bold blueprint of expansion, the Russo-Japanese Treaty of July 1916. Careful appraisal of the available sources indicates that Japan was the instigator of the 1916 agreement, that the third power against which it was directed was the United States, and that Russia, a victim of its own weakness in the East (a weakness which the war in Europe had greatly accentuated), was at least an unenthusiastic partner in this, the last of the Russo-Japanese treaties prior to the revolutions of 1917.

Russian-American relations, in contrast to the relative friendship and alienation which had characterized them before and after 1900 respectively, were in a state best described as indifferent, subsequent to the withdrawal of the American group from the consortium in 1913. The sudden ascendancy of Japan in Asia introduced a new factor after 1914; henceforth Tokyo was to become the mirror through which Washington and Petrograd viewed each other, and it was within the framework of their individual relations with Japan that, for the most part, the attitude of the two states toward each other found meaning and direction. Apart from this framework, however, certain points of contact and friction did exist. In 1915 the United States concluded a "Treaty for the Advancement of General Peace" with the Tsar's Government, similar to a series of "cooling-off" treaties which have since been intimately linked with the name of William Jennings Bryan. But in the Far East the American loan policy in China called forth the diplomatic protests of Russia as well as the objections of each of the Allied powers. But although American financial sorties were irritating to the monopolistic ambitions of the Tsar in North China, it is difficult to believe that they exerted any appreciable influence on Russia's decision to join Japan in the 1916 treaty.

On the other hand, the forthright opposition of Tokyo to American economic activity in China and the antagonism aroused by Washington's aversion to the Japanese imperialist program had the same catalytic effect on Japan as previous American "interference" had had in stimulating the earlier Russo-Japanese agreements.

However, Washington could not take all the credit for the Russo-Japanese Treaty, which represented a confession of the mutual fear and suspicion with which each signatory regarded the Far Eastern motives of the other. On the Japanese side Viscount Ishii frankly admitted that it was his country primarily which desired the agreement and that Japan's motives were "fear of and protection against Russian treachery." [6] And in Petrograd, Foreign Minister Sazonov advanced as a reason for Russian adherence to the treaty apprehension lest German diplomacy succeed in "detaching Japan from the allies." [7] Other equally somber factors influenced the Tsar. In the winter and spring of 1916 Petrograd was hard pressed on the battlefields of Europe; the main source of Russia's munitions was Japan and the latter was therefore in a unique position to apply pressure. It was with an appreciation of these matters that the American Ambassador to the Tsar's Government suggested to President Wilson in January 1916 that "Russia desires no treaty of alliance with Japan," and "realizes that such a treaty . . . might . . . interfere with her freedom of action in Asia on subsequent occasions." "The situation is so embarrassing and the pressure [from Japan] so persistent," Ambassador Marye wrote, "that it is hard to see what will be the outcome. The . . . question is, will Russia be able to temporize until the pressure is relieved by a change of circumstances." [8]

Events supplied a negative answer. A strictly Asiatic view of the balance of power militated strongly against further alignment with Japan, but the Tsar of necessity had to sublimate the Far East to the requirements of the European war. Nor was it possible for America, pursuing an armchair diplomacy and, even more importantly, not yet a participant in the war, to prevent the conclusion of the Russo-Japanese Treaty despite her aversion to it. In the end

[6] Viscount Kikujiro Ishii, *Diplomatic Commentaries* (Baltimore: Johns Hopkins Press, 1936), p. 107.

[7] A. L. P. Dennis, *The Foreign Policies of Soviet Russia* (New York: E. P. Dutton & Co., Inc.), p. 273. Copyright, 1934, by E. P. Dutton & Co., Inc.

[8] Marye to Wilson, January 25, 1916 (Department of State file 761.94/157).

Petrograd went along with Tokyo, preferring the uncertain advantages of a fourth treaty to the certain disadvantages of no treaty, and in thus casting its lot Russia once again provided the tail to the Japanese expansionist kite.

The relative power position of the two signatories was clearly evident in the published terms of the treaty. Article II constituted tacit Russian recognition of the position won in China by Japan through the Sino-Japanese Agreement of 1915.[9] In Washington the State Department, which for months had refused to place credence in the rumors of the impending accord largely because of the negligible benefits it would have for Russia, regarded the treaty as a major Japanese victory: ". . . the Convention appears to be onesided, Russia gains nothing comparable to the concessions made to Japan." [10]

The treaty at once raised numerous questions in official American circles. What would be its effect on the open-door doctrine and, more specifically, on American interests in China? Were there secret provisions in the agreement? And, once these were fairly reliably ascertained, against what nation were the secret articles directed?

In mid-July, Ambassador Francis cabled from Petrograd that Sazonov was "profuse in expression of friendship" and that the United States, according to the Russian Foreign Minister, had "no occasion for fear or suspicion." This attitude was more bluntly (if less politely) reiterated in the Japanese press. Nevertheless, the State Department desired more official assurances and solicited them through messages to Tokyo and Petrograd on August 16. In response both powers reaffirmed their pacific intentions.[11]

---

[9] Russia and Japan declared that in case the "territorial rights or special interests, in the Far East, of one of the High Contracting Parties, recognized by the other Contracting Party, should be menaced" they would confer regarding possible joint action. John V. A. MacMurray, ed., *Treaties and Agreements with and Concerning China, 1894–1919* (Washington: Carnegie Endowment for International Peace, 1919), Vol. II, p. 1327.

[10] E. T. Williams, Division of Far Eastern Affairs, to Lansing, August 12, 1916 (761.94/127).

[11] Foreign Minister Sturmer (Sazonov's successor) assured Francis that it was the definite Russian policy to maintain unimpaired the convention of 1907 and 1910 in regard to the territorial integrity of China and the "principle of

Although the United States could thus console itself concerning the honorable purposes of Russia and Japan, the question of the existence of secret terms in the 1916 treaty was still unanswered and remained so for another year. It was not until the Bolsheviks had seized power in November 1917 that the full text of the treaty was published as part of their extended propaganda campaign to reveal the perfidy of the Allies and thus to create an atmosphere conducive to a general peace. In December, Francis sent his government a translation of the six articles comprising the secret part of the 1916 agreement. Of most significance were Articles I and II, which stated:

I. The Powers, recognizing that their vital interests demand that China shall not fall under political domination of any third Power whatsoever, which may be hostile to Russia or Japan, shall in the future enter frankly and honestly into communication whenever circumstances demand, and shall agree on the measures to be taken to prevent the occurrence of a like situation.

II. In the event that . . . a war should be declared between one of the Contracting Parties and one of the third Powers . . . the other Contracting Party, at the demand of its Ally, shall come to its aid, and in such case each of the . . . Parties shall undertake not to make peace without a previous agreement with the other . . .[12]

At once speculation was rife over the identity of the "third Power" referred to in the treaty. Washington preferred not to state its

equal opportunity for the commerce of all nations in that Empire." Francis to Lansing, August 29, 1916 (761.94/124). On September 13 the Japanese Government stated its desire "to assure the American Government that the new convention is in no sense designed to repeal or to modify the provisions of . . . the convention concluded between Japan and Russia on July 31, 1907. Nor have the Imperial Government entertained for a moment any intention to depart from the policy to which they have avowedly committed themselves respecting the maintenance of the independence and territorial integrity of China as well as the principle of equal opportunity for the trade of all nations in that country." *For. Rel.*, 1916, p. 446.

[12] The full text of the secret treaty is not printed in *Foreign Relations*, but can be found in the State Department archives (761.94/138). Victor A. Yakhontoff, *Russia and the Soviet Union in the Far East* (New York: Coward-McCann, 1931), pp. 380–381, gives perhaps the most official text available among published sources.

beliefs publicly, for reasons which were most compelling at the time: in April 1917 the United States had become an "Associated Power" in the Allied war against Germany and as recently as November of that year America and Japan had superficially shelved their conflicting interests in Asia through the Lansing-Ishii notes. Accordingly an embarrassing predicament confronted the State Department with the publication of the secret Russo-Japanese Treaty and its potential thrust at America. In an interview with the press (December 21, 1917), the government mildly declared that it was unlikely it would seek an explanation "of the meaning and purpose of these secret articles"; instead, "it is rather expected that [Russia or Japan] will voluntarily come forward with a statement concerning them."

It was conceivable that the treaty was aimed at either Germany or the United States, and arguments were advanced then (even as today) which favored each country respectively as the hypothetical third power. The officials of Tsarist Russia were the chief supporters of the anti-German thesis; from the time the open convention was published Sazonov had taken pains to convince Francis that the treaty had no implications for the United States.

Notwithstanding the more logical basis (so far as Russia was concerned) for an anti-German rather than an anti-American treaty in 1916, the circumstantial evidence would seem to indicate that Japan was the chief author of the agreement and that consequently the terms would reflect the views of Tokyo to greater degree than those of Petrograd. While Japan may have had one eye on the possibility of a German victory in the war it is extremely unlikely that this was a decisive factor in impelling the treaty with Russia. The one power which might have frustrated the Japanese march to empire during the first years of the World War was the United States, and just as Russo-Japanese accords had been conceived at least partially to counteract American policy in Asia, so in 1916 it was not unnatural that the two states should continue their defensive efforts against Washington. At any rate this was the construction given the treaty by the State Department. In a memorandum in March 1918 it was noted that Article I was "undoubtedly aimed at the United States which country is continually represented in Japan as seeking political control in China and as constantly aiming to thwart Japan's legitimate ambitions in that country."

If this interpretation was correct, the wording of the secret articles absolved Russia from too great hypocrisy in its statements to Washington, for "any third power whatsoever" could with equal honesty have spelled Germany to the Tsar and America to the Japanese. Nevertheless, the important fact remained that through the treaty Russia had not only sanctioned the Japanese gains of 1914 and 1915 in China, but committed itself to future support for Tokyo's expansionist efforts.

Between the date of signature of the 1916 treaty and the upheavals in Russia the ensuing year the Japanese Government continued unabated its calculated Far Eastern policy and in so doing took the next two strides by which it intended to encompass China within the exclusive framework of Tokyo's sphere of interest.

The first of these steps was the conclusion, between January and March 1917, of a series of secret agreements with Japan's Allies. Cognizant of the Inter-Allied treaties of 1915 in which the European states had agreed upon the territorial spoils each desired subsequent to the defeat of the Central powers, Japan had cautiously waited for a propitious moment at which to press its own claims in the Far East. Such a moment appeared to have arrived early in 1917 with the conjunction of several factors which made the Allies amenable to Tokyo's wishes. On the one hand was the enervating war-weariness of the European belligerents who saw as yet no end in sight to the conflict then in its third year. To this was added an intangible fear lest Japan should deal separately with Germany, a fear which had been nurtured by recurrent rumors of unofficial German-Japanese conversations.[13] Finally, emphasizing and implementing this fear were the consistent refusal of Tokyo to dispatch troops to Europe and the equally consistent Japanese policy of pressuring China to remain aloof from the Western struggle.

[13] *Robert Lansing Papers.* "These secret agreements were obtained by Japan pressing her allies at the [to them] darkest moment of the war, in the winter of 1917, and many facts now known indicate plainly that Japan obtained those agreements by virtually threatening otherwise to treat with Germany." From a memorandum by T. F. Millard, sent to Lansing in July 1919.

The request of the Allies that Japan reverse the latter position by bringing China into the war provided the ostensible rationalization for the secret treaties of 1917. At the same time the price which Tokyo demanded for these services suggested that the purely conjectural value of Chinese participation was perhaps of lesser importance to the Allies than some of the other factors already noted. As paraphrased by the Russian Ambassador at Tokyo, Japan's desires "represent the inheritance of all the rights and privileges belonging to Germany in the Shantung, and the acquisition of the [German] islands north of the equator . . ." [14] In the treaties signed respectively with Great Britain, Russia, and France the Japanese conditions were met without modification. Almost immediately thereafter China severed relations with Germany, for reasons less connected with Japanese urging than with internal Chinese politics, and the following August war was declared.

It now remained for Japan to settle accounts with the United States, and to this end a special diplomatic mission was sent to Washington in the summer of 1917. Coupled with the grievances which Tokyo had already chalked up against America, the latter's position regarding China's entry into the war provided Japan with additional reason for seeking a *modus vivendi* with the State Department.[15] Moreover, the Russian Revolution of March 1917 had palpably weakened the Russo-Japanese Treaty of the preceding year, and an understanding with the American Government, if favorably slanted, could be regarded as partial compensation for the loss of Russia. Finally, the participation of the United States in the war after April 1917 carried with it the psychological necessity of quieting the prevalent rumors of American-Japanese discord.

[14] From *The Bulletin of the Soviets*, December 1/14, 1917. Enclosure in Francis to Lansing, December 18, 1917 (761.94/138). See also F. Seymour Cocks, ed., *The Secret Treaties and Understandings* (2nd ed.; London: Union of Democratic Control, 1918), pp. 84–85, for the same, but with a discrepancy in dates.

[15] Washington had proposed to Britain, France, and Japan that identic notes be sent China "to restore national unity and maintain internal peace as of first importance to itself and to the world and to relegate the question of relation to the world war to secondary place." *For. Rel.*, 1917, pp. 48–49. The United States was officially unaware at this juncture of the recently concluded secret treaties between Japan and the Allies.

Following an exchange of notes in June and July between the Japanese Ambassador at Washington and Secretary Lansing, the ground was cleared for the negotiations with Special Ambassador Viscount Ishii. These were carried on in the course of several "conversations" [16] between the two diplomats in September 1917 and culminated in the now famous Lansing-Ishii Agreement of November 2. As the signatories were motivated by essentially contradictory purposes, the final document was naturally a hybrid compromise in which each state found that which it most desired.

For Japan the agreement was an admission of Tokyo's "special interests" in China. Moreover, Japan was equally confident that in case of misunderstandings its version of the Lansing-Ishii exchange would prevail. The Russian Ambassador in Tokyo cabled his "impression," after conferring with Foreign Minister Motono, that the Japanese statesman, while recognizing the "possibility of misunderstandings," felt that Japan would be better able to carry out her interpretation than would the United States. [17]

In contrast the American Government viewed the notes as a strong reaffirmation of the principles of the open-door and the territorial integrity of China. On November 7, 1917, in answer to Minister Reinsch's distressed cable concerning the effect of the Lansing-Ishii Agreement on China, President Wilson wrote to Lansing, "There has not only been no change of policy but there has been a distinct gain for China." [18] Perhaps the clearest statement of Washington's hopes was made by the Secretary of State in August 1919 in a letter to Senator William H. King. According to Lansing it was the final paragraph of the agreement that required emphasis, the part in which the contracting parties admitted their opposition

to the acquisition by any government of any special rights or privileges that would affect the independence or territorial integrity of China or

[16] The most inclusive account of these conversations is found in the personal memoirs of the two principals. See Ishii, *op. cit.*, Ch. VI, and Robert Lansing, *War Memoirs* (Indianapolis: The Bobbs-Merrill Company, 1935), Ch. XX.

[17] Krupensky to the Russian Foreign Office, November 1, 1917, Cocks, *op. cit.*, p. 88.

[18] *Ray Stannard Baker Papers.*

that would deny to the subjects or citizens of any country the full enjoyment of equal opportunity in the commerce and industry of China.

This declaration [wrote Lansing] applies to *all* governments and, therefore, includes the United States and Japan. Is is not a "Monroe Doctrine" for the Far East, but is analogous to the "hands-off" doctrine of Pan Americanism. . . . I think the "special interests" mentioned should be read in connection with this declaration and interpreted in the light of it.[19]

Notwithstanding this statement Lansing was fully aware of the ulterior Japanese motives in suggesting the exchange of notes, and his inability to mitigate the "special interests" clause or to treat more sternly with Viscount Ishii could be regarded only as a confession of temporary American weakness.

In the ultimatum to Germany in 1914, the Twenty-one Demands on China in 1915, the Russo-Japanese Treaty of 1916, the secret treaties with the Allies in 1917, and the Lansing-Ishii Agreement of 1917, Japan had taken advantage of the war to apply pressure when and where it could be least withstood. The results provided graphic proof of Japanese proficiency as an imperialist power and of the inadequacy of unilateral American diplomatic protests. The United States, aspiring to a role in the Far East but loath to assume foreign commitments, had still to resolve the contradiction inherent in its dual position; had still to recognize that in the harsh game of international politics words cannot balance power.

Gradually, in the ensuing months, the lesson was learned and applied in the first real attempt to halt the onward march of Japanese empire in Asia.

[19] *Lansing Papers.*

PART TWO

CHAPTER IV

Prelude to Intervention:
The Long Debate

Almost simultaneously with the publication of the Lansing-Ishii Agreement came the first tidings of the Bolshevik Revolution in Russia. Its implications for the balance of power in Asia were momentarily overshadowed by the more immediate repercussions of the revolution in Europe, but before a month had elapsed the struggle between the United States and Japan was resumed. This time the focal point was Siberia, and the pretext, Allied intervention. There is strong evidence that the American attitude toward intervention was almost wholly determined by the reaction to the imperialistic Japanese program of 1914–1917. In other words, Tokyo's ambition had at length over-reached itself, as far as Washington was concerned. Accordingly, it was in the pattern of this latest American opposition to Japan that the paradoxical policy of the State Department to Soviet Russia was to find its meaning.

The November Revolution had been preceded in March 1917 by the initial Russian upheaval which had ousted the Tsar and established the so-called "Provisional Government" under the auspices of the more moderate socialist parties. In contrast to its later aversion to the Bolshevik leaders, the United States was broadly sympathetic to the first revolutionists and accorded diplomatic recognition within a week of the establishment of the new regime. In so doing it was the first foreign state to recognize the Provisional Government. The fact that America was drawing nearer to the European conflict at this time quite naturally influenced the cordial regard extended to Russia, for President Wilson's "war to make the world safe for democracy" was less an anachronism once Russian autocracy had been overthrown.

Subsequent to recognition the State Department took several specific steps to demonstrate its friendliness and its desire to aid the Provisional Government. The first of these was the decision to send a Railroad Commission, under the supervision of John F. Stevens, to inspect the Trans-Siberian line with a view to increasing its efficiency. The commission reached Petrograd in July 1917 by way of Japan and Vladivostok, and a few months later Stevens was made official adviser to the Minister of Ways of Communication under the Russian Government. At the request of Stevens a Russian Railway Service Corps of 350 American engineers under the direction of Colonel Emerson was organized in November. However, chaotic conditions and the Bolshevik Revolution prevented either of the American organizations from achieving much during the life of the Provisional Government.

The next expression of solicitude by the United States was embodied in the sending of the Special Diplomatic Mission to Russia in the early summer of 1917. Headed by Elihu Root, the mission included a conglomerate medley of assorted bankers, industrialists, military personnel, social workers, and a labor leader.[1] According to the Secretary of State the purpose of the group was to encourage the Russian Government by expressions of good will and confidence, and to explore "the most efficient means of cooperating" with Petrograd in the prosecution of the war. But behind these hopeful official words was a very real fear lest Russia, despite the firm avowals of her rulers, be forced to a separate peace with Germany.

A month after the Root party had left Russia an American Red Cross Mission arrived under the command of Colonel William Boyd Thompson.[2] The evidences of American sympathy, however, were neither all in one direction nor limited to political, moral, and industrial help, vital though such aid was. At the request of Petrograd, the United States indicated its willingness to receive a Commission from Russia, which arrived in June accompanied by the Provisional Government's Ambassador to Washington, Boris

[1] The list included Major General Hugh L. Scott, Rear Admiral James H. Glennon, John R. Mott, Charles R. Crane, Cyrus H. McCormick, Samuel R. Berton, Charles Edward Russell, and James Duncan.

[2] Thompson remained in Russia only until the end of November, at which time Colonel Raymond Robins became head of the Red Cross Mission.

Bakhmetev. Moreover, under the terms of the War Loans Act a credit of $100,000,000 was extended to Russia on May 16, followed by other sizable loans in August and October. Finally, it remained for America to demonstrate its friendship with one last gesture on the eve of the November Revolution. On October 9 the ambassadors of Britain, France, and Italy had addressed a collective note to Prime Minister Kerensky in protest against the slackening of Russian war effort. By his abstention from this Allied rebuke Ambassador Francis earned the deep gratitude of the tottering Kerensky regime.

The overthrow of the Provisional Government came as a tremendous shock to the Allied nations, particularly as the willful blindness of those closest to the scene had prevented any real comprehension of the Russian picture from sifting into the battle-wearied minds of the statesmen at home. Initial incredulity (matched by a woeful underestimation of the holding power of the Bolsheviks) gave place to keen anger at the audacious suggestion of Foreign Commissar Trotsky that all the warring states cease fighting and conclude a general peace. The antiwar slogan of the Bolsheviks (no victory, no annexations) was a sharp knife cutting at the morale of tired peoples throughout the world and, although it rallied support for the Communists within Russia, it was hardly a boon to the victory-pledged leaders of the Allied powers. The United States hastily assured Ambassador Bakhmetev that the Soviet Government would receive no comfort from America (although both the Red Cross and the railroad missions remained in Russia, as did the American and Allied diplomatic representatives).

In January 1918, following the publication by the Bolsheviks of the network of secret treaties among the Allies, the Soviet leaders issued a decree repudiating Russia's international financial obligations. Earlier in the month Francis began to hint of the inevitability of a separate peace with Germany; negotiations between representatives of the two powers had been opened on December 22, 1917, and after a fortnight's recess were again continued. Finally, on March 3, 1918, the treaty of Brest-Litovsk was signed. A few days later, in answer to a Japanese query regarding Russia's status as far as the Allies were concerned, the American position was enunciated in what, on the surface at least, could best be described as an equivocal statement. The United States did "not feel justified in regarding Russia either as a neutral or as an enemy, but . . . as an ally," the note declared. However, because of its policy of nonrecognition of the Bolshevik regime, the State Department denied that there was, at present, any Russian Government to deal with. Nevertheless, it still behooved the powers "to treat with Russians as in all respects our friends and allies against the common enemy."

The possibility of Russian defection from the European war had plagued the Allies ever since the March Revolution, and the American declaration was manifestly an indirect plea to the Russians to continue their resistance to the Central powers. This was not the only motive, however, nor was it of greatest importance. For more than three months the question of intervention in Siberia had spasmodically raised its head and the Washington pronouncement in March was aimed obliquely at those nations which favored such a policy. The explanation of the American opposition was to be found not primarily in terms of the requirements of the European war, although these were frequently mentioned and exerted some influence, but rather in the compulsions of American Far Eastern policy. The State Department viewed with alarm a potential invasion of Siberian soil by an Allied force which of necessity would have to consist predominantly of Japanese troops. As a result the United States was forced into the awkward and contradictory role of protector of Russian sovereignty, while its loathing of the Russian political system increased. Beginning in December 1917 and continuing through 1922, the old American principle of "the territorial integrity of China" was broadened to include Soviet Asia and, indeed, in a very real sense the United States went further in its efforts to safeguard Russian sovereignty than it had ever done for the traditionally beleaguered Chinese.

In contrast to the consistent refusal of Washington to countenance intervention prior to July 1918, the Allied powers began to commit themselves favorably as early as the previous summer, and in the months pursuant to the November Revolution the United States was subjected to a recurrent diplomatic pressure which eventually caused it to fall in line, however reluctantly. In their efforts to gain American sanction the Allies employed a variety of motives, real and assumed, to rationalize their projected invasion. Included among them might be listed: the re-creation of an Eastern front against the German army; the oft-repeated fear of German control of Siberia, which would include the Allied stocks located there; the alleged danger arising from the existence of Austrian and German prisoners of war in Siberia; the moral necessity to "rescue" the Czechoslovakian legions in their long trek across Russia to Vladivostok; the admitted terror evoked by the menace of bolshevism.

Behind these motives lay others of a less publicized nature, but equally forceful—if not more so—in explaining the Allied attitude. On the part of France an anathema to communism was inextricably associated with the Soviet repudiation of debts, the vast percentage of which were owed to French stockholders. Moreover, the danger to the Third Republic resulting from Russian withdrawal from the war was more immediate and serious than to any of its colleagues, and French statesmen were therefore less sober in their appraisal of the need for intervention than they might otherwise have been. At the same time France and Britain together feared the probable expropriation of their Russian industrial and commercial properties by a surviving Communist government. Empire was a major motivating factor to the British: reports of a potential German-Turkish invasion of India, coupled with rumors of a German-Japanese rapprochement which would likewise spell disaster for England's imperial holdings, disposed Downing Street to support the interventionist schemes.

For Japan, anxiety over a possible threat to existent colonial possessions was not so great as the desire to take advantage of the sudden Russian weakness by further expanding Japanese holdings on the Asiatic mainland. While the proponents of this frankly aggressive policy eventually won out, they were opposed in Japan by a more moderate, less militaristic element composed mainly of liberal business men and the enlightened intelligentsia, who seized every opportunity to soften the harsh ambitions of the general staff. Nevertheless, the army was aided immeasurably by the genuine Japanese suspicion of communism, a factor which can

doubtless be better appreciated by Americans of the present genera·
tion than by those of three decades ago.

The motives, genuine and fabricated, of the Allies in proposing
intervention, together with the evolving American position, arose
from and were peripheral to Russia's weakened condition. Here
was a radical and unproved government exercising unrecognized
jurisdiction. Beyond the limited radius of effective Soviet rule
Russia consisted of a political vacuum and this drew the powers with
the force of a magnet. An irresistible desire to fill the political
empty spaces made intervention of some sort inevitable; the
rivalry of nations paradoxically lent to the intervention its Allied
character.

In the summer and autumn of 1917 the press in the United States
and Japan began to feel its way around the still unofficial subject of
intervention in Siberia. It was believed by contemporary authors
that this newspaper propaganda originated in the Japanese Embassy in London; whether or not this conviction was justified, the
fact remained that the press spoke of Japan as the power to which
France and Britain would turn if the worsening conditions in Siberia
demanded Allied action. In view of Tokyo's geographical propinquity to Siberia and the military situation on the Western front
this was a logical inference and, moreover, one borne out by the
diplomatic record beginning a few months later.

Apparently trial balloons on the subject of intervention were first
sent up almost simultaneously by France and Britain in late November and December 1917. In the instance of France, Clemenceau
specifically named Japan as the nation which should supply an expeditionary force; the British Ambassador at Tokyo used a more
general approach in discussions with the Japanese Government,
but this did not represent any opposition to a unilateral Japanese
occupation.

The immediate negative reaction of Tokyo, which recurred
periodically throughout the winter and spring of 1918, was motivated primarily by the basic desire that military intervention in
Siberia should redound to Japan's imperialist advantage. This desire was forthrightly and unequivocally stated by the Japanese Ambassador in Washington: if America and England "claim certain

rights in countries not belonging to them," they "must allow Japan to claim similar rights." [3] This attitude was behind the long efforts of Tokyo to forestall intervention of an inter-Allied character which would perforce circumscribe Japan's freedom of action. For if Britain and France could be prevailed upon to sanction a Japanese intervention, it was certain that Washington could not. But it was not diplomatically feasible so early in the game to veto an international army in favor of a lone Japanese expedition. Consequently, in December 1917 Tokyo went on record as being opposed to any intervention [4] while simultaneously hinting that for security purposes Japan might be compelled to send a token force to Siberia. The result of this double-edged diplomacy was, initially, to endow Japanese policy toward intervention with a "now we're for it, now we're not" quality which was strongly disconcerting to the Allies. The discrepancies between the various Japanese statements rankled Cecil, who wrote Balfour that the Japanese would not inform Britain of their plans, and were irritated by the suggestions of others.[5]

By the end of 1917 the American position with regard to intervention had crystallized into approximately the form it was to maintain until the following summer. Despite the suggestion of Ambassador Francis in November that troops be sent via Vladivostok and Siberia to aid European Russia in the lingering struggle against Germany; despite his forebodings concerning the alleged pro-German attitude of Lenin and Trotsky; and notwithstanding the anti-bolshevism of the American Secretary of State, the general opposition of Washington to Siberian intervention remained intact. This was partially explained by the uncompromising resistance of the War Department. At the same time, Wilson's close friend and adviser, Colonel Edward M. House, urged a noninterventionist

[3] Memorandum of an interview between Cecil Spring Rice and the Japanese Ambassador, Washington, December 29, 1917 (sent by the former to President Wilson, same date), *Woodrow Wilson Papers.*

[4] "I spoke this afternoon to the Japanese Ambassador. . . . He did not receive the suggestion very favourably and expressed the hope that everything would be done by peaceful means such as conceding local Government in that part of Siberia, to avoid intervention." Robert Cecil to President Wilson, January 1, 1918, *Wilson Papers.*

[5] Blanche E. C. Dugdale, *Arthur James Balfour* (London: Hutchinson & Co., 1936), Vol. II, p. 255.

policy, on his return from Europe at the close of 1917. Moreover, the absorption of the government in the war needs of the Western front, the general mistrust of any policy which would sanction the presence of Japanese troops on the mainland of Asia, and an historic aversion to foreign intervention seemed to eliminate any alternatives to the policy adhered to by the State Department. With the passage of time the Allies were able to soften the American attitude somewhat, but with few exceptions Washington's position was undeviating.

Early in January a French suggestion that a military mission (composed predominantly of French troops) be sent to Harbin and Irkutsk evoked a negative rejoinder from Tokyo, which for the first time pressed openly its campaign for a unilateral Japanese intervention. Following a notice that a cruiser would shortly be dispatched to Vladivostok, Japan asked that the occupation of that city and of the Chinese Eastern and Amur Railroads be left to her if such action were necessary. And at the end of January the Foreign Minister "rather intimated" that the landing of American troops would not please the Japanese people.

President Wilson had already enunciated the guiding principles of United States policy toward Russia in his message to Congress on January 8.

Whether their present leaders believe it or not, it is our heartfelt desire and hope that some way may be opened whereby we may be privileged to assist the people of Russia to attain their utmost hope of liberty and ordered peace . . . The treatment accorded to Russia by her sister nations in the months to come will be the acid test of their good will, of their comprehension of her needs as distinguished from their own interests, and of their intelligent and unselfish sympathy.

This was reinforced by Lansing's rejection, a week later, of the French-proposed mission to Siberia, and by an American statement to the Japanese Government on January 20.

Regardless of the American position, Japan and the Allies continued their propaganda for intervention, and in an effort to make their pressure more forceful they emphasized the possible alternatives should the United States remain intractable. One of the most frequently repeated arguments employed was the alleged necessity of preventing the spread of German influence in the Far East as well as in European Russia. Side by side with this thesis was the statement that intervention would compel the German armies to stay in Russia, and so prevent their concentration on the Western front. The German menace was played up most effectively in private Anglo-French approaches to Washington, where it was inferred that Japan might possibly align herself with Germany if not permitted to act alone in Siberia. From this highly dubious reference to Japanese honor it was but a short step for the British and French to hint at the likelihood of a unilateral Japanese policy should the United States continue in its opposition to intervention.

Advices reaching the State Department from China tended to substantiate this hypothesis. Moreover, at the end of February the Japanese Foreign Minister confided to the French Ambassador that preparations were concluded "for immediate action"; that regardless of Washington's disapproval, "if only England and France agreed Japan could go ahead," and that "the time would soon come when Japan would not be able to wait any longer." [6]

In a letter to Colonel House earlier in the month President Wilson had reiterated his conviction that "it would be a great political mistake to send Japanese troops into Siberia." But in the face of the Allied barrage the first tentative crack appeared in the wall of American resistance. In a communication to the President on February 27 Lansing noted that Japan was "ready to promise disinterestedness and even to say so publicly" and, of equal importance, "to pledge . . . to act as far as the Ural Mountains." [7] In view of the prior information that Tokyo contemplated independent action in Siberia, this latest news was partially responsible for the shift in Lansing's opinion.

Other influences caused doubt concerning the American position at this time. The opinion of the Supreme War Council was one of these. Summarized, the argument advanced by the Council was

[6] *For. Rel.*, 1918, Russia, Vol. II, p. 56.

[7] *Wilson Papers*. This pledge was considered significant in Washington, for it was the opinion of military officialdom that a Siberian intervention which did not proceed west to the Urals would have questionable military value in the German war.

that the Bolshevik Government might dispose of the "enormous stores of military supplies" at Vladivostok "to the advantage of Germany." This accounted for the formulation of the so-called Joint Note No. 16 in February 1918, which recommended the occupation of the Siberian railroad from Vladivostok to Harbin by a Japanese force ("after obtaining a suitable guarantee from Japan") "together with a joint Allied Mission." Notwithstanding Wilson's abrupt dismissal of this attempt by military officials to determine "political and diplomatic questions," army pressure supplemented by that of the Allied statesmen gave further pause to the State Department.

Another source of argument for intervention was revealed in the gradual crystallization of opinion within the American Diplomatic Corps. John F. Stevens, engrossed in the problem of operating the Russian railroads, emphasized the danger of German control (or even Japanese) unless "America takes over"; in China, Minister Reinsch stressed the advantages to be obtained by "quick action on the part of the United States and Allies" in Siberia; Ambassador Francis urged "that we assume control of Vladivostok." These views were seconded by American consular officials in Moscow and by the military attaché at Peking.[8]

In sharp contrast to these exchanges was the antiinterventionist attitude of non-Bolshevik Russian groups. On the whole the representatives of the Provisional Government maintained a consistently solid front against any Siberian expedition manned exclusively by the Japanese, and although this had little effect on the desires of Tokyo and the European Allies, it was bound to appeal to Washington. Just as common hostility toward a third power had stimulated American-Russian friendship in the nineteenth century, so in the months following the Russian Revolution the mutual antagonism of the Provisional Government and the State Department to Japan produced a solicitude on the part of each for the views of the other. Naturally the representatives of the defunct Russian Government had no means of implementing their opinions, but the very existence of their opposition to inter-

[8] *For. Rel.*, *op. cit.*, Vol. III, pp. 219–220; Vol. II, pp. 53, 54, 61; Vol. I, p. 384.

vention played into the hands of Wilson and Lansing whenever the two American statesmen wished to utilize it to advance their own position.

To the Russian opposition were added the undoubtedly more effective arguments of Wilson's own advisers. A composite of the objections of Colonel House, Senator Elihu Root, William C. Bullitt, and others suggested that Japanese intervention would precipitate highly undesirable problems of moral, military, and political content. These were illustrated plainly and representatively in a memorandum by Mr. Bullitt to the President on March 2:

> The moral position upon which our whole participation in the war is based will be irretrievably compromised unless we protest publicly against Japan's invasion of Siberia. Japan pretends that she must at once invade Siberia . . . to prevent the supplies . . . from falling into the hands of the Germans. The Germans are at present 2,550 miles away. . . . We are about to assent tacitly to Japan's invasion. . . . We fear that if we oppose Japan, she will switch to the side of Germany . . . because of her desire to annex eastern Siberia, which she covets so intensely that if she cannot obtain it with the consent of the Allies she will take it with the assistance of Germany. . . . Are we going to make the world safe for . . . Russian democracy by allowing the Allies to place Terauchi in Irkutsk, while Ludendorff establishes himself in Petrograd? [9]

This brand of persuasion held a singular appeal for an idealistic President and a practical Secretary of State. Wilson was particularly prone to moral reasoning, while the logic of the Bullitt argument could not help but attract Lansing.

Three days later the President issued a statement in the form of a note to the Allied ambassadors in Washington which, notwithstanding some redundant phraseology, reflected the influence of the antiinterventionists. While admitting the precariousness of the Siberian situation and the "imminent risk" of "German invasion and domination," while agreeing that "if intervention is deemed wise" Japan "could accomplish it most efficiently," and while reiterating confidence in Japan, Wilson felt impelled to question "the wisdom of intervention":

[9] *Wilson Papers.*

If it were undertaken the . . . United States assumes that the most explicit assurances would be given that it was undertaken by Japan as an ally of Russia, in Russia's interest, and with the sole view of holding it safe against Germany and at the absolute disposal of the final peace conference. Otherwise the Central powers could and would make it appear that Japan was doing in the East exactly what Germany is doing in the West . . . even with such assurances given, they could . . . be discredited by those whose interest it was to discredit them . . .[10]

The American note caught the Japanese midway in their preparation for a large-scale military intervention. Not only did Tokyo's attitude immediately undergo a "marked change," but for several weeks thereafter Japan appeared to have lost all interest in the Siberian project. Although government leaders attributed this *volte face* to a shift in public opinion, more realistic considerations had in fact dictated the change in policy. Japan had no desire for a Siberian venture under the stringent chaperonage implied in the Wilson statement. At the same time she was not free to ignore the American conditions for the very elemental reason that without American financial and material support Japan could not undertake a project as ambitious as she had in mind. This dependence on American largesse was made clear to the British Ambassador at Tokyo within forty-eight hours of the Washington note.[11] The American diplomatic victory was further acknowledged in the formal reply of Tokyo on March 19. After a face-saving reminder to the State Department that the concept of intervention had not originated "from any desire expressed or any suggestion made" by Japan, the memorandum declared that in the Japanese view the success of intervention required the prior understanding of "all the great powers," without which Tokyo would "refrain" from action. A confession of weakness to the United States, the Japanese note was also an invitation to France and England to redouble their

[10] *For. Rel., op. cit.*, Vol. II, pp. 67–68. After learning of this note Colonel House reported that he was "happy beyond words at the absolutely perfect way you have handled this most worrying situation." *Wilson Papers.*

[11] Paraphrase of a cable from the British Ambassador at Tokyo to the British Foreign Office, March 7, 1918. Sir William Wiseman handed this cable to Colonel House with the request that it go no further than the White House. *Wilson Papers.*

efforts to convert America to an interventionist policy. The necessity for achieving this conversion had been borne in upon the two Western powers a fortnight before, however, and the Japanese declaration simply bolstered what had now become the determined policy of Britain and France. On March 2 the Soviet Government had signed the "ignominious unconditional peace with the Central powers"; from then on the dual fear of communism and a German-controlled Russia conflicted with the more sober judgments of many English statesmen, at times replacing them with the less-reasoned advices of the interventionists. So that even before the Wilson note to Japan, Britain had instructed its ambassador at Tokyo to prepare the groundwork for an Allied-sponsored Japanese occupation of eastern Siberia: "No Russian authority exists which can be trusted to guard the stores . . . at Vladivostok . . . Allied intervention seems . . . to be practically inevitable, and . . . it is clear that the task must be undertaken by Japan for geographical reasons." [12] The noncommittal response of Tokyo to the British suggestion, reflecting the Japanese reaction to the Wilson note of March 5, caused London and Paris to concentrate their pressure with renewed vigor on the American Government.

In the middle of the month the Allied Supreme War Council convened in a two-day conference to consider the question in detail. The excited Clemenceau, supported by M. Pichon, urged that if America refused to sponsor an invitation to Japan to intervene, the Allies "must act on [their] own responsibility." The British, a shade more reluctant than their Latin Allies, counseled some delay in the hope that the United States would change its attitude and that the Soviet authorities might perhaps approve of the contemplated Japanese action. The net result of the conference was the formulation by Balfour, on behalf of the Allied powers, of a note placing the case for intervention before the American Government. After summarizing all the familiar arguments and applying a generous whitewash to Japanese motives,[13] the whole problem was

[12] British Foreign Office to the British Ambassador at Tokyo, March 4, 1918; enclosure in Polk to Wilson, March 5, 1918, *Wilson Papers*.

[13] "There are many observers who think that, if that assistance now took the form of a Japanese army operating on Russian soil, it would be regarded with distrust . . . If this be so, it is doubtless due to the fear that Japan would

left at Wilson's door. Without the support of the United States, Balfour concluded, "it would be useless to approach the Japanese Government, and even if the Japanese . . . consented," intervention without American approval "would lose half its moral authority." [14]

The question of intervention was by no means of exclusively Allied concern, however, for while the European states, America, and Japan were debating among themselves, the Soviet Government was manifesting an acute interest in what was, after all, a problem of prime importance to Russia. Motivated by an opportunism nowhere more forcefully illustrated than in the peace negotiations with Germany and in the humiliating terms of the final settlement, the Bolshevik leaders from the outset regarded intervention with cold calculation: What would be its effect on Germany? How dangerous a "guest" would the Japanese prove? To what extent would an intervention in Siberia (and in Northern Russia) aid or weaken the Communists in their hold on the Russian Government? There were no simple answers to these questions, however; indeed, the very situation which had created them was too complicated to be reducible to pat formulae. Mixed inextricably into the fabric of intervention were problems of high policy concerning the war in Europe, American-Japanese rivalry in Asia, and the antagonism of East and West alike to the revolutionary doctrines of Marxism. The frequently conflicting considerations arising from these problems produced ambiguities in Allied and American at-

---

treat Russia in the East as Germany is . . . in the West, would rob her of her territory. . . . No such suspicion can be entertained by those associated with Japan in the present war. If she intervenes . . . it will be as the friend of Russia. . . ." This provided an interesting contrast to the confidential cable from Balfour to Wilson, via Colonel House, on the preceding January 30: "With regard to Japan it is hardly necessary for me to assure you that I fully appreciate the difficulties of the situation . . . It may be said that Japan's aggrandizement, whether territorially (*it might, for instance, prove impossible to get her out of the maritime provinces after she is once established there*) or morally, as saviour of the situation as consequence of her successful intervention, would appear to be a grave danger from the point of view of the spectator. There is force in this." *The Intimate Papers of Colonel House*, edited by Charles Seymour (Boston: Houghton Mifflin Company, 1928), Vol. III, pp. 390–391. Italics mine.

[14] Balfour to Lansing, March 16, 1918, *Tasker H. Bliss Papers.*

titudes which were consequently reflected within the councils of Soviet Russia. For their part Communist officials were in an unenviable predicament: on the West stood an avaricious Germany; on the East, a greedy Japan. It therefore behooved the Russians to minimize the potential threat to their territory inherent in the designs of both powers, but in their dire weakness this could be achieved only through the aid of states whose innate opposition to communism was axiomatic.

Regardless of this triple dilemma, between March and June 1918 the Bolsheviks toyed with the concept of Allied intervention. In the first instance it was conceived as an anti-German policy.[15] Having just affixed its signature to the Brest-Litovsk "diktat," and fully aware of the storm of disapproval which ratification of the treaty would precipitate within Russia, the Soviet Government approached the Allies with a view to ascertaining the amount of help which would be forthcoming should Russia reject the treaty. The Soviet communication was sent March 5 by Raymond Robins to Ambassador Francis, and forwarded by the latter to Washington a week later. In the meantime, on March 11, the State Department had dispatched a message from President Wilson to the Russian people; although it was sent before the details of the Trotsky inquiry reached America, it constituted the only answer ever given to the Russian note. After expressing his sympathy for the people of Russia, then at the mercy of Germany, the President continued:

Although the . . . United States is unhappily not now in a position to render the direct and effective aid it would wish to render, I beg to assure the people of Russia . . . that it will avail itself of every opportunity to secure for Russia once more complete sovereignty and independence in her own affairs and full restoration to her great role in the life of Europe and the modern world.

The reticence of Washington to aid Russia with anything but pious wishes made further delay in ratifying the treaty of Brest-

[15] Early in March, German troops had entered Finland, a move which had been countered by the British occupation of Murmansk. The Soviet Government approved this step and continued to sanction the English occupation until June, at which time an effort to evict the Allies was unsuccessful.

Litovsk superfluous. The Soviet leaders had no intention of respecting the German settlement any longer than was necessary, however, and therefore the matter of intervention continued to interest them. Moreover, in its Siberian aspects Russia viewed intervention equally in terms of the Japanese menace, a factor which explained the larger ramifications of Communist policy in the spring of 1918 and contributed to the earlier decision to ratify the German treaty. In his communication of March 5 Trotsky had sought a statement on the American position should Tokyo conspire with Berlin to "seize Vladivostok and the Eastern-Siberian Railway." The deep anxiety in the Russian capital over the likelihood of an exclusive Japanese intervention had caused Francis to remark upon the "unwisdom" of such a contingency, and to suggest that the ultimate vote regarding the German treaty might well depend on the Allied attitude toward Japan.

The fear of Nippon continued to haunt Moscow in the weeks following the Brest-Litovsk settlement and accounted for the unofficial soundings within Russia concerning a multilateral intervention which, from the Soviet viewpoint, might conceivably check both German and Japanese designs on Russian territory. In all the numerous dispatches emanating from Bolshevik, Allied, and American sources in Russia in the weeks after Brest-Litovsk, two themes prevailed: the probable Soviet acquiescence in an inter-Allied expeditionary force; the adamant Soviet denunciation of a unilateral Japanese intervention, accompanied by the veiled threat that it might cause the Communists to seek an alliance with Germany.

Among all the states warring against the Central powers, the American Government shared most closely the views of Russia in regard to Japanese intervention in Siberia, and it was one of the ironies of history that the two nations, pursuing parallel policies because of a common hostility to Tokyo, were ideologically so far apart that the gap between them was unbridgeable. This was made manifest in the latter part of March in a Soviet statement which declared: "An alliance [with America] is impossible. . . . Russia . . . cannot align itself . . . with capitalistic America." On the other hand, the belief prevailed in the State Department that the Soviet Government was seeking to aggravate American-Japanese friction in the interests of world revolution and that the Communists would "avail themselves of every means to embroil Japan and the United States." [16] These sentiments did not lessen American distrust of Japanese motives, but they did preclude a cooperative approach with the Soviet Government to the whole problem of intervention, while the uncompromising revulsion of Secretary Lansing toward communism indubitably worked to soften his opposition to a Japanese expedition.[17]

Meantime the British Foreign Office launched a new offensive to win Washington's consent to intervention. Instead of pressing for a solitary Japanese force the British took their cue from the Soviet attitude and in one move catered to the anti-Japanese sentiment of both Russia and America by suggesting a joint intervention in which United States troops would participate in sizable numbers. In view of the numerous evidences of Bolshevik interest in such a project it is not inconceivable that an American acquiescence at this time would have been followed by some sort of *modus vivendi* with the Soviet Government. However, Wilson was still undecided, and before he had finally cast his lot with the interventionists, Russia and the Allies had become hopelessly alienated.

An event early in April had repercussions which ultimately were more influential in turning the American Government to intervention than all the verbose arguments of the Anglo-French diplomats. Seizing upon an old guise dearly familiar to the imperialistic powers of the West, Tokyo took advantage of the slaying by armed Russians of a Japanese national in Vladivostok and expeditiously occupied the city. Twenty-four hours later (on April 5) the British followed suit, although with fewer troops involved and a semi-apologetic gesture to Trotsky. Both powers were sufficiently adept at this game to assure each other (and thus the world at large) immediately of the disinterestedness of their motives, and the British Government took the extra precaution of urging the United States to join the party.

[16] Frank L. Polk to the American Legation in Copenhagen, February 10, 1918 (761.94/139).

[17] The attitude of the Secretary of State toward the Bolsheviks and his inherent conservatism were repeatedly attested in letters included among his private papers.

The reaction in Moscow was spontaneous, bitter, and aimed mainly at Tokyo, with a few pertinent questions directed to London. Nor could the American Government escape the inquisition of the Soviet; on April 7 Foreign Commissar Chicherin, in a note addressed to Raymond Robins, referred to "the highly unfavorable influence" which the Anglo-Japanese landing might have "upon the relations between the Soviet republic" and the United States (a curious statement in view of the absence of formalized contact between the two governments). In concluding, the Foreign Minister demanded "a full and definite immediate statement of the [American] attitude toward the occurrence." Such a report was not forthcoming for a long time, however. A clue to Washington's reticence was given by the President in mid-April. "Unfortunately," he wrote, "the whole state of sentiment in Russia is so confused and even problematical that I have found nothing more difficult than determining what course would be the best to pursue."

One of the major elements to complicate the picture for Washington was the gathering strength of indigenous anti-Soviet factions in Siberia throughout the late winter and early spring of 1918. The existence of these groups was significant to the State Department both for their avowed opposition to communism and for the rumored intrigue of England and Japan with certain of their leaders. Early in February the British interest in Captain Semenov had been acknowledged. A month later the American chargé at Harbin had reported a proposal to restore a Far Eastern army and government in Siberia under Admiral Kolchak.[18] And on April 4 the American consul at Harbin sent a cable to Washington which quoted an alleged telegram from General Tanaka to Horvat.[19] The Japanese general, after expressing his inability to assist the Russians prior to the establishment of a local Siberian Government, stated that following the formation of such a government Japan would be in a position to render aid. In return, Tokyo's "compensation" included:

[18] Kolchak was former commander of the Russian Black Sea Fleet under the Tsarist and Provisional Governments, and had made his way to Shanghai in the winter of 1918, where he began to organize an anti-Bolshevik army.

[19] Horvat was a key Russian (non-Soviet) official in the administration of the Chinese Eastern Railroad.

(1) dismantling of all fortifications at Vladivostok, which should be an open port;

(2) full fishing rights in all Siberia;

(3) open navigation of the Amur River;

(4) preferential forest and mining concessions similar to those demanded of China.

The cable also contained a message from Horvat to the State Department: "Can we secure the support of the United States at all and if so would it continue to the point [of] standing by in case of dispute [with] Japan, or would we be abandoned for commercial reasons?" No sooner had Washington received the Horvat message than a telegram arrived from the Prime Minister of the newly formed autonomous Siberian Government. In tone and language the incipient Russian state echoed the democratic united front promises of the deceased Kerensky regime, and to these pledges it added a vociferous denunciation of all things Bolshevik and an invitation to the Allies to intervene in Russia.

Regardless of the growing distaste with which the American Government viewed the Soviet leaders, President Wilson could not bring himself to encourage "any of the movements for a government of Siberia." Combined with a traditional respect for the right of peoples to self-determination were, on the one hand, an acute suspicion of the control which the Japanese might exert over any Far Eastern Russian government which Washington supported and, on the other hand, the contradictory information in the possession of the State Department concerning the need for Allied intervention.

For several weeks the advocates of a Siberian expedition had been concentrating on the threat posed by German and Austrian prisoners of war who, released following the Brest-Litovsk Treaty, were supposedly about to seize control of Siberia in the interests of the Central powers. Depending on their personal attitudes toward intervention, the German threat was respectively highlighted or discredited by American observers in their reports to Washington, and the consequent discrepancies in these reports made policy-forming uncommonly difficult. In March, Admiral Knight, aboard the U.S.S. *Brooklyn* outside Vladivostok, termed "preposterous" Japanese newspaper statements anticipating the arrival of German forces in eastern Siberia. But early the following month word from Harbin stressed that the only way to save Siberia from the Central powers was through "complete control of the railroad with ample military support." This unqualified opinion was substantiated by the "anti-Bolsheviks" in the United States Foreign Service, including Messrs. Macgowan, Jenkins, Thomson, and Nielsen.[20] Conversely, Paul Reinsch declared emphatically that there was "no evidence of a concerted plan on the part of the Germans to control Siberia through the prisoners, nor could such an attempt succeed"; and in answer to a request from Washington, Professor Thomas G. Masaryk, distinguished leader of the embryonic Czechoslovakian movement, further disparaged the German danger in Siberia and urged closer relations with the Soviet authorities. After sifting the contrary evidences the State Department temporarily acquiesced in the "pro-Soviet" view of the problem:

The reports of German influence in Siberia appear to have been greatly exaggerated . . . prisoners are for the most part Austro-Hungarian subjects—not German—and . . . who . . . are joining the Bolsheviki in order to fight capitalistic governments. . . . So long as the Bolsheviki are not antagonized by the Allies they and their Austrian confederates may be regarded as co-belligerents with us against the autocracy.[21]

[20] With regard to Macgowan, General Graves wrote: "The representatives of England, France, and Japan had found in Mr. MacGowan a ready and willing listener to reports as to the danger to be expected from the . . . prisoners . . . in Siberia. . . . Mr. MacGowan . . . was making reports from Irkutsk . . . and should have been able to ascertain the truth about prisoners . . . who, according to his report, made very little or no effort to conceal their identity. As these prisoners . . . were not in Irkutsk . . . I am forced to the conclusion that he [MacGowan] was desirous of getting information that would justify his reports to the State Department. His consular associates from other countries were all interested in making him believe there was a menace from these war prisoners, so all information given [him] . . . naturally would be calculated to form the impressions the Allied representatives desired." William S. Graves, *America's Siberian Adventure, 1918–1920* (New York: Jonathan Cape and Harrison Smith, 1931), p. 31.

[21] Memorandum, Division of Eastern European Affairs, April 19, 1918, *Breckinridge Long Papers*.

This attitude, with its concomitant of nonintervention, was maintained for the next six weeks despite the resurgence of fresh Anglo-French arguments, supplemented in turn by American consular reports and the pressure of various Russian groups. The chief weapon employed by Paris statesmen to batter down American resistance was the suggestion that independent Japanese action was probable —a contingency which had become all the more plausible since the Japanese landings at Vladivostok on April 4. This approach was also adopted by the Italian Ambassador to Russia, and although Francis wired from Vologda that he "did not believe . . . Japan would intervene against our wishes," he was forced to admit the existence of a "situation which gives a grasping nation a magnificent opportunity."

Only too clearly aware of Tokyo's capacity for infiltration on the mainland of Asia, and stung into further skepticism by the forthright Communist efforts to sow dissension between Japan and America, Secretary Lansing had a long discussion with the newly appointed Japanese Ambassador on April 29. The 1918 version of the Lansing-Ishii conversations produced no executive agreement, but the Secretary of State was nevertheless able to record his gratification that the Japanese agreed "fully" with the American viewpoint, and "do not see at present the military compensation for the danger of uniting the Russian factions to resist intervention and of throwing them into the arms of Germany." [22] On the basis of these reassurances Washington became more emphatic in its opposition to a Siberian expedition.

Meanwhile both France and Britain were stressing the imperative need for intervention to offset the critical situation on the Western front. Toward the end of April, Balfour suggested that London and Washington simultaneously approach the Soviet Government with an offer of Allied intervention and a guarantee of withdrawal at the end of the war, that the American Government agree to participate in the expedition, that the military command be left in Japanese hands. The American response showed the influence of military as well as diplomatic considerations on the Department of State. Regarding the latter, Lansing's political wariness

[22] *For. Rel.*, 1918, Russia, Vol. II, p. 144.

of any cooperative policy with Trotsky had been revealed almost as a reflex immediately after the receipt of the British proposal; moreover, the American statesman was anxious to avoid the alienation of the anti-Soviet forces in Siberia and this would hardly be possible if Washington entered into formal agreements with the Moscow Government. On the military side, the Secretary of State told Lord Reading, the British Ambassador, on May 11 that the United States had thus far been unable "to find any advantages in sending troops to Siberia."

As far as pure strategy was concerned, the American General Staff was pursuing a course of iron logic in its resistance to intervention. In contrast, the Japanese military were of the opinion that something very "effective" would result from an armed expedition into Asiatic Russia, and beginning the middle of May all reports pointed to the rising supremacy of the army group in Tokyo's ruling circles. In over three and a half years of participation in the World War, the Japanese had never been noted for their solicitude regarding the Allied struggle, nor had they been receptive to any suggestions that Japanese troops be sent to the European fighting fronts. Consequently the eager persistence with which Tokyo now pressed for intervention could be explained only on three possible grounds: a genuine fear of a German-controlled Siberia, a similar terror of a Communist regime in the Russian Far East, or an overriding desire to extend the Japanese empire at a crucial moment. That the last of these alternatives was the determining one, and that the other two were employed largely to rationalize an imperialistic policy, was the final verdict of Washington and, indeed, of later history. So that although Ambassador Morris cabled on May 16 that Tokyo was emphasizing "the necessity of establishing order, supporting more moderate elements and repressing Bolshevik movement," its soldier-diplomats were busily taking steps to advance the power position of Japan in Siberia. On one side this was illustrated in the policy adopted toward Kolchak and Semenov, whereby promises of support were offered in turn for questionable "compensation," and in which the two leaders were unscrupulously played off against each other to their common detriment. Thus, following the split between Kolchak and Semenov in mid-May, Tokyo's

General Nakajima declared that he would "continue to support with arms and ammunition both factions." In the light of later events, this was an open invitation to fratricide.

Another aspect of Japan's policy was demonstrated in its relations with China. As early as February, Reinsch had been informed of Tokyo's confidential advances to Peking regarding the "disorder" in Siberia, and in March and May respectively the two countries exchanged notes providing for armed collaboration against the enemy, the March agreement in particular being focused on China's northern frontier where the activities of the "Reds" in Siberia were allegedly endangering the interests of Peking and Tokyo. American skepticism of the usual Japanese variant of "joint cooperation" and American anxiety lest Japan, under the pretext of a possible Siberian intervention, occupy and eventually annex Manchurian territory were added factors in the diplomatic relations of the two countries in the ensuing months.

A third illustration which emphasized the imperialistic basis of Japanese policy was found in the purposeful press campaign by which the suspicions of the peoples of both Siberia and Japan were aroused as to ulterior American intentions in Asiatic Russia. In the main the activities ascribed to the United States were economic, and the following news dispatch, which appeared in papers throughout Japan on May 18, was typical of Tokyo's method:

The United States is making steady progress in its activity in Siberia and it is now reported that the Washington government, as a result of recent agreement with the Bolshevik government, has obtained an exclusive control of the Siberian Railway and Emerson and several other engineers now believed soon to start from Vladivostok for Moscow.

The press in Vladivostok and northern Manchurian cities were fed variations of this, including charges that Washington "means to share with Germany in despoiling Russia."

Official disclaimers from Tokyo sought to blind the State Department to the origin of these sniping news dispatches as well as to Japan's esoteric motives in Siberia. However, unlike previous instances when the proponents of Japanese aggrandizement had been temporarily defeated by the nonmilitary groups, the tacking and weaving of Nippon's policy from May onward represented mere feints to cover an undeviating ambition to intervene in the Russian Far East. At the same time, and notwithstanding Japan's efforts at deception, far more was being perceived than was admitted in Washington, and this gradually led to an about-face in the Wilson policy. Diplomatic etiquette prohibited the two powers from acknowledging their rivalry or the relation of their mutual antagonism to their respective Siberian policies and, ironically, it was left for the blunt-spoken Soviet leaders to forecast the future with cynical realism. On May 14 Lenin prophesied that an "inevitable conflict will arise between Japan and America for supremacy of [the] Pacific and its coasts," and pointed to "the conflicting interests" of the two "imperialistic countries" which, "screened by an alliance against Germany," checked "the movement of Japanese imperialism against Russia."

On June 1 in Paris a special Allied conference considered afresh the Siberian question. A very important factor in the decision to call this meeting was the official interest manifested in intervention by the new Japanese Government under the premiership of Baron Goto. At the Paris session the prime ministers of the European Allies, in conjunction with the Supreme War Council, elaborated three conditions subject to which they would approve Japanese intervention. Japan "should promise to respect the territorial integrity of Russia," to "take no side in the internal politics of the country," to "advance as far west as possible for the purpose of encountering the Germans." [23] According to the advices forwarded to Washington, on the receipt of a satisfactory Japanese response the American Government would be approached "as it was well known that the Japanese Government would not act" without United States approval and consent.

With this latest evidence of Japanese interest in intervention came a new surge of Allied pressure on the President, the War Department, and the American commanders in the field. According to General Bliss, the endless remonstrances to which he was subjected by his European colleagues touched only upon the al-

[23] Frazier via Sharp to Lansing, June 10, 1918 (763.72 Su/55).

leged advantages of intervention and significantly abstained from
any references to conceivable drawbacks. At the same time the
American general was strongly impressed by the increasing hatred
of the Allies for the Soviet Government, a hatred which made
mockery of the later pledges to abstain from interference in internal Russian politics. But although Bliss remained wary of the
interventionist arguments, others, including General Pershing on
the Western front and diplomatic and private persons in Russia
and the Far East, were urging that serious consideration be given
to the merits of such a program. To these voices were joined those
of official Britain and France, and the anti-Soviet Russians. To the
British, intervention was conceived of as a grandiose Japanese invasion to offset German pressure in the West and to safeguard
British possessions in the East; to the French it was all this plus a
morale-building enterprise in the face of the forty-mile proximity of
the Germans to Paris. Meanwhile opinions of non-Communist Russians were flooding into the State Department, containing invitations to the Allies to intervene from both private citizens and
members of the Provisional Government. The essence of these appeals was that intervention should be Allied in character, although
predominantly Japanese in numbers; that the alternative to an
Allied expedition would be a Bolshevik-German domination of
Russia and Siberia to the common misfortune of the Allied powers
and the "democratic" Russians; that America had a unique hold
upon the confidence of the latter.

These expressions received added weight with reports, on the
one hand, of reverses suffered by Semenov in skirmishes with
armed German and Austrian prisoners of war and, on the other,
with the receipt of new evidences of alleged Soviet perfidy. On
June 16, War Commissar Trotsky had voiced the opinion that if
a choice between German and Japanese troops were forced upon
him, "I would say . . . better the German army than the Japanese. . . . Any policy in connection with the Allies is the most
wicked treacherous policy with respect to the Russian people." [24]
This sort of vitriol, as injudicious as it was inflammatory, was grist

[24] Dennis, *op. cit.*, p. 286.

for the mill of the American anti-Bolsheviks, who seized upon every
kind of rumor in their dispatches to the State Department to il-
lustrate Moscow's "betrayal." According to Bruce Lockhart, the pro-
Soviet British agent, Trotsky's new position of defiance was traceable
at least in part to the moderating German attitude.[25] At any rate,
on June 22 the Soviet leader declared unequivocally:

> We cannot regard the intervention of the Allied imperialists in any
> other light than as a hostile attempt on the freedom and independence
> of Soviet Russia . . . Only fools can imagine that the Japanese would
> enter this fight for no other purpose than to help the Allies free Russia
> from the Germans . . . As between Japanese and German occupation
> . . . the former is more dangerous for . . . Russia since there is much
> less reason to expect an early internal change in Japan than in Germany
> . . . Those who twist this statement into an argument that we plan
> an alliance with the Germans against the "Allies" are either naturally
> stupid or are being paid to be stupid.

By mid-June, Colonel House was "convinced that it was no longer
possible simply to return a blank negative to Allied demands for
intervention." In a letter to the President on the 13th, duplicated
by a Lansing memorandum on the same date, he suggested that
an Allied relief commission be sent to Russia to precede (if not to
obviate) any armed intervention. The desire to reconcile American
deeds with the Wilsonian expressions of sympathy and respect for
the rights of the Russian people could not be thus easily achieved,
however. To the Allies relief could be considered only as an ad-
junct to military intervention, and this view was shortly to prevail
within the State Department.

Of invaluable moral assistance in the conversion of Washington
was the anabasis of the Czechoslovakian legions across Russia in

[25] On May 29 Lockhart had cabled his government to the effect that prior
to May 1 the Communists, fearful of Germany, could have been persuaded to
accept Western intervention. Thereafter, however, "owing to the great change
in the attitude of Germany towards the Bolshevists, it is hardly probable that
the latter will consent to intervention by the Allies." Paraphrase of telegram from
Lockhart to the Foreign Office, May 29, 1918 (861.00/2087½). Before dispatching this message, Lockhart discussed it with the military attachés of the
Allies in Moscow and found that "they completely agreed." *Ibid.*

the late spring and early summer of 1918. But while this eventually produced "the first plank in the platform of the interventionists," [26] arousing as it did the sentimental fervor of the Allied peoples in general and the Americans in particular, later history disclosed that there was more method than madness in the seemingly fruitless trek of some forty-five thousand Czech soldiers from the Ukraine to Vladivostok, the first lap in a hypothetical round-the-world journey to the battlefields of France.

Following the Bolshevik Revolution and the Soviet-German peace negotiations, the Czech National Council in Paris had announced the incorporation of its forces in Russia with those in the West and arranged with London and Paris for financial aid in transporting the troops to France. Perceiving an opportunity to use the dependent Czechs as a nuclear force around which to build an Allied Siberian expedition, Great Britain persuaded the French Government to its point of view, whereupon it was decided in late May that the Czechs would remain in Russia. Uninformed of the Allied plan, the United States had been observing with sympathetic interest the eastward journey of the Czech troops across Russia. Equally oblivious of the decision taken by the Czech military commanders to violate their agreement with the Soviet Government providing for the surrender of Czech arms at way stations across Siberia, Washington was angrily stirred by the news of the Cheliabinsk affair on May 14 with its explosive repercussions. At Cheliabinsk station a train filled with German and Austrian prisoners going west had passed the Czech train. When one of the prisoners struck a Czechoslovak he was lynched, and when Soviet officials promptly arrested the lynchers, their comrades intervened. Trotsky then ordered the Czechs to forfeit their weapons; the refusal to comply and the sporadic resistance to the Bolsheviks which followed was a prelude to the later organized Czech efforts to fight the Communists.

On June 4 Ambassador Francis joined his diplomatic colleagues in a caveat to the Russian Government to the effect that the

[26] R. H. Bruce Lockhart, *Memoirs of a British Agent* (New York: G. P. Putnam's Sons, 1932), p. 284.

"disarming of the Czechs would be considered . . . an unfriendly act." [27] This charge was denied by Foreign Commissar Chicherin on the grounds of Russia's neutrality.

Given the emotional reaction of American public opinion on behalf of the Czechs, the rising antipathy between the Soviet leaders and the Western powers, and the relentless interventionist pressure of the latter on Washington, it was scarcely conceivable that the American Government would ignore the existence of a situation which offered an easy solution to the moral dilemma confronting it. Throughout June the records of Washington officials and agents in the field stressed the connection between intervention and the allegedly beleaguered Czechs; where hitherto it had been a solemn obligation of the United States to uphold the internal integrity of Russia it now became a duty of equal solemnity to rescue the valiant Allied legion. But while a valid excuse might have been projected for intervention directed to the removal of the Czechs *from* Siberia, it was soon obvious that the reverse of this procedure was contemplated by various American diplomats and the Allied Governments. A cable from Reinsch was characteristic of the trend at this time:

It is the general opinion of Allied representatives here in which I concur that it would be a serious mistake to remove the Czecho-Slovak troops from Siberia. With only slight countenance and support they could control all of Siberia against the Germans. Their removal would greatly benefit Germany and further discourage Russia.[28]

To Wilson this information provided "the shadow of a plan that might be worked, with Japanese and other assistance." From this time forward American policy evolved steadily toward

[27] In a letter to his son on the same date Francis wrote: "I am now planning to prevent if possible the disarming of 40,000 or more Czecho-Slovak soldiers, whom the Soviet Government had ordered to give up their arms . . . *I have no instructions or authority from Washington to encourage these men to disobey the orders of the Soviet Government*, except an expression of sympathy with the Czecho-Slovaks sent out by the Department of State. I have taken chances before, however." David R. Francis, *Russia from the American Embassy, April, 1916–November, 1918* (New York: Charles Scribner's Sons, 1922), p. 303. Italics mine.

[28] *For. Rel.*, 1918, Russia, Vol. II, pp. 206–207.

intervention. The voices of the opposition were gradually stilled. The Wilson Administration, which had been like unto a ship at the mercy of willful storms, now began to steer its course by the prevailing wind. Irritated, but no longer fettered by competing and contradictory advices, it picked up strength and purpose as it moved ineluctably toward intervention. But although the presence of the Czechoslovaks provided the focal point around which the far-flung advocates of intervention at last rallied in outward agreement, unanimous accord on what constituted the "rescue" of the Czech contingent was never realized, even among United States officials. The consequences were inescapable. As soon as Allied forces arrived in Siberia, Wilson was to find that, as Paul Reinsch had suggested earlier, the British, French, and Japanese, as well as many American Foreign Service personnel, defined "rescue" as the reinforcement of the Czechoslovaks in the *interior* of Siberia, and not, as the President had apparently intended, their evacuation *from* Siberia. This divergence of interpretation was to confuse still further an already confused and distorted picture.

On July 4 Lansing noted that "a sentimental element" had been introduced "into the question of our duty" by the Czech capture of Vladivostok. He distinguished between intervention "to restore order" and intervention to furnish protection to the Czechs, concluding that the United States was now confronted with "a moral obligation to save these men from our common enemies, if we are able to do so." Two days later the Secretary of the Navy quietly confirmed this obligation in a cable to Admiral Knight at Vladivostok. In order that the city remain available "as a base for the safety of the Czechs and as a means of egress for them should the necessity arise," Daniels authorized the Admiral to "utilize the force" at his disposal and to "request similar action by Allied naval forces in holding the city." [29] This was indeed a revealing note! So solicitous had the United States become for the welfare of the Czechoslovakian regiment that for once the Allies had no need of requesting American cooperation in Siberia; an American official had already requested Allied aid!

Beneath the outward manifestation of concern over the plight

[29] *Ibid.*, pp. 263–264.

of the Czechs, which was purposely exaggerated in the interests of the interventionists, the main current of American anxiety continued apace, manifesting itself indirectly throughout the records of the period. On June 18 Wilson informed the French Ambassador to Japan that he "was considering anew the entire situation, and would express his conclusions within the next ten days." [30] Commenting on this statement afterwards, the French Ambassador to Russia remarked that Wilson's protestations revealed his hostility to an expedition which "by the nature of things would have to be executed by the Japanese." [31] This, of course, was the crux of the whole issue as far as Washington was concerned. Aside from Ambassador Francis, whose naïveté regarding power politics was demonstrated in this, as in frequent other instances,[32] the State Department had little faith in Japanese declarations, no matter how eloquently phrased. Thus the official reply of Tokyo to the Allied communication in early June, in which the "conditions" of Japanese intervention had been outlined, was only partially satisfactory to the Wilson Government. After reiterating its disinclination to consider intervention without American sanction, and its willing-

[30] *Ibid.*, p. 219. In contrast to the Department of State, the War Department was still unreconciled to intervention. On June 19 Secretary Baker wrote: "If I had my own way about Russia . . . I would like to take everybody out . . . except the Russians, including diplomatic representatives, military representatives, political agents, propagandists and casual visitors, and let the Russians settle down and settle their own affairs." Later on he referred to the intervention program as "nonsense . . . one of those sideshows born of desperation." Quoted by Foster Rhea Dulles, *The Road to Teheran* (Princeton: Princeton University Press, 1944), p. 137.

[31] Joseph Noulens, *Mon ambassade en Russie sovietique, 1917–1919* (Paris: Plòn, 1933), Vol. II, p. 114.

[32] In a telegram to Lansing, dated June 22, Francis said: "In my judgment no promises should be exacted of Japan and no promises made to her if she will consent to intervention without them. If Japan can be induced to join with us in intervention we need have no fear concerning her exactions or demands when the war ends. War will certainly terminate in our favor . . . when the end comes, the Entente will dominate the peace table and Japan will be compelled to accept the just terms offered whether she likes them or not. We have announced the principle of self-determination of peoples and our Allies have agreed thereto, consequently Japan cannot afford to object in the final peace conference." *For. Rel., op. cit.*, p. 222. Lockhart, *op. cit., passim*, noted several instances in which the American ambassador demonstrated his "innocence" concerning international politics.

ness, in the event that such a sanction were obtained, to abide by the first two Allied conditions, the Japanese note stated:

With regard to the third condition, requiring the Allied expedition to advance as far West as possible, the Japanese Government regret that they should find it impossible for them to engage to extend Westward their military activities beyond the limits of Eastern Siberia, in view of the grave difficulties with which such operations will be practically confronted.[33]

The utility of such limited intervention in terms of reestablishing the Eastern front, capturing the majority of escaped prisoners of war, and protecting the sizable Allied stocks between Lake Baikal and the Urals was highly doubtful to Washington, and therefore the motives of Tokyo were once again questioned. But by the end of June there were indications that intervention in Siberia would eventuate in the not-distant future, with or without American approval; and given the myriad pressures on the State Department, the Czechoslovakian "justification," the admitted dislike for the Bolsheviks, and the implications for America's Far Eastern position in a Japanese-sponsored expedition, the United States had little latitude in formulating its policy. Accordingly, President Wilson summoned to the White House on July 6 the Secretaries of State, War, and Navy, General March, and Admiral Benson. The conferees discussed in detail the ramifications of the Siberian issue, and emerged with a document which was a tribute to the confusion surrounding the problem and which anticipated the public statement of American policy a few weeks later. In brief, the imploring Allied appeals for the establishment of an Eastern front were repudiated as a valid cause for intervention; evacuation of the Czechs from Russia was unhappily omitted in the numerous references which stressed solely the need to protect these exiles in their march to join their compatriots in the *interior* of Siberia; and the inter-Allied expedition to accomplish this was

---

[33] Copy of a note handed by the Japanese Ambassador at London to the British Secretary of State for Foreign Affairs; given to Wilson by Reading, June 29, 1918. *Wilson Papers*. See also F. Palmer, *Bliss, Peacemaker* (New York: Dodd, Mead & Co., 1934), p. 301, for a partial summary of the note.

to consist of seven thousand Americans and an equal number of Japanese, armed with weapons of war and promises of noninterference.[34]

From a memorandum on July 8 Lansing appeared to be convinced that Viscount Ishii shared the American point of view as to the purposes of intervention and the numerical strength to be employed.[35] The underlying discordance between the two countries was sufficiently manifested in the next ten days, however, to belie the outward aura of calm and mutual trustfulness. In the first place, information relating to the newly formed Horvat Government in Siberia, reputedly monarchist in sentiment and backed by Tokyo, was extremely disquieting to the State Department. Although the Japanese Foreign Minister, in response to an American note, promptly assured Ambassador Morris that "Japan would pledge herself not to support any group or interfere in the internal politics of Siberia," other points of irritation persisted. In the main these were centered on Japanese activities in Manchuria and along the Chinese Eastern Railroad, where it was apparent that Tokyo was seeking to infiltrate under spurious pretenses. For example, Washington had been notified by China three months previously that

[34] *For. Rel.*, *op. cit.*, pp. 262–263. Consistent with the practically undeviating attitude of the War Department, General March stood alone as the only dissident to the Wilson plan for intervention. Peyton C. March, *The Nation at War* (New York: Doubleday, Doran & Co., 1932), p. 124.

[35] On July 6 Colonel House had a conversation with the Japanese Ambassador which revealed the superficial knowledge of Wilson's adviser concerning the Far East. In a letter to the President on the same date, House wrote: "He [Ishii] stated that within recent years there had been a growing tendancy [sic] upon the part of Russia to exclude the Japanese from Siberia, although they continued to let Koreans and other Asiatics go in. He thought that the position of Japan would become intolerable if her citizens were to be deprived of such an outlet.

"I expressed my sympathy with this view and believed he would find the United States cooperating with the Japanese to bring about a more liberal policy. If this could be done, he was sure that Japan would be willing to follow our lead in any policy that might be determined upon regarding Siberia. It has been my opinion for a long time that unless Japan was treated with more consideration regarding the right of her citizens to expand in nearby Asiatic, undeveloped countries, she would have to be reckoned with—and rightly so." *Wilson Papers.*

Japan was opposed to any arrangement whereby American assistance would be used on the railroad in northern Manchuria. And in May the Horvat faction, always associated with Japan in the Washington mind, had reached an agreement with China which reorganized the board of directors of the C.E.R. with the result that the legal connection with the Russian Government, dating back to the treaty of 1896, was dissolved "until [the] complete restoration of order in Russia." In reply to the report in July that China was contemplating action to regain control of the line— a control which, once again, was inalterably linked to Japanese maneuvers, by the State Department—the American Government felt compelled to defend the rights of the State of Russia and to protest any untoward step by Peking.[36] Moreover, a similar démarche was sent to Tokyo on July 19 after Morris had telegraphed: "The General Staff is urging upon the Cabinet the immediate occupation of Manchuria by Japanese troops . . . The plan submitted includes taking over the control of the Chinese Eastern Railroad." [37] While the twin problems of Manchuria and the C.E.R. continued to worry the United States long after American troops had entered Siberia, they were simultaneously additional factors in precipitating the decision to intervene.

On July 17 the Secretary of State dispatched an *aide-mémoire* to the Allies and Japan which proposed that America and Japan each send seven thousand troops to "assist the Czechoslovaks in Siberia." Surrounding the core of the declaration were successive layers of platitudes and inconsistencies which were intended to soothe Russian feelings, delimit by inference Japanese activity, and outline broadly America's motives. Thus, the memorandum stated emphatically:

[36] *For. Rel.*, 1918, Russia, Vol. II, p. 292. This elicited the following response by the Acting Minister for Foreign Affairs, on July 20: ". . . Chinese Government has no intention of attempting to oust Russians from the control of the Chinese Eastern Railroad . . . however . . . two days ago such a course was strongly urged upon the Foreign Office by a representative of 'a certain nation' . . ." In cabling this message, Chargé MacMurray noted that the "certain nation" obviously was Japan. *Ibid.*, p. 298.

[37] *Ibid.*, pp. 281, 297–298. Japan ignored the United States admonishment and proceeded to occupy Manchuria. Griswold, *op. cit.*, p. 230.

We felt that by sending troops in not only without any limitation as to number, but even indicating that more troops would be sent if the occasion demanded, the natural impression would be created in the Russian mind that this was an expedition which had more in view than merely assisting the Czechs. We felt . . . that the number should be limited, and if later it appeared that this force was not adequate, the question could be discussed and this Government would then . . . decide whether they would continue or . . . withdraw, leaving the Japanese and the other Governments to proceed if they saw fit.

I also called his attention to the words "having regard at the same time to the special position of Japan," and said that it hardly seemed necessary to put that in, as the Lansing-Ishii agreement very clearly indicated our attitude toward Japan . . . but putting it in might create difficulties in Russia . . .[41]

Nor was the Japanese declaration the only source of American anxiety. On July 24 MacMurray telegraphed from Peking that China had been notified of the Japanese plan, and that Tokyo expected automatic Chinese approval of the establishment of Japanese railroad patrols along the Chinese Eastern Railroad in Manchuria, on the basis of the Sino-Japanese military convention. Two days later Assistant Secretary of State Long sought to counteract Tokyo's move by informing Chinese Minister Koo that in the event of a Siberian intervention the United States felt it would "be advisable" for China to control "alone . . . that part of the Chinese Eastern Railroad which lies within Chinese territory." This advice was passed along to Japan on July 29. The receipt of word at the end of the month that Tokyo had ordered "a number of torpedo boats to Nicolaievsk to protect Japanese interests," added to the above instances of Japan's policy toward intervention, caused Wilson to complain bitterly that "the Japanese Government is trying to alter the whole plan in a way to which we cannot consent and for the time being . . . the whole matter is in suspense."[42]

[41] Polk to Wilson, July 26, 1918, *Wilson Papers*. See also Ray Stannard Baker, *Woodrow Wilson: Life and Letters* (New York: Doubleday, Page and Co., 1939), Vol. VIII, pp. 297–298, and Polk to Morris, July 27, 1918, *For. Rel.*, *op. cit.*, p. 307.

[42] Wilson to Daniels, August 1, 1918, *Wilson Papers*; Baker, *op. cit.*, Vol. VIII, pp. 310–311.

This atmosphere did not prevail for long, however. On August 1 and 2 Japan yielded sufficiently to the American position to win final approval for the Siberian expedition. In the first place the Minister for Foreign Affairs let it be known that while the situation concerning the Chinese Eastern was a difficult one, Tokyo would doubtless agree to Washington's suggestion that only Chinese troops be utilized to guard the railroad "simply because . . . [the Japanese minister] and his colleagues desired to act in full accord with our views." In regard to the Siberian intervention in particular, Viscount Ishii presented the State Department with an undated memorandum on August 2 which omitted the most disturbing features of the July 24 pronouncement. Although Tokyo still balked at committing itself to round numbers in describing its military contingent, the Wilson Government was apparently satisfied with the oral explanations of the Japanese Ambassador [43] and on the afternoon of August 3 the official American declaration on intervention was given to the Allies and the press. In every important respect the August statement was almost identical with that which had been circulated among the Entente powers on July 17; in other words, the criticisms of the Allies were not incorporated in the final American draft and the latter was as replete with contradictions

[43] Ishii told Polk that "his Government still felt a larger force than proposed was essential, but in view of the necessity for immediate action, and in view of the attitude of this Government, his Government authorized him to say that they accepted our proposals, reserving the question as to the sending of additional troops . . . until circumstances should arise which might make it necessary.

"He said that his Government had explained this last point by saying it might be necessary for the troops to move out of Vladivostok in order to prevent the slaughter of the Czechs, or it might be necessary to send reinforcements for this same purpose . . . He said that in such an emergency it was his Government's intention to consult this Government and the other Governments, but it was conceivable that there might be no time for consultation, in which case the Japanese Government wished to say frankly that they would be compelled . . . to move without consultation . . .

"I asked him two or three times whether it was his understanding that the Japanese forces would be limited to ten or twelve thousand men, and he said that in view of the fact that such a number had been mentioned by me in our previous conversation, and in view of the fact that his Government stated they accepted our proposal, he felt there was no question on that point." *For. Rel.*, *op. cit.*, pp. 325–326.

as the initial proposal: Washington consented to an intervention of which it heartily disapproved; it sought to limit the action of the Allies by freeing them of its own self-imposed restrictions; and it renounced political interference by offering assistance to those Russians who desired it.

Wherein lay the explanation for this bundle of diplomatic inconsistencies which, through its ambiguity, provided a platform on which the Principal Allied and Associated Powers could stand in superficial agreement, the while they clung to their respective, and frequently antithetical, motives for intervention?

In the preceding eight months Britain and France had gradually swung to an espousal of a large-scale intervention; one in which a million or more Allied troops, predominantly Japanese, would invade Siberia and march west through Russia in order to halt the movement of German forces from the Eastern front to France. The growing terror of a German victory and the accompanying dread of the loss of the Anglo-French colonies in southeast Asia were mainly responsible for the Allied position, and these factors had relegated to the background the pardonable fear of Japanese entrenchment in Siberia after the war.

In contrast, Tokyo was opposed to the creation of a "second front" in the Russian Far East. To the general staff the German danger was as incidental to Japanese policy as it had been for the past three years, and accordingly Japan was explicit in its unwillingness to dispatch troops west of Irkutsk—a point too many hundreds of miles from the European battle lines to have any important bearing on the struggle. At the same time, Tokyo was equally adamant in its refusal to countenance a "small" intervention, reserving ultimate freedom of action in determining the number of troops it would send to Eastern Siberia.

The American high command, averse on grounds of strategy to *any* intervention, large or small, had provided the Wilson Administration with one of its most convincing arguments for many weeks. Secretary Baker recounted some years later that the President had told him of his satisfaction "with the soundness of the War Department's view but that, *for other than military reasons, he felt obliged to cooperate* in a limited way in both proposed expeditions." [44] The sense of obligation which moved Wilson to participate in an intervention which he believed to be unjustified from a military standpoint could have stemmed only from political considerations. To what extent, it may then be asked, did these considerations of high policy emanate from a hatred of communism, and to what extent from a fear of Japan?

The anti-bolshevism of the American press and people was unqualifiedly articulate throughout the spring and summer of 1918, and the President expressed his own feeling for the Soviet when he wrote: "I don't think you need fear any consequences of our dealing with the Bolsheviki, because we do not intend to deal with them." [45] With this in mind, the August declaration that the United States desired "to steady any efforts at self-government . . . in which the Russians themselves may be willing to accept assistance" could not have been intended to console the Soviet rulers. This was confirmed by the sharp reproof cast upon American motives by the Bolsheviks a few weeks later. Nevertheless, logic required that anti-communism be dismissed as the guiding motive in the American policy. In the first place, it in no wise explained the unremitting attempts of the State Department to forestall intervention from December 1917 through June of the following year; and secondly, an expedition limited by American insistence to a few thousand men could not conceivably have unseated the Soviet Government. Once the decision to intervene had been made, the emotional antipathy of the American people to bolshevism played the role of an accessory, a role which was overemphasized simply because the principal motive behind the American intervention was never openly revealed. The closest which Washington came to such a revelation was in that part of the August statement which solemnly assured the Russian people that the United States contemplated no action which would in any way impinge on Russia's sovereignty and territorial integrity. In view of the historic aloofness of America to foreign conquest this pledge was intended to tie other hands than its own, specifically those of Japan.

[44] Graves, *op. cit.*, p. ix. Italics mine. Apart from the Siberian expedition, American troops also participated in the North Russia intervention.

[45] Wilson to Senator James Hamilton Lewis, July 24, 1918, *Wilson Papers*.

In essence, the United States consented to intervene after a policy-duel of several months had failed to turn the Japanese from their desire to send an army to Siberia, a desire in which Tokyo had received support and encouragement from London and Paris. Having witnessed the penetration of Japanese imperialism on the mainland of Asia between 1914 and 1917, Washington had no illusions concerning the true intentions of Tokyo in Siberia. Similarly, the State Department was at last fully cognizant of the impotence of diplomatic protests unaccompanied by physical commitments. Viewed from the perspective of history, the August pronouncement on the purposes and goals of the Siberian expedition was therefore an integral part of American Far Eastern policy: Czechs, Germans, the war in Europe, and the interests of the Russian people provided a moral rationalization for what was basically a political struggle between Japan and the United States. In the summer of 1918 the scales of power in Asia were weighted heavily on the side of Tokyo, and the twin principles by which America had traditionally sought to protect its interests—the open-door and the preservation of the territorial integrity of Asiatic states —were in danger of lasting effacement. The necessity to stop the Japanese drive for empire was accordingly imperative. By virtue of war and revolution Soviet Russia became the scene of the battle, and the United States emerged as the defender of Russian sovereignty in the Far East.

CHAPTER V

Intervention in Siberia: I

It would be difficult to find a period in American foreign relations more rampant with confusion, less understood by its contemporaries, and superficially more diffuse in purpose than the nineteen months during which seven thousand United States troops occupied Siberian territory. The incongruous *aide-mémoire* of August 3 which comprised the orders of commanding General William S. Graves was an invitation to ambiguity, reflecting the discordant influences which had determined the American course of action. Ensnared in its own contradictions, the State Department oscillated markedly in applying the August declaration, finding ample justification therein for the widest extremes of policy. Several factors contributed to the general confusion.

In the first place, the Siberian expedition was at best a recurrent sideshow to the men in the Wilson Administration who were progressively engrossed in the problems attendant on the conclusion of the war and the Paris Conference. This meant that the Far Eastern intervention never received the systematic and conscientious attention of top-flight experts, but was relegated instead to the pigeonholes of diplomacy, from whence it was drawn spasmodically as events dictated. In the second place, the obfuscation of the official statement, coupled with the Armistice in November 1918, undoubtedly contributed to a restiveness in the American people toward an expedition which became increasingly incomprehensible to them. This in turn evoked Congressional resolutions demanding the recall of the Siberian contingent. In the third place, the general staff in Washington, never reconciled to the wisdom of intervention, and regarding it steadfastly in terms of its military, rather than its political significance, staunchly upheld General

87

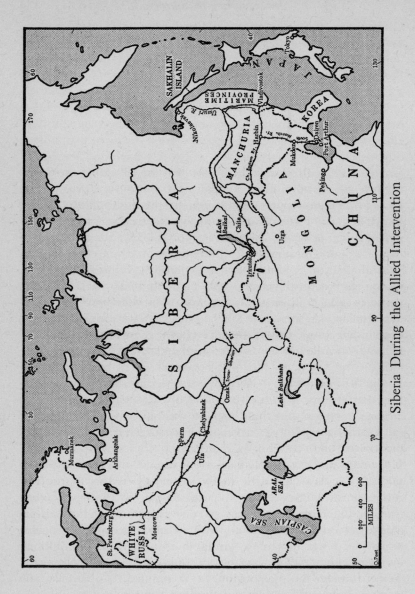

Siberia During the Allied Intervention

Graves in his rigid refusal to interfere in internal Russian politics, with the result that the Departments of State and War were frequently embroiled in "family" disputes over the interpretation of the August memorandum. Finally, Secretary Lansing and his colleagues, at least partly because of their absorption elsewhere, vacillated between two opposite poles in their attitude toward intervention, the one anti-Japanese and the other anti-Soviet. The most effective means of countering Japanese ambition lay in maintaining Siberian territory intact, to the ultimate benefit of the Soviet Government; conversely, the surest way of blocking the Communists was to promote and protect anti-Bolshevik groups in the Far East, thereby weakening Siberia to the advantage of Japan. While the anti-Japanese policy was always essentially more compelling because of its ramifications for the balance of power in Asia, the anti-Communist drive also exerted a strong influence on Washington. As a result, an attempt was made over a period of months to syncretize the two policies by shuttling back and forth between them and even by pursuing both simultaneously. This not only clouded the whole Siberian issue to an extent hitherto unknown, but aroused the antagonism of every nation and group in any way concerned with intervention, including the Moscow Government.

The decision of the United States to withdraw its forces from Russian territory in the early spring of 1920 was attributable in large measure to public pressure and was officially justified on the ground that with the evacuation of the last Czech troops the original purpose of intervention had been served. In terms of American-Japanese rivalry this simply meant that the scene of conflict was removed from Siberia to the respective foreign offices of the two countries where it continued unabated while Washington, sorely tried by the Japanese victories at Paris as well as by the Russian occupation, sought new levers with which to swing the balance of Pacific power into more favorable alignment. In the ensuing five years the State Department scored an ephemeral success over Tokyo through the medium of the Washington Conference and pressure-diplomacy, and by 1925 Russian territory was finally freed of Japanese troops.

The antagonism of America and Japan was duplicated in the hostility of Moscow to Tokyo in these years. Following the November Revolution of 1917, the Russo-Japanese understanding of the preceding decade was shattered, and despite the "warmed-up" condition in which it was served in a treaty in 1925, the two states never achieved more than a nodding confidence prior to the Second World War. Because their Asiatic policies were forged in the common crucible of their suspicion of Japan, it was indeed perverse logic that the Soviet Union and the United States were unable to adjust their mutual differences and establish harmonious relations. On the contrary, Russia sought to offset Japan by an ardent courtship of China, and the American Government, even as it strove valiantly to protect Moscow's Far Eastern possessions from the rapacious Japanese, endeavored to undermine Soviet influence at Peking. American-Russian relations from 1918 to the end of 1925 were thus determined both by common need and by common antipathy: fear of Japan drove the two countries to pursue parallel policies, while fear of each other prevented the coalescence of those policies into a united front.

On September 4, 1918, a fortnight after the first United States troops had disembarked at Vladivostok, General Graves arrived to assume active command of the American Siberian army. In the course of the preceding month the underlying disparities between the American and Allied policies had begun to be manifest and, notwithstanding instances of cooperation and accord, the lines once drawn remained fundamentally distinct in the weeks to come. The first Anglo-French act to provoke the State Department was the introduction of politics into what was professedly a purely strategic military engagement. On August 11 the British Government informed Lansing of its decision to appoint a high commissioner to represent British interests in political questions. The next day French Ambassador Jusserand suggested the establishment of an inter-Allied civilian group to supervise and connect the Vladivostok and Archangel expeditions. Among other duties the board would act as a mediator of political disputes and determine the relation between the Allies and the local governing authorities.

To make the pill more palatable, France coated it with an American chairmanship.

At the end of the month Washington responded to the Paris communication with a statement of policy which was adhered to until shortly after the Armistice. Emphasizing its strict impartiality "as between contending political parties," the American Government accordingly considered political cooperation impossible, and as "unnecessary" as it was "undesirable." Instead, it preferred to stand by, "ready to help in the most practical and wholehearted manner."

To the British such aloofness was hard to accept. A few weeks later Downing Street again sought to persuade the State Department of the necessity for a specially constituted body to act on questions of economic, social, and political content. The farthest that Washington was willing to go at this time, however, was to blueprint a comprehensive plan for the economic relief of the Czechoslovaks and those parts of Russia under Allied control; but the organization by the War Trade Board of a Russian Bureau was followed by a continual stalemate because of the unwillingness of the Allies to pursue disinterested policies in Siberia and north Russia.[1]

Another source of irritation in the autumn of 1918 was the American unwillingness to reinforce the Czech soldiers in western Siberia. On the basis of reports testifying to the critical position of these troops, Lansing sought the advice of Wilson in mid-August and even urged that the newly formulated American declaration be revamped in the interest of a broader intervention. The President's opposition was reflected in a memorandum dated August 20, in which he categorically refused either to countenance an enlarged expedition, Japanese or American, or to dispatch Allied forces west of Irkutsk. Meantime British commanding officer Poole, in North Russia, sent instructions to the Czechoslovaks to seize the

[1] *For. Rel.*, The Paris Peace Conference, 1919, Vol. II, pp. 474–475. Illustrative of the economic competition among the intervening powers was the muddle over the currency problem and the introduction of different currencies in different parts of Russia; the Japanese, for example, sought to displace the ruble by the yen, thus tying the Siberian economy to Tokyo.

city of Perm and thence to join the Allied troops. Although such a scheme was wholly consistent with the British-held concept of intervention, whereby infiltration of the Czechs *into* Russia rather than their evacuation *from* Russia was the goal, Wilson was visibly disturbed by "the utter disregard" of Poole and the Allies for "the policy to which we expressly confined ourselves." Writing to Lansing in early September he queried: "Is there no way . . . by which we can get this comprehended?" Pursuing the matter a fortnight later he told his Secretary of State:

We must either insist that the Czecho-Slovaks give up their purpose of establishing an Eastern front . . . and that they move eastward and unite with the Allied forces in Eastern Siberia and ultimately be transferred to some other front, or we must fall in with the design which has all along underlain this matter, namely . . . of drawing us into the formation of an Eastern front composed of troops of the Allied nations.[2]

This, of course, was the choice of alternatives which ought theoretically to have been faced in July when the American Government formulated its *aide-mémoire*. Had a decision clearly been made at that time, there would have been no moral justification for the Allied efforts to keep the Czech troops in Siberia. But the August memorandum avoided all mention of the evacuation of the Czechoslovaks; and if this had been the President's ultimate objective it was nowhere officially listed in the policy statement. Consequently, as Lansing indicated on September 21, the ambiguity of the *aide-mémoire* left only one avenue open to the Wilson Administration: emphasis upon the impractical (in contrast to the illegal or immoral) aspects in creating an Eastern front.

If the American declaration was sufficiently broad and confused to permit the Allies to pursue policies with which the President was wholly unsympathetic, it was also productive of widely divergent interpretations by American Foreign Service personnel. Thus in contrast to Wilson's concept of a small and limited intervention, Consul General Harris cabled from Irkutsk at the end of September that a minimum of fifty thousand Allied forces was

[2] Wilson to Lansing, September 18, 1918 (861.00/3009).

imperative for the welfare of the Czechs; at the same time the need for reinforcements was substantiated by Ambassador Morris in Tokyo, who urged that General Graves be allowed to proceed to Omsk to form a winter base in order to be of support to the Czechs farther west. These messages were countered at once by a forthright communication from the State Department.

The ideas and purposes of the Allies with respect to military operations in Siberia and on the "Volga front" are ideas and purposes with which we have no sympathy. We do not believe them to be practical or based upon sound reason . . . Consequently, while we have said that we do not desire to set the limits . . . of our associates, we are not prepared and do not intend to follow their lead and do not desire our representatives to be influenced by their persistent representations as to facts and as to plans for action which, to us, seem chimerical and wholly impossible. You will . . . impress upon the . . . authorities of the United States . . . at Vladivostok that . . . they are expected to be governed wholly and absolutely by the policy of this government as expressed herein.[3]

In effect this was an amendment to the declaration of August 3. But while reducing the equivocation of the latter by clarifying American opposition to the establishment of an Eastern front, the Washington note evoked strong resentment among the Allies and anti-Soviet Russians. Regardless of the selfish reasons behind their reaction, the resentment itself was in a sense justifiable, for the State Department, which had expressly abstained from efforts to limit Allied activity "even by implication" in the August statement—before intervention had occurred—was now apparently exerting moral influence against the Allied program. It did not matter that this latest note was addressed solely to American representatives in the Far East and was intended to brief *them* on official policy; the psychological effects were felt well beyond the American diplomatic circle. Czechs, British, French, Japanese, the non-Bolshevik Russian army, and the Provisional Government's spokesman in Washington alike expressed disapproval of Wilsonian obstructionism. The net result, it was predicted by these prophets of gloom,

[3] *For. Rel.*, 1918, Russia, Vol. II, pp. 392–394.

would surely be the betrayal of the Czech legions and the turning of the non-Soviet Russians to Germany for aid in preserving order.

The stiffening of American policy was a reflection of three separate considerations, each of which influenced the State Department for different reasons. These were public aversion in the United States to an increased expeditionary force, American military opposition to any depletion of men or resources from the Western front, and the State Department's own reluctance to sanction an extension of intervention in terms of both men and territory, because of the added temptation it would present to the imperialists of all countries, and notably to those of Japan.

Although Tokyo had impressed upon Ambassador Morris its firm intention to cooperate "with America both in present Siberian problems and in future policies vis-à-vis China" and had illustrated the former by refraining from the appointment of a high commissioner to Vladivostok, burnt offerings such as this, so glibly proffered by the Japanese diplomats, did little to erase Washington's skepticism. Within only a few days of the official American decision to intervene the State Department rejected a British plea that the United States request Japan to send to Siberia whatever military assistance Czech and Japanese military experts deemed desirable and necessary. The occasion for the British note arose from the "critical position" of the Czech troops, and was in reality a Japanese-inspired request sent by a third power to Washington. This oblique approach, coupled with Tokyo's unwillingness to wait even a fortnight before seeking to undermine the American doctrine of a limited intervention, only deepened the suspicion of the State Department regarding Japanese motives.

No sooner had Japan been turned down than its cause was sponsored by the French who, after rendering lipservice to the views of President Wilson, felt compelled to "place the facts before him." Briefly, the Czechoslovak, French, and Japanese staffs in Vladivostok had concluded that "immediate and powerful reinforcements . . . three or four Japanese divisions" were a prerequisite to the Czech advance westward to Irkutsk.

On the basis of these "unmistakable signs" that Japan was planning to increase its military forces, and fearful lest changing conditions jeopardize the American position in Asia, Assistant Secretary Long drafted a proposal in which the American Government would express its approval of an increase in the number of Allied troops in Siberia. Incorporating part of this note in a letter to the President, Lansing reverted to what had become, in American-Japanese relations, a recurrent piece of rhetoric:

If the Japanese Government indicate their purpose to take such action what ought we to say? If we reach the conclusion that Japan will follow this course in any event, would we or would we not be in a better position to control the situation in the future by asserting that present conditions require Japan to send sufficient troops to open the railroad to Irkutsk and to keep it open so that we can send supplies to the Czechs? [4]

While these questions were circulating among Washington officialdom, Tokyo assumed the burden of its own defense. Resting its case on the "overworked" Czechoslovaks, Japan proclaimed its intention of sending about ten thousand additional troops to the Maritime Provinces and others to the Trans-Baikal region. A query to the Secretary of State three weeks later reflected Presidential anxiety over Japanese actions, but it did not go beyond Pennsylvania Avenue for two months:

Do you not think it would be wise to ask Japan in some courteous but nevertheless plain way, what she is now proposing to do with the large army which she has sent to Siberia? . . . I can see no necessity for a large Japanese force in Siberia, and think the purpose of its continuance there needs to be defined.[5]

At the end of October, Tokyo made another gesture to Washington by notifying Ambassador Morris of its refusal to honor a recent British request to dispatch more soldiers to the Asiatic mainland. Nevertheless, by November 6 the Japanese were sufficiently dispersed along the coast so that they occupied every entrance into both Siberia and Manchuria.

[4] *For. Rel.*, The Lansing Papers, Vol. II, p. 374.
[5] Wilson to Lansing, September 17, 1918 (861.00/3009).

Taking advantage of the military agreements concluded with China in the spring of 1918, Japan had duplicated its rapid influx into Russian territory by sending sizable forces to northern Manchuria beginning in mid-August. Disclaiming any ulterior motives the Japanese Foreign Office politely but firmly informed Washington that the troops had as their only purpose the support of Chinese militia against Bolshevik incursions on Chinese territory, that the situation was not comparable to the joint intervention in Vladivostok, and that "the only nations that have interests involved are Japan and China." This was at once countered by Chinese Minister Koo's repudiation to the State Department of Tokyo's precipitate and needless intervention in Manchuria; and sensing that the situation in the Far East was rapidly deteriorating to its own disadvantage, the American Government cabled a strong protest to Japan on November 16:

The United States has viewed with surprise the presence of the very large number of Japanese troops now in Northern Manchuria and eastern Siberia . . . the number of these troops [is] . . . so great as to constitute a definite departure from the express understanding for cooperation between Japan and the United States and quite unwarranted by any military necessity. This Government . . . is convinced that any monopoly of control such as that now exercised by Japan . . . will arouse suspicion and prove open to charges of exploitation. Such monopoly is . . . opposed to the purpose of this Government to assist Russia [and] . . . also to its views regarding China . . .

The substance of this note was communicated to London and Paris, where it evoked ambiguous rejoinders containing no concrete promises of cooperation with the American view. The Japanese Government, which had changed hands earlier in the month and was temporarily under the aegis of a more moderate political party, made no attempt to justify the action of the preceding ministry. However, the Foreign Minister admitted that the total Japanese contingent, which had reached 72,400, "had now been reduced to 58,600," a figure which he did not deem excessive.

It was not merely the numbers of Japanese soldiers shipped to Vladivostok which alarmed the American Government; but of even greater concern was the frankly opportunistic use which was made of them. This was evidenced in general by the army of concession hunters which followed in their wake, and in particular by the attitude adopted in regard to the Trans-Siberian and Chinese Eastern railroads and to the anti-Communist factions in Siberia.

Had the intervening powers—and this included the United States —been sincere in their splendid avowals of noninterference in internal Russian politics, Washington would have been saved one of its most prolonged diplomatic headaches, for the end of the German war in November 1918 necessarily implied the termination of the officially stated grounds for intervention. However, Japan had the tacit and, to the limit of their ability, the positive support of England and France [6] in its efforts to challenge Soviet sovereignty in Asia, and if the American Government had not been convinced that Tokyo's ultimate goal was either the perpetuation of anarchy in Siberia or the creation of a weak puppet regime, rather than the establishment of a strong and unified Siberian government which could have neutralized effectively Soviet claims in the Far East, it is conceivable that the Japanese would have received the sanction of the United States. Instead, America found itself— in Trotsky's metaphor—between the hammer and the anvil, repelled alike by Soviet communism in the West and by Japanese imperialism in the East, with the result that it continued to participate in an anti-Bolshevik intervention even as it waged diplomatic warfare with Japan.

In the early spring of 1918 Washington had tentatively harbored the thought of collaborating with the Soviet authorities against the Central powers, and to that end it had conceived of intervention in Siberia under Soviet auspices. But by mid-July, when the State Department formulated its initial pronouncement on intervention, there was no longer the remotest desire on the part of

[6] The western Allies rationalized their post-Armistice anti-Bolshevik intervention mainly on the ground that the indigenous Siberian groups had remained loyal to the Allied cause, and accordingly France and Britain could not leave them to the merciless Soviet Government without first permitting them to try their strength against the Communists. The fact that the Soviet leaders would mete out even harsher punishment, after the eventual departure of the Allies, apparently did not occur to them.

either America or Russia for a cooperative effort. In subsequent months the hostility entertained for all things communistic in American governing circles was poorly concealed; quotes taken at random from the private correspondence of Robert Lansing are illustrative of the then-prevailing sentiment:

> In Eastern Germany Bolshevism is raising its abominable head, and a Germany crushed might become a prey to that hideous movement. If it did, Europe might become a seething mass of anarchy . . . We must take no chances on this war culminating in such a frightful catastrophe, beside which "the Terror" of 1792 would be a happy epoch.[7]

> I am anxious over the question of how we can check Bolshevism and the dangers which threaten the very structure of society . . . The sacrifice which was made to overthrow autocracy would be useless, if it results in the triumph of a proletariat despotism which menaces liberty and human rights more than the most powerful autocrats. Bolshevism must be suppressed. It is the worst form of anarchism.[8]

The American Ambassador to Russia, writing from London in January 1919, expressed his belief that "the Bolshevik Party . . . [has] no cohesive principles other than opposition to organized government and well ordered society wherever it may exist." [9] It was the prevalence of this kind of conviction, supported by the mountainous reports of Communist "butchery" and "slavery" and by the wholesale liquidation of all the pillars of bourgeois social order, that helped to determine American nonrecognition in the years ahead.

For its part, the Moscow Government reacted with cold fury to the Allied intervention. The landing of the troops at Vladivostok in August 1918, preceded by the Allied-encouraged revolt in North Russia, could not have been planned for a more acute psychological moment. The staying power of the Bolsheviks was still an unknown factor and the anti-Soviet groups were keyed to a resistance which was as yet undulled. On August 5 the first in a long series of protests, varying from standard diplomatic courtesy to crude and turgid

[7] Lansing to E. N. Smith, October 12, 1918, *Lansing Papers.*
[8] Lansing to R. S. Hungerford, November 14, 1918, *ibid.*
[9] Francis to Lansing, January 17, 1919, *ibid.*

harangues, was sent to Washington and Tokyo from Moscow via
the Soviet representative in Switzerland. The substance of the note
was a proper refutation of the Allied arguments used to justify intervention, namely the danger to the Czechoslovaks in Siberia and
the menace created by the Austrian and German prisoners of war.
This was followed on October 24 by an acrid message addressed to
Wilson personally. After quoting from the President's message to
Congress in January 1918, and reiterating point Six of the Fourteen Points,[10] Foreign Commissar Chicherin remarked:

> You expressed the deep sympathy which you felt towards Russia
> which at that moment . . . was carrying on negotiations with . . .
> German imperialism . . . you assured [the Soviet congress] . . . that
> Russia could depend on the support of America. This was six months
> ago and the Russian people have had ample time to experience *de facto*
> the good feelings of your government . . . of your allies, the realization
> on the part of the allies of Russia's needs and the wisdom and the dis-
> interestedness of their sympathy. These feelings have been expressed
> firstly through the fact that with financial assistance on the part of your
> allies and with the diplomatic support of your government the con-
> spiracy of the Czecho-Slovak was organized on Russian territory . . .
> During a certain period attempts were made to create a *casus belli* be-
> tween the United States and Russia . . . You have given promise to
> offer Russia your assistance . . . this has . . . found expression in the
> attempts made in Archangel, Murmansk and the Far East by Czecho-
> Slovak troops and later on by your allies to impose by force on the
> Russian people the power of the subjugators . . . The touching story
> of the relations between the United States and Russia have not given
> quite the results which could be expected from your address to Con-
> gress.

The note concluded with an outspoken query regarding the "price"
for evacuation by the Allies of Soviet territory:

> When do you . . . and your allies intend to withdraw your troops
> from . . . Siberia . . . Do the governments of America, England and

10 "The evacuation of all Russian territory and such a settlement of all questions affecting Russia as will secure the best and freest cooperation of the other
nations of the world in obtaining for her an unhampered and unembarrassed
opportunity for the independent determination of her own political development and national policy."

France intend to stop shedding the blood of the Russian citizens if the Russian people consent to pay ransom? In that case what payments do the governments . . . expect . . . ? Do they demand concessions, delivery of railways . . . ? Or territorial concessions, part of Siberia, or the Caucasus, the Murman Coast? We expect you, President, to declare decidedly what are your demands and those of your allies . . .[11]

In January 1919 Senator Hitchcock attracted Moscow's attention by his defense of Wilson's decision to intervene. Retorting a few days later Chicherin emphasized the fact that all the motives listed in the Senator's speech, "regardless of any former validity, had lost their force" with the end of the war. "We are therefore at a loss to understand how the maintenance of American troops in Russia can be justified." According to Consul Poole in Archangel no justification was required. Instead, the question confronting the State Department was one of future American policy in regard to the Soviet regime.

Because the formal communications of the Bolsheviks were never acknowledged by Washington this question was considered in its earliest stages by the Paris Peace Conference. There the constant dilemma of the United States regarding the Russian problem infected the Allied powers sufficiently to result in stalemate. Caught between the two logical alternatives of expanding their intervention and thereby overthrowing the Communists, or dealing with Moscow on the basis of any one of its numerous approaches, the Allied states hedged and sidestepped, leaving the problem no nearer lasting solution at the end of the conference than it had been in the summer of 1918.

On the one hand there were the proponents of White Russia, representative of every non-Communist Russian faction including the unburied corpse of the Provisional Government, and these were tolerated and even encouraged by the conferees. At the same time, representatives of the Provisional Russian Government found their most ardent promoters in the Allied camp; France was undivided

---

[11] Quotation taken from State Department file 861.00/3393 (The American Minister to Norway to the Secretary of State, November 2, 1918). A more polished translation is given in Henri Barbusse, *The Soviet Union and Peace* (London: Martin Lawrence, Ltd., 1929), pp. 48–57.

in its hatred and fear of bolshevism, and Clemenceau discovered in Englishmen like Winston Churchill unqualified advocates of an anti-Red war. Notwithstanding the opposition within his cabinet to the Soviet leaders and a Proteus-like tendency of his own, Lloyd George proposed in January 1919 that some consideration be given to Moscow as the *de facto* Russian Government. In this the British Prime Minister was upheld by President Wilson, who said:

We should be fighting against the current of the times if we tried to prevent Russia from finding her own path to freedom . . . If the Bolsheviks refrained from invading Lithuania, Poland, Finland, etc., he thought we should be well advised to allow as many groups as desired . . . to send representatives to Paris. We should then try to reconcile them, both mutually and with the rest of the world.[12]

On the basis of the Anglo-American stand and of advices affirming the conciliatory spirit of the Soviets, the Allies agreed that Wilson should compose a proclamation inviting all factions, including the Communists, to an international conference at Prinkipo Island to discuss the Russian question in detail.

Despite immediate acceptance by Moscow the proposal was still-born, essentially because of Allied duplicity. Still ideologically partial to the White Russians, the Paris delegates (exclusive of Wilson) allowed these anti-Bolsheviks to wreck the Prinkipo plans by their refusal to attend any sessions at which Red Russia was represented. The same factor was responsible in March and April 1919 for the collapse of a second attempt to reach an agreement with the Soviet. The Bullitt mission, dispatched to Russia in March, had emerged with peace terms to which the Bolshevik Government promised adherence if the Allies should confirm them by April 10. The failure to do so stemmed from the resurgence of the Kolchak offensive in Siberia, and the Allies, falsely estimating the strength of the latter, once again ignored the Moscow Russians.

"There is no use in concealing the fact," Churchill wrote in a

[12] David Lloyd George, *Memoirs of the Peace Conference* (New Haven: Yale University Press, 1939), Vol. I, p. 221.

memorandum which received the assent of the Paris statesmen, "that we are helping the anti-Bolshevik forces of Russia against the Bolsheviks and that with our help their position is rapidly improving." [13] On April 18 this was confirmed by Moscow in a bitter tirade against the Entente powers:

It is only with the help of your governments that the most furious counter-revolution is kept alive in those parts of the former Russian Empire where Allied or German intervention has crushed the people's Soviet power . . . Wild reaction prevails in the domain of Kolchak, the hireling of your rulers, in Siberia, where the most persevering and desperate of the Russian monarchists have rallied, where not only the supporters of the Soviet Government and the people's revolution, but even the supporters of the bourgeois Constitutional Assembly, not sufficiently ardent servants of reaction, are slaughtered *en masse*, while every new advance of the Dictator Kolchak's troops is accompanied by mass destruction of the working class population.[14]

The Paris Peace Conference concluded with no further reference to Soviet Russia, its attention in the final weeks being wholly absorbed in the still rising star of the Kolchak clique. President Wilson returned to America to plead for the ratification of the Versailles settlement and in the course of his western tour in September 1919 his hostility toward the Bolsheviks was evidenced repeatedly. Thus, a "little group of men just as selfish . . . ruthless . . . pitiless, as the agents of the Tsar" governed Russia; bolshevism was synonymous with anarchy; only brute force could explain the survival of the Communist power. On January 8, 1920, the Secretary of State further elucidated the American attitude toward Russia:

With respect to suggestions . . . that the time has come to establish relations with the Russian Bolsheviki, it is the view of the . . . United States that past experience has proved the futility of endeavoring to arrive at a satisfactory understanding with them. Their ultimate purposes are inimical to all established governments and any seeming compromise which they may make with such Governments is vitiated by their avowed opportunism.

[13] *Ibid.*, pp. 248–249.
[14] Barbusse, *op. cit.*, p. 73.

. . . The United States is convinced that Lenin and his immediate disciples will never permanently forego the dream of world revolution or enter loyally into amicable relations with non-Bolshevik governments.[15]

This suspicion of the Soviet Government constituted one of the two principal reasons for the growing tolerance which Washington evinced toward the autonomous Kolchak movement in Siberia following the Armistice in 1918. The other reason reflected the determination of the State Department to foster a group in Asiatic Russia which, in contrast to the political faction headed by Ataman Semenov, would not be subject to Japanese overlordship. Guided by these twin motives, American policy toward Russia in the Far East throughout the period of intervention was directed to the preservation of Russian sovereignty; but the sovereignty was by implication that of the anti-Bolshevik Russians, and only when their defeat was regarded as inevitable did the American troops withdraw. Subsequently, American diplomacy acknowledged and eventually supported—albeit vicariously—the Soviet claim to the Pacific seaboard.

The decision to aid the Kolchak Government at Omsk was arrived at laboriously by the United States; furthermore, it was made only when the Omsk directorate emerged as the strongest and most representative of the numerous Siberian governments which mushroomed into existence in the summer of 1918 after the initial successes of the Czechoslovaks.[16] As a result, just as the obstinate refusal of Washington to commit itself to intervention for month after long month in the winter and spring of 1918 had provoked the exasperated anger of the Allied powers, so in the early autumn its tactics of watchful-waiting, coupled with the confused declaration on intervention of August 3, left the more vocal of the anti-

[15] *For. Rel.*, 1920, Vol. III, pp. 444–445. It was this sentiment which caused the State Department to ignore Martens, the official Soviet representative in the United States, who remained from March 1919 until January 1921, at which time he left voluntarily to escape a pending deportation warrant.

[16] The Siberian governments included the Provisional Government of Western Siberia, the Siberian Cossack Government, the Transbaikal Voisko Government, General Horvat's Government, and the Provisional Government of Autonomous Siberia.

Bolshevik Siberians with a distinct feeling of irritation bordering at times on actual hostility.[17]

In September the first bid was made for active American political support following the convening of a state conference at Ufa. The conference formed an all-Russian government which was declared the successor of the Provisional Government of the March 1917 Revolution. In answer to a communication from Bakhmetev (the Provisional Government's Ambassador at Washington) Lansing replied with what amounted to back-handed support; while this fell far short of the hopes of the Ufa representatives and the Allies it was at least a straw in the wind, indicative of the unexpressed desire in the United States for a strong anti-Soviet state in Siberia. But reports from the strongly anti-Communist Harris, consul general at Irkutsk, in October and early November, claimed that the Ufa Government was practically synonymous with that of Soviet Russia ideologically and urged that recognition be postponed indefinitely. This attitude was confirmed in a more general way by Ambassador Morris, who cabled on October 18 that no central government in Siberia exerted any genuine authority and therefore recommended that no recognition or assistance be accorded.

In November, however, the Ufa Government attached itself to the Omsk directorate, and although Harris continued to berate the Bolshevik affiliations of the directorate and to urge American aloof-

[17] The newspaper *Primorskya Zhizn* (Vladivostok), on August 14, 1918, printed the following remarks: "The declaration of the United States . . . has produced a marked disenchantment among the Russian people . . . the readiness to come to the aid of Russia during the period of her greatest stress is expressed in very vague terms . . . Russia, withering away under the yoke of Germanism and under its tool, Bolshevism, will be benefited but little by the occupation of Vladivostok by the Allies and by the guarding of stores . . . or by the protection of the rear of the Czecho-Slovaks . . . And who is to blame that negotiations, in connection with united Allied intervention in the Far East, have been so prolonged, that active military operations will not commence until autumn . . . It is a matter of great regret that the American Government is still lacking reliable information in regards to the actual situation in Russia and to the ordinary wants of the nation." Enclosure in Caldwell to Lansing, August 23, 1918 (861.00/2978). The above, and editorials of similar content, overlooked the fact that a vital element in Washington's seeming dilatoriness was the absence of a common policy among the Siberian anti-Bolsheviks. If the United States was confused, its confusion stemmed at least in part from a similar atmosphere in Siberia.

ness, France and Britain began to display an interest in this group which bolstered it and, in so doing, eventually attracted Washington's support. On November 6 the political high commissioners of the two Western Allies entered into an equivocal but nevertheless helpful association with the all-Russian Government. They announced that agents would be appointed to carry on unofficial relations with the directorate until such time as the latter should become sufficiently strong and acceptable to the Russian people to warrant official recognition.

Given this encouragement the Omsk Government immediately gained ground and within a fortnight elected Admiral Kolchak as dictator. On two separate counts the regime of Kolchak appealed to the Allies: it represented a violent swing away from both communism and questionable liberalism, and almost as its first act it solemnly vowed to assume the debts owed the Allies by the Tsarist Government. These intentions naturally exerted a favorable influence on Washington; to them were added in the course of the next few weeks reports of the growing strength of the Kolchak movement and its determination to concentrate on western Siberia until its position was more widely acknowledged in the extreme Far East. But perhaps the one factor which more than any other disposed the United States to a friendly sponsorship of Kolchak was the persistent rumor concerning the Japanese policy in eastern Siberia, where disorder and chaos dominated and where Captain Semenov, under the protective wing of the Japanese military command, sought to undermine the foundations of the Omsk Government to the ultimate benefit of the imperialists in Tokyo.

Nor was this rumor without substantiation. As early as September 11 Morris had correctly estimated the temper of Japan's expansionists when he cabled his conviction that the general staff had "a definite policy in Siberia" which it proposed to pursue, "leaving to the Foreign Office and Viscount Ishii the task of explaining after the event." Part of this policy was revealed shortly when the Japanese generals agreed to support, with arms and money, several Cossack atamans in eastern Siberia in their organization of a Russian force of twenty thousand men. Toward the end of November, Semenov openly declared his independence of the Kolchak movement and termed himself "a sort of commissioner for the Trans-Baikal district." Scarcely a report reached Washington from this time through May 1919 which did not speak of the efforts of Semenov to establish himself in direct opposition to the Omsk Government, and of the tacit backing tendered by the Japanese.

In the face of this threat not only to Russian territorial integrity but to the continued power of the Kolchak faction, the Omsk authorities pleaded frankly for American aid. In a long complaint addressed indirectly to the State Department through the Russian Embassy at Washington, Admiral Kolchak summarized the numerous extra-legal actions of the Japanese, and concluded with a somber warning regarding Japanese imperialistic aims which could not but arouse the apprehensions of the American Government.

On December 16, within a matter of hours following the receipt of the Kolchak communication, Acting Secretary Polk cabled instructions to Morris at Tokyo to "confer frankly" with the Foreign Minister over Japanese political activities in eastern Siberia. But the results were nugatory. Briefly, the Japanese general staff was no more deterred by the brave words emanating from Washington than Kolchak was aided by them. In the first place they represented only a negative policy ("It is not to be understood that this Government desires to support Admiral Kolchak as against General Semenov, but merely its purpose to see that loyal Russians be allowed to manage their own affairs"); secondly, the United States was unable to come to any final decision regarding the Omsk Government for several months, during which the single-minded Japanese pursued their divisive tactics unchallenged. Finally, notwithstanding the open sympathy of many State Department officials, both at home and in Siberia, for the Kolchak group,[18] the Ameri-

[18] Others were less favorably disposed to the Omsk Government. Morris vacillated in his attitude, while MacMurray, viewing the situation from Tokyo in January 1919, was unequivocal in his opinion: "I hope no formal recognition will be extended to Kolchak. His personality is of small significance. He is surrounded and dependent on the support of reactionary elements whose principal idea of government is the reconquest of former grafts. His army is being organized on old lines of Tsarist discipline . . . After allowing the Siberian Government and the Directorate which were both sincere attempts at liberation to collapse from lack of recognition, the Allied support of Kolchak's experiment in reaction is a feature regrettable." *For. Rel.*, 1919, Russia, p. 327.

can army under General Graves remained adamant in its refusal to lend comfort or support to any internal Russian faction.

In January 1919 Secretary Lansing anticipated what eventually became American policy toward the Omsk Government. In a cable to Polk from Paris he suggested that although recognition would be premature and extensive military aid inexpedient, the Allied and Associated governments might well render economic and financial assistance and provide military supplies to Kolchak "until such time" as a central Russian government should emerge.

The avowal by Kolchak at the end of the month that his power would be relinquished to an all-Russian government whenever it was created by an accredited constituent assembly; the conclusion of Harris in March that the "Kolchak government is stronger than ever before and growing in power"; the consensus of Harris, Admiral Rodgers, General Graves, Charles Smith (of the American Railroad Commission), and Consul Caldwell in mid-April that Kolchak should be given all aid, financial and material, short of actual recognition; [19] the positive program of support proffered the Omsk authorities by England and France throughout the early months of 1919; and the continued insidious Japanese policy of divide and rule in its dealings with the Siberian factions served finally to crystallize American opinion in favor of the Kolchak Central Siberian Government.

London and Paris were motivated almost exclusively in their attitude toward Kolchak by their fear of bolshevism, which figured ever more largely in proportion as the Peace Conference failed to reach any satisfactory basis of compromise with Moscow. Although neither of the two Western powers was primarily concerned over Japanese aggression in Siberia *per se*, the establishment of a counter-revolutionary government in Asiatic Russia presupposed the consistent and united Allied support of one, rather than of competing, Siberian parties; and consequently the British, who had abetted Semenov earlier in 1918, repudiated him when the Omsk Government emerged as the "highest Russian power."

---

[19] General Graves' agreement to this suggestion was in sharp contrast to his otherwise studied and consistent aloofness toward the Kolchak and other Siberian groups. Ambassador Morris, while consenting to most of the Harris *et. al.* program, was averse to extending a loan to Kolchak at this time.

The State Department had reason to rejoice in this fact, for the cause of Semenov—and with it that of the Japanese expansionists—was severely handicapped without Anglo-French encouragement and simultaneously the outlook for Soviet control of the Russian Far East was clouded. Indeed, had Consul General Harris or any of the Foreign Service personnel who shared his views been in command of the American expeditionary force it is not difficult to surmise that American policy, through the act of cooperating with the Allies on behalf of Kolchak, would have gone far to block the closing pincers represented by Japan in eastern Siberia and by the Communist Government in western Russia. However, through its own ambiguity as reflected in the ill-famed August 3 statement on intervention, the United States had undermined in advance a program such as that previously described. For, although aid to Kolchak was to most Department officials harmonious with the August declaration, General William S. Graves, heading the American army, viewed the *aide-mémoire* as utterly inconsistent with support for Kolchak or any other Russian group. Accordingly, he pursued a policy of strict neutrality—a policy in which he was supported by the War Department and the President but which very quickly brought upon him the recriminations of England, France, Japan, each of the non-Soviet Russian factions and, not least of all, the United States Department of State.

Interpreting his instructions narrowly, the American general was of the conviction that he "was to take no part in differences between different Russian factions"; that "the American forces were here to . . . defend property and the Trans-Siberian Railway, and force would only be used if this property was endangered by Bolsheviks or others." [20] The basic clash between this view of intervention and that entertained by every other interested party was illustrated in an exchange between British General Knox and General Graves in March 1919. Knox wrote:

I wish we could see more eye to eye in matters here. The objects we wish are undoubtedly very similar but we are falling into different ruts.

[20] Lt. Col. S. L. H. Slocum to Colonel Van Deman, April 28, 1919, *Bliss Papers*.

The policy of our Government is to support Kolchak, and I believe in that policy, for if he goes there will be chaos.

This educed the following remarks from the American officer:

I believe it is well known . . . that the United States does not intend to interfere in the internal affairs of Russia. I have consistently followed this policy. As to the support of Kolchak, I do not feel under my orders that I can support or interfere with any individual . . . I consider it none of my affair as to what the tendencies of any of the contending factions in Russian affairs are.[21]

In ensuing weeks the sharpness of this conflict was accentuated, leading at length to British endeavors to have Washington change Graves' instructions. Such efforts were, of course, wholly undiplomatic and, in terms of great power relations, quite unprecedented; nor were they welcomed by the American Government. For all these reasons, Britain's "interference" provided vivid illustration of the gulf separating Graves from his European colleagues.

Nor were the English the only ones to bring such pressure to bear. In March, Acting Secretary Polk telegraphed to Lansing that in his opinion "the situation is somewhat beyond General Graves . . . his inclination is to interpret his instructions very conservatively." This comment was extended early in May when Polk described Graves as "lacking" in both "a high degree of tact and large experience in affairs"—qualifications required of the American command in Siberia. But of even greater significance in this particular communication was the implication that the real criticism of the American general centered on his neutrality, which undermined effectively the State Department's anti-Soviet policy.

This criticism was echoed with growing fractiousness by the Siberian press throughout this period and found expression also within the ranks of the Omsk Government.

Even General Graves was distressed by the turn of events; and finally, after resisting all attacks on the American position and on himself personally, he was obliged to confess the unhappy predicament into which his adherence to instructions had propelled him.

[21] Graves, *op. cit.*, pp. 189–190.

Every Kolchak adherent I talk to asks the question if we do not intend to fight the Bolsheviks why are we in their country . . . Kolchak
adherents will be disappointed and extremely antagonistic to the
United States if we do not immediately join in active military operations against Bolsheviks after recognition of Kolchak. As long as troops
are in Eastern Siberia and not employed in active operations against
Bolsheviks we can expect bitter animosity from Kolchak.[22]

By the middle of May the logic in General Graves' description
of the situation was no longer controverted and the elements within
the American Government which had favored active support for
Kolchak reaped their triumph, transient though it was. The all-
important decision which signified this victory was made by the
Big Four at the Paris Peace Conference after the question of the
Allied relationship to the Omsk Government had dotted their
agenda at intervals over a four-month period. As early as mid-
February the increasing favoritism with which the American delegation viewed Kolchak was manifested in a telegram to Washington
in connection with the abortive Prinkipo Conference. The message emphasized the desirability for the Omsk Government to be
represented at Prinkipo, because the American attitude toward
recognition might hinge on "information obtained" there.

At the end of April, Polk was able to wire Morris that the American Mission "has been carefully considering the advisability of a
provisional recognition of the Kolchak Government," and in May
the President sent a personal query to his ambassador at Tokyo,
concerning "the kind of men and influences surrounding Kolchak,"
and whether the dictator was "strong enough and liberal enough
to control them in the right direction." [23]

Meantime Wilson was struggling with the uneasy dilemma
posited by Graves. At a meeting on May 9 he outlined the problem
to his diplomatic colleagues in all its subtle ramifications. In essence, American "neutrality" as practiced by General Graves had
served to weaken the Omsk authorities in the eyes of the Siberian
peasants and simultaneously to irritate Kolchak's adherents, a fact

[22] Graves to Adjutant General Harris, May 11, 1919 (861.00/4630).
[23] Wilson to Tumulty, received May 16, 1919 (861.00/4539).

which, the President suspected, was relished by Tokyo. Therefore, "the United States Government found itself faced with the two following alternatives: (1) to take sides with Kolchak and send much stronger forces to Siberia. (2) To withdraw." Ever apprehensive of Japanese tactics, Wilson suggested that if the first alternative were adopted "it was certain that the Japanese would increase" their forces "still more." On the other hand, the withdrawal of the American contingent would leave the field to Tokyo and Kolchak. The ultimate consensus of the President and the Allies to implement their support of Kolchak by endowing his government with a semi-official status illustrated the forcefulness of the anti-Japanese motive in determining Wilsonian policy. At the same time, the decision to retain Allied troops in Siberia some six months after the Armistice, and to employ them to the exclusive advantage of one particular Russian faction which stood in revolutionary opposition to the *de facto* Soviet Government, constituted striking testimony of the hostility of the intervening states to bolshevism and was, by the same token, a solemn breach by Wilson of his pronouncement on intervention of August 3, 1918.

The joint note to the Kolchak Government, dated May 26, was a hybrid concoction reminiscent of the earlier American declaration in the inconsistency of its opening paragraphs. Paying homage indirectly to their heterogeneous activities in Siberia, the five powers [24] expressed their need "once more to make clear the policy they propose to pursue in regard to Russia." This was followed by a statement which was somewhat questionable in view of the Japanese aid to Semenov and that of the other Allies to Kolchak:

It has always been a cardinal axiom of the . . . Powers to avoid interference in the internal affairs of Russia.

[24] The Japanese had not been a party to the Big Four discussions on the policy to be adopted toward Kolchak, and although they declared their solidarity with the Allies by sponsoring the note of May 26, the Japanese Foreign Office was critical of it. In a conference with the Russian Ambassador at Tokyo, Shidehara "explained . . . that it had been presented at a hastily called meeting in Paris and had been adopted without allowing sufficient time for consideration or discussion." Morris to Lansing, June 6, 1919 (861.00/4647).

With the end of the war, the note declared, intervention could be continued only if it would "really help the Russian people to liberty, self-government, and peace." Simultaneously, however, the Allies were

convinced that it is not possible to attain these ends by dealings with the Soviet Government. . . . They are therefore disposed to assist the Government of Admiral Kolchak and his Associates with munitions, supplies and food, to establish themselves as the government of all Russia, provided they receive from them definite guarantees.

Briefly, these included: the promise of a freely elected constituent assembly as soon as Kolchak should reach Moscow; free elections "throughout the areas which they at present control . . . for all local and legally constituted assemblies"; "no attempt to revive the special privileges of any class or order in Russia"; a democratic Russia which would join the League of Nations; confirmation of Kolchak's statement of November 1918 respecting the national debt of Russia.[25]

The reply of the Omsk spokesmen, although couched in generally affirmative phrases, left the ultimate acceptance of the Allied requests to the still hypothetical constituent assembly when and if established; nevertheless, this satisfied the powers, which declared their willingness "to extend to Admiral Kolchak and his Associates the support set forth in their original letter."

As far as Washington was concerned, however, even the auspiciousness of the exchange with the Omsk Government and the subsequent material help which was rushed to Vladivostok did not produce any drastic alterations in diplomatic policy. In answer to a series of questions framed by Bakhmetev, the American interpretation of its new relationship with Kolchak was declared (1) not to amount to *de facto* recognition, (2) not to include the accrediting of diplomatic agents to Omsk, (3) not to imply unlimited financial assistance. Furthermore, despite the rapid deterioration in the strength of the Omsk Government throughout the late spring and summer of 1919 the United States refused to commit itself to the

[25] "Dispatch to Admiral Kolchak," May 26, 1919. *For. Rel.*, 1919, Russia, pp. 367–369.

sending of replacements for the Czech troops, whose withdrawal was considered a growing necessity in view of their largely depleted morale. At a Big Five meeting on July 9 the suggestion had been made by Lansing that the Czechs be repatriated; this had educed from the French the rejoinder that American and/or Japanese troops be dispatched in proportion as the Czechoslovaks left Siberia. The importance of American participation in this replacement had been vouched for by Ambassador Morris on several occasions during a prolonged visit to Omsk. On July 22 he described the extremely precarious situation which was evolving for Kolchak throughout western Siberia. The fact that the only supporters of the Omsk regime were "a small discredited group of reactionaries, Monarchists, and former military officials" had led certain Russians, together with representative Czechs, French, British and Americans on the spot, to conclude that a Czech withdrawal would precipitate "a formidable anti-Kolchak if not pro-Bolshevik uprising in every town on the railway from Irkutsk to Omsk." Five days later Morris and General Graves conferred with Kolchak, and the American Ambassador reported on the 30th that as no further Russian manpower was available to patrol the railroads, the exodus of the Czechs made it imperative that Allied reinforcements be sent. The answer of Lansing to the French proposal for extra American and Japanese soldiers was transmitted on August 8 and stated simply: "the President finds it impracticable to furnish additional American troops for this purpose."

In the face of Wilson's decision six weeks previously to support Admiral Kolchak, the refusal in August to lend him the one form of aid of which he was in direst need found a partial explanation once again beyond the rim of purely Russian-American relations, in the broader framework of American-Japanese rivalry. "I submit," Morris had telegraphed, "that no arrangement with Japan will prove satisfactory which does not provide that the United States shall contribute at least one half of the additional troops."

There is a fundamental difference in purpose governing the Siberian policy of the two governments. The Terauchi ministry, which was military, clearly planned to use the joint expedition . . . last summer as an excuse to take possession of the Chinese Eastern Railroad and thus dominate northern Manchuria and eastern Siberia. The direct method of accomplishing the purpose failed, but the purpose remains. . . . All the evidence convinces me that Japan is pursuing in Siberia the same methods which have produced such tragic results in China.[26]

The Wilson Administration had struggled alone since the beginning of the World War to counter Japanese imperialism in China and the President, in July 1919, had just emerged from the conference halls of Versailles where he had been an uneasy party to the benefits conferred on Tokyo by the Allies in the treaty of peace. In terms of the Russian intervention the State Department had witnessed the facility with which the Japanese had slipped out from under their implied policy of a small expeditionary force within a few weeks of their August 1918 declaration. Consequently the American Government was in no mood to precipitate further Japanese encroachments, an almost inevitable sequel to any decision to increase the number of United States forces in Siberia. In other words, even had the very survival of the Kolchak Government depended on such a move, Washington would probably have sacrificed the latter in the greater interests of its all-inclusive Far Eastern policy. It is generally conceded, however, that by the first of August the Kolchak cause was already damaged beyond repair so that the Wilson decision regarding additional American troops did not, of itself, foredoom the Omsk Government. Nevertheless, Kolchak's Foreign Minister, Soukine, complained bitterly that Russia was being left "out of all consideration while the United States settled her private quarrels with Japan."

Russia will not forgive this but will hate the United States for coming here and encouraging us to expect aid and then to find that there is no intention of aiding us, but that the United States considers her own quarrels with Japan of more importance than her relations with Russia. . . .[27]

[26] *Ibid.*, p. 293.
[27] Enclosure, dated September 17, 1919, in Baker to Lansing, November 7, 1919 (861.00/5608). These remarks were made by Soukine in a conversation with Major H. H. Slaughter, and sent by the latter to General Graves in a memorandum.

The Japanese threat had a double edge, for the mere refusal to expand American troop operations in Siberia in no wise eliminated the numerical superiority hitherto possessed by Tokyo. As Morris stated bluntly in a telegram on August 11, "we will be forced to abandon eastern Siberia to Japanese domination" unless a minimum of 25,000 American soldiers (together with recognition of the Kolchak Government and a liberal extension of credits) were approved immediately. It was not possible, the Ambassador asserted, to check Tokyo "by frank discussion and formal protests. We must speak our determined purpose in the only language the Japanese clique can understand." In words uncannily similar to those to be used by American diplomats a generation later in describing relations with the Soviet Union, Morris declared that firmness on America's part would "not lead to friction," but on the contrary would create a better understanding.[28]

Viewed from Washington, the alternatives presented were identical with those with which Wilson had labored at the Paris Conference prior to the Allied joint note to Admiral Kolchak. In or out of Siberia the United States seemed to be promoting the cause of Japan. As between the two choices, the government found the rough path confronting it in its relations with Congress the deciding factor. In the first place only Congress could authorize either military or commercial credits for the Omsk officials; secondly, the Administration felt that Congress could not be urged to act until the Peace Treaty had been ratified; and finally there was no effective means of convincing the American people or Congress that twenty-five thousand men should be ordered to Siberia a year after the war was over. Morris was therefore instructed to express his government's regrets and to inform Admiral Kolchak that the "limitations" of American aid reflected domestic conditions in the United States rather than lack of confidence in the Omsk directorate. This, of course, provided small satisfaction to Kolchak.

In the last four months of 1919 the strength ebbed from the Siberian Government, leaving in its wake an increasing rancor toward the United States and a general desperation which was

[28] "Memorandum for the Secretary of State, based on digest of Ambassador Morris's dispatches since his trip to Omsk," August 14, 1919, *Long Papers.*

reflected in the willingness of the Russian admiral to court favors from the Japanese and their hirelings in Siberia. Although it would be a misstatement of fact to lay the collapse of the Kolchak regime at the door of the American Government, it was perhaps true that the recurrent fluctuations in Washington's policy hastened the final demise of the Omsk Government. In one sense the American policy was analogous to that which Washington had pursued toward the Soviet rulers in the spring of 1918, before it had definitely abandoned all intention of cooperating with Moscow. Just as the State Department had demanded proof of Bolshevist opposition to the Central powers prior to committing itself to a concrete program of aid, so in 1919 the condition of recognition was evidence that the Kolchak Government had "some stability and some hope of success."

This *quid pro quo* was not unnaturally displeasing to the Omsk authorities, who doubtless realized that the "stability" and "success" of their government depended in the first instance on *prior* Allied and American support. The consequent growing irritation toward Washington found expression in various ways. On the one hand, it was directed at Ambassador Morris, whose original lack of confidence in the Kolchak movement, temporarily assuaged by his visit to Omsk, seemed to have revived on his return to Vladivostok. In the second place, General Graves, never a friend to Kolchak, received vehement castigation for his avowedly critical and aloof attitude. Early in August he had informed the War Department that the Kolchak Government could not possibly survive and that if the Allies supported it they would "make the greatest mistake in history." [29] Several weeks later Graves blatantly ignored the agreement between Omsk and Washington whereby he was to have delivered a quantity of rifles to Omsk, excusing himself on the ground that the agents of Kolchak in eastern Siberia were "threatening to declare war on the United States." In reply Foreign Minister Soukine administered a strong rebuke to Graves and appealed over the general's head to the State Department. Although Graves was at once instructed to carry out the agreement, the bitterness remained. Its next manifestation came at the end of Sep-

[29] Graves, *op. cit.*, pp. 235–236.

tember with the arrival of General Rozanov at Vladivostok. Rozanov
was a Cossack operating nominally under the Omsk Government
in the Priamur military district, but his attitude toward the Allied
military command and the uncontrolled actions of his troops in
Vladivostok provoked the former to demand that Kolchak recall
him. This evoked the strongest protest which had thus far emanated
from Omsk. As in previous instances General Graves was regarded
by Soukine as "one of the chief promoters of the affair." His conduct, the Foreign Minister declared, had become "entirely incomprehensible" and his continued presence in Vladivostok would lead
to "perpetual misunderstandings and to the growing public dis-
content with Americans." Notwithstanding the admonishment
to Graves from a State Department which had long been out of
sympathy with him,[30] Lansing upheld the action of the Allied
military leaders in Vladivostok and subsequently the Omsk Government felt compelled to recall Rozanov.

Early in October, Washington was advised of numerous rumors
regarding a plot allegedly backed by the Japanese military, to make
the Allied position untenable in Siberia. In discounting the more
nefarious allegations charged to Tokyo, Morris cabled that the
Omsk Government was losing power and its collapse would open
the way for Soviet control of Siberia. With such a contingency
in mind the Ambassador stated his conviction that Japan could
not be condemned if it "takes matters into [its] . . . own hands,
and adopts methods, however deplorable, ruthlessly to suppress disorder and to protect [its] . . . national interests." Events in the
following weeks accentuated this trend. By the latter part of November the Kolchak army was "entirely demoralized and scattered"
and the Kolchak ministry had resigned. A new cabinet formed
several days later was characterized chiefly by its suspicion that
America was leaning toward the Communists, and by a determination "to nurse Japanese influence." In view of the steadily dwindling
prestige of Kolchak, the negligible support tendered him by Wash-

[30] On November 1, in compliance with Lansing's wish, Baker telegraphed
Graves: "State Department has requested that in future all representations to
Minister of Foreign Affairs at Omsk be made through Consul General Harris
and not direct by military authorities. Secretary of War approves this request . . ." *For. Rel., op. cit.*, p. 542.

ington, the avowed triumph of bolshevism in western Siberia, and the penetration of Japanese propaganda as far as Lake Baikal, Japan had become "the dominant factor in the Pacific section" and correspondingly its influence at Omsk began to replace that of the United States.

However, a short breathing spell still remained for American aspirations despite the initial apprehension of Lansing and the changeless fears of Russian Ambassador Bakhmetev regarding Japanese motives. At the end of November an extended debate within Japanese governing circles had witnessed the temporary triumph of the Hara moderates over the military faction led by General Tanaka, and for a few weeks thereafter Washington and Tokyo discussed the Siberian crisis with a mutual earnestness and sincerity, motivated preeminently by their common fear of bolshevism.

It was the wish of the United States to buttress the Omsk Government by widening its base through the inclusion of representative popular elements. This desire was apparently shared by the Japanese, who suggested that "a parliament of self-governing bodies in Siberia" would attract the support of the masses. On December 3 Secretary Lansing wrote a long memorandum for the President in which he formulated a plan for a "Russian Bureau, Incorporated," to extend and promote commercial and financial aid in the interests of the Siberian Government. But within a month Washington and Tokyo had fallen out; simultaneously the American consul at Harbin pronounced the end of the Kolchak regime with the supremacy of bolshevism. And on January 30, 1920, the Czechoslovaks delivered Kolchak to the Communists at Irkutsk, where he was shot within the week.

By the end of 1919 it appeared to the State Department that much of what it had struggled for in the long course of the Siberian intervention had evaporated. Communism remained, its virus infecting an ever larger proportion of the population (as well as the Czech troops); Japanese imperialism remained, its tentacles reaching inland to encompass a widening radius of territory; and the Omsk Government, which Washington had hoped to see established as a bulwark against Moscow and Tokyo alike, had utterly disintegrated.

CHAPTER VI

Intervention in Siberia: II

The eclipse of the Kolchak movement accentuated the chaos in Siberia and, more importantly, that phase of the American-Japanese conflict which was focused on the occupation of the Trans-Siberian and Chinese Eastern railroads. Indeed, the struggle between the two powers throughout the unhappy saga of intervention was nowhere more articulate than in regard to the problem of railroad supervision.

In June 1917 John F. Stevens had arrived at Vladivostok, followed subsequently by Colonel Emerson's Russian Railroad Service Corps, with the avowed intention of increasing the efficiency of the Trans-Siberian line under the auspices of the Provisional Russian Government. This had immediately aroused the suspicions of Tokyo whose "special position" in Asia included, in the Japanese view, preferential treatment vis-à-vis the great network of railroads in Manchuria and Siberia.

As early as 1916 the Tsar's Government had agreed to relinquish part of the Chinese Eastern Railroad to Japan in return for war materials; by a series of treaties with China in 1918, and through diplomatic pressure on Peking in July of that year, Tokyo had sought to guarantee its version of "joint occupation" of the railroads in the forthcoming Allied intervention.

An officially declared purpose of the states participating in the Siberian expedition had been the protection of the Czechoslovak forces in their movement across Siberia, and therefore there was implicit recognition on all sides of the necessity of guarding the railroad lines against Bolshevik incursions. At the same time, the unquestioned advantages which possession of the main lines of communication would provide for the imperialist-minded nation were equally obvious. Consequently, professing to see in the American army of engineers its own unaffirmed motives, the statesmen in Tokyo sought relentlessly to limit the scope of American operations and simultaneously to entrench themselves over as many miles of railroad and in as many vital centers as their disproportionate manpower permitted. These tactics precipitated a storm of criticism in Washington which finally led to the creation, under State Department initiative, of the Inter-Allied Board for supervision of the railroads; the Board was at length organized in January 1919 and continued to function until after United States troops had evacuated Russian soil.

Within a month of the dispatch of Allied forces to Siberia, in August 1918, the future pattern of American-Japanese conflict was revealed with prophetic accuracy, albeit in skeletal form, in a communication from Stevens. Reporting that about 18,000 Japanese troops had already reached Vladivostok, he noted that efforts were being made by the Japanese to take over control of railroad operation in eastern Siberia. Stressing the futility of mixed American-Japanese management he urged that the roads be placed under military control and their operation assigned to his commission and the Russian Railroad Service Corps. The situation was critical, he declared, and "should be promptly met by the United States."

A similar report, emphasizing Tokyo's esoteric motives and stressing the fervent desire of the Russian people to avoid Japanese management of the railroads, was sent by Consul General Harris from Irkutsk early in September. The State Department, however, was already stirred to action by Stevens' message which indicated that Tokyo had increased its Siberian contingent by half almost before the ink had dried on its officially sanctioned figure of twelve thousand men. Consequently Washington took the first step in what shortly became the American proposal for the operation of the Trans-Siberian and Chinese Eastern railroads during the period of intervention. Enlarging upon Stevens' suggestion, Lansing telegraphed to Morris on August 30; after reminding the Ambassador that the Stevens mission was the agent of the Russian people and was "being paid and supported by their Ambassador here from funds belonging to them," the Secretary proposed that Stevens, on behalf of the Russians, assume general direction of all the railroads concerned.

The Japanese response took two forms, political and military. On the diplomatic front the astute Baron Goto resorted to a device which had been employed frequently in the prolonged negotiations preceding intervention—aligning the Japanese Government initially on the side of Washington and accusing Britain and France of obstructionism. Thus, "the Allied Governments represented at Vladivostok might not look with favor on a plan which placed the railroads under such control." Goto himself expressed approval of the American suggestion but declared that Anglo-French opposition strengthened that element in Tokyo which was against it, and accordingly made the plan politically difficult of achievement.

The army's answer was less devious; on September 3, while Morris was conferring with Foreign Minister Goto, the Japanese general in Vladivostok issued orders placing the railroads under military control. Because of the pronounced split between Japan's political and army personnel there was always the possibility that the general staff acted quite irresponsibly in Siberia and elsewhere in Asia, as had happened not infrequently in the past. However, it was just as conceivable that concerted schemes for Japanese aggrandizement were furthered under the guise of independent military action, which was taken superficially in spite of the "strictly honorable" intentions of the Tokyo diet. Whichever of these motives was the correct one, the Foreign Minister told Morris that he could not account for the report regarding the Japanese general's action, and "thought it must be due to some misunderstanding. He offered as an explanation," Morris wrote, "the familiar suggestion that the report arose through mistranslation."

Nevertheless, no effort was made at Tokyo to investigate the Japanese military move and by the middle of September the cabinet had shifted its own policy more directly in line with that of the army. In a lengthy memorandum the Japanese Foreign Office presented what constituted, in its view, unanswerable objections to the placing of the railroads in the hands of Stevens. In the first place, respect for the position of General Horvat, the legally appointed director of the Chinese Eastern Railroad and administrator of the

Ussuri line, prohibited his removal from office so that Stevens might assume control. Secondly, although the latter was likewise a legal appointee of the Russian Provisional Government, his function was specifically technical, and neither Stevens' Advisory Commission of Railroad Experts nor Colonel Emerson's Railway Service Corps had received authorization to control the Russian roads. It therefore followed, according to Tokyo, that the American suggestion could rightly be interpreted as "intervention in Russia's domestic administration." The only possible justification for such a program would be "military necessity of supreme importance," the existence of which Japan denied. Moreover, because the Allied military representatives, together with Russian railroad officials, had decided in August that the Russian lines were to remain under the latter, Japan concluded that the American proposal had best be dropped, implying serious consequences if this were not done.

Although the Japanese memorandum was dated September 18, it was written without foreknowledge of an official American statement composed five days previously which had advanced the State Department's case for Allied operation of the railroads under John Stevens and the Russian Railroad Service Corps. The one essential factor motivating Washington, according to the declaration, was the desire to carry out "its original purpose to assist the Russian people in the vital matter of transportation." As the American Government interpreted the situation, the lawful rights of Russia and China in the railroads had in no wise been altered either by the Communist movement or by the presence of Allied forces in Siberia. Moreover, the United States itself had absolutely no selfish interest in mind in pushing its plan for the temporary internationalization of the roads. In the words of the statement, Washington disclaimed "all purpose to obtain any interest or control" in the Russian lines. "Such a purpose . . . would not be tolerated" by the American people.

The concern registered by Tokyo for the safety of Russia's administrative integrity (a concern which was habitually paraded by both Japan and the United States as a means of limiting each other's activities in Siberia) had thus been anticipated by the American Government through its unequivocal disavowal of any hidden

motives in its proposed railroad plan. The resultant acceptance of
the Washington proposal by the Allies cut the ground from under
the immediate Japanese objections but the Foreign Office, unwilling
to abandon its position without further struggle, promptly shifted
its approach. A brief Japanese attempt to stall, by hinting at continued British recalcitrance, was followed by Downing Street's unqualified acquiescence in "any agreement which may ultimately
be reached" by Tokyo and Washington. This forced Baron Goto
to adopt a policy of theoretical endorsement of the American project,
while at the same time the Japanese Government conducted a
prolonged sniping attack on specific parts of the proposal with the
object of delaying its enactment beyond the point of usefulness.
The effectiveness of these tactics was demonstrated by the fact
that while Morris recorded Japanese agreement "in principle" on
September 18, a final compromise proposal was not mutually accepted until four months later.

The question which confounded and plagued American statesmen throughout the intervening weeks was the seemingly secondary
one regarding the "method of transfer" of the railroads from Russian
to American management. A foretaste of the diplomatic snags surrounding this subject was disclosed in a message from Morris the
end of October. Four weeks of fruitless negotiations, during which
identic words had been bandied by Tokyo and Washington to
describe wholly different objectives, had caused the Ambassador
to submit that, without a "clear understanding" with Japan on
the "meaning and purpose" of military occupation of the railroad,
any Japanese assent to the American plan would "be artificial and
dangerous, and Mr. Stevens' position would rapidly become untenable." In the same cable Morris described the continued military
encroachments of the Mikado's troops along the Chinese Eastern
Railroad in Manchuria, their manifest attempts to displace American, Chinese, and Russian forces, and the stoppage of all freight
shipments with the exception of those intended for the Japanese.
The substance of this report was confirmed a week later, thus expanding the evidence that while Tokyo's diplomats procrastinated
its army rapidly extended Japanese control over the disputed railroads. Notwithstanding American representations to the Foreign

Office, Goto did not offer to restrict the army's movements; instead he announced that the Japanese opposition was centered in the general staff, and suggested three possible alternatives to the United States plan: "an Allied committee simply to advise the present Russian management; joint management by Stevens and Kinoshita;" and "sole Japanese operation of the Chinese Eastern." [1]

In the meantime Stevens had voiced his categorical refusal to consider any program whereby a division of authority would exist in the railroad management, and his opposition, plainly and repeatedly stated in the autumn months, prevented the State Department from acceding to Japanese interpretations which would have made even more onerous the eventual Allied operation of the roads.

At the end of November the problem of the railroads was no nearer solution than it had ever been and the exasperated Morris, convinced that "the Siberian situation in itself" was "not hopelessly complex," and that the real difficulty lay "almost wholly with the divergent policies of the Associated Governments," pleaded again for a "united policy, even if a compromise." If this were impossible, he queried whether America's pledges to the people of Russia did not require the adoption and support of a unilateral plan.

This frame of mind was duplicated in recurrent messages from Stevens testifying to the worsening of railroad communications and the unabated infiltration of Japanese forces throughout Siberia. Furthermore, Baron Goto's alternate suggestion that Japan assume full control of the Chinese Eastern appeared to have received the sanction of his government at least, for Washington was informed confidentially that a Russian official connected with the Russo-Asiatic Bank was negotiating for the sale to Japanese interests of a controlling share in the bank. This would involve the transfer to Japan of the railroad with the attendant control of North Manchuria.[2] Confirmation of these rumors was supplied by Stevens, who cabled that Tokyo had made a formal demand that the Chinese President of the Chinese Eastern Railroad turn the line over to the

---

[1] Kinoshita was "Director of the Traffic Bureau of the Japanese Imperial Government Railways." *For. Rel.*, 1918, Russia, Vol. III, p. 283.

[2] Memorandum of a conversation with the Russian Ambassador, November 22, 1918, *Long Papers*. Memorandum on Japanese interests in Russia and China, 1919 (n.d.), *Lansing Papers*.

Japanese. And by mid-December the American military attaché
at Peking reported that nearly 10,000 Japanese were in occupation
of the Chinese Eastern zone.

The State Department had no intention of permitting Tokyo
to usurp any railroad in Manchuria or Siberia, however, and its
freely expressed concern lest "Japanese control . . . and absorption
of the railway for military purposes" render impossible the provision-
ing of the Russian population was a fragile covering for its deeper
anxiety regarding Japanese motives. Nevertheless, the seemingly
inexhaustible intransigence of Tokyo all but reaped a diplomatic
victory when the first Japanese alternative to the American proposal,
which contemplated an Allied committee with purely advisory
powers, received the tentative approval of both Morris and Acting
Secretary Polk. In essence the Japanese plan provided for supervision and assistance by Stevens, rather than the undiluted control
which he had demanded; further than that, it changed the American
engineer's position "from that of general manager with power
to choose his staff to that of president of the technical board,"
which was to consist of one representative from each nation with
military forces in Siberia. Apparently lapsing from his usual per-
ceptiveness, Morris cabled on December 3 that the difference between the Japanese and American plans was small in practice.
As an afterthought, however, the Ambassador was compelled to
admit that the success of the project depended on Japan's future
attitude—hardly a predictable factor. In reply Polk supported Morris
mainly because with the approach of winter it was imperative that
transportation facilities be improved.

This did not shut the door to the possibility of objections by
Stevens, for the Acting Secretary declared that the United States
would not consent to have the American engineer promoted "up-
stairs" where he would have no real authority. Stevens' flat statement at approximately the same time, "I cannot accept ambiguous
position suggested or recommend the plan," terminated that phase
of its existence.

Morris then proceeded to amend the proposal in order to appease
Stevens, only to run afoul of Japanese objections at changes in
the Tokyo formula which Goto termed "vital." Ten days later the

Japanese Foreign Office presented a new compromise and on December 27 Morris wired his conviction that this latest plan represented a sincere Japanese effort to meet Stevens' views. The plan corresponded sufficiently closely to the American requirements so that the Ambassador was able to convert Stevens to its acceptance. Under it the technical board's administrative function was reinstated and definite powers were reincorporated for the president of the board.

Negotiations were finally closed January 9, 1919, when Viscount Uchida, who had succeeded Baron Goto in the Foreign Office, gave his approval to a memorandum which contained the points hitherto agreed upon by the two governments. Among the salient features of the plan as finally adopted were:

The Inter-Allied committee, whose function it would be to operate the railroad lines, would consist of one representative from each of the states participating in the military intervention, including the Provisional Russian Government, and the chairman of the committee would be a Russian. The Allied military forces would protect the railways, and at "the head of each railway shall remain a Russian manager . . . with the powers conferred by the existing law." The Technical Board would be representative of all the intervening powers. Stevens would become President of the Board as well as a member thereof. Both Japan and America would give him "the authority and support . . . necessary to make his efforts effective." The program would be liquidated "upon the withdrawal of foreign military forces from Siberia and all the foreign railway experts . . . shall then be recalled." And the plan would be interpreted as a genuine effort to operate the two roads on behalf of the Russian people, "with a view to their ultimate return to those in interest without the impairing of any existing rights." [3]

This, of course, was the crux of the whole agreement, for without the final clause it was plain that the United States would not have been a party to the plan. It was, in effect, Washington's guarantee equally as much as a guarantee to the Russians that the intervening powers entertained no insidious, imperialist designs on the Trans-Siberian or the Chinese Eastern railroads.

[3] *For. Rel.*, 1919, Russia, pp. 236–237, 239–240.

On February 10, 1919, Acting Secretary Polk addressed a formal communication to Ambassador Ishii which constituted the official inauguration of the American-Japanese plan. After expressing his "gratification" that the two powers had obtained so clear and cordial an understanding, Polk inserted a paragraph which lucidly illustrated the basic American distrust of Japan's motives in Siberia. The joint agreement had stated in part that "the interests of [the] respective Allied powers in charge of . . ." the more important railroad stations "shall be taken into due consideration."

The United States understands [Polk informed Ishii] that the word "interests" in this case, is used as referring to the convenience of the . . . powers . . . and *not as implying any political or territorial rights or spheres of influence.*[4]

At the end of February, Charles H. Smith was appointed American representative on the Inter-Allied Committee, and on March 17 Stevens issued a declaration to the Russian people as to the purposes and objectives of the Allied plan and its direct importance to the welfare of Siberia. Five days later the Russian chargé at Washington transmitted the Kolchak Government's satisfaction that the Allied plan did not in any sense constitute an impingement of Russian sovereignty.

Despite the approval thus accorded, the Omsk group was not entirely reconciled to the railroad program, largely because it had been utterly ignored throughout the prolonged period which preceded its adoption. Although the United States was, at the time, still uncertain of the policy it would pursue toward Kolchak, the fact that a plan which, after all, was of immediate and intimate concern to the Siberian populace had been evolved with only a passing nod in its direction illustrated more eloquently than words the purely secondary nature of American interest in Russia personally, and the contrasting importance of Washington's relations with Tokyo.

The single other power which possessed a direct stake in the

[4] *For. Rel.*, 1919, Vol. I, pp. 594–595. Italics mine. Between February 19 and March 5 France, Britain, and Italy notified the United States and Japan of their approval of the plan. On March 19 the Czechoslovaks were invited to participate in the program.

railroad network, but whose sensibilities were overlooked by the Allies, was China. The Chinese Eastern line, subject to a contractual agreement between Russia and China of twenty years' duration, represented a concrete investment to the latter and, moreover, a definite foothold in northern Manchuria, where Japanese incursions were continually weakening Chinese influence. Consequently the Peking authorities were understandably distraught at the seemingly endless infiltration of Japanese troops, at the "persuasive" methods employed by these forces to dislodge the Chinese guard along the railroad, and at the Allied plan which did not, according to Peking, pay sufficient attention to China's rights in the C.E.R. On February 4 the State Department received a memorandum from the Chinese Government which claimed that a "third party [had] no right to interfere" in the Russo-Chinese treaty regarding the railroad; that therefore Peking should assume control pending the restoration of a *bona fide* Russian government, and that such control should include full responsibility for the operation, maintenance, and military protection of the line within the framework of the Allied plan. Simultaneously China submitted a proposal for the management and reorganization of the railroad with the objectives of maintaining "the sovereign rights of China" and rendering the railroad efficient.

The attitude of Washington was an admixture of condescension and firm pressure. Peking was assured by Minister Reinsch that its interests were provided for and that a copy of the plan would be relayed as soon as final agreement had been reached. The desire of the Chinese Government that its representative on the Technical Board be equal in rank and authority to Stevens was declared wholly inadmissible, if for no other reason than that of efficiency and unified control. Ultimately Peking withdrew this request, contenting itself with the hope that Chinese railroad experts would be enabled to cooperate in the administration of the C.E.R.

In assuming the burden of protecting both Chinese and Russian treaty rights in the railroad the United States Government had taken the first step in what eventually became a virtual trusteeship over the terms of the Russo-Chinese Treaty of 1896, a role which involved it increasingly in the relations of Peking and Moscow and which was vividly illustrated in the Sino-Soviet dispute a decade later.

The initial challenge to the railroad status quo in Siberia and northern Manchuria came from Tokyo. The Japanese decision in December 1918 to concede in large measure to the American proposal for railroad management had represented in part a short-lived victory for the moderate Hara element over the Tanaka military clique. It had also signified the effectiveness of American economic pressure on Japan specifically recommended by Ambassador Morris.[5] However, once the Allied plan had received the approval of the Foreign Office the habitual ogre of Japanese obstructionism again lifted its head, and in the course of the following months the impossibility of cooperating with Tokyo under even the most explicit arrangement was repeatedly demonstrated. In short, the diametrically opposed policies of Washington and Tokyo could not be syncretized; collaboration was a contradiction in terms.

Throughout the winter and spring of 1919 Stevens and the American engineers, together with the representatives of France, Britain, and Italy, strove to increase the operating power of the Siberian lines for the purpose essentially of providing supplies for the anti-Bolshevik groups, notably the Omsk Government. The policy consistently adhered to by Japan—of supporting rival groups and preventing the emergence of a strongly centralized Siberian government—should have forewarned the State Department that Japanese assistance through the railroads in the interests of Kolchak was unlikely; furthermore, viewed in terms of Japanese imperialism the avowed Allied concept of a unified, smoothly operating Trans-Siberian system was wholly undesirable.

As a result Washington and Tokyo were thrown against each other from the moment the Inter-Allied agreement was promul-

---

[5] "Political considerations would suggest the wisdom of postponing action on Japanese applications now pending before the War Trade Board until the Japanese Government has decided how far it will cooperate with us in Russia. The issue is definitely raised by our proposal for the Stevens' operation of the Russian railways. If the Japanese Government refuses assent to a plan which is vital to the immediate future of Siberia I would favor a less generous policy toward Japan." Morris to Lansing, October 31, 1918 (694.119/245).

gated and, despite repeated attempts to span the chasm dividing them, their differences remained irreconcilable. The first indication of this was the utterly impractical suggestion at the end of February that Japan exercise "sole supervision" of "a substantial portion of the Chinese Eastern," despite Stevens' well-founded contention that "the main line cannot be placed under different systems of operation without defeating the whole object of the agreement."

Two months later, following extended efforts to reach some sort of *modus vivendi* whereby the authority of the Technical Board over the military occupation units could be effectuated, Tokyo submitted two memoranda which revealed the difficulty of cooperating with the Japanese military forces in Siberia "through civilian control." In summarizing the substance of the notes Morris pointed out that the Japanese general staff insisted on keeping the initiative and refused either to understand or to tolerate any arrangement "which would deprive them of independent action." It was this attitude, the Ambassador declared, which so fatigued and irritated American representatives in Siberia.

While this question was being discussed a further breach appeared in the form of a Japanese desire to alter the gauge of the Changchun-Harbin section of the Chinese Eastern Railroad. Quite apart from the disrupting effect of such action on transportation along the Manchurian part of the Trans-Siberian system, the State Department perceived in Tokyo's plan an endeavor to join at least one line of the Chinese Eastern with the Japanese controlled road in southern Manchuria. The implications of such a move were apparent; accordingly Washington blocked the project by championing again the legal rights of Russia and China in the railroad.

Meanwhile Tokyo was demonstrating its "separatist" desires by refusing to control the obstreperous Semenov, whose recurrent attacks on the eastern end of the Trans-Siberian line were endangering the lives of American engineers and diverting supplies intended for Admiral Kolchak. In mid-July 1919, except for a few points guarded by American soldiers, the entire road from Irkutsk to Vladivostok was occupied by the Japanese, and they in turn used Semenov's organization to threaten the Allied railroad operation. According to Morris their plan was transparent. Balked by the railroad agreement in their original purpose of appropriating the Chinese Eastern and Trans-Siberian lines (as the key to the control of eastern Siberia and northern Manchuria), they proceeded to operate through the Cossacks.

Semenov based his activities on the argument that as a Siberian leader he had succeeded to the control of the Siberian roads in general and of the C.E.R. in particular; and by September his efforts to make good this claim had aroused grave misgivings among American officials. Stevens cabled on the 26th that he was "positive" that Semenov and Kalmykov (ataman of the Ussuri Cossacks) intended to seize the Chinese Eastern with the tacit consent of Japan. "This action," he concluded, "would be [a] fatal blow to all our good offices." Furthermore, there appeared some evidence that the Chinese Inspector General of Manchuria, Chang Tso-lin, was courting Japan's favor and was therefore not averse to encouraging Semenov, even to the point of elevating him to the directorship of the C.E.R. With these possibilities in mind Polk instructed Reinsch to discuss the matter with the Chinese Government at Peking, stressing the fact that such action would violate the plan of joint operation and would be an extremely injudicious step for China to take. The American protest rested nominally on the desire that the legal status of the Chinese Eastern be kept intact.

It was the accumulation of a myriad grievances such as these which ultimately convinced Washington of the futility of further prolonging the farce of American-Japanese cooperation in Siberia. As a result the government began to think seriously of evacuating its expeditionary force, leaving Tokyo to examine its own conscience in the light of the inevitable publicity which would accompany such a step. In one sense the conjectured action was an admission of weakness by the State Department, for it had never commanded a sufficiently large military contingent in Siberia to insure Japanese respect for the Allied railroad agreement,[6] and an increase in official

[6] Even the inauguration of the Stevens plan had not resulted in an increase in the number of American troops in Siberia. On January 14, 1919, Secretary of War Baker had written to Acting Secretary of State Polk: "The War Department adheres rigidly to the policy laid down for the use of United States troops in Siberia by the President in his memorandum to the Powers. The

notes and protests had not atoned for lack of army personnel. At the same time, it was believed that a decisive and radical change of policy might serve to strengthen the United States by confining the American-Japanese conflict to the respective foreign offices of the two countries, where the superiority of Washington's moral position would exert a possibly telling effect. Consequently the problem was discussed inter-departmentally by the Wilson Administration and on August 30, 1919, an extremely forceful and cogent note was sent to the Japanese Government.

The message traced in detail the successive acts which had culminated in the Siberian intervention and in the Inter-Allied agreement for the operation and control of the Trans-Siberian and Chinese Eastern railroads; it pointed to the essential role of the two lines in the economic and political life of Siberia and the consequent importance of any developments which obstructed them; it narrowed these developments down to the basic dispute between Japan and the United States over the interpretation of the Inter-Allied agreement. As the American Government viewed the situation, the Japanese interpretation precluded a broad cooperation with the associated powers in operating the two roads; conversely, a unilateral approach, limited to safeguarding railroad property and keeping the line open, seemed to characterize Japan's understanding of the agreement. To the United States such an understanding was "wholly inadmissible." In concrete terms the Japanese military commanders had consistently refused to protect "the lives and property of the Allied inspectors" in areas controlled by General Semenov. Yet Japan was fully aware that Admiral Kolchak, whose government the Allies were pledged to support, favored the railroad agreement, and that accordingly the Semenov elements were acting in open defiance of his regime. Therefore the Imperial Japanese Government by its behavior was not only undermining the authority of the Omsk leaders, but silently acquiescing in a reign of terror in eastern Siberia which threatened to sabotage the

War Department does not believe that the small force which we now have there is large enough to give Mr. Stevens support with reference to the policing of the Chinese Eastern and Trans-Siberian Railroads, and cannot approve of sending any more troops to Siberia for such purpose." Baker to Polk, January 14, 1919 (861.00/3651).

railroad agreement by forcing the withdrawal of the Allied engineers.

The American note then registered the grave concern with which Washington regarded the situation. Declaring that it could not "be held responsible for that for which it is not in fact responsible," and pointing to Japan's failure to support a plan which was predicated on inter-Allied cooperation, the United States indicated that the time had come to fix the responsibility "for the failure of the enterprise." The government now had to decide whether the only course left was "an entire withdrawal from all further efforts to cooperate in Siberia," followed by "a public statement of the reasons" for withdrawal.

The concluding paragraph of the document must have drawn a tolerant smile from the more practical foreign ministers of all the governments to whom copies were sent, for it reflected that strong idealism of the American President which, in preceding months, had motivated the writing of the Covenant of the League of Nations. The United States was

firmly convinced that the future welfare of all Governments is to be based upon a community of interest which is about to replace permanently the former balances of power and other bargains of self-interest and aggrandizement on the part of one nation or group of nations at the expense of others. With the deepest regret [the American Government] . . . finds that the attitude of Japan in this matter raises the question as to whether this view of international relations is shared by the Imperial Government.[7]

Copies of the note were communicated to the Allied governments, China, and Russian Ambassador Bakhmetev at Washington. After a conference with Assistant Secretary Long, Bakhmetev consulted by cable with the Omsk Government and also with Sazonov, representing Kolchak at Paris. In the middle of September, Sazonov replied that an American exodus would "never in the world be understood by the Russians," who would view it as a capitulation to the Japanese at Russian expense.

The British were similarly anxious over the proposed American evacuation, and cryptic reference was made to the fact that

[7] *For. Rel.*, 1919, Russia, pp. 573–578.

"the withdrawal of United States troops would leave Japan as the only country maintaining forces in Siberia."

Tokyo was silent for two months following the receipt of the American note and its reply at the end of October was neither indignant nor servile; instead, the Japanese Foreign Office sought to excuse itself by a series of wordy rationalizations. It first reiterated the old dilemma of the government wishing to pursue one path while the general staff proceeded independently to set its own course, thus leading to the unfortunate absence of Japanese cooperation with the Allied plan. However, this was remedied by renewed assurances of Japan's intentions to fulfill its obligations. Finally there appeared the time-gaining device whereby Tokyo invited formal discussion of specific instances in which "Japanese troops have refused to protect the lives and property of Allied inspectors."

The comment of Ambassador Morris in forwarding the note included a shrewd critique of American policy:

It is of no value to discuss at this time and in the abstract the views or purposes of the Japanese Government. I see no advantage to better relations between Japan and America in reiterated statements of policy, rather we should put Japan's national purposes . . . to the test of action. When we are prepared as a Government and people to support constructive action in the Orient then we should seek Japan's cooperation and at the same time be ready to proceed without it. Mere . . . protest simply accentuates differences and may lead to serious complications. In the face of crying needs such as exist in China and Siberia we cannot be placed in the position of seeming to stay the hand of Japan while failing to offer any alternative plan . . . We are not in a position to do more than we are doing although the conditions call for much more. Under these circumstances we can only make the best of our limitations and with patience continue our efforts to cooperate with Japan. Such a policy may seem unsatisfactory but it is . . . far better than entire withdrawal.[8]

Notwithstanding the vigorous American protest and its own conciliatory answer, Japan continued to pursue with single-minded de-

[8] *Ibid.*, pp. 588–594. For the American answer to the Japanese note, see pp. 594–595.

termination its policy of infiltration in Siberia and North Manchuria. On December 4 Stevens informed Washington that the
Chinese Eastern officials were seeking a loan of Japanese yen and
that if the United States planned to keep the open-door in Manchuria it would perforce have to block Japanese efforts to secure
financial control of the C.E.R. In February 1920, shortly after
the execution of Kolchak, Stevens reported further that Japan
was offering the Chinese Eastern a five-year loan of twenty million
yen without security, "simply receipt of railway." If consummated,
Japanese domination of the road was assured. And simultaneously
Tokyo's closest ally, England, again intimated its concern over
conditions resulting from the collapse of authority in Russia and
the importance of preventing the control of the C.E.R. from
falling under one power exclusively. The British, like the Russian
Provisional Government, thought this could best be done by maintaining the American military contingent in the Russian Far East.
But although Washington was equally exercised over the precarious
situation which had developed, the State Department was already
committed to the termination of the Siberian expedition. This did
not mean the repudiation of the time-honored policy in Asia, but
rather that henceforth other channels would be used for its implementation.

The decision to withdraw was the result of four major factors
which bore down on the Department of State and made any other
alternative impracticable. They included domestic pressure within
the United States, the defeat of the Kolchak movement, inability
to check the Japanese through the retention of troops in Siberia,
and the continuing evacuation of the Czechoslovaks. The last of
these played the same part in American policy in 1920 as in 1918,
providing a moral justification and an immediate pretext for the
action the United States was about to take. This and the second
factor distracted attention from the third motive, which was never
published for obvious reasons.

Opposition to the American intervention in Russia began to
find expression within a month of the Armistice and the records
of Senate proceedings at the time indicate not only an almost total
lack of information by the Senators regarding the diplomacy prior

to the Allied expedition, but a pronounced aversion to the program as a postwar project.[9] In answer to a cable from Polk in January 1919 about continued Senate pressure, Wilson authorized the Acting Secretary to discuss the whole problem before a secret hearing of the interested Senate committees. Although Polk and the Cabinet did not agree with the President's suggested approach to Congress it is worth noting because it reveals so implicitly the "extracurricular" quality of the American policy. Thus Wilson wished Polk to mention to the Senate committee the "potential value" of the Trans-Siberian Railroad "as a means for developing American commerce particularly from the west coast of the United States to Russia." The Acting Secretary was then to describe the friction with Japan and the latter's practical seizure of the Chinese Eastern Railroad, "thereby in effect controlling all intercourse to and from Russia via the Pacific." [10] Moreover, the root of the President's Far Eastern program was expressly admitted in a telegram on February 9 in which Polk was given discretion to talk with Congressional committees when and if he wished. According to the cable American policy was utterly divorced from the Russian problem as

irrespective of what our policy may be toward Russia, and irrespective of future Russian developments, it is essential that we maintain the policy of the open-door with reference to the Siberian and particularly the Chinese Eastern Railroad.[11]

This was indeed a revealing commentary, not on Wilsonian policies in particular but on international politics in general. Re-

[9] See *The Congressional Record*, Vol. 57, Part 1, pp. 342–346 (December 12, 1918) for Senate Resolution 384 (65th Congress, 3d Session) and the accompanying speech of Senator Johnson. The resolution contrasted the "various incidents indicating a state of war," with the August 3 declaration on intervention, and asked the Secretary of State to provide available data "so that the Senate and the Nation may know why and for what purpose our soldiers are in Russia and what is the policy of the Government in reference to Russia." In committee the resolution failed to pass by a tie vote. *For. Rel.*, Paris Peace Conference, 1919, Vol. II, p. 483.

[10] Polk was further instructed to develop at length the difficulties the American Government had had with Japan in Siberia. *For. Rel.*, 1919, Russia, pp. 246–248, 249.

[11] *Ibid.*, p. 251.

gardless of the idealism which motivated Wilson as much as idealism ever moved any statesman, the harsh fact remained that without a balance of power American commercial and financial interests in the Far East were in mortal danger, and that Japan was the nation which threatened the Asiatic equilibrium. Therefore, as Wilson indirectly admitted, the question of Russia's future government, whether Communist or something else, was secondary. The compulsions of a balance of power overrode every other consideration and dictated Wilson's approach in 1919 even as they are shaping national foreign policies today.

With the signing of the Versailles Treaty in June 1919 the Siberian venture was subjected to renewed attack in the Senate as the restiveness of the American people increased. To men of Senator Borah's insight the intervention was strictly an aggressive Japanese plot, consciously aided by England out of fear of communism and sanctioned by the American State Department. It was "without constitutional authority" and involved an attempt to establish a government within Russia satisfactory to England, Japan, and America and which would promote Japanese imperialism. By the end of the year the public mood had so manifested itself that Lansing and his aides could no longer temporize; Assistant Secretary Long had recommended in August that the United States withdraw, and toward the end of December the Secretary of State formulated a memorandum which, with little change, became the official American note to the Japanese Government of January 9, 1920, setting forth Washington's decision to evacuate Siberia, and the reasons therefor.[12]

Taking advantage of an earlier communication from Tokyo, the Wilson Government incorporated the main points raised in the Japanese message with its own conclusions. The United States could not, the note declared, "send a reinforcement of sufficient strength" to "act on the offensive in cooperation with anti-Bolshevik forces." Furthermore, "under present conditions" (the collapse

[12] In a note which accompanied the December 23 memorandum to the President, Lansing declared: "The truth of the matter is the simple fact that the Kolchak Government has utterly disintegrated . . . if we do not withdraw we shall have to wage war against the Bolsheviki." *For. Rel.*, Lansing Papers, Vol. II, pp. 392–393.

of the Omsk Government and the rapid ingress of the Communists) it was considered impracticable to "continue to participate in guarding the districts . . . under Allied military protection," for this might well involve "an undertaking of such indefinite character" and so great an armed force that Washington "would not feel justified in carrying it out." Consequently, in line with the third alternative included in the Japanese note of a month before, the United States had decided to withdraw its forces.

In drawing the balance sheet between the announced objectives of the expedition in the August 1918 declaration and the situation which precipitated the removal of American troops a year and a half later, Lansing was able to satisfy at least his own government that "the main purposes for which American troops were sent to Siberia are now at an end." By omitting all mention of the fact that the Czechs, to whose alleged rescue the United States army had been sent, had purposely remained in Siberia to fight bolshevism until they were near mutiny in their desire to leave Russia, the Secretary of State could properly note that an agreement had been reached with Great Britain for the repatriation of the Czech troops from Vladivostok, and that, once evacuation began, "the first purpose for which American soldiers were sent to Siberia" might be "regarded as accomplished." He found that the "second purpose, namely, the steadying of efforts at self-government or self-defense on the part of the Russians," was impossible of achievement because of the continued presence of foreign troops on Siberian soil. In other words, Lansing confessed to the unlikelihood of unseating the Bolsheviks.

The decision to remove the American expeditionary force had as its corollary the withdrawal of the American railroad experts in accordance with the terms of the Inter-Allied railroad agreement of January 1919; and of this the Japanese were likewise notified. In concluding his note, Lansing took occasion simultaneously to express his government's confidence in and warning to Japan concerning its Far Eastern policy. Therefore, while regretting the necessity for withdrawing because it marked the end of a cooperative Japanese-American effort to assist the Russian people, and while expressing appreciation for "the friendly spirit" [*sic!*] of Tokyo in the undertaking, the communication served notice that the American Government retained its "deep interest" in the political and economic fate of the Siberian people and its desire for future cooperation with the Japanese "in all practical plans which may be worked out for the political and economic rehabilitation of that region." [13]

On January 22 Ambassador Shidehara transmitted the formal reply of his government; after repeating the American explanation of its precipitate decision to withdraw, which had allegedly allowed no time for prior consultation with Japan, and accepting Washington's assurances to that end, the Japanese memorandum took the occasion to untie Tokyo's hands in Asia regardless of American policy. Accordingly the note reiterated a portion of Lansing's declaration of a fortnight earlier to the effect that the United States would not object to any Japanese decision to retain troops in Siberia, to send reinforcements, or to continue to aid in the operation of the Trans-Siberian and Chinese Eastern railroads.

In its answer a week later the State Department was careful to define more explicitly the intended meaning of the Lansing statement. While it confirmed "the intimation" given by the American Secretary of State, Washington emphasized its confident belief that Japan, "in the exercise of the trust devolving upon it," would pursue a policy consistent with that agreed upon by the two governments in 1918 and 1919, "particularly in connection with the operation of" the two railroad systems.

The tenor of these exchanges was vivid indication that no single step by either of the Far Eastern protagonists could resolve the American-Japanese conflict or, by the same token, the problems posed by the unstable political condition of Asiatic Russia. The departure of General Graves and the last American troops from Vladivostok on April 1 was, in the longer view, merely a curtain behind which American diplomats busily shifted scenes for the next act.

In the light of history and the perspective of time, what epitaph can be pronounced on the American Siberian policy? Its divergence

[13] Lansing to Shidehara, January 9, 1920, *For. Rel.*, 1920, Vol. III, pp. 487–490.

from established principles of international law regarding non-interference in the internal affairs of sovereign states has been stressed by numerous authors. (The factor of "military necessity" was an Anglo-French concoction, never subscribed to by the State Department, which intervened in spite of the contrary advices of the Department of War.) The effect on the people of Siberia resulting from the Allied occupation was painful and protracted; Wilson had unerringly described its inescapable tragedy in February 1919, when he told his colleagues at Paris:

The troops of the . . . Powers were doing no sort of good in Russia. They did not know for whom or for what they were fighting. They were not assisting any promising common effort to establish order throughout Russia. They were assisting local movements, like, for instance, that of the Cossacks, who could not be induced to move out of their own sphere . . . [He] pointed out that the existing forces of the Allies could not stop the Bolsheviks, and that not one of the Allies was prepared to reinforce its troops.[14]

In other words, while the American and Allied forces remained, remnants of hope were clung to by the anti-Soviet elements of the population; but in terms of the hardships endured and the retribution which followed in the wake of the Allied exodus, the price paid for a transient reprieve was exorbitant. At the same time the psychological effect of the Allied action on the Moscow Government was hardly calculable. Seeds of distrust already deep-planted in the mutually antagonistic minds of capitalist and Communist society broke through the earth and flowered with the Siberian invasion, contributing not a little to the atmosphere of suspicion which has, with brief exception, characterized American-Soviet relations over the past three decades. Finally, as indicated above, the United States action was preeminently called forth by the requirements of the Far Eastern balance of power, but intervention did not checkmate the Japanese in their search for empire, and when the American troops left they were unaccompanied by their Japanese cohorts.

[14] Minutes of the 14th Session of the Supreme War Council, February 14, 1919, *For. Rel.*, 1919, Russia, p. 57.

Against all the black marks in the American intervention, however, was one relieving gray: the State Department had decided to intervene only after failing to dissuade the Allies from it, and throughout the nineteen months of its participation the United States exerted a steadying influence on the ambitions of Japan, drawing formal pledges from that country regarding both the scope and the intentions of its Siberian policy. In this respect, at least, the American Government went far in preventing the alienation of the Siberian Far East from the sovereign rule of the Russian state, and to that extent upheld the status quo in the Pacific. Moreover, through its active role in the Allied venture Washington was in an indisputably better position to impress its will on Japan in the next few years, and so to assume a leading part in the gradual Japanese evacuation of all Russian territory.

In essence, President Wilson's Siberian expedition was an act of political expediency directed primarily at Japan, and therefore an integral part of American Far Eastern policy. In so far as a nation's diplomacy tends to be judged by reference to the so-called "realities" of power relationships, the decision adopted by the State Department in the summer of 1918 was, accordingly, both "right" and inevitable.

CHAPTER VII

Diplomacy by Protest

Between April 1920 and the assembling of the Washington Conference at the close of 1921 the United States continued in its efforts to restore the equilibrium in Eastern Asia. With the collapse of organized Siberian resistance to the Bolsheviks and with the evacuation of American troops, the State Department was gradually forced into the embarrassing position of upholding Soviet sovereignty in the Far East as against Japanese incursions, although the actual admission of this fact was withheld as long as possible. This position was the more equivocal in that Washington consistently rebuffed all Soviet attempts to open diplomatic relations and to promote trade even as it protected the Russian claims to Siberia.

In the meantime Moscow looked alternately to Tokyo and to Washington for the opportunity to strengthen its own hold in the Far East. Lenin and Trotsky, acute realists and opportunists, entertained no hesitation concerning the policy that the Soviet Government should adopt: if Japan could be prevailed upon to accept a generous settlement, that would be satisfactory; or if the State Department could be persuaded to forgo its aloofness toward Moscow, that would be equally pleasing. And if neither of these alternatives were feasible at the time, it was still open to the Kremlin to foster American-Japanese rivalry and encourage the mutual suspicions of the two nations in the almost certain gamble that such tactics would eventually force one of the rivals to approach the Soviet in search of a "friendly" balance to its antagonist.

In February 1920 the Russian leaders made a formal bid for Washington's friendship and recognition, stressing in the main the immense economic benefits which would ensue with American financial assistance in the task of Russian reconstruction. This brought forth no encouragement from the State Department; consequently Russia redoubled its efforts in the direction of Japan. Already on February 26 Morris had reported that "a wireless telegram regarding peace" had been sent to Tokyo which pointed "to the mutual advantages of an understanding especially in view of Japan's great economic interests." [1] The following week this proposal was confirmed and implemented by further details relative to the Soviet offer. Thus Morris cabled: "The possibility of giving recognition to domination by Japan in Asia is rather cleverly suggested." Russia apparently was prepared to recognize special Japanese interests which as yet had been conceded by "no other country." The only "compensation" asked in turn by Moscow was the immediate evacuation of Soviet territory by Japanese troops.[2]

The government of Japan was unimpressed by these sweeping offers; in the foreknowledge that the American expeditionary army was shortly to withdraw from the Far East, leaving the Siberian harvest to Tokyo, there was small incentive to enter into an agreement with Moscow which could serve only to limit the scope of Japan's aggressive ambitions. Furthermore, there was a genuine terror of bolshevism within Japan which, judged by the semi-hysteria evoked by communism in distant America, was certainly worthy of some consideration in explaining the Japanese policy. As a result, the official cabinet decision in February to withdraw the Japanese forces from all Siberia except Vladivostok and Nikolsk and along the Chinese Eastern Railroad (with joint Sino-Japanese contingents guarding the Manchurian frontier) was intended not as a first step in evacuation, but as the consolidation of Tokyo's defense against communism (and perhaps as the springboard for future Japanese advances).

Japan's policy was stated in full at the end of March in an article in the *Official Gazette*, organ of the government. Stressing the difference in geographical relation to Siberia between Japan and the Allies, and the peculiar danger to Japanese residents on the

[1] Morris to the Secretary of State, February 26, 1920 (861.00/6446).
[2] *For. Rel.*, 1920, Vol. III, p. 449.

Russian mainland under the continued Bolshevik threat, the article stated:

This is the reason why the Empire is not able to withdraw the troops immediately. The Empire entertains no political ambitions towards Russia. As soon as the political conditions in the territories adjacent to our country settle down, as soon as the menace to Manchuria and Chosen has been removed, the safety of the lives and property of the Japanese residents assured and the freedom of communications guaranteed, we hereby reaffirm our pledge that the Empire will evacuate Siberia provided the Czecho-Slovaks have been completely withdrawn.[3]

The protective attitude of the Japanese Government toward its nationals in Siberia, forcibly expressed in the spring and summer of 1920 in Vladivostok, the city of Nikolaievsk, the island of Sakhalin, the greater portion of eastern Siberia, and along the Chinese Eastern Railroad, was to convince Moscow [4] and Washington alike that whatever the basic justification for Tokyo's action, the Mikado's army had no intention of leaving Russian soil without a struggle. Nevertheless, in response to renewed Soviet feelers, Secretary of State Colby adhered to the ambiguous Russian policy of his predecessor. On August 10 he informed Moscow through the Italian Ambassador at Washington that while the United States recognized the right of every nation to choose its own form of government, a Sovietized Russia could never expect diplomatic, not to mention economic, relations with America. The fervent Russian denials of Washington's castigations and the reaffirmation of the common need of both countries to promote political and commercial intercourse fell on ears "that would not hear," and the American attitude of negativism—nonintervention and nonrecognition—was faithfully passed on to the incoming Harding Administration in March 1921.

[3] The substance of this article was embodied in an official Japanese communication to the State Department on April 3, 1920. *Ibid.*, pp. 505, 506.

[4] On August 18 the Communist Party paper in Vladivostok accused Japan of flagrantly violating its international obligations in Siberia and of plotting to establish a puppet regime. This precipitated the seizure of the paper by the Japanese authorities at Vladivostok. Caldwell to Colby, August 31, 1920 (861.00/7524).

The Soviet Government reacted to the position of the State Department by resorting again to the theme of an American-Japanese war in the Far East. For example, Lenin in November 1920, in an address before the Moscow District Conference of the Russian Communist Party, referred to the "differences between our enemies" (Japan and the United States), which had "recently increased."

We have rightly estimated this imperialist rivalry and we have made up our mind as to the necessity of systematically utilizing this rivalry in order to make their fight against us difficult . . .

At the same time, however, the Soviet leaders were too perceptive to push the American-Japanese antagonism beyond its proper limits. Regardless of Washington's aversion to Moscow, the cause of Russia was being furthered by the State Department through its efforts to delimit Japanese imperialism, and therefore Soviet blasts against the United States were usually tempered by expressions of hope for the future of American-Russian relations in Asia, resting as they did on the common platform of hostility to Japan.

Harding may also try to crush Soviet Government (wrote *Pravda* on November 11, 1920) but he will probably do his best to preserve Russia from economic and political exhaustion because value of having strong state at back of Japan is appreciated.[5]

In two months this was followed by a cable from Charles H. Smith, the American representative on the Inter-Allied railroad commission, who spoke of the Russian "trust" in the United States and suggested that the Siberian authorities (representing the Far Eastern Republic which, formed in 1920, was little more than a Soviet mouthpiece) would willingly accept American operation of the railroads if Japan would comply with the agreement. And in

[5] Quoted in a dispatch from the American consul at Viborg to the Secretary of State, November 19, 1920 (711.61/413). A year later *Izvestia* advocated American-Soviet cooperation, for the reason that "in many cases their interests and ours coincide, more particularly in regard to Japanese imperialism." Enclosure in the American Commissioner, Riga, to the Secretary of State, December 20, 1921 (711.61/57).

June 1921 the United States was auspiciously omitted from a Soviet note to the British, French, and Italian governments which protested vigorously against Japanese encroachments in the Russian Far East and stated the conviction that all the Entente powers were "morally responsible for this new link in the chain of intervention."

However, Moscow's gestures to Washington, whether threatening or cajoling, altered neither the American attitude toward the Soviet nor American policy in Asia, both of which were deep-rooted and mutually exclusive. To the State Department, the form of government in Russia was a deplorable calamity and a disease which required isolation; but it did not follow that Japan should be encouraged or permitted to compress the area of Bolshevik infection through amputation of Russian territory. This conviction stemmed not from any diagnosis of Marxism but from the basic dictates of America's Far Eastern policy, which demanded that the Japanese march to empire be halted whenever and wherever this was diplomatically possible.

In other words, Siberia was simply a place-name—of no greater or lesser significance than China, Manchuria, or the islands of the Pacific—in the comprehensive map of American political strategy; and the preservation of its sovereignty was as integral to the balance of power in Asia as the maintenance of the open-door in China. Washington's anathema to communism, while sufficiently strong to prevent the establishment of diplomatic relations with the Kremlin until 1933, was throughout secondary to its policy in the Far East, and accordingly the United States fought to uphold the Russian right to Siberia despite a persistent refusal to recognize the existence of the Russian Government.

In the months following the decision to withdraw its armed forces from Asia, Washington was confronted with growing evidences of Tokyo's design for expansion in Siberia and northern Manchuria. The relatively minor progress by the State Department toward containing the Japanese imperialists, coupled with the deterioration of the American position vis-à-vis Japan in China, were primarily responsible for the alacrity with which Secretary Hughes seconded the British suggestion of including the problems of the Pacific on the agenda of the Washington Conference in 1921.

The first of two "incidents" which provoked the Japanese to extend the radius of their Siberian occupation occurred in March 1920 with the wanton massacre of an alleged seven hundred Japanese subjects by Bolshevik partisans in the city of Nikolaievsk. This prompted Tokyo to transport a contingent of troops to the Russian-owned northern half of the island of Sakhalin, of which Nikolaievsk was the capital city, although located on the Siberian mainland at the mouth of the Amur River.[6] The actual troop movement did not take place until April 19, but the Moscow Government had forewarned the Western nations and the United States a month earlier. Accusing Japan of a plot to take possession of Sakhalin, the Soviet Government drew European and American attention to the "new unjustified aggression of which Russia is the victim" and pointed out "the disasters which will follow for those powers themselves." Ambassador Morris was at once instructed (March 27) to ascertain Japan's reason for landing on the Russian end of Sakhalin instead of at Nikolaievsk.

It was not until five days after Tokyo had ordered its armed division to Sakhalin, however, that the government offered a partial explanation of its move through a formal statement on April 24. Because of ice conditions, the note averred, Nikolaievsk was temporarily inaccessible, and therefore the Japanese force was being sent via Sakhalin "where they will stay until the freezing season is over, in the meantime protecting the Japanese residents in the locality of Alexandrovski" (a port on Sakhalin). This was hardly a straight answer to Washington's question, but by the time the ice had melted Tokyo was able to account for its action quite explicitly. In a memorandum on July 3 Ambassador Shidehara emphasized the duty of his government to uphold "the dignity of a nation so wantonly assailed." Moreover, he added, until a legal Russian govern-

[6] The city of Nikolaievsk had historically been an integral part of the Maritime Province on the mainland of Siberia, but by a Russian imperial decree in 1914 the town and its environs were separated from the Maritime district and incorporated in the province of Sakhalin, which included the northern portion of that island. The American Government was unaware of this until after it had dispatched a strong note to Japan on July 16; the American Consul at Vladivostok confirmed the incorporation of Nikolaievsk with Sakhalin Province on August 7, 1920. *For. Rel.*, *op. cit.*, pp. 518, 521, 523.

ment were established (in the absence of which negotiations were patently impossible) Japan could do nothing other than to occupy salient points on Sakhalin.

Unwilling to hasten the formation of a "legal government" in Russia by sanctioning the Soviet regime, the State Department took the only alternative and lashed out at Tokyo with a biting note which must have provided some solace for Moscow. Claiming that the Japanese policy was "entirely at variance with the trust . . . jointly assumed" by Japan and America two years previously, and that "other nations" had refrained, "despite provocations and injuries" similar to those sustained by Japan, "from the adoption of any course that involves encroachment upon Russian territory in the time of Russia's helplessness," the Secretary of State concluded:

I am compelled to advise you that this Government cannot participate in the announced decision of your Government with regard to Sakhalin, nor can it recognize the occupation of said territory by any non-Russian authority.[7]

The first response to the note took the form of increased Japanese activity on Sakhalin. On July 23 Chargé Bell cabled from Tokyo that an extra division was to be sent to the Russian part of the island and that government preparations were in progress to send out "mining and other experts" to "exploit the natural resources of the island" while it was "temporarily" occupied. This was followed on August 13 by an official Japanese disclaimer of all the charges in the Washington memorandum, and an intimation that Tokyo's action was brought about by the pressure of a thoroughly aroused public.

Unable to adopt more telling means of persuasion, the State Department watched in silence as Japan extended its grasp on Sakhalin; in October, Smith reported from Vladivostok that the Japanese planned to "keep not only Sakhalin but also all of eastern Siberia that they can." Every Japanese action tended to confirm this plan, he declared. If steps were taken at once Tokyo's

[7] Colby to Shidehara, July 16, 1920, *ibid.*, pp. 518–519.

ambition might be frustrated; later on it would prove infinitely more difficult.

But Washington remained unmoved and Smith's prediction slowly unfolded. In March 1921 the Japanese War Office issued a bulletin that Japan would shortly enlarge the area of its occupation in the hope that through the introduction of civil administration peace and order would be maintained.

After two months had elapsed Secretary Hughes took up the American diplomatic attack where it had been left by the expiring Wilson Administration. In a long memorandum on June 3 the Secretary placed on record the continued American opposition to the presence of Japanese troops and civil administration in various parts of Siberia and Sakhalin, and in a combination nonrecognition, open-door doctrine declared

that the Government of the United States can neither now nor hereafter recognize as valid any claims or titles arising out of the present occupation and control, and that it cannot acquiesce in any action taken by the Government of Japan which might impair existing treaty rights, or the political or territorial integrity of Russia.[8]

The Japanese rejoinder, five weeks later, left Washington approximately where it had been before its initial move. Tokyo distinguished between the Allied occupation of Siberia and the Nikolaievsk affair, abjured any ulterior motives, but suggested that Japanese forces might be removed at an early date, contingent on

[8] The "protective" nature of America's attitude toward Russia was vividly indicated in the closing paragraph of the note: "The purpose of this Government is to inform the Japanese Government of its own conviction that in the present time of disorder in Russia, it is more than ever the duty of those who look forward to the tranquilization of the Russian people and a restoration of normal conditions among them, to avoid all action which might keep alive their antagonism and distrust towards outside political agencies. Now especially it is incumbent upon the friends of Russia to hold aloof from the domestic contentions of the Russian people, to be scrupulous to avoid inflicting what might appear to them a vicarious penalty for sporadic acts of lawlessness, and above all to abstain from even the temporary and conditional impairment by any foreign power of the territorial status which, for them as for other peoples, is a matter of deep and sensitive national feeling transcending perhaps even the issues at stake among themselves." The Department of State to the Japanese Embassy, June 3, 1921, *ibid.*, pp. 702–705.

the outcome of certain plans which were even then receiving the consideration of the government.[9]

Paralleling the Nikolaievsk incident in the spring of 1920 was a conflict between Russian and Japanese troops at Vladivostok. During February and March the relations between the provisional government of the city and the occupation army had become increasingly taut, and on April 2 the Japanese military commander had presented a forty-eight hour ultimatum to the Vladivostok regime. In brief the Japanese demanded that the Russian authorities adopt a strict laissez-faire attitude in all matters pertaining to Japan's armed forces, that virtual diplomatic immunity be accorded them, and that all activities and articles considered harmful to the Japanese Empire be suppressed and prohibited. A tentative acceptance of these terms on the evening of April 4 was followed, according to Tokyo (this was denied by the Vladivostok Government), by an attack on a Japanese patrol a few hours later. This precipitated a rapid succession of steps by Japanese General Oi, culminating at the end of the month in a very profitable settlement for Tokyo. The Russians were allowed to retain their army, but they were effectively barred from sources of military supplies; within a wide radius of Vladivostok the Japanese assumed control of all railroads and nearly all the major towns and cities; finally, the borders connecting Russia, China, and Korea were declared closed to the Vladivostok regime, whose forces were to be withdrawn at least thirty kilometers.

On May 25 Consul Caldwell reported that the last of the Czech troops had reached Vladivostok, thus removing one of the concrete bases on which Tokyo had rested its case for continued intervention after the American evacuation. By this time, however, the allegedly exigent conditions in and around Vladivostok precluded the recall of Japanese troops. In reply to a formal Japanese communication to this effect in July, Secretary Colby evaded the issue temporarily, pleading ignorance of the necessary facts and reserving "an expression of . . . opinion." On August 13 Japan elaborated the Siberian situation at length in a palpable effort to convince

[9] These plans centered on the Dairen conference between Japan and the Far Eastern Republic, in the fall and winter of 1921–1922. See below.

Washington that the lives of some seven thousand Japanese in
Vladivostok were threatened by its lack of stable government; that
lawless Koreans under Communist influence were penetrating into
Korea, a situation "almost tantamount to a state of war"; that accordingly the maintenance of the Japanese forces was a measure of
self-defense. As a result of the continuing "menace" Tokyo still
had fifty thousand troops in the Vladivostok district in the autumn
of 1920; the city government had practically collapsed, its economy
was ruined, and civil insurrection was rife. The familiar pattern of
imperialism seemed inescapable, with Stevens cabling in November:
"Vladivostok Government practically gone, Japanese absolutely
control remnants . . . and now have the three ocean entrances
to this country in their possession."

Meanwhile Tokyo was pursuing a similar policy in the Siberian
hinterland and in northern Manchuria. Shortly after the last American troops had embarked from Vladivostok, Ambassador Morris
sent a gloomy telegram to Colby giving his "personal interpretation of the recent developments in Eastern Siberia."

I regret to say I have never doubted for the past two years that the
Japanese General Staff has not only contemplated but has carefully laid
plans for the permanent occupation of Vladivostok and the Chinese
Eastern Railroad should conditions so develop as to render such action
practicable. Since the armistice every development has led to the realization of this ambition, cherished by the Japanese military leaders. The
increasing disorder and conflict in China, the collapse of anti-Bolshevik
movements in Russia, the failure of our Senate to ratify the peace treaty
and the consequent postponement of any effective League of Nations
and finally our withdrawal from claim of interest in Siberia have all
combined to create a situation peculiarly favorable to a policy of aggressive action by Japan. . . . For the moment the military group appear
to be in control and they have lost no time in putting their plan into
operation.[10]

To these forebodings were added others of an equally disturbing
nature from Stevens. In mid-May he cabled Japanese plans to
establish a monarchy in Siberia under a member of the former

[10] Morris to Colby, April 27, 1919 (861.00/6832).

Tsar's family; three weeks later he reported that the Japanese War Office was again courting Semenov, whose cause it purportedly wished to promote as against the Socialist provisional Vladivostok Government. Furthermore, during the summer of 1920 the situation in Manchuria was again clouded with the receipt of news in September that Tokyo's forces had consolidated their strength south and east of Harbin in order to prevent northern Manchuria from being invaded by Soviet troops. This action was taken, despite official notice to Japan by the Chinese Government that it was prepared to assume full responsibility "in dealing with this menace." Two months later Stevens warned of a forthcoming attempt by Tokyo to intervene in the Trans-Baikal region, from which Japanese troops had only shortly been withdrawn. Rumors of similar tenor continued to reach the State Department throughout the winter and spring of 1921, so that Washington had ample evidence pointing to Japanese efforts to perpetuate anarchy in Siberia. On June 18 Secretary of State Hughes listed the charges against Japan from both public and private sources of information and sent them to the Japanese Ambassador, but a routine denial was the only response from Tokyo.

While the American Government sought vainly to delimit and discourage Japanese control in eastern Siberia, Vladivostok, and on the island of Sakhalin, Tokyo demonstrated the full diversity of its Russian policy by its attitude toward the newly formed Far Eastern Republic and its acute interest in the Chinese Eastern Railroad.

The former was a short-lived "sovereign" state created out of compromise between Japan and the Kremlin, regarded by each as a potential lever for the advancement of its own purposes, and destined for self-liquidation as soon as its utility had been spent. By the spring of 1920 the Soviet armies had halted to the west of Lake Baikal out of deference to the superiority of Japanese strength from there eastward. Between Baikal and the Pacific coast four "independent" republics had formed: Verkneudinsk, Chita, the Amur, and the Maritime. The first of these was politically the most sympathetic to Moscow; Chita was in the hands of Semenov; the Amur Republic never achieved political stability; and

Vladivostok (capital of the Maritime Province), although under Japanese occupation, was governed chiefly by the Kerensky Socialist Revolutionaries.

In short order the Bolsheviks had penetrated into the Verkneudinsk Government which, encouraged by Moscow, urged political union with the remaining Siberian Republics except (temporarily) Chita, and with the provinces of Sakhalin and Kamchatka. The Japanese Government—which had recurrently expressed its desire to see the establishment of a legal government in the Russian Far East with which it could settle the questions arising out of the Nikolaievsk massacre and the Vladivostok incident—regarded the evolving buffer state with growing interest during the summer of 1920. Negotiations had brought assurances from Moscow that the new government would be both independent and non-Communist, and Tokyo thereupon seized the opportunity to support the Far Eastern Republic—not out of convictions stemming from the Soviet promises, but in the belief that Japan could control and direct the infant state as a bulwark against bolshevism.[11] Moreover, if the republic could be "managed" by Tokyo, Japanese imperial designs could proceed apace in Siberia.

The United States was informed in May 1920 of the organization of the Far Eastern Government with Alexander M. Krasnoshchekov, perhaps the leading figure behind the movement, as Foreign Minister. Declaring itself to be a republic with democratic liberties guaranteed "to all classes of society," and claiming to include the territories of Trans-Baikal, Amur, Primorskaia (the Maritime Province), Sakhalin, and Kamchatka, and the right of way of the Chinese Eastern Railroad, the government warned both Moscow and Tokyo against attempted interference, demanded the

[11] Morris to Colby, May 6, 1920, *For. Rel.*, 1920, Vol. III, p. 548. For their part, the Soviet leaders naturally entertained the opposite belief. According to Ivan Maiski of the Foreign Commissariat the Soviet Government regarded the Far Eastern Republic "merely as a make-shift creation," designed to protect Russia from Japan. In this it was successful, for the F.E.R., instead of becoming a "knife at the heart of Soviet Russia," was turned into a base against Japanese aggression. By 1922 the buffer state had fulfilled its "mission," and its liquidation was "only a question of time." Quoted by Dennis, *op. cit.*, p. 330, note 9, from Ivan Maiski, *The Foreign Policy of the Russian Soviet Federated Socialist Republic, 1917–1922*, pp. 177–179 (in Russian).

recall of all foreign troops, and made a bid for friendly relations with the "Allied Powers." Within six months of its founding the Far Eastern Republic had succeeded in ridding the Chita Government of Semenov, and thereafter the city of Chita became the virtual capital of the Siberian state. In April 1921 Washington received a communication from Krasnoshchekov identic with messages sent to "all governments and nations of the world," in which the constituent assembly of the F.E.R. repeated the essence of the earlier declaration and stressed *in extenso* the sovereign quality of the state and its absolute independence of Moscow.

While exerting great effort to present their case favorably to the Western powers, the authorities at Chita were even more earnest in their endeavors to draw the solicitous interest of the United States. This was especially true as Japanese intentions became weekly more obvious, and therefore the Far Eastern Republic, taking its cue from Moscow, sought to attract American support as a potential check on Tokyo. The initial approach was made on March 22, 1921, in an appeal to Washington to define its position regarding the Siberian intervention. It quoted copiously from the August 1918 American declaration and summarized Japanese activities in Siberia after the evacuation of the United States expeditionary force. "The American Government made no statement to the Russian people of the Far East at the time of the departure" of its troops, the message noted.

It is therefore not quite clear . . . whether the American Government had achieved the purpose for which it sent troops to Siberia. . . . Does the United States . . . adhere to its declaration of August . . . 1918? If [so] . . . how does [it] . . . explain the continuance of the intervention after the evacuation of the Czecho-Slovak troops? . . . When will the United States . . . which invited the Japanese Government to a military cooperation in the Russian Far East require a definite end to the intervention which began in 1918 by that invitation? [12]

Four days later Ignatius Yourin, the president of a special Far Eastern Republic mission to Peking, gave American Minister Crane

[12] *For. Rel.*, 1921, Vol. II, pp. 739–741.

a second communication from his government, the essence of which was a bid for the opening of diplomatic relations with Washington. To make the prospect more attractive, at the end of April, Yourin addressed still another message, emphasizing the untold economic benefits which the Republic could confer on American business interests through the investment of capital in the development of Siberia's natural resources. The note closed, however, with an admonition that Chita could not wait indefinitely on Washington's pleasure. If the United States expressed no interest in the fate of the Russian Far East its peoples might be compelled to "throw themselves on the side of the enemy in the face of possible conflicts in the East."

Several weeks before this message was received the State Department had already taken a tentative step in the direction of the Siberian Government with the decision to send an observer to Chita. Instructed to avoid any statements regarding possible future American policy, Major W. J. Davis, who was appointed to the task, was to report on the nature of the Far Eastern Republic in terms of political philosophy, voting, property rights, and so forth; the extent, respectively, of Japanese, White Russian (Semenov), and Soviet influence at Chita; "immediate trade possibilities"; the stability of the government; and the desirability of stationing a consular officer there. No effort was made, however, either at this time or apparently in succeeding months, to provide Chita with more than oblique answers to its earlier questions concerning the American attitude toward the Siberian intervention. Nevertheless, the Far Eastern Republic had assessed American Asiatic interests correctly, and the renewed activities of the Japanese in Siberia and on Sakhalin in the summer of 1921 spurred the State Department to more precipitate action regarding the Chita Government than might otherwise have occurred.

In May a quick revolution overthrew the Socialist Government at Vladivostok and replaced it with a conservative regime which immediately broke with the Siberian Government at Chita. Both Chita and Moscow at once protested against the purportedly Japanese-sponsored coup. Yourin sent a peremptory note to Tokyo demanding the cessation of interference with the Russian Far East

and, specifically, with Chita's efforts to quell the revolutionists at
Vladivostok. On June 6 the Far Eastern mission at Peking informed
Crane that all the states which had participated in the Siberian intervention shared equally the responsibility for the "grave consequences" which had ensued, and expressed the hope that Washington would strive to effect an early evacuation of Japanese troops
from Siberia.

This incident, coupled with the information that Tokyo was
preparing for a conference with representatives of the Chita Government at Dairen to discuss the bases for the Japanese withdrawal,
convinced Washington that more positive expression of its concern over the Russian problem offered the only possible means of
limiting the Japanese demands. Yourin had stated as much the
first week in August when he informed the American chargé at
Peking that the "form of negotiations" between Tokyo and Chita
was "dependent upon American interest in them," and that the
F.E.R. would "have to concede more if the United States" did not
"take such interest." [13]

On August 22 the Japanese Ambassador at Washington sent a
memorandum to Secretary Hughes relative to the approaching
Dairen Conference. After stating that the initiative for the meeting had come from Chita, the Japanese note listed the proposed
agenda. This included

the conclusion of commercial arrangements, the removal of the existing
menace to the security of Japan and to the lives and property of Japanese residents in Eastern Siberia, the provision of guarantees for the
freedom of industrial undertakings in that region and the prohibition
of Bolshevik propaganda over the Siberian border.

These negotiations, the note continued, were not intended to secure
unilateral Japanese rights or advantages but, on the contrary, were
directed to the guarantee of Japan's national safety and welfare.
If the conference were successful Tokyo would proceed "to the
complete withdrawal of Japanese troops from the Maritime

[13] *Ibid.*, p. 713.

Province." [14] Notwithstanding these generous assurances the State Department was apprehensive, the more so as Ambassador Shidehara declared that the Chita Government was in no position to discuss the Nikolaievsk massacre and that the question would consequently have to be reserved for the future. Accordingly Consul John K. Caldwell was instructed to proceed to Chita immediately on special duty. His mission, not intended as a precursor to recognition, was viewed by Washington as an indirect form of pressure on both the Far Eastern Republic and Japan.

For its part the Chita Government, naturally averse to trading away Russian territorial and commercial rights in return for the questionable pledges of Tokyo, regarded the sending of an American consular official to the F.E.R. as only one-half of a necessarily reciprocal exchange. In July, Krasnoshchekov had sounded out Washington for permission to send a delegation to the United States simply "to state their case and their needs promising to abstain . . . from propaganda"; the importance of such a step became progressively clearer as the Dairen Conference developed. "Japan is the only nation willing to enter into negotiations" with Chita, Chargé Bell telegraphed in mid-September. Despite the onerous concessions demanded, the Russian Far Eastern Government was faced with the alternative of no foreign trade relations (which would have been the equivalent of economic suicide) or of trade on Tokyo's terms. On the other hand, "if Chita [were] allowed to have representatives sent to Washington," Bell concluded, it could afford to "break off present conference with Japan." [15] And early in October, Minister Schurman cabled that public opinion in Peking predicted that American unwillingness to receive a com-

---

[14] *Ibid.*, pp. 714–715. Commenting on this memorandum, Poole wrote Hughes: "From this appears what was already understood, namely, that Japan is making troop withdrawal a basis of bargaining for concessions . . . It is hoped that . . . you will agree that we cannot let Japan proceed without serious protest. If we do so, we are defaulting on our promises to the Russian people, made publicly in 1918 when the joint military expedition was sent to Siberia, and prejudicing in advance the work of the approaching conference." Poole (Division of Russian Affairs) to Hughes, September 16, 1921 (861.00/9025½).

[15] *For. Rel., op. cit.*, pp. 715–716.

mercial mission from Chita would tend to throw the Far Eastern Republic "into the arms of Japan"; this might even cause the Republic to cede Northern Sakhalin to the Japanese.

Moved by these reports the State Department at length acquiesced in the desire of Chita to send an unofficial delegation to Washington. But it was clearly indicated that this in no sense implied formal recognition. Chita, at least, had achieved more than its parent state, the Soviet Government. However, the American decision reflected no particular friendship for the Far Eastern Republic, but a deep-seated suspicion of Japan.

In the meantime one final area of contention had further roiled the troubled waters of American-Japanese relations from 1920 to the end of 1921—the status of the Chinese Eastern Railroad.

It will be recalled that the Inter-Allied agreement of 1919 for the operation and protection of the C.E.R. had been specific in its phrasing that the intervening states would not alienate railroad rights, by whomsoever held. It was also a part of the agreement that the road personnel representing the Allied and Associated powers would be withdrawn following the evacuation of the troops of the participating nations. These two statements had been incorporated at the urging of the American Government mainly because of its distrust of Japanese intentions. So far as the second provision was concerned, the withdrawal of the military contingents of all countries except Japan in 1920 meant that, unless a compromise arrangement were evolved, Japan alone would keep its railroad experts and its armed forces along the C.E.R. This was the immediate problem confronting Washington in the spring of 1920. The first provision in the Inter-Allied agreement gave the State Department a knottier dilemma, one which intruded in government offices for the next decade. In brief, the preservation intact of rights, by whomsoever held, involved Washington in disputes not only with Tokyo but with Peking and Moscow. The copious flirtation conducted by the Soviet Union with China in 1919 and 1920, and the later relations of the two countries, were to give the American State Department many anxious moments as to the possible fate of the Chinese Eastern Railroad. In the first instance, however, America's protective instincts were aroused

by the willful tactics of the Japanese Government and general staff,
to whom the exit of the Western states from Siberia was the
signal for Japanese entry and domination.

Nor was the United States the only nation to be alarmed by
Tokyo's encroachments on the C.E.R. Several months prior to
the departure of General Graves and the American soldiers the
British Foreign Office had tried to dissuade Washington from
withdrawing, by casting indirect aspersions on the motives of its
Japanese ally. Moreover, within three weeks of the American em-
barkation from Vladivostok a member of the British Embassy
reported the outbreak of hostilities on the Chinese Eastern line
between Japanese and Chinese troops, and asked informally
the State Department's views "as to the possibility of preserving
status of that railway and preventing extension of Japanese control
over it." [16] The twin problems herein presented commanded the

[16] *For. Rel.*, 1920, Vol. I, p. 685. This attitude was in sharp contrast to the
opinion of the British Ambassador at Tokyo, Sir Charles Eliot, who in April
informed Morris: "British interest in Siberia was wholly an incident of the
war. The creation of the Kolchak Government was simply a step in the attempted formation of a new eastern front. The signing of the armistice rendered further efforts of that character unnecessary and the subsequent British
support of Kolchak during . . . 1919 was induced by a sense of honorable
obligation not to desert the movement simply because it had no further use.
The fall of Kolchak discharged this obligation. Great Britain had no further
political or national interest in such a remote territory as Siberia and he could
see no reason why his Government should interfere in the national aspirations
of Japan; differing with all other countries the interests of Japan in Siberia were
vital and exacting; the threat of Bolshevikism [*sic*] in Korea and Manchuria was
in his judgment real. Japanese citizens and business interests in the Maritime
provinces were endangered and it seemed to him only natural that Japan
should adopt rigorous measures to protect these interests. He could see no
essential difference between such action by Japan and the past action of his
own country in Egypt." Morris to Colby, April 14, 1920 (861.00/6762). At
the end of April, in reply to American inquiries, the State Department was
informed that the British Government did not "share the views expressed by
Sir Charles Eliot . . ." but that it wished "Inter-Allied Railroad Board continued for the present with ultimate return . . . to Chinese in trusteeship for
Russian interest." *For. Rel., op. cit.*, pp. 687–688. The British opposition to
Japanese control was further indicated in a communication from Chargé Bell
at Tokyo, June 19, 1920. And on August 5, following conferences with the
British Minister to Peking (who was in Washington en route to England), the
British Ambassador to the United States, Ambassador Morris, and the Under
Secretary of State, Secretary Colby wrote: "From this talk and others . . . I
have been gratified to realize the common interests of Great Britain and the

attention of the American Government between the first of April 1920, and the end of October 1921, when the practical failure to resolve them accounted for the inclusion of the Chinese Eastern Railroad on the program of the Washington Conference.

Early in May, Ambassador Bakhmetev proposed in Washington that the railroad be in effect internationalized through an international committee with either national or joint financial support. A few days later England, purportedly speaking also for the French, suggested that the C.E.R. be managed under the original Inter-Allied arrangement (except for the military board), that Sino-Japanese troops patrol the line, and that the consortium finance it. This would, it was reasoned, control Japan, stabilize China, limit the Communist menace, and make the initial step of the consortium one of broad international value.

While expressing general approval of the British plan, Washington felt that the projected means of financing the railroad would meet with Japanese objections, a theory which was shortly verified by Foreign Minister Uchida, who indicated in June "that he did not like the idea of having the consortium connected with the Chinese Eastern Railroad" and that "the Cabinet must consider this matter . . ." The ensuing "consideration" was sufficiently protracted so that Tokyo had arrived at no conclusions by the end of the year. Meanwhile sporadic Chinese efforts to dislodge the Japanese troops from that part of the Chinese Eastern which was nominally under the exclusive protection of Peking were unavailing. Moreover, the State Department was informed in July of the likelihood that Semenov, losing ground in the battle between the Far Eastern Republic and his disintegrating forces based at Chita, was contemplating a retreat to the concession zone of the C.E.R., a prospect which might easily bring added American-Japanese conflict within the zone.

All these factors, linked with the continued temporizing of Tokyo in regard to the British project, contributed to the formulation in

---

United States in the Far East and to find the British willing to work with us in opposition to the exploitation of particular spheres of interest and to make the open door policy and the maintenance of the administrative and territorial integrity of China a reality." *Ibid.*, p. 705.

Washington in January 1921 of an alternative plan for operating and financing the railroad. The one outstanding feature in the American proposal was the unparalleled authority with which it endowed the Technical Board. In addition to the powers granted under the original Allied agreement the Board was to possess "full control" over all financial matters pertaining to, and all personnel · connected with the railroad. Simultaneously, the President of the Board was to become its unquestioned head.

This amended plan was too drastic even to solicit the support of the British, who squeezed out from a direct negative by declaring that the proposal would never receive Japanese or Chinese support. London's answer, given in mid-May 1921, was followed in three months by disheartening news from the American banking participants in the consortium, who expressed regret that there was "little immediate possibility of offering in the United States a loan" to the C.E.R. The final blow was registered on October 28 with the official Japanese rejection of the American formula. Ironically, Tokyo assumed the mantle of sanctimonious righteousness in defense of Russia and China, whose legal rights in the railroad were declared endangered by the "radical" American plan. Although Japan was prepared to offer a modified proposal of its own, the outline was so vague and the powers it granted to the Technical Board so curtailed in comparison with the 1919 agreement that the United States was unable to consider it. Accordingly the question of the Chinese Eastern Railroad (together with its companion problems regarding the liquidation of the Siberian intervention) was carried over to the deliberations of the Washington Conference.

CHAPTER VIII

Diplomacy by Conference

In terms of the space and time devoted to the respective subjects on its agenda, the conference which convened in Washington in the winter months of 1921–1922 was preëminently concerned with naval disarmament. Questions relating to the Far East comprised the other major topic, under which were discussed in proportionately brief order the status of Russian rights and the Chinese Eastern Railroad. The problem of Asiatic Russia was more accurately a side-issue than a matter of high policy to the American Government throughout the years following the revolutions of 1917; and this was still true in 1921, notwithstanding Washington's interest and participation in Siberia's international politics. The significance attached to the Russian Far East had tended at any given time to reflect the existing relations between the United States and Japan, and only as the balance of power in Asia favored the Japanese did the State Department become genuinely solicitous for the safeguarding of Siberia's political sovereignty and territorial integrity. At Washington in 1921–1922 the problems inherent in the confused situation in Asiatic Russia constituted a relatively minor phase in the general picture of American-Japanese rivalry.

By the end of the European war Tokyo had gone far in the consolidation of its position on the Asiatic mainland. In accordance with the Sino-Japanese treaties of 1915 and 1918, and the secret treaties between Japan and the Allies in 1917, the Versailles settlement transferred all German rights in Shantung to Japan. President Wilson was able through sheer persistence to obtain a statement from the Japanese delegates which mitigated the full force of the Shantung provision, although it was not included in the Paris treaty. Specifically, Japan affirmed its intention of restoring Shantung "in full sovereignty" to China, "retaining only the economic privileges granted to Germany." At the same time Japanese annexationist designs on the German islands north of the equator were theoretically frustrated by awarding the islands as trusts to Tokyo in the form of mandates. Wilson, an uneasy party to these arrangements, looked upon the League of Nations as the guarantor of Japan's fidelity; nevertheless, there was little question that participation in the war had yielded most promising dividends to the Japanese.

Regardless of the *volte-face* in American policy toward Europe heralded by the Harding victory in 1920, the Republican Administration was no more willing than its predecessor to forfeit American interests in the Far East. Consequently the manifest desire of the Japanese general staff to press its advantage throughout Asia was viewed with the utmost misgiving in Washington. In view of these facts the State Department was seriously concerned in late 1919 and early 1920 over the reports of a pending renewal of the Anglo-Japanese Alliance. The Siberian expedition two years previously and the British support of Japanese claims at the Paris Peace Conference had convinced Washington that regardless of Downing Street's anxiety over the C.E.R. or the incursions of Tokyo in China, as long as the alliance between the two states prevailed the Japanese would continue their aggressive policy on the Continent of Asia and, in the last analysis, England would be unable to check them. This belief was reenforced by two cables in January and April 1921, from the American consul at Harbin. According to the first the Japanese Foreign Minister had declared that London was in absolute sympathy with Tokyo's program. The second stated that in an exchange with Britain and France regarding the Siberian question the two Allies had intimated their approval of Japan's plans, and therefore apprehensions over American resistance were groundless ("thanks to diplomatic measures taken through powers friendly to Japan").[1]

By the first of June the British Government had become thoroughly aware of the American attitude toward renewal of the Anglo-

[1] Johnson to Secretary of State, January 24, April 5, 1921 (861.00/8006, 8449).

Japanese Alliance and the cognate wish that the treaty, if retained, be brought in line with American Far Eastern policy. The British were also sensible of the State Department's desire to convene an international conference on the limitation of armaments. It was but a step to blanket the two questions under a single heading, and on July 8, at the suggestion of Lord Curzon, the American Ambassador cabled Secretary Hughes and proposed that President Harding call a conference to consider both Far Eastern questions and those relating to naval armaments.[2]

Harding was agreeable, and on July 10 tentative announcements were dispatched to the interested nations.

Five days later Secretary Hughes raised the question of the subjects to be included on the assembly's Asiatic agenda; in a telegram to the British Foreign Office he stated the American view that the powers should consider "all such Pacific and Far Eastern problems as are of international concern." These embraced, beside the standard questions on the status of China, the "integrity of Russia." In response, London suggested that the "conference should ignore but leave for later determination and action" the problem of Russia's integrity.[3] But Hughes was unwilling to omit from the prospectus any area of American-Japanese conflict, and consequently insisted on the inclusion of the Siberian problem. In order that none of the participating states restrict the scope of the discussion at the forthcoming conference, and thus tie American hands regarding specific Far Eastern problems, Hughes couched the formal invitations to the powers in these words:

It is not the purpose of this Government to attempt to define the scope of the discussion in regard to the Pacific and the Far East, but

[2] *For. Rel.*, 1921, Vol. I, pp. 19–21. On the same day Hughes telegraphed Ambassador Harvey (in London) to ascertain the British reaction to a conference on the limitation of armaments.

[3] England was apparently not eager for the agenda to be too broadly inclusive regarding Asiatic problems. In this respect it is noteworthy that the original British acquiescence in a Pacific conference stemmed in large part from the attitude of Canada, as revealed in the Imperial Conference at London in the late spring of 1921. Canada was insistent that the Anglo-Japanese Alliance be dropped, and suggested in its place a Pacific four-power understanding (British, American, Chinese, and Japanese) to be arrived at by a conference on Pacific problems.

rather to leave this to be the subject of suggestions to be exchanged by the meeting of the Conference, in the expectation that the spirit of friendship and a cordial appreciation of the importance of the elimination of sources of controversy will govern the final decision.[4]

So far as Asia was concerned, therefore, the decision of the United States to hold an international conference represented an attempt to implement its Far Eastern policy by weakening (if not terminating) the Anglo-Japanese Alliance, and by bringing the light of world opinion to bear on every Asiatic question at issue between Washington and Tokyo. This included the various phases of the Siberian problem. The State Department had been unable, by unilateral diplomacy, to force the Japanese from Vladivostok, Sakhalin, or the Chinese Eastern Railroad, and to moderate Tokyo's demands on the Far Eastern Republic at Dairen. Through its sponsorship of the Washington Conference, however, the American Government counted on achieving a decisive moral advantage by assuming the role of disinterested partisan of the legal rights and interests of Asiatic states as against the imperialism of any potential aggressor. The net result of this policy was that once again the United States emerged as the protector of Russian sovereignty in the Far East; and once again the guiding motive was found in concern not for Russia, but for the open-door and the balance of power throughout Asia, threatened as they were by the foreign policy of Japan.

In view of these facts it could hardly be expected that Tokyo would react enthusiastically to the Hughes program. There was no alternative to acceptance of the American invitation, however, for a Japanese refusal to confer on questions which were of paramount importance to her would arouse the pardonable suspicions of all the major powers regarding her deeper motives.[5] Moreover,

[4] *Conference on the Limitation of Armament* (Washington: G.P.O., 1922), p. 6.

[5] In a letter to John W. Davis, October 4, 1921, ex-Secretary Lansing commented on the Japanese position at the forthcoming conference: ". . . whoever thought of tying the Far East onto the Conference was pretty shrewd and showed political sagacity. There can be no doubt that Japan did not want to have these matters discussed here, but she was in no position to refuse without inviting general condemnation and without apparently indicating an ar-

in such a contingency the likelihood of extending the alliance with England would be jeopardized, and the consequent isolation of Tokyo in the Far East would inevitably mitigate the effectiveness of its Asiatic policy. At the same time, participation in the conference offered no assurances that Japanese claims in the Pacific area would be respected; the Mikado's Government was therefore confronted with an uneasy dilemma and placed on the defensive for the first time in a score of years in its dealings with the West.

In an initial effort to resolve the issue Japan sought to restrict the agenda to the subject of arms limitation, and, failing in this, to define beforehand the precise topics which would be included in the discussions on the Far East. On July 26, after every other power had signified its willingness to attend the conference,[6] Tokyo's acceptance was forwarded to the State Department. From its redundant verbiage it was possible to draw three main points in the Japanese note. It was assumed in the first place that the conference agenda was still open to limiting amendments; secondly, that Pacific and Far Eastern problems were included only because of their close bearing on the question of naval armaments; thirdly, that because armaments comprised the main object of the conference, the introduction "of problems such as are of sole concern to certain particular powers or such matters that may be regarded accomplished facts should be scrupulously avoided."

This was no more and no less than a Japanese counter-invitation to sabotage the Washington Conference by excluding from it the specific questions which the State Department was most

---

rogant and aggressive policy. In fact the Japanese had no choice. They had to come. They are going to be in the same difficulty about limiting the subjects on the agenda. How can they refuse to discuss a matter in regard to China without being credited with improper motives. They hate to come and they can't stay out . . ." *Lansing Papers.* In contrast to this point of view, see Yamato Ichihashi, *The Washington Conference and After* (Stanford: Stanford University Press, 1928), p. 21.

[6] Japan's temporizing was due in part to a desire to ascertain the attitude of England and France to the conference before determining its own position. The further delay in Tokyo's answer (nearly two weeks after the other powers had responded) was partially explained by a cable from Stevens, July 27: ". . . I hear the Japanese Government making every effort possible to make treaty with Far Eastern Government before deciding clear attitude toward proposed Pacific conference." Stevens to Hughes, July 27, 1921 (861.00/8876).

eager to discuss. If adhered to, the exception from the agenda of "problems . . . of sole concern to certain particular powers . . ." would have obviated the Far Eastern aspect of the conference by removing the area of American-Japanese discord from the legal scope of the agenda. Secretary Hughes met the suggestion from Tokyo indirectly; without further correspondence with the Japanese Foreign Office he informed the press that all the powers had accepted the proposal for a conference. On August 11 this was followed by invitations to Britain, France, Italy, Japan, and China which, as noted above, expressly rejected any advance limitations on the range of the discussions.

Japan was not the only country to regard the Washington policy with misgiving. Soviet protests at the omission of Moscow from the conference were both loud and abusive, notwithstanding the fact that the United States had explicitly proclaimed its intention to protect Russian interests. The first Soviet démarche revealed what was perhaps the major source of Russia's indignation, namely that the conferees were still anticipating the forcible overthrow of the Communist regime. Thus Moscow referred to the declaration of the powers "that they will . . . reserve the matter of inviting eventually a new Russian Government, which should replace the present one, to accede to the decisions . . . they adopt."

The Russian Government can in no case agree to other powers taking upon themselves the right to speak for it, especially since this ostracism is intended to apply only to the [Soviet Government] . . . while any counter-revolutionary government which might replace it would not be subjected to such ostracism. Such an attitude on the part of the . . . powers can only be interpreted as clearly favoring the Russian counter-revolution, and as a fresh manifestation of the interventionist system.

This theme was reiterated in the closing sentence of the note, which called the "preference eventually to be shown" to a counter-revolutionary regime "a hostile act" against the Bolshevik Government. The remainder of the communication constituted a challenge of the legal power of the conference to consider questions which touched the rights of Russia without consulting its government.

Moscow elaborated its own "nonrecognition" doctrine regarding Washington decisions, and announced that it would reserve "complete freedom of action" in all questions discussed.[7]

The substance of the protest was repeated in a second note to the powers on November 2, following a three-and-a-half-month interval during which no one of the states concerned acknowledged the original Soviet communication. Pointing to the galling fact that the nations "that now intend to take upon themselves the guarding of [Russia's] . . . interests are the same governments" which intervened on behalf of the White armies, the note further warned:

The working people of Russia understand quite well that if these powers will take upon themselves the decision of questions which concern Russia, these will be reached under the influence of interests quite different from those of Russia, and the solution which will be found will be detrimental to the Russian Nation . . .

Whatever will be the ostensible agreement come to at Washington, the suspicion, nearly the certainty, will always exist that secret agreements have been concluded to the detriment of Russia, and one more element of defiance and suspicion will be introduced into international relations. In these conditions the decisions of the Washington Conference will inevitably be the source of new conflicts, new troubles, and new shocks. Far from bringing pacification they will bring trouble, struggle, and hatred into the international life of nations and will only be the cause of new calamities for humanity.[8]

Apart from these official protests the Russian press carried a running attack against the conference powers during the autumn of 1921. In a series of articles in *Izvestia* and *Pravda* a single theme emerged: the necessity for the peoples of the Far East (China, Mongolia, and the Far Eastern Republic) to unite with the Soviet Government in warding off the inevitable incursions of the West and Japan. "This Conference [*Izvestia* editorialized on September 2] is only an attempt to harmonize the interests of the most important Anglo-Saxon imperialistic robbers, at the expense of the

[7] Chicherin to the Governments of the United States, China, France, Great Britain, Italy, and Japan, July 19, 1921, *For. Rel., op. cit.*, pp. 41–43.
[8] Same to same, November 2, 1921, *ibid.*, pp. 86–87.

weaker Japanese robber, . . . China and Soviet Russia." The Executive Committee of the Communist International called "on the popular masses of China and Korea" and eastern Siberia "to draw more closely to Soviet Russia" in the face of the menace of world imperialism. A month after the conference had opened a Soviet official in Harbin spoke of the negotiations at Washington as "the division among [the powers] . . . of the globe and the enslavement of the weaker nations," and warned China not to "expect for herself any good result from the conference." [9]

But if Moscow could not gain entry to the proceedings at Washington through the respectable front door, it was not averse to a back entrance or to representation by impersonation. To these ends, the Soviet authorities urged the sympathetic Far Eastern Republic to seek access to the conference. Consequently Chita's Foreign Minister wrote to Secretary Hughes on September 10 stating the case for participation by the Republic. His words and reasoning reflected the influence of the Soviet Government, but contrived a politeness and deference to the United States which were conspicuously lacking in the Moscow notes. Resting the claim of interest in the conference on the geographical position of the Far Eastern Republic (an extensive Pacific coastline) and its authoritative right to speak for the Siberian peoples, he announced that it would "oppose the open violation of the sovereign rights of the nation" by the powers and would refuse to recognize decisions made without its consent. However, it was clear that the Republic did not wish to be forced into this awkward position, for the Foreign Minister went on to express the conviction that the United States had no ulterior motive in calling the conference and would agree that a peaceful settlement of Far Eastern problems could be effected only through Siberian participation in the proceedings at Washington.

No formal response was made to this letter, on the grounds that Chita had not been recognized by the American Government; but Hughes did instruct the American Minister at Peking to convey

[9] Schurman to Hughes, December 19, 1921 (861A.01/153). The quotation is from the Peking newspaper accounts of an interview by the press at Harbin with the Soviet "extraordinary plenipotentiary," Pai Kestler.

to the Republic's Foreign Minister "informal observations" regarding Washington's attitude. In so doing the Secretary of State
paid a courtesy to Chita which Moscow had never received; on
the other hand the nature of the reply could by implication have
been intended to answer the Soviet charges of the preceding month.
"In the absence of a single, recognized Russian Government," the
message read, "the protection of legitimate Russian interests"
devolved as a "moral trusteeship" on the conference powers. It
regretted that these circumstances precluded Russian cooperation,
but it was "not to be conceived" that decisions would be taken at
Washington "prejudicial to legitimate Russian interests" or in
violation of Russian rights. The United States hoped and expected
that the results of the conference would merit the support "of the
people of Eastern Siberia and of all Russia" because of their "justice and efficacy in the settlement of outstanding difficulties."

But although the Far Eastern Republic was denied official representation at the Washington Conference, it shortly achieved
American permission to dispatch "unofficial" individuals to the
United States for "commercial" purposes. Consequently, American arguments at the conference against the maintenance of Japanese forces in Siberia were reinforced by means of the information
provided to the press by the "delegation" from Chita.

In contrast to the attempts of the F.E.R. and the Soviet Government to plead and threaten their respective ways to Washington,
the officials of the Provisional Russian Government adopted a
meek attitude in keeping with their humble status. The American
reply to the Far Eastern Republic's note had been issued to the
press September 17; five days later the ambassador at Paris of the
extinct Kerensky regime called at the American Embassy to express the appreciation of the anti-Bolshevik Russians in France
for the American attitude. On November 10, the day before the
conference assembled, Bakhmetev presented Secretary Hughes with
a detailed memorandum on Russia's Asiatic interests—political,
economic, and legal. The central theme of the document exposed
the core of fear, not only in the Provisional Government, but in
Soviet Russia, in the F.E.R. and, not least of all, in the United
States. The aim of Japan, wrote the Ambassador, could be ex-

plained only as one phase of a "coveted plan" to dominate "the whole eastern part of the Asiatic continent and to transform" the Sea of Japan into a "closed Japanese basin." If Japan succeeded in establishing control over the Russian Far East, it would have "military domination over China"; and of signal importance—even after a stable Russian government emerged, this would be blocked from "harmonious cooperation . . . with the other White Powers in the realm of the Pacific." In view of the ominous prospect, the belief prevailed in orthodox Russian circles that, as a consequence of the Washington Conference, Japan should be importuned to leave Siberia at once and without reservations.[10]

It was not difficult for the Department of State to agree with these sentiments; and, with the opening of the conference on the third anniversary of the Armistice, Washington issued a diplomatic declaration of war on Japanese pretensions in eastern Asia.

The first order of business on the agenda was the limitation of naval armaments; this was followed by "Pacific and Far Eastern Questions," with the third and final topic concerned with electrical communications on the mandated islands of the Pacific. Under the second heading provision was made for the termination of the Anglo-Japanese Alliance at such time as a new Four-Power Pacific treaty was ratified by its signatories—Britain, France, Japan, and the United States. The effect of the new agreement was to enlarge the membership of the expiring Anglo-Japanese treaty and to replace its military sanctions with a pledge of respect by each of the four nations for the possessions of the others in the Pacific. Thus while Japan now had a moral guarantee of its Asiatic holdings by three Pacific powers, it had the military guarantee of none.

So far as Russian interests were concerned, they were considered under the dual topics of the Chinese Eastern Railroad and Siberia. It was the officially declared purpose of the United States to ascertain that the legal rights of Russia and China in the railroad would in no way be jeopardized; to that end the American Government sought a formula which would bind all the countries at Washington to the principle of non-alienation. In view of Sino-Soviet relations and contractual arrangements regarding the line in 1919–1920, the

[10] Enclosure in Bakhmetev to Hughes, November 10, 1921 (861A.01/129).

State Department's efforts were directed to the preservation of the C.E.R. from the exclusive control of China and to the removal of Japanese influence therefrom; for nominal Chinese management, in its weakness, could easily become a front for Moscow as well as for Tokyo, and in either event American Far Eastern policy would suffer. Therefore to the extent that America's diplomacy sought to mitigate Soviet influence in China, the paths of Moscow and Washington diverged yet more sharply.[11] In regard to Japanese infiltration, events preceding the conference had given advance notice of Tokyo's motives; and the staying power of the Mikado's armed forces in the Chinese Eastern zone was scarcely conducive to confidence on the part of the United States. Accordingly the receipt of information to the effect that Peking was contemplating the seizure of the C.E.R. augmented American determination to forestall the Chinese action by obtaining an international agreement at Washington. "If the railway were confided to China at this time as a trusteeship for Russia," Hughes cabled Schurman December 24, "financial control by Japan would certainly ensue probably through the purchase by the South Manchuria Railway [owned by Japan] of the new issue of bonds which would be necessary." An "international conservancy" was thus the best guarantee against national aggression until it should become possible to return the road to its legal owners.

Two months prior to this message Tokyo had vetoed the American proposal for the implementation of the 1919 Inter-Allied railroad plan, and Britain had withheld its support pending Sino-Japanese approval. Now, in aspiring to win the consent of the powers to a new project (and thus to commit Japan to a policy of cooperation), Washington discovered that its most vocal opponent was China, whose delegates at the conference and whose officials at home remained frankly apprehensive of the efforts expended on their behalf. This was traceable in part to a feeling that China's

[11] At the end of January 1922 the State Department received a strong protest from the Soviet Government regarding the Washington Conference deliberations on the C.E.R. For this and more detailed treatment of the Chinese Eastern as part of the American-Russian-Chinese diplomatic triangle, see Chapter X. The current chapter treats the railroad problem primarily in terms of its relation to American-Japanese rivalry.

assent would provoke the hostility of Japan, but it also represented a natural reaction to the continued "meddling" of the nations in matters respecting the sovereign rights of China, particularly in the face of Soviet offers to end the unequal relationship between Peking and Moscow.[12] As a result the conference emerged with the problem of the railroad no nearer ultimate solution than before. The states resolved that:

the preservation of the Chinese Eastern Railroad for those in interest requires that better protection be given to the Railway and the persons engaged in its operation and use; a more careful selection of personnel to secure efficiency of service, and a more economical use of funds to prevent waste of the property.

These requirements were to become the subject of regular diplomatic exchanges between the conferees, but as the months passed it was China and Russia which met the question, and not the foreign offices of Tokyo and the West. In agreeing to this so-called Root resolution, the powers other than China reserved

the right to insist hereafter upon the responsibility of China for performance or nonperformance of the obligations towards the foreign stockholders, bondholders and creditors of the Chinese Eastern Railroad Company which the powers deem to result from the contracts under which the railroad was built and the action of China thereunder and the obligations which they deem to be in the nature of a trust resulting from the exercise of power by the Chinese government over the possession and administration of the railroad.[13]

This reservation was intended essentially to insert a legal claim into the future operations by Peking of the C.E.R. and stemmed from the contract concluded between China and the Russo-Asiatic

[12] For the Soviet declarations of 1919 and 1920 see Appendix A. Chinese delegates Hawkling Yen and Wellington Koo registered their protests against the reports of the Subcommittee of Technical Advisers (on the C.E.R.) and the resolutions of the Conference in regard to the railroad, largely on the basis that the powers were ignoring the legal rights of China as a sovereign political entity. See *Conference on the Limitation of Armament*, pp. 1376, 1380, 1504, 1506, 1508.

[13] *Ibid.*, pp. 316–318.

Bank in October 1920, whereby China assumed a virtual trusteeship over the line, notwithstanding the objections of the powers.
By the Washington Conference declaration Peking was thus notified that its future acts with respect to the railroad would elicit
the interest and potentially the intrusion of the remaining states.

The Chinese Eastern was a subject on which the anti-Japanese
and the anti-Soviet policies of the United States, ordinarily pursuing parallel lines, definitely converged. Until 1922 American
diplomacy had ignored Russia but simultaneously had tried to protect Russian rights as against Japan. In that year the State Department determined to halt the alleged encroachments of both Moscow and Tokyo on the C.E.R., and correspondingly aroused their
joint antagonism as well as that of the Chinese Government. However, Japanese sensibilities were more easily quieted in this particular instance because, regardless of Washington's endeavors to
frustrate the China policy of Tokyo, Secretary Hughes was indirectly
playing the Japanese game in so far as he sought to prevent a close
accord between Moscow and Peking. This did not, however, lead
to any genuine reorientation of American-Japanese relations. Following the adjournment of the conference the Japanese delegates
suggested a preliminary American-Japanese agreement on the subject of the Chinese Eastern Railway to precede the formulation of
a definitive international arrangement. But the purpose behind
this was revealed in the further statement of the Japanese officials
that they desired an organization which would afford Japan "a
position of equality"; and their objections to any program in which
the existent Technical Board would have increased powers (and
a continued American chairmanship) were undisguised.

The lines of respective national policies were more clearly drawn
in the second topic of immediate concern to Russia, namely the
continued presence of Japanese troops in Siberia. Here once again
the United States was promoting Moscow's cause (the while it
hoped that the Bolshevik Government would collapse), and there
was no other construction possible of American policy than that
it was exclusively anti-Japanese. This fact was apparent not from
the conference records as such, for the entire Siberian problem was
disposed of in approximately fifteen minutes, but from the more

informative dispatches of the period which, without exception, exhibited a strong aversion to Japan and its ruthless Siberian policy.

The fact that a fairly large percentage of these reports emanated from the Far Eastern Republic was in itself indicative of their content. Sporadic protests from Chita punctuated the Washington Conference throughout December, focusing international attention on the ultra-imperialistic nature of Tokyo's offensive in Siberia. Hammering at the theme that Japan intended to "seize our territory and turn it into a Japanese colony," the F.E.R. addressed an appeal "to all Nations" on December 20, which cited chapter and verse for the charges against Tokyo.

To these complaints Chita added others concerning the demands of Tokyo at the Dairen Conference. Earlier in December the State Department was informed by the Far Eastern trade delegation that Japan had presented to the Republic a seventeen-point treaty containing three secret clauses. Allegedly these provided for the dismantling of all fortifications on the Siberian Pacific coast, the removal of Russian troops to a distance of not less than thirty miles from the Korean border and, most significantly,

the Chita Government should recognize as valid all treaties and agreements made by Japan with the various governments which had existed in Russia and Siberia (not only the Tsar and Kerensky Governments but also all provisional and minor governments such as [those] . . . at Vladivostok and the so-called governments set up by Semenov and other Siberian leaders).[14]

A fortnight later Consul Caldwell telegraphed: "The Japanese . . . at Dairen have become more insistent in their demands since the Washington Conference opened." There followed a summary of the "most objectionable" Japanese demands, which included, beside the secret clauses given above, preferential economic and commercial treatment for Japanese nationals in Siberian ports and

[14] Memorandum by the Acting Chief of the Division of Russian Affairs, December 8, 1921, *For. Rel.*, 1921, Vol. II, p. 752. These terms were in marked contrast to the very moderate demands listed by the pro-Japanese author, K. K. Kawakami, in his *Japan's Pacific Policy* (New York: E. P. Dutton & Co., Inc., 1922), pp. 239–240.

on Siberian rivers, and an anti-Communist pledge by the F.E.R. The latter considered these ultimata so unacceptable that for over a month negotiations were practically suspended.

The American Government was closely attentive to these reports and made no effort to disrupt the publicity with which they were paraded in Washington by the commercial representatives of Chita. In the light of the F.E.R. "propaganda" (which was verified by American Consul Caldwell from Dairen) and the numerous cables from Stevens corroborating the worst Japanese motives, the Department had given little credence to Premier Hara's statement to Ambassador Warren on November 9 that "the Government was anxious to withdraw its forces as soon as possible from Siberia" and would do so after "guarantees" had been obtained from the Far Eastern Republic. On the contrary Hughes and his colleagues were deeply concerned lest Tokyo escape from the Washington Conference without committing itself on the floor as to its Siberian policy.

Yet notwithstanding the burden of proof cast upon Japan and the admittedly superior moral position of the United States, the time devoted by the conference to Siberia was so microscopic in relation to that reserved for China as to constitute an insult in the eyes both of Chita and of Moscow. On January 23 Baron Shidehara addressed the twenty-fourth meeting of the Committee on Pacific and Far Eastern Questions with an apologia on Japanese activities in Siberia over the preceding two years. Everything of which Tokyo was accused was roundly denied. Japanese troops were in restricted portions of the Russian Far East at that time only because the presence of Japanese residents and the "geographical propinquity" of Korea made occupation imperative. In refutation of the charges of Japanese support for Semenov, Shidehara explained the reluctance of Tokyo "to abandon their friend whose efforts in the allied cause they had originally encouraged." But Japan had "no intention whatever" of interfering in Russia's domestic affairs, and when once it had been ascertained that the help afforded Semenov was "likely to complicate the internal situation in Siberia" relations were broken. The Dairen negotiations, the Baron asseverated, were "in no way intended to secure for Japan any right or advantage of an exclusive nature."

They have been solely actuated by a desire to adjust some of the more pressing questions with which Japan is confronted in relation to Siberia. They have essentially in view the conclusion of provisional commercial arrangements, the removal of the existing menace to the security of Japan and to the lives and property of Japanese residents in Eastern Siberia, the provision of guarantees for the freedom of lawful undertakings in that region, and the prohibition of bolshevik propaganda over the Siberian border. Should adequate provisions be arranged . . . the Japanese Government will at once proceed to the complete withdrawal of Japanese troops from the Maritime Province.

On the other hand, the occupation of Northern Sakhalin was "wholly different . . . from the stationing of troops" on the Siberian mainland. The Nikolaievsk massacre demanded "a measure of reprisal" pending the establishment of a responsible Russian government.

Nothing is further from the thought of the Japanese Government [Shidehara concluded] than to take advantage of the present helpless conditions of Russia for prosecuting selfish designs . . . the Japanese Delegation . . . is authorized to declare that it is the fixed and settled policy of Japan to respect the territorial integrity of Russia, and to observe the principle of nonintervention in the internal affairs of that country, as well as the principle of equal opportunity for the commerce and industry of all nations in every part of the Russian possessions.[15]

It all sounded so familiar, for it was in effect a paraphrase of Japanese communications to the American Government in answer

[15] *Conference on the Limitation of Armament,* pp. 1394–1400. In commenting on this speech, Ichihashi declared: "This statement of the Japanese representative is astonishingly candid, almost undiplomatically so. The position of the Japanese Government was made unmistakably clear." Reprinted from *The Washington Conference and After,* p. 316, by Yamato Ichihashi with the permission of the author and of the publishers, Stanford University Press. For the crackling rejoinder of the Far Eastern Republic to the Shidehara statement see *For. Rel.,* 1922, Vol. II, pp. 844–846.

to the latter's protests at each new Japanese incursion over the two-year period covered in the Shidehara speech. Short of challenging Tokyo's honesty on the floor of the conference which, in the diplomatic protocol of that day, would have been tantamount to a rupture in relations between the two countries, Secretary Hughes could only reiterate the American position and express his sincere hope that Japan would be able to fulfill its intention of withdrawing from Siberia in the near future. Therefore, on January 24 he took occasion to supplement the Shidehara history of intervention by placing on record the successive American notes to Tokyo and the continuing American conviction that, despite the recognized Bolshevik threat to Japanese interests,

the public assurances given by the two Governments at the inception of the joint expedition . . . required the complete withdrawal of Japanese troops from all Russian territory—if not immediately after the departure of the Czecho-Slovak troops, then within a reasonable time.

As to the occupation of Sakhalin, the United States regretted that Japan had deemed necessary "the occupation of Russian territory as a means of assuring a suitable adjustment with a future Russian Government." [16]

Following these remarks the Committee on Pacific and Far Eastern Questions unanimously resolved that the statements of the two diplomats be reported to the conference and spread on its records. That ended the Siberian discussion. When the conference adjourned on February 6, 1922, the aggregate of its deliberations concerning Russian problems was starkly unimpressive: a few score of words buried among hundreds of pages dealing with other subjects. The Japanese had acknowledged their sins without confessing them, and had departed from Washington unfettered by any specific date for the evacuation of their troops from Siberia. The ultimate settlement of that question, similar to the problem of the Chinese Eastern Railroad, was removed from the boardwalk of open conference to the more devious and shadowy channels of diplomacy. And finally, neither the ambiguous position of the Soviet

[16] *Conference on the Limitation of Armament,* pp. 1402–1412.

Government nor that of the Far Eastern Republic was in any way clarified; instead they, too, were consigned to the foreign offices of the powers and to the dictates of the future.

The reaction of Moscow to the Washington "failure" was accented by a florid spate of invectives; [17] and, in less colorful language, the critique of many serious observers was inclined to disparagement or apprehension regarding the net results of the conference.

And yet the final balance sheet was not without its credit ledger —a fact which emerged with the realization that the limits of American achievement were determined, not by American intentions, but by the anarchic framework of international political society within which they operated. Secretary Hughes could exhort and plead for the open-door and for the territorial integrity of Russia; he could expose Japanese imperialism directly and by implication; and these things he did with a frankness which was refreshing. But neither he nor his government nor the powers convened at Washington could legislate Japan out of Asia, and there was not a state at the conference or outside which was equipped to apply economic or military sanctions. The American Government, sensitive through experience to the currents of public pressure, accordingly chastised Japan with the only weapon at its disposal, and haling the criminal before the bar of world opinion it pointed the long finger of guilt where all could see. This was done without the co-operation or support of any other nation, and despite the obvious discomposure of Tokyo; and later events disclosed that it was to

[17] The "working masses of enslaved colonial peoples" were left unprotected from the menace of "an armed capitalistic peace," Soviet leaders declared. The Four-Power Treaty was condemned as a "quadruple alliance of bloodsuckers." Quoted by Dennis, *op. cit.*, p. 307. Several months later, however, *Izvestia* (July 6, 1922) credited the United States with the achievement of a notable victory over Japan and England at the conference: "The Washington Conference demonstrated that the United States must be considered one of the most active political powers in Eastern Asia. By attaining the abolition of the Anglo-Japanese alliance, America succeeded in dividing the forces of its most important opponents in Asia: England and Japan. This is a very advantageous strategic manoeuver and one which enables the United States to increase its influence at the expense of Japan and England. This especially relates to China, which on account of the present political situation in Eastern Asia represented the main field of the American activity . . ."

exercise a degree of restraint on the appetites of Japanese expansionists. That the American efforts did not provide a lasting solution to the problems besetting China and Siberia should have been a foregone conclusion, however, for in the obsolete vocabulary of the balance of power a solution is merely a compromise of expediency.

CHAPTER IX

Washington Aftermath

Three years following the Washington Conference irony poked fun at the United States in the form of an ephemeral Russo-Japanese rapprochement. In one sense the situation which developed was not unlike that subsequent to the Russo-Japanese War, when the mutual antagonism of the Tsar's Government and Tokyo to the interference of Roosevelt and Taft contributed to the series of four treaties between the two countries. But although the Soviet authorities were disgruntled at the Washington negotiations (a sentiment which they shared with Japan albeit for palpably different reasons), and at the subsequent attitude of the United States, the gradual amelioration of Russo-Japanese relations resulted as much from practical necessity on the part of each power as from American stimulus.

But before Tokyo and Moscow tentatively approached each other the distance between them was further widened. Initially this was evidenced by the precipitate break-up of the Dairen Conference in mid-April, 1922, approximately ten days after the Far Eastern Republic's delegation at Washington had warned Secretary Hughes of the deepening crisis between Chita and Tokyo. Each party to the Dairen negotiations accused the other of bad faith in terminating the discussions; from the published correspondence, however, it seems likely that Chita, probably at the behest of Moscow, rebelled at the unreasonableness of the Japanese *quid pro quo* for the evacuation of its forces, and that a stalemate ensued.

The next incident to aggravate Russo-Japanese relations was the abortive conference at Changchun the following September. Three months previously Tokyo had made a public announcement of its decision to "withdraw all the Japanese troops from the Maritime Province . . . by the end of October, 1922." The added declaration that "suitable measures" would be taken "for the protection of resident Japanese subjects" gave point to the Changchun proceedings during which Tokyo strove to squeeze every possible concession from Chita (and Moscow) in return for its pledged evacuation of the Siberian mainland. Thus among the demands ostensibly directed to the safeguarding of Japanese residents were: the internationalization of Vladivostok, revision of the fisheries convention, the open-door for Japanese merchants, the destruction of fortifications in the territory of the Russian Far East, and the neutrality of the Far Eastern Republic in the contingency of a war between Japan and a third power. Moreover, in the course of discussions Tokyo expressed a desire to obtain Northern Sakhalin "either by purchase or by a long-term lease. If this cannot be done the Japanese wish the exclusive privilege of holding concessions in Russian Sakhalin." [1] The Chita delegation, supported by Moscow, not only rejected this proposal but doomed the conference by making the continuation of negotiations contingent on the immediate agreement by Tokyo to a deadline for the removal of its forces from the Russian half of the island.

During the summer and fall of 1922, while these frictions prevailed, there was thus a passing chance for the United States to forestall the reorientation of Russo-Japanese relations by a shift which would have brought Washington's policy in closer alignment with the realities of the Far Eastern picture, instead of leaving it as it was—a product of wishful thinking. However, with an anathema

---

[1] Thomas (consul on special detail at Chita) to Hughes, via Warren, October 6, 1922, *For. Rel.*, 1922, Vol. II, p. 862. This desire was anticipated the previous January when the Japanese Foreign Minister informed the House of Representatives in Tokyo: "Japan will never make use of her present occupation to secure privileges for Japan improperly. At a future date when a legitimate government is established and when we enter into negotiations with it careful attention will be paid with the idea of being able to protect fully the rights acquired by our people at the time of its occupation, and in compliance with the requests of our nationals an examination will be made into them . . . We are taking care to avoid trouble to ourselves against the future time when a legitimate government may be established in Russia. Therefore be easy on this score." Enclosure in Warren to Hughes, February 1, 1922 (500A4/369).

toward communism coloring its outlook (an anathema which was certainly not minified by the Soviet press or propaganda), the American Government missed its cue at the psychological moment. The State Department had followed up the Japanese announcement of its intended withdrawal from Siberia with a note which not only approved Tokyo's contemplated action but emphasized the continuing concern with which Washington regarded Japanese occupation of Sakhalin. "By no inference," Ambassador Warren was told on June 27, "should there be any surrender of the position of our Government in this regard." Nevertheless, during the Changchun deliberations Chita was rebuffed in its attempts to seek American pressure on Japan for the relinquishment of the island. Furthermore, in 1922 and succeeding years while the Japanese remained on Sakhalin, Washington was adamant in its refusal to protect the concession obtained by the Sinclair Corporation from the Far Eastern Republic (and verified by Moscow following the union of Chita with the Soviet) for petroleum explorations on the island. That the Japanese refused to let an advance group of company officials make even preliminary surveys was apparently unimportant to a State Department obsessed with the notion that, by upholding the rights its citizens had achieved by a contract with the unrecognized Soviet regime, the United States would in effect be recognizing that government.

In the light of this attitude Karl Radek went unheard by Washington when he advocated a Soviet-American alliance in the Pacific in September 1922, and so, too, did the delegates of Chita when in November they expressed their appreciation for America's friendly help in bringing about "the evacuation of the Siberian mainland" by Japan. Ten days before this communication was received Department officials had reached the conclusion that Chita was so nearly a part of the Soviet Government that its recognition as an independent state had ceased to be a practical question, and therefore interest in the remarks of its representatives was scant. These factors, coupled with the recurrent friction of Washington and Moscow in China, removed any possibility of American-Soviet cooperation in the Far East for another decade.

In the meantime the practical requirements stemming from the geographical propinquity of Soviet Asia and Japan gradually impressed the two countries with the necessity for regularized contact. This was emphasized by the formal extension of the Russian boundaries eastward following the absorption of the Far Eastern Republic into the Soviet orbit on November 19, 1922; simultaneously the political atmosphere was lightened by the evacuation of the last Japanese troops from Siberia on October 25. This step, and the exodus of Tokyo's forces from Sakhalin two and a half years later, were a reflection of the potentially weakened political position of Japan in the Far East after 1921; a result in large measure of American efforts in behalf of the territorial integrity of both Russia and China.

The Hughes policy at the Washington Conference had robbed Tokyo (at least theoretically) of some of the victories it had attained over China by the 1917 treaties and the Versailles settlement. Moreover, the termination of the Anglo-Japanese Alliance had left the Japanese general staff without the potential military support of Great Britain in its imperialistic ventures. To this were added the cancellation of the irksome Lansing-Ishii Agreement in April 1923 and the unrelenting American protests against the continuing Japanese occupation of Sakhalin.

Economic considerations between 1921–1925 further contributed to the reorientation of Nippon's policy. On the one hand provisional trade agreements were signed with Soviet Russia by Britain, Germany, Norway, Austria, and Italy in 1921 (followed by unconditional *de jure* recognition by England's Labor Government in February 1924), and these substantially influenced Tokyo's attitude. At the same time, the occupation of both Siberia and Sakhalin had proved an immense drain on the Japanese treasury, in return for which the gains had been minuscule.

Economic and political compulsions were also responsible for the renewed Soviet efforts to reach a *modus vivendi* with Japan subsequent to the Washington Conference. Moscow was eager for the improved status which would accompany diplomatic recognition by the major powers of the world; and, of paramount importance, the Communist Government was in dire need of trade and economic assistance. Spurned by Washington, the Kremlin reappraised the advantages which would accrue from normal relations with Japan, and to this end it dispatched A. A. Joffe of the Foreign Commissariat to Tokyo in early 1923. But the Mikado's Government was determined to drive a hard bargain—an attitude no doubt strengthened by cognizance that Soviet overtures to America had been rejected in their entirety. On July 25, 1923, Joffe reported that Tokyo desired "to sell her recognition of Russia at the highest price attainable." This evoked a further bid from Moscow which combined a warning to Japan regarding its Siberian policy with the following significant statement:

Soviet Russia is the only country on earth that makes no distinction of race and color. She will give the Japanese the same opportunities and rights as she will any other foreigners for the utilization of their skill and labor on Russian territory. . . . she hopes that, if the Japanese Government will really give up its policy of enmity toward her, permanent peace and close relations between the two peoples will become possible, and peace and progress will thus be established at least in one portion of the Pacific.[2]

The deadlock continued, however; and not until the following April, when the unsatisfactory circumstances surrounding Japanese fishing in Russian waters were finally resolved by the two countries, did Tokyo commence formal negotiations for a treaty of recognition. After this time the more exorbitant of the Japanese demands and the calculated obdurateness of Soviet resistance were respectively diluted by the force of external events which made each more amenable to the conditions required by the other. Thus, for example, the sudden conclusion of the Sino-Soviet Agreement in May 1924 was a stunning shock to the Japanese Foreign Office. On June 7 the American Ambassador at Tokyo cabled that the Ministry was "more concerned than they care to admit" over the treaty and felt, as a result, that the difficulty of solving the problems with Russia was increased. Accordingly efforts to that end were redoubled. By mid-November the Moscow Government was further relieved following a telegram from Soviet representative Karakhan,

[2] *Izvestia,* July 30, 1923.

who was conducting the negotiations with Tokyo. The Japanese "will make certain concessions," he informed Foreign Commissar Chicherin, "as they fear that we might decline to continue negotiations." And two days later he stated:

The negotiations this time will come to a satisfactory conclusion, as the Japanese evidently intend to reduce many of their demands with respect to concessions in Sakhalin and Kamchatka in order to come to an agreement with the S.S.S.R. for the purpose of forming a block against Anglo-American policy in the Far East.[3]

For its part, Russia too evinced a more moderate attitude in the late autumn of 1924. A temporary resurgence of strong Japanese demands for concessions from Moscow had moved Karakhan to advise breaking off negotiations; but the contrary opinion prevailed in the Foreign Commissariat, and it was decided to continue the parleys. The chief reason listed was revealing of the inescapable Russo-Japanese-American Asiatic triangle. Deliberations were pushed, "particularly as the prospect of improving relations between Russia and America was on the whole unfavorable." [4]

On January 20, 1925, Japan and the Soviet Government signed a Convention (including two protocols) which provided for the establishment of diplomatic and consular relations, the final evacuation of all Japanese troops from Northern Sakhalin by May 15, and far-reaching concession agreements to be concluded subsequent to the withdrawal of the Japanese forces (see Appendix C). Chicherin's comment to the press was guardedly mild:

The Russo-Japanese agreement certainly signifies the consolidation of the Union of Soviet Socialist Republics in the Far East, while to Japan it means the creation of friendly relations reassuring in case of complications that might be pending for her.

More significant than this labored statement of the obvious was an editorial in *Izvestia*, February 24 (italics mine):

[3] Enclosure in Coleman (American Legation, Riga) to Secretary of State, December 23, 1924 (761.94/290).
[4] Enclosure in White (chargé, Riga) to Secretary of State, November 29, 1924 (761.94/287).

It must be stated that in respect to the United States . . . it can be said . . . that the interests of that country do not in any way conflict with the interests of the Soviet Union. . . .

All sources from which news of the changed attitude of the American Republic to the Soviet Union is coming, including also American sources . . . are unanimous . . . that this impetus has been supplied by the conclusion of the Soviet-Japanese treaty. As the United Press Agency informs, it was just the treaty between the Soviet republic and Japan that definitely convinced Coolidge of the necessity of starting as soon as possible negotiations with the Soviet government. *The opinion that the treaty of the Soviets with Japan is just likely to lead to such a result we have voiced as soon as it became known that the Governments of Japan and of the Soviet Union had come to an agreement on all principal points.*

If this and the quotation above can be regarded as representative of Soviet thought, it would appear that the Russian Convention with Japan was at least partially expedited by continued American aloofness and that the Communist leaders, who had been unable to attract the United States with an alliance based on antagonism to Tokyo, hoped to achieve the same results by befriending the Japanese.

This "friendship" lasted nominally for several years, superficially cemented by the scrupulous Japanese evacuation of Sakhalin on May 1, 1925, and testified to by V. M. Molotov in his report to the Congress of the Soviets in March 1931. For the Russian Government, however, it was and remained an expedient, analogous to that adopted by the Tsarist regime in the years 1905–1917, and for essentially the same reason. Then, as in the 1920's and 1930's, Japan nurtured dreams of expansion which flowered on the Continent of Asia in the fullness of time; then, as in the decades after, Russia lacked the physical power to halt the predacious Nipponese, and the darkening crisis in Europe demanded Moscow's first attention; then, as in the twenties and thirties, the American State Department mixed mighty protests with feeble actions.

So far as Russian hopes for a closer accord with the United States were concerned, the treaty with Japan (with its contingent economic concessions) went diplomatically unheeded on Pennsylvania Avenue, notwithstanding the role which American Far Eastern policy had played in fomenting it. The removal of the last Japanese soldiers from Sakhalin—symbolizing the fulfillment of the American "obligation" to preserve Russia's territorial integrity—along with the softening of Japanese policy toward China, caused the State Department temporarily to relax the Pacific vigil it had assumed in relation to Tokyo throughout the months of intervention and the years that followed.

Had proof been required, the events in Eastern Asia between 1918 and 1925 illustrated clearly the mainsprings of American policy: the balance of power, rent asunder by Japan, had called forth the unstinted efforts of President Wilson and his successors to right the wrong wherever found, for the dread terror of communism itself had been viewed a lesser evil than Japanese hegemony on the continent. Accordingly, the integrity of Russia's soil had been zealously guarded even as the integrity of its soul had been doubted. But when the war of intervention had ceased, and the last echoes had faded from the conference halls at Washington, the U.S.S.R. remained an outcast more thoroughly shunned by the nation which had protected it than by any other major power in the world.

Nor was the American policy one of negation alone: between 1920 and 1929 the United States waged intermittent battle to counteract the influence of Soviet Russia in the councils of Peking.

CHAPTER X

Rivalry in Asia:
The Second Stage

During the first few years of Bolshevik rule
Russia's weakness was its strength in its relations with the peoples
of continental Asia. Significantly, it was in this period that communism as a philosophy attained its largest following prior to the
Second World War, for in those darkest days when the future of
Russia was uncertain it was somehow easier to believe in the mil-
lennium—that classless paradise which would be ushered in on
the wings of world revolution. Unable from sheer exhaustion to
subscribe to the diplomacy of the Tsars, and sufficiently imbued
with a crusading zeal—supplemented by sharp political insight—
to sacrifice their own boundaries for the preservation of "the
great idea," the new rulers at Moscow were consequently willing
to forgo the imperial Russian stake in the Far East for a foothold in the minds of their Asiatic neighbors. Marxism, the gospel
of the dispossessed, found ready adherents in the ferment of China
and Asia, where the long tutelage to the foreigner and the im-
maturity of indigenous political organization, combined with the
lushly extravagant Soviet promises of equality and freedom, produced fertile and receptive soil.

Together with fear of the possible repercussions of Soviet communism on the capitalistic world, the United States might well
have felt the gravest apprehension over the penetration of Russian propaganda in China. In the first place, Communist ambition was not limited to the Peking Government; its tentacles extended as far south as Canton, where it embraced and nourished
the rising Nationalist Party of Sun Yat-sen. Secondly, the possibility existed that Russian influence, if unchallenged, would
eventuate in a Soviet government at Peking, which in turn would

189

furnish a powerful lever in the Communist plot to overthrow the Western economic system. Furthermore, in disclaiming the fruits of Tsarist conquest, the Soviet authorities were establishing a wholly unwelcome precedent for the West: by implication they challenged the Western nations and Japan to prove their moral fibre through following Russia's lead; and, failing in that, they tendered a Russian blessing to Peking if it should seek unilaterally to dispossess itself of foreign rights and privileges in China.

But communism, inasmuch as it was a policy based on weakness, slowly receded from the forefront of Soviet strategy as the Bolsheviks consolidated their hold on the Russian Government; and power politics, characteristic of the stronger state, unobtrusively assumed the dominating role in Moscow's foreign relations as it had done in the days of Tsarist rule. Marxian theory continued to be proclaimed and subscribed to, but just as the transition from the dictatorship of the proletariat to the classless, ruler-less society seemed to have been postponed indefinitely, so too were world revolution and the end of the imperialist state. Instead, Russia found itself in 1923 and succeeding years a sovereign entity harassed by an international political system in which aggression and warfare still threatened the unprepared, and in which the balance of power was a more persuasive force in the affairs of nations than the Communist International. Consequently Russia—the tide of power gradually rising on its shores—turned a different cheek to China and, under the guise of Communist brotherhood, attempted to infiltrate into Chinese governing circles so as to tip the scales of foreign influence at Peking away from Japan and other potential intruders, and in the direction of Moscow.

So far as the United States was concerned, the shifting emphasis in Soviet policy meant that Washington could resume its traditional role of protector of Chinese sovereignty against all potential assailants, including Russia. But although the Soviet-befriended Asiatics were cooling in their ardor for Moscow since its manifestation of older-type chauvinism, Asia generally and China in particular had experienced a sufficient degree of freedom in the decade prior to 1925 to resent increasingly the custody in which their sovereignty was kept by the West. As a result the privileged status of the

United States in China was pricked and questioned throughout the twenties, and the State Department in 1929 was forced into the equivocal position of protecting foreign rights in China against the Chinese themselves—not China against the rapacious foreign powers! To make the irony absolute, the nation whose self-appointed guardian the United States became was none other than Soviet Russia.

Hardly a month had elapsed after the November Revolution of 1917 before the Bolshevik authorities, carving opportunity out of defeat, granted to all peoples within the Tsarist domains full equality and the right of secession from the Russian state. This was the harbinger of that imperialist renunciation which found expression in the Russian Declarations of 1919 and 1920 respectively.

On July 25, 1919, the Soviet rulers issued an elaborate statement to the Chinese people and the Northern and Southern governments, renouncing Tsarist acquisitions in China, abolishing extrality, and (according to the Chinese text of the Soviet note) returning the Chinese Eastern Railroad to China without compensation. Later Soviet editions of this document, however, scrupulously avoided any mention of the C.E.R. In October 1920 China was handed a second note which confirmed the basic content of the first, but suggested that a specific arrangement be made for the management of the Chinese Eastern, with due "regard to the needs" of Russia.[1]

Although the Peking Government officially ignored the Soviet offers and no treaty was negotiated for several years, the Western powers did not attempt to conceal their uneasiness, a feeling which was in no way assuaged by the second Congress of the Third International in July–August 1920, and the Pan-Asiatic Conference at Baku in September, at which the Soviet leaders openly pleaded for an alliance between Asia's "eight hundred millions of people" and Russian communism.

In the early months of 1919 preceding the initial Soviet gesture and, in fact, throughout most of the year, the American Government had evinced a genuine sympathy on behalf of China's efforts to free itself from some of the more onerous obligations which had

[1] The two Russian documents are given in Appendix A.

been pressed upon it by the Tsarist regime. While reiterating its conviction that no country had the right to infringe upon the existing status of the C.E.R., the State Department tended to overlook the representations of Ambassador Bakhmetev (of the Russian Provisional Government) and his associates regarding all other matters. For example, in May a memorandum from the Russian Embassy in Washington concerning Chinese intentions "to hinder the activities of the Russian Legation" went unanswered. In response to the Provisional Government's note to the Allied and Associated powers at Paris in December on the subject of Peking's violation of the 1913 and 1915 Russo-Chinese Mongolian agreements, the United States declared that it had never been informed of the treaties and therefore felt incompetent to evaluate the Russian charges. And in answer to further communications from Bakhmetev, the consensus of the Department was illustrated in a memorandum which, while noting American opposition "in principle" to the prejudicing of Russian rights, confessed that from "a human point of view" it was "easy to sympathize with the Chinese." [2]

This frame of mind was abruptly dispelled, however, when the Chinese actions were connected in the press and in diplomatic reports with a premeditated Bolshevik program to supplant Tsarist influence at Peking with that of the Soviet authorities. The widely scattered rumors regarding the Soviet Declaration of July 1919 were eventually sifted into a cohesive pattern which Ambassador Bakhmetev found far more persuasive in his messages to the State Department than the fears he had hitherto expressed. The unilateral repudiation of treaties (suggested by the Soviet emissaries at Peking) was consequently made the subject of a carefully reasoned letter to the Acting Secretary early in April 1920, and in direct conversa-

[2] *For. Rel.*, 1920, Vol. I, p. 758n. This attitude was reflected in a conversation between Breckinridge Long and Bakhmetev on December 18, 1920: "The Russian Ambassador . . . asked if we would send a word of advice to China to dissuade her from her unfriendly activities toward Russia in derogation of Russia's treaty rights. I asked him if he was a Chinese citizen what he would do? He replied just what China is doing. I told him that under the circumstances that we would not feel justified in speaking to China about matters which concerned purely Chino-Russian treaty relations." *Long Papers.*

tion Bakhmetev urged that China be warned not to listen to the Bolsheviks, a plea which found Polk amenable.

Five months later "the first tangible victory in China" of the visiting Communists was witnessed in Peking's decision to close the old Russian Legation and consulates and to terminate diplomatic relations with the Russian Provisional Government. This precipitated the first of several notes from Washington intended to protect preexisting Russian rights and to counteract Soviet influence by indirectly impugning Moscow's deeper motives.

On September 21, Minister Crane was instructed to express orally the American Government's perturbation. Fear was expressed that Peking might consider the Soviet offer to renounce Russian treaty rights in China or, while holding to the letter of those rights, to jeopardize them in practice. The United States assumed that this was not China's intention, but it nevertheless felt obliged on behalf both of Russia and of China to warn the latter against "conniving" with the Communists at the expense of the "treaty rights of the Russian people."

Simultaneous with the communication to China, Washington toyed with a French-sponsored scheme whereby an international commission would administer in trust the Russian interests in China until the establishment of a "duly constituted" Russian government—that is, a government more acceptable to the Western powers. Because by this time the Soviet regime had been the *de facto* government nearly two years, the American attempt to discredit its right to speak for the Russian masses could hardly be deemed either friendly or fair, the more so as Washington was still listening to the Russian Provisional Government's spokesmen, whose claim to speak rested solely on an eight-month tenure of office.

The Chinese authorities were not unnaturally dubious regarding the French proposal; nor were they more favorably disposed by the knowledge that France, Italy, and Japan strenuously objected to an exclusive Chinese control in Russia's absence.

In the meantime the effectiveness of Western and Japanese protests against the contemplated action of Peking was diluted by the traditional unwillingness of the United States to implement its words with physical pressure. The most that Washington would do was to dispatch still another note to China in early October 1920 which revealed in full measure American alarm over Soviet inroads throughout Asia. This alarm was twofold. It expressed American fright over the ideological menace of communism, and American apprehension lest Bolshevik incursions precipitate demands on China by other nations. Thus Peking was informed, on the one hand, that in agitating for the recovery of Chinese rights the Soviet Government envisaged an anti-foreign movement in China which could be used as a weapon against capitalistic states. On the other hand, Washington warned Peking that to submit, even tentatively, to Communist influence would conceivably alienate the "friendly regard" of those same capitalistic states and might even provide an excuse for their further aggression, undertaken superficially to protect legal Russian rights from being confiscated "on behalf of the Russian Reds."

This lightly veiled threat was all but ignored by China's Foreign Minister who declared, however, that treaty relations between the state of Russia and China were in no wise ended by the Chinese closure of the Russian Legation, but were merely suspended temporarily; that China adhered to its attitude of noninterference in internal Russian politics; that Peking intended to "protect and administer the Russian settlements" unilaterally; and that, although Russian consular courts were abolished, Russian laws—in so far as they did not conflict with Chinese laws—would be applied to Russian subjects in Chinese courts.

This declaration provoked the powers at Peking to indulge in a prolonged dispute with the Chinese Government over specific points in the Chinese response. But the latter stubbornly refused to retract anything from the substance of its formally stated policy.

In the spring of 1921 a circular from the Dean of the Diplomatic Corps in Peking to the member states set a date for the further discussion of the question of maintaining Russian treaty rights in China. But the United States, foreshadowing the failure of united action, abstained from participation in the diplomatic conference of the Allied representatives. In so doing the American Government was at length trying to adjust to the new role into which Soviet tactics had forced it, and simultaneously to retain the friendly tolerance characteristic of its historical approach to the China problem.

The advances in Soviet popularity credited to the about-face in the Russian attitude had indeed posed a dilemma for American diplomats—a fact which was to become increasingly apparent in the ensuing years. The problem before Washington was to maintain China's respect while countering Soviet influence—a problem nowhere more clearly understood than in Moscow. As succinctly stated in *Izvestia* (July 6, 1922), the United States was painfully discovering that Bolshevik influence was growing "in precisely the young Chinese circles on which America was counting." This unhappy situation was further augmented by another obstacle, "the outbreak of a sharp Chinese nationalism." American diplomacy was finding it "rather difficult" to continue the role of "protectors of China," because China's regeneration required no "protection"; China was, in fact, "trying to get rid of protection" by all foreign elements.

The avowed Soviet policy of helping China to achieve this goal further added to the American predicament, particularly as Moscow poured the oil of its propaganda into the wheels of Chinese politics, thus putting the worst possible light on American intentions in the Orient. In the article from *Izvestia* quoted above, for example, the Russian paper suggested that Washington, confronted with problems in the implementation of its Asiatic policy, had decided that it must coordinate its program with that of Moscow. Cooperation was hardly feasible, the article concluded, "since America wants to colonize China and Soviet Russia wants to see China free and independent."

Equally typical of the Russian publicity was a later news account (*Izvestia*, November 7, 1922) which pictured the United States laying its hand "on that wealth of coal and iron" in China for which it was competing with Japan. It devolved upon the Communists to frustrate this effort to turn China "into a mere colonial dependency."

Nor was the Soviet offensive confined to Peking or limited to a war of words against the West. In 1921 a Chinese Communist

Party had been organized in Shanghai under the guiding impetus of Comintern agents. And in the next five years the anti-imperialist activities of the Communist International were nowhere more pronounced than in South China. One patent reason for this concentration was that Marxian dialectics depicted the Far Eastern colonial dependencies of the Western states as the most vulnerable salient of capitalist society. In the second place the Communists were concentrating their fire on British imperialism in particular, and the English stake in China constituted a tempting target to the Chinese and the Marxists alike. But of even greater importance was the pregnant opportunity presented by the struggling Nationalist Party of Sun Yat-sen. Although he had been instrumental in the establishment of the new Chinese Republic following the revolution of 1911, Dr. Sun had never cooperated with the reactionary elements (led by Yuan Shih-kai) who contrived to gain control of the Chinese Government. Instead, Sun and his followers had established themselves in Canton, where they worked tirelessly to create a strong and popular movement to supplant the Peking authorities. By the close of 1922, when the Communists appeared on the scene, the prospects of the Nationalist Party were at their lowest ebb, and so it was that Sun, while rejecting communism as a philosophy for his country, seized the proffered Russian hand of Albert Joffe as the last great hope whereby to consummate the Chinese Revolution.

The Soviet agent, who alternated between official missions to the Chinese Government and clandestine trips to Shanghai, agreed to render Comintern aid to the Kuomintang faction. He also acquiesced in the Sun thesis that conditions in China were not conducive to a Communist experiment, although this divorcement of aid from ideology was manifestly a mere tactical concession. Indeed, Michael Borodin, a skilled Communist organizer, soon arrived to take over the revolutionary planning of the Kuomintang movement. Propagandists were trained, cells were developed, a Party Congress was called, and Chinese Communist Party members were brought into the Nationalist organization even as the Communist Party retained its individual existence.

Four months before these activities were launched in southern China, Soviet envoy Joffe had arrived in Peking with the purported objective of concluding a defensive agreement between his government, China, and the Far Eastern Republic. On September 2, 1922, the Russian spokesman made an offer to Wellington Koo to negotiate all questions between Russia and China, based on the Soviet declarations of 1919 and 1920. According to *Izvestia* (September 16) the Chinese response was affirmative. By the end of the month American Minister Schurman was sufficiently impressed by the efforts of the Soviet mission to cable Washington about Joffe's progress and the large number of "educated Chinese" who regarded bolshevism "as merely another phase of democracy."

But the pathway to Soviet-Chinese accord was not without its quota of snags, and these became increasingly apparent as the two parties, even in the midst of their feast of friendship, dickered to advance their respective interests. The Russian representatives complained at Peking's attempt to discuss the outstanding questions on the agenda separately. This protest was accompanied by the recurrent Soviet charge that the Chinese authorities were taking no steps to prevent the concentration of White Russian forces in northern Manchuria where their presence constituted a serious threat to the Russian people—so serious that in December, Consul Hanson reported the massing of nearly ten thousand well-equipped Soviet forces on the Siberian-Manchurian border.

The fact that Moscow was able to command a potential resistance of this scope was indicative of the gathering stability of the Soviet Government, a stability further demonstrated by the manner in which Adolph Joffe expatiated on the 1919 and 1920 Russian declarations to China. On November 6, 1922, the Soviet emissary, "with a view again to avoiding any misunderstanding whatsoever," stated that "it was quite wrong to draw the inference from these declarations that Russia renounces all her interests in China." A distinction was drawn between the rights accruing to Russia from the "predatory and violent policy" of the Tsarist regime and Russia's "local and just interests" in China. This, of course, constituted that tool of qualification by which bargains are struck and compromises are made in diplomacy. It prefaced the inclusion of "conditions" in the table of contents of Sino-Soviet relations. The obvious first condition: Reciprocity. The act of renunciation, once unilaterally made, was claimed to depend for its validity on two-way discussions leading to "a free accord" between Moscow and Peking. The second condition: Haste. The Russian promises of 1919 and 1920 could not, "after all, be valid forever." China must "discontinue its ignoring of Russian interests" and quicken negotiations, or the Soviet Government might "after all be obliged to consider herself free" from the earlier declarations.[3]

Another area of Sino-Soviet discord was Mongolia. Despite the Soviet renunciation of Tsarist acquisitions, under which Mongolia had severed its relations with China in 1915 and become a virtual protectorate of Petrograd, the capital of Outer Mongolia was occupied by the Red Army in March 1921. This was nominally to defeat the counter-revolutionary forces of Baron Ungern Sternberg, but the Communists made no effort to withdraw following their victory. On the contrary, a puppet government was established at Urga under Soviet auspices; and by the time the Joffe mission had reached Peking, Russia and Mongolia had concluded a treaty which, by establishing "friendly relations" between the two countries, left no doubt of the ascendancy of Soviet influence. In answer to the Chinese protest against Russia's activities in Mongolia, Joffe asserted that Red troops remained only at the request of the Mongolian inhabitants. Moreover, as long as China permitted reactionary White Russian movements to organize on its territory, Moscow would feel compelled (in China's "real interests") to retain forces at Urga. But regardless of Joffe's rationalization, the Mongolian

[3] *For. Rel.*, 1922, Vol. I, p. 333. "It is interesting to observe the change in tone of these declarations. In the beginning they are extraordinarily friendly to China and give the impression that the Soviet Government is so anxious to restore friendly relations and win China as an ally that it is prepared to renounce all Russian rights and interests in China, including extraterritoriality, concessions . . . and other special privileges. Later, however, when the Moscow regime had become stronger and had seized Mongolia in a more arbitrary manner than the Tsar's Government would have dared to do, the attitude changes and the communications are almost threatening to China." From a memorandum by Mr. Douglas Jenkins, Division of Russian Affairs, Department of State, December 20, 1922, *ibid.*

issue provided the stumbling-block in the 1922 negotiations between the Kremlin and Peking, and no treaty was achieved.[4]

In contrast to the fluctuations of Soviet-Chinese relations, American policy toward Russia remained impassively aloof throughout the 1920's. The only positive evidence that Washington was cognizant of the consolidation of Soviet power came with the decision, at the suggestion of Bakhmetev, that the Provisional Government's Ambassador relinquish his post on July 1, 1922, at which time Chargé Ughet was given custody of the property of the defunct government and accorded diplomatic status. The Moscow Government was not willing to extend a like courtesy to the American consulate at Vladivostok; Consul Tuck was informed that, pending official recognition or "some other form of mutual agreement" between the Soviet Government and the United States, Russia would not grant the usual diplomatic immunities and privileges. Therefore Washington ordered the consulate closed in May 1923.

Meanwhile the American stand on nonrecognition of the Soviet regime was reiterated by Secretary Hughes in March and by President Harding at the end of July. On December 6 President Coolidge outlined the conditions for recognition in his message to the Congress:

Whenever there appears any disposition to compensate our citizens who were despoiled, and to recognize that debt contracted with our Government . . . whenever the active spirit of enmity to our institutions is abated; whenever there appear works mete for repentance; our country ought to be the first to go to the economic and moral rescue of Russia. We have every desire to help and no desire to injure. We hope the time is near at hand when we can act.

This elicited a fresh attempt by Soviet Commissar Chicherin to enter into negotiations for the removal of "all misunderstandings between the two countries." In reply Secretary Hughes stated bluntly that it required "no conference or negotiations" for Moscow to restore confiscated American property or to repeal the decree repudiating foreign debts, and that until these were accomplished,

[4] In May 1923 Moscow received a Mongolian mission, and a year later a Soviet Republic was proclaimed in Urga.

and Communist propaganda directed against American institutions was abandoned, the Soviet Government could expect no discussions with the United States looking to recognition.

Regardless of the respective merits and drawbacks in Washington's policy, the absence of mutual representation in Russia and America could only hinder the solution of problems in the Far East in which both states professed a direct interest. More than that, nonrecognition ineluctably augmented the deep-seated misunderstanding of each other's motives in Asia, a fact which became increasingly manifest as the years passed and Moscow, more confident of its strength, lapsed back into the routine politics of a major Asiatic power.

One of the chief problems which illustrated the disadvantages of nonrecognition was the Chinese Eastern Railroad—a problem destined to haunt American diplomats for well over a decade, and connected with the more general question of Soviet-Chinese relations between 1920 and 1930.

With respect to the latter, the collapse of negotiations in 1922 was viewed by both states as only a temporary break; and in the next two years Soviet propaganda and pressure continued to leave an imprint on Chinese thought, and to evoke the perennial suspicions of Japan and the West. Receiving its information from the back-handed channels which alone were available to the State Department in its sterilized treatment of Russia, Washington learned in June 1923 that the Soviet leaders were assiduously pushing China toward friction with Japan over the Liaotung Peninsula, with promises of unofficial and undercover aid; and that Peking was being importuned to oppose the "excessive demands" of the powers concerning guarantees to foreigners on the ground that these constituted interference in China's domestic affairs— an infringement of Chinese sovereignty.

The arrival at Peking of the Karakhan delegation in the late summer of 1923 inaugurated a second protracted series of negotiations which finally culminated in the agreements of May 1924 between Soviet Russia and China, and in the settlement of September 1924 between Russia and the Three Eastern Provinces of the Republic of China. The major single problem considered by the contracting parties was the Chinese Eastern Railroad, which by itself was sufficient to arouse the keen interest of Washington.

It will be recalled that every effort had been expended by the State Department to achieve a mutually satisfactory agreement with Japan for the operation and management of the Chinese Eastern and Trans-Siberian systems during the Allied Siberian intervention; and the recurring theme of the American Government in 1918, 1919, and ensuing years had been that previously existing rights in the C.E.R., by whomsoever held, should not be alienated. In the first instance American solicitude was a by-product of Washington's fear of Japanese motives. However, the status of the railroad was being protected not only against Japanese penetration, but against each and every hypothetical challenger, including if need be China and the Soviet Union. Accordingly the United States watched anxiously as Peking, taking advantage of the collapse of Russian strength in the Far East in 1919 and 1920, began to exercise unilateral control over matters which were, by treaty-law, the proper subject of Sino-Russian negotiations.

On October 2, 1920, China notified the Russo-Asiatic Bank of its decision to "assume provisionally," pending a railroad agreement with a "Russian Government that may be recognized by China," "supreme control" over the road, and to "resume the advantages and particular interests" which accrued to China by the 1896 operating contract. In line with this declaration the Chinese Government increased the number of its nationals in the joint administration of the railroad and converted it into a purely commercial concern.[5]

In response to the pointed query of the State Department a few weeks later, the Chinese Minister of Communications assured the United States that China continued "actively to support the Inter-Allied agreement for the control of the Siberian railways and the Chinese Eastern Railroad."

Meanwhile the Soviet Government had enunciated its declaration of October 1920. This included a statement of Russia's willingness to negotiate a special treaty in regard to the C.E.R. According to the Soviet proposal the Far Eastern Republic was also to

[5] *For. Rel.*, 1920, Vol. I, pp. 713–715, 716–721, 722.

participate in such a settlement. Consequently, in a communication to Secretary Hughes (March 22, 1921) the F.E.R. announced the reversion to it of former Tsarist rights in the Chinese Eastern. The State Department was informed that these rights were therefore "subject to revision conjointly" by Chita, Moscow, and Peking.

Although Washington was wholly opposed to the seizure by China of railroad rights which belonged equally to Russia, it was perhaps even more disconcerted to discover that the Bolshevik Government and its Far Eastern satellite were approaching China with a view to a joint settlement of the railroad problem exclusive of any other power. Consequently the arrival in Peking toward the end of 1921 of the so-called Soviet Ambassador, Paikes, augmented American apprehensions. At the end of the year Minister Schurman was instructed to "impress" Chinese officialdom with "the questionable validity of any agreements" concluded between the Soviet Government and China on the C.E.R., and with the "impossibility" of obtaining the assent of the West to any attempt to "nullify the 1896 treaty."

This reminder received added emphasis because the Washington Conference, then in session, had slated for discussion the status of the Siberian and Chinese Eastern railroads. This was displeasing to China and perhaps even more to the Moscow Government. The reaction of the Soviet to exclusion from the conference has already been noted; on December 8 Chicherin sent a formal protest by Paikes and Schurman against any discussion by the conferees of the C.E.R. on the ground that the question concerned Russia and China alone. The two nations were even then negotiating the conditions for the return of the road by Moscow to Peking, the note averred, and as soon as the latter had accepted "certain indispensable guarantees" the transfer would take place. For these reasons the Soviet Government stated that it would refuse to recognize any infraction of Russian rights by conference decision at Washington. In other words, the Bolsheviks did not wish their generous gesture to China meddled with, weakened, or in any way sullied by Washington Conference resolutions which, they were convinced, were intended to bully both China and Russia in the interests of Western and Japanese imperialism.

Peking's resentment was expressed to Schurman on January 5, 1922, when the Foreign Minister declared that China preferred that the road be converted to state property but, if this were impossible, favored the existing status. The people of China "were unanimous in their opposition to international control." Nor did the minister "see why the Washington Conference should consider the Chinese Eastern Railroad," especially as the Soviet Union was unrepresented. Notwithstanding these protests from the two principals, the powers adopted a resolution and a reservation which, as noted earlier, met the American objective of providing legal grounds for complaint should China or Russia, individually or together, pursue a policy toward the C.E.R. which jeopardized the contractual arrangements of 1896.

Throughout the conference Peking had displayed a sharp reluctance to amend or strengthen the original 1919 Inter-Allied agreement, a project which had been foremost in American minds since the rebuff by Japan of the American railroad proposal of January 1921. The success of the Chinese delegates in frustrating Washington's hopes forced the latter to resort to diplomatic pressure after the conference, but the most that could be accomplished was the reiteration by Peking of its ability to handle its responsibilities in the C.E.R. without foreign aid. The Anglo-American plea to Foreign Minister Yen in late February that the latter "voluntarily take the lead" and invite international "consultation and cooperation," coupled with the assertion that the "Powers would deplore using pressure against China" and therefore hoped that "China would voluntarily request cooperation," evoked an unofficial explanation of the Chinese attitude which did not in the least mitigate Peking's position.

On March 22, C. C. Wang, acting head of the railroad, summarized the situation. China was opposed to foreign "cooperation," because the C.E.R. was a Sino-Russian enterprise, Russian rights were in the custody of China, and it would be easier to reach an agreement with Moscow in the future if the existing status of the line were maintained; both Russia and Peking were opposed to other alterations unless and until sufficient reasons should arise; Chang Tso-lin was "master of Manchuria" at the time, and his "susceptibilities" could not be ignored; the interest of the powers in the line was based not on formal investment, but only "on the fact that through the Technical Board . . . they . . . expended money on the railway"; the fear of the powers of a potential Japanese control was exaggerated in view of the visible lessening of Japanese aggressive designs. On the basis of these remarks Schurman opined that China desired to remain aloof from "political, territorial or other arrangements" regarding its rights in the C.E.R., and that informal Sino-Soviet discussions were an immediate probability.

Within the next few months the intimation that Great Britain, as part of its economic retrenchment program, desired to withdraw from the Technical Board, the opinion of Secretary Hughes that "it is not wise to spend more money at present" in connection with the road, and the impending evacuation of the last Japanese troops, which would definitely end the Inter-Allied railroad agreement, convinced the State Department of the necessity for providing some sort of understanding to replace the 1919 accord. As a result of American-inspired negotiations over the summer of 1922, on October 31 the government of China was presented with similar, though not identical, notes from all the powers involved in the Inter-Allied program of the preceding three years.

The substance of the American note called attention to the termination as of that date of the activity of the Inter-Allied committee at Vladivostok and of the Technical Board at Harbin. After repeating the resolution and reservation adopted by the Washington Conference relative to the C.E.R., the State Department made special reference to the railroad by reserving "to itself all rights including those with respect to advances in money and material which have been made by it in aid" of the Chinese Eastern, either unilaterally or through the agencies established by the Inter-Allied agreement. Furthermore, the American note reaffirmed "concern in the preservation of the Chinese Eastern Railway with a view to its ultimate return to those in interest without the impairing of any existing rights," and "continued interest" in the maintenance of the road "as a free avenue of commerce open to the citizens of all countries without favor or discrimination." In view of its interest in these matters, Washington notified China that it would continue to observe "the manner in which" Peking discharged its obligations, and would stand ready to "assist or cooperate" "at any time in any practicable way" to conserve the railroad and assure its "efficient operation in the interest of all concerned." [6]

This educed from the Chinese a statement of the progress achieved in the operation of the railroad, together with a brief reminder that the responsibilities assumed by Peking were, notwithstanding the heavy importance attached to them by the United States, "merely those" formerly exercised by Russia, and "now exercised by China" provisionally because of "the absence of a formally recognized Russian government."

In the meantime the Joffe mission had arrived at Peking, wholly unsatisfied with the conditions existing on the Chinese Eastern and determined that the railroad would constitute perhaps the leading question in the discussions with China. According to the Soviet envoy, Moscow alone had the right to interfere in the line, being more than any other government concerned with its future since Russian funds had built it and it comprised Russian property. The foreign source of the vast percentage of these funds and the Soviet repudiation of Tsarist-contracted foreign debts were conveniently overlooked by Joffe. Moreover, he asserted, not even the 1919–1920 Soviet declarations of abnegation altered the legal status of the road, for even if Russia should vest her title "in the Chinese people," her interests in the line would survive simply because the C.E.R. was "a portion of the Great Siberian Railway" and united various parts of Soviet territory. This point of view was reaffirmed to DeWitt Poole by Skvirsky, chairman of the Far Eastern Republic's commercial delegation at Washington, when he spoke of Russia's "vital" interests in the C.E.R., saying that China "would have to consent to joint" control, and that the prevailing situation, in which the railroad zone harbored White Russians, could not be tolerated.

The failure of the Joffe mission to accomplish any concrete results and the continuing need for a *modus vivendi* to regulate Sino-Soviet relations resulted in a retreat by both countries from their

[6] *For. Rel.*, 1922, Vol. I, pp. 925–926.

mutually aggressive diplomacy of 1922. By the following May, China recorded its eagerness to negotiate all outstanding problems with Russia, including the C.E.R.; and in June the State Department was informed that the railroad question would be settled through joint concessions. Consequently the Soviet delegation was able to meet with greater success in the ensuing conversations with Chinese officials; and in mid-March 1924 the two states signed a preliminary draft, in which it was declared that "the future of the Chinese Eastern Railway shall be determined by the U.S.S.R. and . . . China, to the exclusion of any third parties or party."

A Russian newspaper in Harbin anticipated America's interest in the negotiations when it referred to Schurman's speeches and public utterances as proof that the United States had "no intention of remaining a passive onlooker" when the existing status of the Chinese Eastern was destroyed.[7] Nevertheless, the State Department would not go as far as the financially interested French Government, which wished to induce China to avoid an agreement with Moscow that did not include a "formal reservation of the rights of foreign stockholders and creditors of the railway company." In order to avert any misunderstanding with the Chinese, Schurman was instructed not to join the representatives of France or other countries in protesting Peking's negotiations with Russia. At the same time, however, the American Minister was to send a separate note to the Chinese Foreign Office, reminding the latter of its continuing responsibility as railroad trustee under Resolution XIII of the Washington Conference, a responsibility which negotiations with no other state could supersede. "This note," Hughes declared, should "make it clear . . . that the United States Government stands for the protection of all interests including Russian and is not endeavoring to prevent the conclusion of a Sino-Russian agreement." [8] Accordingly Schurman addressed the Peking Government on May 3 in the sense requested, but it could hardly have been expected that the American disclaimer of any attempt to forestall a Sino-Soviet rapprochement would be received with much credence by a Russian government which had been scorned

[7] Enclosure in Hanson to Hughes, March 19, 1924 (761.95/458).
[8] *For. Rel.*, 1924, Vol. I, pp. 486–487.

and mistrusted by Washington almost since its inception. Indeed, the logical inference to be drawn from the conditions surrounding the Hughes statement was that Washington, recognizing the impossibility of preventing a Russo-Chinese accord, filed for the record its continuing "interest" in the railroad.

On May 14 the response of Soviet representative Karakhan to the American communication (which had leaked to the press) was published in the Peking newspapers. The question of the railroad, the Bolshevik emissary recalled, "related only to China and Russia, and if other powers intervene, it is only to hamper understanding" between the two principals. The Washington Conference resolution was invalid without the participation of the Soviet Government, and the present action of the State Department was typical of the imperialistic policies of the West. Finally, the Russian Government, having "taught all great powers not to meddle with Russian affairs," now hoped "to teach them not to interfere with Russo-Chinese affairs," and to this end Moscow would protect China's sovereignty and national dignity against any attacks.[9] Moreover, the American statement of disinterest in the Sino-Soviet negotiations was sharply refuted by a member of the Russian mission after the conclusion of the agreement:

Our negotiations with China were conducted in a condition of extraordinary pressure on the Chinese ruling circles on the part of States which [look] . . . on China as on a colony of world capital. The pact . . . did not at [the] time receive its confirmation, *exclusively owing to the pressure of America and France.*[10]

On May 31, 1924, two agreements were concluded by Peking and Moscow, one on "General Principles for the Settlement of the Questions" between the two countries and the second on the "Provisional Management of the Chinese Eastern Railroad." Under the terms of the former, diplomatic relations were established; Russia denounced all treaties and agreements concluded by the Tsarist regime with any third powers which affected sovereign

[9] *Ibid.*, pp. 489–490.
[10] "Comrade Rykov on the International Situation." Excerpts from *Izvestia,* June 8, 1924. Italics mine.

Chinese rights, and both governments agreed that neither would conclude such treaties in the future; Chinese sovereignty over Outer Mongolia was recognized (although in view of the virtual Soviet protectorate over the territory this article had little real significance); the two states promised not to allow within their respective territory the existence and/or activity of organizations (or propaganda) aimed against each other's government; and Tsarist concessions, the Russian portion of the Boxer Indemnity, extraterritoriality, and consular jurisdiction were renounced by the Soviet. All these matters were to become the subject of special negotiations at a conference to be called within a month following the signature of the agreement, when the details of the C.E.R. convention would also be settled.

As far as the convention was concerned, the May 31 agreement on the railroad (and Article 9 of the "General Principles" accord) provided for the eventual redemption of the line by China and the transfer to Peking of all outstanding shares and bonds. Moreover, the purely commercial nature of the enterprise was confirmed, and the contracting parties declared their exclusive right to decide all questions arising from the status of the road.[11]

In the light of later events the May agreements represented a major Soviet victory, both in terms of Moscow's successful flaunting of foreign objections and in regard to the treaties themselves. Although Karakhan had acceded to China's desire to repurchase the C.E.R. at some future date, the interim arrangement for joint management placed Russia in an extremely advantageous position: the right of appointing the general manager of the road was given to Moscow, the powers of that official were purposely left ill-defined but extensive, and under the agreement the U.S.S.R. was to exercise "a preponderant influence in the affairs of the railway and . . . to retain the essential parts of its economic interests in North Manchuria . . ."[12]

The full extent of the Soviet triumph was not appreciated by

[11] The May treaties and the Soviet agreement with the Three Eastern Provinces (September 20, 1924) are given in Appendix B.

[12] League of Nations, *Appeal by the Chinese Government—Report of the Commission of Inquiry (The Lytton Report)*, 1932, p. 35.

Peking at the time the agreements were consummated, however; on the contrary China was sufficiently pleased with the results of the negotiations to express itself quite abruptly in a note to Washington, Paris, and Tokyo on June 16. Peking declared that the establishment of Sino-Soviet relations had entirely altered the status of trusteeship which had been exercised by China over the C.E.R. at the time of the Washington Conference, so that in the future the governments of Russia and China would deal with the railroad without benefit of foreign advice. This attitude was somewhat modified two weeks later when the Chinese Legation informed the State Department that the agreements with Russia did not "prejudice any claims which other Powers may wish to prefer against" the road "on account of money advanced to it by them."

But Washington was not so easily placated, and on July 11 Secretary Hughes reaffirmed a direct financial claim on the Chinese Eastern of $4,177, 820.06, the sum advanced to the technical board "for the purpose of saving the Railway from breakdown and deterioration." That debt, wrote Hughes, comprised an obligation of which the Chinese Government could not divest itself merely by "devolving" its trusteeship of the C.E.R. "upon another party." As a result the American Government "felt it necessary" to renew the reservation made in the American note of May 3.[13]

The general disapproval of Washington over the Sino-Soviet agreements furnished Moscow with an excellent opportunity to inveigh against the United States, and this was done by Soviet Ambassador Karakhan in an interview with the Peking press at the end of June. Hughes had "evidently decided to punish China" and to chastise the Russian Government, the Soviet spokesman declared, and Washington's nonrecognition policy was directly trace-

[13] *For. Rel.*, *op. cit.*, pp. 504–505. In refuting the Hughes arguments the Chinese author Weigh states that the four million dollar loan made by the United States was not solicited by China, that it was intended primarily for the protection of Allied forces in Siberia and to facilitate transportation for the Czech troops. Moreover, China had never agreed to Resolution XIII of the Washington Conference, at which Russia was unrepresented. Finally, the Russo-Chinese agreement contained nothing resembling "a repudiation of any obligation on the Chinese Eastern Railway . . ." Ken S. Weigh, *Russo-Chinese Diplomacy* (Shanghai: The Commercial Press, Ltd., 1928), p. 244.

able to the alleged evil influence of Moscow on Peking. The Soviet, however, was unperturbed,

well knowing there is not a single honest and reasonable American who . . . supports [the] short-sighted Russian policy of Hughes. [The] Soviet has outlived many governments and will certainly without injury to itself outlive [the] present rulers of America.

The Washington Conference resolutions, he continued, were "nonexistent" in Russian eyes; and judged by the attitude of the powers toward China, they were equally unimportant to the states which had signed them.[14] Earlier in the month (June 12), *Izvestia* had jubilantly hailed the rapprochement with China, terming it a "fundamental blow" against the "imperialist designs of Japan and America" on China and signifying the end of "foreign military intervention in the Far East."

The dénouement of American-Soviet friction regarding the May agreement came a few months later when China turned the Russian Legation over to the Soviet representatives. The Diplomatic Corps at Peking, which had been holding the legation keys on behalf of the deceased Provisional Government, had no alternative but to restore them to Karakhan. This was thoroughly distressing to the United States, which bitterly resented Moscow's action in elevating its envoy to ambassadorial rank—thereby automatically making him Dean of the diplomatic body. Moreover, the acute discomfiture of the Coolidge Administration over China's recognition of the Bolshevik Government was an established fact. On August 18 the American mood was transmitted to the Soviet Union in a postscript to the note of the foreign diplomats at Peking that accompanied the legation keys to Karakhan. The tenor of this addendum was that American acquiescence in the joint note to the Russian Ambassador neither constituted nor implied recognition of the Soviet Government.

The redundant and impolitic nature of this communication invited a prompt Russian rejoinder. In a note to the Japanese Minister at Peking (in the latter's capacity of Dean), Soviet Ambassador

---

[14] *For. Rel., op. cit.*, pp. 502–503.

Karakhan berated Tokyo for accepting the "American commission at a time when Japan is herself engaged in negotiations . . . to restore normal relations" with Russia. Karakhan further chided both Japan and the United States by his sarcastic reference to the fact that

there does not exist in international law . . . a method of restoration of diplomatic . . . [relations] between two governments by way of returning to one of them a legation belonging to the latter government and situated in the capital of a third power by the other of those two governments, which, but accidentally and without the consent of the real owner, has in its [hands] the keys from the buildings of such a legation.[15]

But this was not all; diplomatic channels were too stereotyped to permit the full expression of Moscow's sentiments, and these were consigned to the Bolshevik Rosta News Agency, which issued a crackling statement on the idiosyncrasy of American diplomacy and the "hypocrisy and Christian bigotry" enveloping American policy toward China, all of which were contrasted with the "sincere and straightforward policy" of the Kremlin.

A month later, September 20, 1924, Russia signed an agreement with the Manchurian Government of General Chang Tso-lin, whereby the terms of the C.E.R. settlement of May 31 with China were reenacted. Although the Soviet Government gave as its reason for the conclusion of a separate treaty with Mukden that "the people of [the] provinces have the right to state they adhere to the Peking agreement . . . and that foreign interference in the railway will thus be eliminated," [16] and although the Russian Embassy announced that the Mukden agreement would be canceled whenever Manchuria was brought within the radius of Peking's effective control, American representatives in the Far East were inclined to a cynically pessimistic attitude. Thus Consul Hanson, at Harbin, cabled that the September convention

[15] *For. Rel., op. cit.*, pp. 454–455.
[16] Hanson to Hughes, September 30, 1924 (761.93/535); Bell to Hughes, October 15, 1924 (761.93/551).

amounts to the recognition of Manchuria as an independent state by the Soviet Government which, by appointing a vice Minister of communications and the local Soviet Consul General on the board of directors and a radical communist general manager, has commenced a suspected scheme to Sovietize Manchuria as they have done in outer Mongolia. Thus their work to undo the results of the Washington Conference as far as China is concerned has commenced.[17]

And the American chargé at Peking found in the treaty

the singular situation of the government which declares itself the best friend of China and most anxious to uphold its sovereignty taking advantage of a situation when the Central Government of China is weak to do something which is calculated to cause increased disintegration; whereas the imperialistic powers . . . maintain a strict neutrality in order that Chinese sovereignty may be maintained.

The Soviet rulers were placing "a premium upon the success of Chang Tso-lin," the message concluded, because his failure would precipitate the cancellation of the Mukden-Soviet agreement.[18]

Notwithstanding the questionable and esoteric motives of the Soviet Union in concluding the treaty with the Manchurian regime, the United States took no official steps either to protest or to register its complaint at the Russian move. Nevertheless, Soviet Far Eastern policy was the object of considerable speculation in Washington in the ensuing years.

Four months after the treaty with Chang Tso-lin, Moscow and Tokyo established diplomatic relations under the convention of January 1925. This action gave rise then and in later months to rumors concerning a potential Asiatic grouping, consisting of Russia, Japan, and China, directed against the Western powers. The credibility of this and similar hypotheses was vouched for by their appearance elsewhere than in Washington. A Danish newspaper, on January 22, 1925, printed an editorial on "The Great Game in the East," which stated in part:

[17] Hanson to Hughes, *op. cit.*; Hanson to Bell, October 2, 1921 (761.93/546).
[18] Bell to Hughes, *op. cit.*

Chicherin's best man, Karakhan . . . has by clever diplomacy and cash in hand succeeded in bringing about an agreement between the Soviets and China. Karakhan's second triumph—the Japanese Entente —seems to indicate a veritable concentration under Soviet leadership of the Asiatic peoples against the white world, viz., Europe and America.

This caused the American Minister at Copenhagen to note:

It will be interesting and important for us as Americans to observe how far the present Russo-Chinese-Japanese Entente will be successful in promoting the aims of the Soviets. That there is a menace to the entire West in such a combination seems self-evident.[19]

In July the Japanese Minister at Peking approached the American Legation with an informal bid for closer cooperation between his government and the United States and Great Britain. This was not intended to discredit the concept of a Sino-Soviet-Japanese block, but rather to utilize the possibility of such a combination to strengthen Japan's bargaining position with the West. As Chargé Mayer reported: "The Japanese must sooner or later decide whether to join an Asiatic block with China and the Soviet Union or to remain, so to speak, a Western power." This decision would hinge on the kind of understanding obtainable with respect to "cooperation" in China. And the chargé concluded his observations with the suggestion that "by aligning ourselves in such an association . . . it would be a move toward detaching Japan, at least for a time, from a pan-Asiatic alliance with the Soviet Union." [20]

But although a memorandum from the State Department in September called attention to the alleged Russian desire to use Japan and Germany "as pawns to check the activities of the Western Powers in China," the American Government resisted the temptation to turn the tables on Moscow through even so much as an informal understanding with the Japanese. The basic argument in support of this position had been cogently put by the American Minister to China in July 1925:

[19] Enclosure in and comment by J. D. Prince to Hughes, January 22, 1925 (761.93/556).

[20] *For. Rel.*, 1925, Vol. I, pp. 772–774.

In the present undeveloped stage of Chinese political thinking, hatred first of the British and secondly of the Japanese is the consuming passion. The United States is being eagerly watched to see whether it is pro-Chinese or whether it is pro-British or pro-Japanese. I think we can work honorably with the British and Japanese and yet not quixotically identify ourselves with them in such a way as to bring upon ourselves a share of the odium in which the Chinese hold them.[21]

In the broad concept of a Soviet-sponsored "co-prosperity sphere," a Moscow-Peking rapprochement and a Moscow-Tokyo accord were alternately sought between 1925 and 1928—both being distinguished by an anti-Western foundation. Moreover, the sharp recrudescence of civil war in China found Russia volubly associating itself with the forces of Chinese nationalism in their struggle to terminate China's bondage to the West. In December 1925 Josef Stalin told the annual Communist Party Congress:

Truth and justice are altogether on the side of the Chinese revolution. That is why we sympathize . . . in [the] . . . struggle for liberation of the Chinese people from the yoke of the imperialists . . .

Throughout these years the practiced infiltration of Moscow-inspired Communists into the ranks of the Kuomintang had proceeded apace. The Nationalist leaders, eager to widen the base of popular support by appealing to all dissident groups, had welcomed the Communists and, while Sun Yat-sen lived, had kept the Bolshevik element in a subservient role. But after Sun's death in March 1925 the amorphous Nationalist Party quickly coalesced into two separate wings. While both were committed to the freeing of their country from onerous foreign obligations, they clung to opposite poles in the policies they advocated as a means to this end.

In the period after the Washington Conference the United States had taken a sympathetic attitude toward the Chinese "evolutionists"—those who desired to achieve full sovereignty through the demonstration of Chinese political and legal maturity. On the other hand the Russian Government, created in chaos and dedicated to revolution, bent its energies to the strengthening of its Chinese

[21] *Ibid.,* pp. 786–787.

counterparts—those elements which sought, by anti-foreign riots and the outright repudiation of foreign debts and treaty commitments, to force China's equality on a resisting West and simultaneously to tighten Sino-Soviet bonds. Accordingly the Shanghai outbreaks in May and June 1925, directed against British policy, received the full support of the Moscow press, leading eventually to strained relations between Britain and Russia in Asia. The prestige of the Comintern and the success of its violent tactics in southern China caused Minister MacMurray to write that the "new spirit of Chinese nationalism" recognized "no obligations of friendship except with Russia"; that the United States was classed with England and Japan but for the attenuating fact that America was considered less aggressive and was therefore less feared. Cognizant that a Chinese government united under the aegis of the Communists would spell the permanent alienation of China from the West and the wholesale infraction of its foreign commitments, the American envoy cabled to Secretary Kellogg in late November 1926 that "some friendly words of warning" were imperative in the interests both of "China and ourselves."

There is no clear evidence that the United States deliberately sought to support the conservative wing of the Kuomintang as against the Communist-led left wing in 1926–1927. Nevertheless, the successful establishment of the Nationalist Government in Nanking in 1927 precipitated an ugly cleavage within the Party and the excommunication of the Communists, who withdrew to Kiangsi Province in Central China.

In part the rupture of relations between the two Chinese factions represented the Nationalist desire to rid China of all foreign limitations on its sovereignty, including those exacted by Russia; in part it was evoked by an overplaying of the Soviet hand in China. The net effect was that Russian influence began a toboggan slide from which it never fully recovered.

Already in the spring of 1926 Moscow had sensed the cooling political atmosphere and had adopted two measures to counteract it, neither of which was successful. In the first place the equivocal railroad agreement of two years previous had begun to produce friction between Chinese and Russian officials, and the Soviet

Government accordingly made one of its "strategic retreats, with the hope of being able to strike back later." The Kremlin was "apparently willing to sacrifice its material advantages in North Manchuria," Consul Hanson cabled, referring to a Soviet decision to yield on all Chinese demands regarding the railroad, "in order to gain some indefinite profit from the Chinese in the future." But as Hanson pointed out, the Russian action showed an ignorance of Chinese psychology, "for the weaker the Soviet Government shows itself the more the Chinese authorities will demand now and in the future." [22]

At the same time Russia sought to counteract its poorer relations with China by drawing closer to Japan. The initial effort occurred with the visit of Vice-Commissar of Railways Serebriakov to Tokyo in 1926, and was unsuccessful. The Soviet proposal amounted to a spheres of influence project which the Japanese rejected ostensibly for that reason. In essence Serebriakov suggested that in return for a Japanese pledge to construct no railroads north of the Chinese Eastern without Russian consent, Russia would respect a Japanese railroad monopoly south of the C.E.R. But despite solemn assurances to the American Ambassador that the Japanese intended to adhere to the principles established at the Washington Conference, rumors persisted throughout 1927 that Moscow and Tokyo were engaged in preliminaries tending toward an understanding in regard to Manchuria and Mongolia.[23] These were denied by Debuchi, Vice-Minister for Foreign Affairs, who told Ambassador MacVeigh that Japan "would not make any political agreement with Russia in reference to north or south Man-

[22] Hanson to Kellogg, April 16, 1926 (761.93/609).

[23] An informant told Hanson that at a meeting of the Japanese Privy Council, "It was decided to continue negotiations with Soviet Russia up to the point where something advantageous could be secured by Japan, and then use the results of these negotiations as a weapon to force the Chinese to comply with Japan's wishes. In regard to the proposals that Japan aid Soviet Russia to maintain the latter's rights on the Chinese Eastern Railroad it was decided to give the impression to the Soviet side that Japan was willing to render such aid, without taking any real steps in this direction. At the same time it was to be intimated to the Chinese officials that Japan had no objection to China's policy in regard to the Chinese Eastern Railroad." Hanson to Johnson, November 8, 1927 (793.94/1639).

churia." Yet on January 30, 1928, Consul Hanson forwarded the details of an alleged Russo-Japanese convention. Aside from supposed economic concessions granted to Tokyo in the Amur, Maritime, Trans-Baikal, and Ural areas of the Soviet, Baron Goto purportedly obtained from Moscow a pledge that the Chinese Eastern from Changchun to Laoshako on the Sungari River would be transferred to Japan for one hundred and fifty million yen. Half of the amount would be spent in Japan on orders for railroad equipment; the rest would be paid to Russia after the 1914 status quo in northern Manchuria was restored. The onus of establishing this condition was placed on the Soviet Government, for, according to the agreement, Japan would allow Russia to organize a revolutionary party in Manchuria (with the proviso that Communist propaganda would not spread to Korea).[24]

Few references to this alleged convention exist. The terms were never publicly verified by either party; and, if the agreement was *bona fide*, it was obviously half-hearted on both sides. In the light of their later relations, there were perhaps no more than two "attitudes" that could conceivably have been traced to the 1928 discussions: the Japanese reaction during the Sino-Soviet dispute of 1929, and Soviet willingness to sell the C.E.R. to Japan in 1935.

The only other Russo-Japanese treaty in these years was public and essentially nonpolitical. In 1928 the two nations concluded a basic fisheries convention which was periodically extended after its eight-year term had expired. But neither fisheries nor territorial agreements with Japan atoned in any real sense for the rapid falling-off of Sino-Soviet friendship.

Throughout the latter part of 1926 while relations between Moscow and Peking underwent consistent deterioration, the American Government adhered formally to a strict neutrality. Notwithstanding the efforts of Chinese officials to ascertain "the view we would take . . . if the Chinese Foreign Office gave Karakhan his passport," MacMurray informed Peking:

It must not be assumed from the fact that my Government had no official relations with the regime of the Soviets that we were hostile to

[24] Same to same, January 30, 1928 (761.94/387).

Russia. We are merely aloof . . . If [Karakhan's] . . . functions as [Dean of the Diplomatic Corps] . . . were to be terminated by the Chinese, the question for us would be equally determined by that act. His status is a matter wholly between the Chinese and the Russians. We are completely unconcerned, even though we may deplore the fact that an attitude of active hostility has been taken openly by the Soviet representative in regard to what we deem our just rights in China.[25]

This point of view was confirmed by Washington on August 19, when Acting Secretary Harrison wired the American Minister that the "question of the Soviet Ambassador's status concerns only China and the Soviet Government," and "No doubt as to this fact should be left in the minds of the Chinese." Nevertheless, Washington's aversion to Communist tactics and philosophy, and its innate sympathy with the more conservative Chinese factions, were plain to the Chinese and certainly afforded no deterrent to China's anti-Soviet policy.

In April 1927 Chinese authorities raided private Russian properties and the compound of the former Russian Legation with results which convinced the government that the Bolsheviks were conducting extensive subversive activities. On May 10 MacMurray cabled that the evidence gathered amply proved that Moscow had consistently incited "the Kuomintang to anti-foreign violence." In the meantime, on April 17 the Soviet Embassy at Peking was closed—a sharp defeat for the Communists. Russian interference in internal domestic politics purportedly continued throughout the remainder of the year, culminating in an abortive Communist uprising at Canton on December 11. This precipitated the severing of diplomatic relations with the Soviets by the government of the Nationalist regime, three days later.

Seen in perspective, Russian diplomacy in the Far East between 1920 and 1928 was its own worst enemy. Reflecting, perhaps, the uncertainty of the domestic political scene prior to the consolidation of the Stalinist forces, it was marked by a superficial erraticism and fluctuation which was almost its undoing. Moscow had suc-

[25] August 18, 1926. *For. Rel.*, 1926, Vol. I, p. 1098.

ceeded, as a result of sedulous efforts, in exchanging diplomatic representatives with both Japan and China by 1925; but in many respects this indication of a mutual desire for harmonious relations was in effect the high-water mark of friendly accord. In the case of Japan, relations moved in an uninspired rut, never sincerely cordial, gradually backsliding. In the instance of China, diplomatic contact and ideological prestige were unabashedly exploited for political gain. Surprisingly, the nascent Chinese Nationalist Government struck back, at first hesitantly, then more firmly, and finally boisterously—with consequences of unexpected and potentially grave import.

CHAPTER XI

America and the Sino-Soviet Dispute

In contrast to the abrupt dismissal of Soviet envoys by the Chinese Government in the closing days of 1927, relations between the Manchurian regime of General Chang Tsolin and Moscow were for some months unspectacular. Although harmony was noticeably absent, the Chinese Marshal could ill afford to arouse active Russian displeasure. Not only did the Chinese Eastern Railroad traverse Manchuria, thus giving the Kremlin a legal interest in that territory, but the extensive frontier between Siberia and the Three Eastern Provinces was inadequately garrisoned. At the same time, the exigent relations of Moscow and Peking ultimately had a strong reaction in Manchuria. The realization by Marshal Chang of the strategic and vulnerable position of his country, Soviet-Manchurian friction in the operation of the C.E.R., and the unfortunate excesses of Communist propaganda, at length converted the Mukden Government to a tentative (and, as events proved, a precarious) cooperation with the newly established Nanking regime of Chiang Kai-shek. This drawing together of Chinese forces accentuated Chinese nationalism and in turn augmented the resistance, both of Mukden and of Nanking, to alleged Russian efforts to dominate the Chinese Eastern. Given these circumstances, open conflict was only a matter of time.

On May 27, 1929, the Soviet consulate at Harbin, which had not been affected by the closing of Russian consulates in China proper, was raided by Chinese representatives; six weeks later (July 10) the C.E.R. was seized. These two events marked the formal inception of the Sino-Soviet dispute. While so localized that it never attained the international importance of a Balkan conflict, the Russo-Chinese dispute possessed a unique significance because of its bearing on American policy in the Far East and, specifically, on American-Soviet relations.

Apportionment of responsibility for provoking the conflict and appraisal of internal Chinese motives have never revealed unanimity of opinion by students of the crisis; there was, however, no question that the 1924 agreement on the Chinese Eastern Railroad invited confusion in its implementation, that numerically the Chinese were impotent to limit the activities of the Russian general manager, and that the Chinese were eager to assume more positive control of the line as a means of asserting their claim over Manchuria (as against both Russia and Japan). There was equally no question that in arbitrarily seizing the railroad, regardless of cause, the Chinese had unilaterally violated a treaty with another sovereign state.

The Chinese action had been anticipated the preceding January, when the local authorities at Harbin had forcibly taken over the city's telephone system which had been managed by the C.E.R. The subsequent raid on Russia's Harbin consulate in May was allegedly conducted to break up a Communist meeting and to expose subversive Soviet activities, but the general consensus of opinion indicated that "the real issue" was control of the railroad. Russia's "inexhaustible patience" with respect to the earlier repressive measures of Mukden and the Nationalist Government was momentarily waived when Acting Foreign Commissar Karakhan assailed the illegality of the Harbin act; but the Russian protest was ineffectual and on July 10 and 11 Chinese officials consummated their anti-Soviet program with the seizure of the Harbin telegraph system, the arrest of a dozen Communists connected with the railroad, and the dismissal of the Soviet general manager, assistant manager, and all the Russian heads of departments.

The Chinese coup could not have been better calculated to alienate Western sympathy had it been conceived with no other end in view. If, as the Russian author Yakhontoff suggests, the Nationalist and Mukden leaders anticipated approval, or at least the indulgent tolerance of the powers in the move against the unpopular Soviet regime, their perspective on international politics was strangely out of focus. Stalin's "logic of things" was "stronger than any other logic" in 1929 as it had been a decade before: specifically, Washington could and would protect the Soviet Union, in spite of its aversion to the Soviet philosophy and government, whenever the force which threatened Russia was feared by the State Department more than it feared Russian Communism. This had been implied in the period of Siberian intervention; it was now to be attested in the Sino-Soviet dispute of 1929.

The policy of the American Government toward the dispute was determined by two main factors, neither of which had more than an indirect relationship to Russia. In the first place the Chinese violation of the 1924 agreement represented the forcible infringement of treaty obligations, which Washington and the Western states had consistently opposed in their sponsorship of the Chinese "evolutionists." Paradoxically, the tactics of the Harbin authorities against Moscow were precisely those which Russia had fostered in its propagandist support of the radical elements throughout China. Consequently the quixotic situation developed in which the United States and Europe found themselves protecting the Soviet Government against the revolutionary Chinese actions which Moscow had done so much to encourage. Moreover, in 1929 Russia was again an imperial power notwithstanding its Communist professions, and accordingly the Chinese challenge to legal Russian interests on Chinese territory was viewed by Washington as symbolic of Nanking's desire to throw off every treaty fetter imposed by the West. The prospect was disquieting. If successful, Nanking might seek through strong-arm tactics to liquidate all foreign interests in China —a contingency specifically brought home to Washington in a cable from MacMurray pointing to the connection between Nanking's seizure of the railroad and American extraterritorial rights in China. Thus the United States was deeply self-interested in the outcome of the Sino-Soviet conflict.

The second factor which shaped American policy was the potential effect of the dispute on the Kellogg-Briand Peace Pact, signed the year before with the adherence of both the Soviet Government and China. Notwithstanding the fatal weakness of the Pact, which outlawed war but contained no means of enforcing its provisions except moral suasion, the State Department had assumed a leading role in negotiating the agreement; and in the late 1920's the post-Locarno glow of international good will blinded men and nations alike to the shallow foundation of peace. As a result Secretary Stimson was understandably perturbed over a situation which threatened to nullify the Paris accord almost at its inception, and his recurrent efforts to provide a solution to the crisis were launched officially on behalf of the Kellogg Pact.

On the basis of its Asiatic interests and its commitments to world peace, therefore, the United States felt directly involved in the outcome of the conflict. Moreover, by a perverse irony America was compelled to favor the Soviet side of the argument. Both because Moscow lacked diplomatic representation at Washington, and because the latter's cold attitude toward recognition was undisguised, the Kremlin had no way of knowing or appreciating the American espousal of Soviet rights in the dispute; conversely, Moscow had been for so long the recipient of American barbs that it automatically interpreted Washington's interference as anti-Russian and accordingly unwarranted. This in turn led the Soviet authorities to cast undiplomatic obloquies at the State Department, thus widening the gulf between the two countries.

The United States made three separate attempts to effect a settlement of the Russo-Chinese dispute, the superficial results of which were nil. On the basis of the relative strength of the two contenders and their respective preparedness for war, it has become fairly evident that both states wished to avoid formal hostilities; however, high political tension has frequently overcome the saner judgments of statesmen, and such tension existed at various points in the Sino-Soviet conflict. Therefore the spotlight of world attention which Washington focused on the Siberian-Manchurian border and the pressure it brought to bear on Nanking and Mukden inevitably exerted a moderating, if not a conceivably decisive, influence in the bilateral negotiations of the opposing powers.

Within a few days of the Chinese seizure of the railroad the Soviet Government dispatched a memorandum to the Nanking chargé d'affaires at Moscow, the substance of which accused China of treaty violations in the face of repeated Russian offers to negotiate points of difference in the interpretation of the 1924 agreements. Despite the Soviet conviction that the Nationalist Government regarded a willingness to confer as a sign of weakness, the Kremlin reiterated its suggestion of arbitration, but on the basis of a prior revocation of the unilateral Chinese acts of the preceding months. If, after three days, an unsatisfactory answer were received from Nanking, Russia gave warning that it would "be obliged to resort to other means of defense of the lawful rights of the U.S.S.R."

The Chinese response on July 16 utterly ignored the Soviet *quid pro quo*, stressing instead China's willingness to discuss the problems at issue if Moscow in its turn would "respect the law and sovereignty of China and refrain from making any proposals contrary to the facts of the case." The tenor of this note was regarded by the Kremlin as "unsatisfactory in content and hypocritic in tone"; consequently the Soviet Government declared that the means of settling the dispute amicably had been exhausted and therefore all communications and political contact between the two countries would be terminated, although Russia reserved its rights arising from the 1924 treaty.

Washington's initial reaction to news of the Far Eastern conflict had been one of aloofness, but the growing seriousness of the situation was soon a matter of concern to the State Department. While Moscow and Nanking were exchanging their first bitterly obstinate notes, Secretary Stimson prepared to employ the diplomatic means at his disposal to ward off what then appeared to be an imminent clash between Soviet and Chinese forces. On July 18 he conferred individually with the British, Japanese, and French ambassadors and stressed the grave responsibility imposed by the conflict on the Kellogg-Briand signatories. In a conversation with C. C. Wu on the same day, Stimson spared few words in impressing the Chinese Minister with the American conviction of his government's guilt. Moreover, from the information at hand the Secretary of State believed that the dispute was of an "eminently justiciable nature" and "peculiarly fitted for arbitration." Despite Wu's rationalization of the Chinese behavior, Stimson insisted that China had acted too hastily, and, regardless of motives, the neutral world considered Nanking guilty of an attack on a sovereign power. But in response to a Chinese query, the Secretary stated that American good offices could not be offered except at the request of both parties and that he "did not believe Russia would make such a request."

Thus this first effort of the United States to hasten a solution of the conflict was characterized by a unilateral, rather than an international approach, by undisguised pressure on China, by reference to the obligations of both disputants under the Kellogg provisions, and by an unwillingness to tender good offices unless approached by Russia and China alike—a remote contingency.

The American suggestion that the major powers approach Moscow and Nanking in the sense in which Stimson had discussed the crisis with C. C. Wu was immediately approved by Britain and France. In contrast, Japan dissociated itself from the Stimson policy, superficially because of resentment that Washington had not officially consulted Tokyo regarding the substance of its remarks to the Chinese Minister. However, the Japanese were too acutely interested in every problem concerning Manchuria to ignore the Russo-Chinese dispute; and at approximately the same time that Stimson was conferring with Wu, Baron Shidehara addressed himself to the "placation of China and Russia." [1] This wholly independent and separate Japanese attitude was maintained in the following weeks and gave rise to various conjectures seeking to account for Tokyo's refusal to cooperate with the other interested powers. Although the likelihood of a secret Russo-Japanese understanding was discounted later by Ambassador Castle, State Department officials were uncertain as to its credibility, especially as it provided a conceivable explanation for Japan's aloofness from the international protests which were later so strongly resented at Moscow. At any rate, throughout the dispute the sympathies of the Japanese people were "entirely with the Soviets," either by reason of prior agreement or, as in the case of the Western states, because of the threat to foreign interests implicit in the Chinese coup. So far as Japan explained the isolation of its policy from that of the other powers, it expressed a conviction that no danger of war existed

[1] Neville (chargé at Tokyo) to Stimson, July 26, 1929 (861.77C.E./210). "By computing the difference in time between Tokyo and Washington and adding the time necessarily occupied for the transmission and translation of messages, the explanation that Baron Shidehara acted without any knowledge of the conversations at Washington does not deserve to be doubted."

from the Sino-Soviet clash, and therefore no necessity for interference by the Kellogg-Briand signatories.

The first response of Nanking and Moscow to the overtures of the
Western states indicated the willingness of each to abide by the
stipulations of the Paris agreement provided no warlike act were
committed by the other. "Our signature of the Kellogg pact was
not just a diplomatic gesture," stated Jan Radzutsk, Commissar
of Railroads and acting head of the government.

We know the masses demand drastic action. We know our strength
and the Chinese weaknesses, but our pacific pronouncements are not
just words . . . When we talk of peace we mean peace, and when we
condemned the imperialist policy of foreign powers defending their
interests in China by force we were sincere. No other country ever received such provocation as we have received from the Chinese. But we
shall not fight unless our country is invaded.[2]

On the Chinese side, a government manifesto declared that
China would "devote itself to peace" and respect the Anti-War
treaty "to the utmost of her ability and consonant with the right of
self-protection." But it was noted:

The right of self-defense is an undeniable right, and should the Soviet Government flagrantly violate it, the responsibility for the breach
of peace must rest entirely upon the Soviet Union and not upon China.[3]

The lip service rendered to the treaty to outlaw war on July 24
when it came into effect undoubtedly resulted in part from the international publicity directed at the disputants at the behest of Stimson. This was especially true in the case of the Chinese, who had lost
some of their original enthusiasm, following the stern and unfriendly
reaction of the powers to their *coup*. On July 25 MacMurray reported that Nanking was prepared to return to the *status quo ante*
with respect to the railroad if an effectual guarantee could be provided against the recurrence of Soviet propaganda.

[2] July 19. Reported by Walter Duranty in *The New York Times*, July 20,
1929, p. 1:7.
[3] *For. Rel.*, 1929, Vol. II, pp. 228–231. (Message received in Washington
July 23.)

The influence of the American move on Moscow was less easily evaluated because of the force of domestic conditions in determining Soviet policy. Russia was absorbed in the problems and requirements of the Five Year Plan, and its leaders were loath to curtail their efforts by involvement in a struggle in Asia or elsewhere.[4] At the same time, notwithstanding international pressure or the desire to avoid military action, the Soviet made the acceptance of its conditions precedent to any negotiations with China regarding the dispute. Thus Karakhan informed the French Ambassador that M. Briand's proposal that Russia and China mediate their quarrel was "without point in view of the refusal of the Chinese authorities to restore the legal bases" which constituted the "necessary prerequisite for an agreement," by fulfilling the three-point ultimatum contained in the Soviet note of July 13.

The theoretical willingness of both parties to confer on the problems involved, but their apparent inability to agree on preliminary conditions before meeting in conference, convinced Secretary Stimson that the deadlock could be broken only by further international action, and this resulted in his second attempt to solve the dispute, on July 25. Expressly disclaiming mediation "by any nation or group of nations" because such a course "might excite unfounded suspicion," the Secretary of State suggested that Russia and China, "in the exercise of their own sovereign action," create conciliation machinery through which "a full and impartial investigation of the facts" could be undertaken. Moreover, pending such an investigation Stimson proposed that the two powers "agree to commit no act of hostility," continue the regular operation of the Chinese Eastern, appoint a neutral as president and general manager, and restore the former Russian and Chinese directors in accordance with the 1924 agreement. The further terms of the C.E.R. treaty should likewise be respected—namely, neither party should permit in its respective territory the organization of groups and the use of propaganda directed against the other.

[4] At a session of the Communist Party's Central Committee on July 17 "Smirnov expressed a hope for peace, because the grain-stocking campaign would be upset and the internal situation complicated by war. Smidovitch and Brukhanov also spoke similarly . . ." Coleman to Stimson, July 25, 1929, *ibid.*, p. 240.

The second Stimson plan, representing international consultation of a much more advanced character than the first, never evolved beyond the embryonic blueprint stage at which the Secretary confided it, in deepest secrecy, to the British, French, Italian, Japanese, and German governments. Its premature death was attributable to three causes: the inhospitable reception accorded it by Japan and the uncertainty of Britain and Germany and, to a degree, France, regarding the plan; the violent resentment of Soviet Russia to the American "imperialist plot"; and the wish of Nanking and Moscow alike to reach a settlement by direct negotiations, without the suggestions or interference of a third power.

It was this last reason which provided the ostensible basis for Tokyo's objection to the proposal, although in the light of the traditional American-Japanese rivalry for position in Manchuria it perhaps could not have been expected that the latter would openly embrace the Stimson project. An interesting sidelight was cast on the impotence of the Kellogg Pact, in the Japanese reply on July 30:

Should the plan . . . be rejected by either or both of the contending parties, the Powers will find themselves in a peculiarly embarrassing position. It is presumed that none of the Powers have any intention of exercising material and effective pressure upon the unwilling parties to force acceptance of the plan.[5]

The preference of Russia and China for a bilateral settlement also provided Britain and Germany with cause for their veto of the American conciliation scheme. Out of loyalty to their common sponsorship of the Paris Pact the French Government couched its reply to Washington in generally approving terms, but counseled delay in launching the plan until Moscow and Nanking should fail to reach an accord "by direct communication between themselves."

Although the Soviet Government had never been notified of Secretary Stimson's project, Moscow was "fairly accurately" informed of its content; and on August 6 *Izvestia* lashed out at the proposal, accusing the United States of leading the "imperialist powers" in a "direct intervention . . . for the purpose of taking

[5] Memorandum by the Secretary of State of a Conversation with the Japanese Ambassador, July 30, 1929, *ibid.*, pp. 259–260.

the Chinese Eastern Railroad into their own hands . . ." According to the Counselor of the Soviet Embassy in Berlin, the American plan "seemed to reflect a desire to effect American control of the railway." [6] Suspicious for over a decade of Washington's attitude toward the C.E.R., and mindful of earlier American attempts to continue and amend the 1919 Inter-Allied agreement for the operation and control of the line, it was not surprising that Moscow saw in this latest covert project a new attempt at internationalization under the neutral chairmanship of an American national.

Soviet distrust of American motives in particular and of international interference in general accounted for Karakhan's remark to the Japanese Ambassador on July 30 that "there was no need for intervention or mediation by a third power." So far as China was concerned, the Minister of Railroads acknowledged to MacMurray that his government preferred direct discussions with Russia to the good offices of a foreign power; and during the last days of July, Washington was informed that the Chinese representatives in Berlin were trying to arrange for negotiations with Moscow through the medium of the German Government.

Notwithstanding the preference of all the powers, including the Soviet Union and China, for a settlement exclusive of foreign cooperation, Moscow and Nanking were seemingly unable to find common ground even for exploratory conversations, and in the course of the next three months the situation on the Siberian-Manchurian frontier rapidly worsened. A proposal by the Young Marshal (Chang Hsueh-liang, son of Chang Tso-lin) on July 22, while conceding certain of the Soviet demands, was sufficiently mangled in a further exchange between Mukden and Moscow to be unsatisfactory to the latter. At the same time reports reaching Nanking stated that the Soviet Union was reluctant to deal with China, as no relations existed with the Nationalist Government, and that Russia expected to play Mukden and Nanking against each other to its own advantage.

On August 19 the State Department sought again to bring pres-

[6] Report of an interview of Louis Fischer with Brodovsky. Schurman to Stimson, August 10, 1929 (861.01/1502).

sure on the Chinese Government. Assistant Secretary Johnson, in a conference with the Chinese Minister, noted that the Soviets "were prepared to send new appointees to take the place of those" China had dismissed; if this were true, which the Chinese diplomat averred, he (Johnson) could not see why Nanking was dissatisfied. But he was unable to convert the Minister to his point of view. The latter stated in rebuttal that to accept the Soviet condition "would be to admit" China's error, which Wu was not prepared to do. Whether or not this was "overstating the case," as the American official declared, the Chinese Minister was immovable.

By mid-August the first reports of actual armed clashes between Russian and Chinese troops were received. On the 19th the Soviet Foreign Commissariat announced that Red Army border crossings were in retaliation for previous raids on Soviet territory by White Russians and Chinese detachments. The precarious and inflammatory situation precipitated by military conflict, and the great difficulty of assessing correctly the charges of each side, naturally augmented the anxiety felt in Washington. By August 26 Stimson was apprehensive lest the Soviet Government was preparing for "the eventuality of war," and accordingly he sounded out the British Ambassador with a view to further consideration of the problem by the Kellogg-Briand powers. The two statesmen agreed that the original guilt in the dispute had been China's, that China had also been amiss in refusing to "make amends and [in not] restoring the status quo," but that neither of these acts "would justify an act of war upon China," particularly because she had agreed (in the Kellogg Pact) "to settle such controversies only by pacific means." The naïveté of this assertion led Sir Esme Howard to venture the biased suggestion:

If Russia should go to war and invade Manchuria, particularly if China could be persuaded to offer to restore the status quo, Russia would be so clearly in the wrong that it would probably be easy to eventually rally public opinion of the other nations of the world to put an embargo on trade with her and thus check her military operations.[7]

[7] *For. Rel., op. cit.*, pp. 296–297.

The British Government, however, had little sympathy with Stimson's desire to "do something"; the only action which should be contemplated was of a sort both disputants were amenable to and which would be "incapable of interpretation as in any sense prejudging the issue." This neatly excluded all action, but the British Foreign Minister was not inclined to despair. Neither Russia nor China wished or was prepared for war, he asserted; therefore pacific settlement of the dispute was a fairly computable certainty (a revealing commentary on the efficacy of the Paris Pact!).

The American Government did not share the optimism of Downing Street, however; and the continued news of armed attacks in the Soviet-Manchurian border area, combined with the failure of renewed attempts by Moscow and Nanking to effect a preliminary *modus vivendi*, persuaded the State Department to repeat its pressure on China. Between August 27 and September 10 the contending powers had exchanged proposals for discussion, marked by Soviet moderation and Chinese evasiveness, and consequently on September 17 Assistant Secretary Johnson openly accused Nanking of sabotaging a settlement. Pointing out that negotiations were collapsing because China had refused to accept the appointment of a new Russian manager and assistant manager prior to a conference, Johnson emphasized that the Soviet request was compatible with the 1924 agreement. Unwillingness to accept the Russian appointees indicated that the Chinese "were not quite reasonable in their attitude and that this attitude created a bad impression" in the United States. Moreover, the Assistant Secretary inferred that Nanking's illegal seizure of the road and infraction of the Sino-Soviet treaty gave the Russians no alternative to the use of force to recover their position. The world "could hardly hold China guiltless if matters should go on to a situation where there would be open conflict."

Even as these remarks were being addressed to the Chinese chargé, the Soviet Government rejected China's truncated proposal of September 10, and in so doing pointed out that "the responsibility for further development of the conflict devolves fully upon the Nanking Government."

A few weeks later Germany took a hand in the negotiations by suggesting that each party should immediately liberate all persons held by the other in connection with the C.E.R. affair. The refusal of Moscow to accept the proposal furnished the Chinese Government with an excellent pretext for a manifesto to the Kellogg-Briand powers at the end of October. In essence the Nanking declaration was an attempt to absolve China of all its sins regarding the dispute; Russia's refusal to exchange prisoners was characteristic of the Kremlin's unwillingness to reach an amicable accord; Russian "acts of aggression" on Chinese territory were unmatched by any Chinese attacks on Siberian soil; consequently, "if a state of war should eventuate from the Soviet Government's incessant provocation, the responsibility . . . must be borne" by Moscow.

These words and the obstinate bravado of Nanking were hardly compatible with China's internal powers of resistance, however; and the continued diplomatic impasse created by its rejection of the preliminary Soviet terms redounded to Nanking's own disadvantage. The core of the difficulty lay in domestic Chinese politics, where the recurrent struggle for supreme political control between Marshal Chang in Manchuria and General Chiang in China made a united front impossible. This inevitably advanced the Soviet position, for the longer the Chinese stalled the more confused the internal political crisis became, and the greater was Russia's opportunity to play off the two Chinese governments, thereby decreasing the staying power of each. Consequently, the unreasonable conditions which Nanking had attached to negotiations in September boomeranged during the ensuing weeks; but in October the apologetic eagerness of Marshal Chang to meet the Soviet requirements of July 13 elicited only silence from Moscow.

Nor did the gravity of the Chinese predicament evoke sympathy from the United States. In response to a Chinese query on November 21 as to whether Washington was "going to do anything" about conditions in eastern Asia, Stimson stated frankly that "he thought the United States had done everything it could do in the matter"; that "the Chinese were in their present predicament because they had acted very unwisely" in rejecting the Russian-proposed settlement.

But the American reprimand afforded neither solace nor relief to the hard-pressed government of China; and failing to obtain any solution to their dilemma from the State Department, the Nanking authorities seriously considered an appeal to the League of Nations.[8] On November 26 a general statement was sent to Geneva as well as to the individual signatories of the Pact of Paris, urging that steps be taken to stop the Soviets and to punish them for violation of Chinese territory. On the same day, however, Chinese diplomats ascertained that the major powers were not favorable to a formal appeal to the League, mainly because neither the Soviet Union nor the United States was a member.

Meantime press reports indicated that the Japanese were exerting their influence to effect a settlement of the dispute. Allegedly informal conversations were being conducted by the Soviet Ambassador and the Chinese Minister at Tokyo under the auspices of Japan. The latter's interests in Manchuria, it was conjectured, militated against exclusive Chinese control of the Chinese Eastern for both political and economic reasons. Therefore, it was surmised, Tokyo would seek to resolve the dispute by restoring the equivalent of the *status quo ante*. As a result, the opportunity might soon present itself for Japan "to play the role of mediator under very favorable circumstances"—as the protector of "Manchuria from Russia" for a second time and as the "champion of the vested interests of the Soviets." [9]

This telegram had scarcely reached Washington when Secretary Stimson sent for the Japanese Ambassador and informed him that it might be necessary for the American Government to issue "a public statement, calling the attention of the Chinese and Russians to their obligations under the Pact." The alacrity with which the State Department seized the initiative, coming so shortly after the purely negative remarks made to China a week before, and following so quickly the news of Japanese endeavors to facilitate a Sino-Soviet settlement, suggested strongly that American interest in the dispute was motivated not solely by an abstract concern for peace, but at least partially by a desire to forestall the Japanese efforts and,

[8] The possibility of such an appeal had been suggested as early as the preceding August. MacMurray to Stimson, August 7, 1929 (861.77C.E./182).
[9] Myers to MacMurray, November 20, 1929 (861.77C.E./687).

by the same token, to corner whatever prestige might accrue from a solution of the controversy. At any rate, on November 26 the American Government addressed a circular note to the Kellogg Pact signatories. After a reminder that Russia and China were both adherents to the Pact and that hostilities between them approximated "a condition of actual warfare," the communication inquired whether the various powers would join Washington in individual public statements, to bring pressure on Nanking and Moscow to expedite the pacific settlement of their conflict.

With the exception of Japan, all the powers consulted signified their general approval of the Stimson plan, although Germany, Italy, and Britain expressed preference for a joint note over separate statements. Tokyo's abstention was based on its rejection of the American proposal of the preceding July. The Foreign Minister told the American chargé on November 27 that "he doubted the practical benefit which would ensue" from Stimson's plan; furthermore, "the Russians regardless of the facts in the case would regard any such public statement as instigated by the Chinese." And two days later he added that "nothing could be accomplished by outside pressure" in view of the information just received that the Chinese Government had empowered Marshal Chang to negotiate with Russia on the basis of the original Soviet demands.

On the same day Ambassador Schurman, in Berlin, telegraphed a copy of a Chinese note to Russia, dated November 14. In substance the communication proposed "the formation of a mixed commission in order to investigate and to establish the responsibility for the serious" Sino-Soviet situation. The note also advocated the withdrawal of the armed forces of both countries from the frontier and stated that if these conditions were acceptable to Moscow, the National Government, "as a signatory of the Pact of Paris," would be prepared "to submit the entire dispute to a neutral, impartial resort for adjustment."

In the meantime, on November 28, the Soviet Government, finding Marshal Chang amenable to its conditions of July 13, notified Mukden that as soon as the Russian Manager and Assistant Manager of the C.E.R. were reinstated, a Soviet agent (Mr. Simanovsky) would confer at Khabarovsk with an accredited Chinese representative as to technical questions and the time and place for the projected Sino-Soviet conference.

Before the news of these exchanges had reached Washington the corresponding wheels of American diplomacy were already turning, and on November 30 Secretary Stimson launched his third attempt at a solution of the Sino-Soviet dispute. On that date telegrams were dispatched to France, Germany, Great Britain, Italy, and Japan which, reminiscent of an old American practice, ignored fine points of qualification and distinction by lumping together the replies of the powers to Washington's circular note of November 26. "Having received replies from all the Governments addressed, and finding [them] in general favorable in principle [*sic!*] to [the American] proposal," Stimson declared his intention of sending a note direct to the Chinese Government and, by way of France, to the Soviet Union. This communication expressed American concern over the Manchurian crisis, recalled the initial American effort to draw Sino-Soviet attention to the obligations of the Kellogg-Briand Pact signatories, refreshed the memories of the two powers regarding the relevant clauses of the treaty, and voiced the hope that they would "refrain or desist from measures of hostility" and find a peaceful solution to their conflict. The American Government felt, the note concluded, "that the respect with which China and Russia will hereafter be held in the good opinion of the world will necessarily in great measure depend upon the way in which they carry out these most sacred promises." [10]

Under instructions from Washington this note was not to be published until December 2, but at the later behest of the French Government, which desired that the statements of France and America be released simultaneously, the date of publication was delayed twenty-four hours. Before that time arrived the State Department had received information that preliminary discussions looking toward a Sino-Soviet conference were under way between Moscow, Mukden, and Nanking. Notwithstanding these reports, however, no effort was made to postpone or recall the official Ameri-

[10] *For. Rel., op. cit.*, pp. 366–368.

can statement. Meanwhile every nation which had adhered to the Pact of Paris was informed of the American note and urged to follow Washington's precedent in addressing itself to the Russian and Chinese governments. If the Manchurian dispute were ignored (the American Government declared) by any of the adherents to the Kellogg-Briand agreement, the force of public opinion, which was its only sanction, could not but be impaired.

The response of the major powers to the Stimson declaration was divided. France, as co-author of the Kellogg-Briand Pact, copied the American text verbatim in its appeal to China and Russia. The British note, though not identical, was substantially similar, as was the Italian. Germany and Japan refrained from issuing statements. Germany was already a channel for communications between the disputing parties and felt that it would be highly undiplomatic simultaneously to fall in with the American scheme. Moreover, Berlin possessed information confirming the fact that direct negotiations between Russia and China had been initiated. Knowledge of this likewise provided the main reason for Tokyo's abstention from the Stimson démarche. The attitude of most of the lesser states was favorable; so that in the early days of December by far the great majority of the Kellogg Pact signatories appealed to the Soviet Union and China.

The response of Moscow and Nanking to the public pressure thus applied was a study in contrasts. China was conciliatory, dulcet, and politely firm in pledging itself to maintain the Anti-War Treaty and in justifying its behavior throughout the dispute. The Soviet Union, congenitally suspicious of the alien and capitalistic West, ignorant of the efforts expended on its behalf by Washington in conversations with the Chinese Minister throughout the autumn of 1929, and instinctively convinced that international interference could not, by definition, be disinterested, couched its reply in language appropriate to its mood. The seizure of the Chinese Eastern marked the culmination, according to Moscow, of a "policy of provocation" which had characterized Nanking's relations with Russia through the preceding few years. Such conduct, if directed against America, Britain, or France, would have been regarded as "sufficient pretext for invoking the reservations made

when signing the Treaty of Paris for the Renunciation of War." [11]
But the Soviet Government, for its part, had chosen not to recognize these reservations and "had no intention of invoking them."
The fact that Washington had forwarded its statement at a time
when Russia and China were negotiating a settlement could "not
fail to be considered as a pressure, which nothing justifies, on the
pourparlers, and consequently" it could in "no way be considered
as a friendly act." Moreover, the Kellogg-Briand Pact contained
no means for its own implementation, and Russia had never agreed
that the signatories should "arrogate to themselves" the right of
enforcement. The Sino-Soviet dispute could, therefore, be settled
only by the parties involved. In concluding its statement, Moscow
could not resist an extraneous jibe at the United States:

The Government of the Union cannot fail to express its astonishment
that the Government of the United States, which, by its own will, does
not entertain any official relations with the . . . Soviet Union, should
find it possible to address to the latter advice and recommendations.[12]

The full expression of Russia's resentment could not be confined
to a formal diplomatic rejoinder, however uninhibited this might
be. Accordingly the Moscow press was given free rein in an attempt

[11] The "reservations" referred to were, in the first instance, those made by
the British Government in Paragraph 10 of its note of May 19, 1928, to the
effect that "there are certain regions of the world the welfare and integrity of
which constitute the special and vital interest for our peace and safety. His
Majesty's Government have been at pains to make it clear in the past that
interference with these regions cannot be suffered. Their protection against attack is to the British Empire a measure of self-defense. It must be clearly
understood that His Majesty's Government . . . accept the new treaty upon
the distinct understanding that it does not prejudice their freedom of action
in this respect . . ." In the Soviet note to France (August 31, 1928) anticipating Russian adherence to the Kellogg-Briand Pact, Foreign Minister Litvinov
had called attention to this British reservation, had labeled it "an attempt to
use the Pact itself as an instrument of imperialistic policy," and had declared
that the reservation could "not be considered as binding on the Soviet Government . . ." Russia likewise scored other restrictions mentioned in the diplomatic correspondence of the principals prior to the conclusion of the Pact, and
asserted that it would not be bound by them. See *For. Rel.*, 1928, Vol. I,
p. 68 (for the British reservation of May 19) and pp. 174–175 (for the Soviet
note of August 31).

[12] December 3, 1929, *For. Rel.*, 1929, Vol. II, pp. 404–406.

to discredit American motives absolutely. Even before the Stimson statement had been dispatched the "confidential" and "secret" Washington circular of November 26 had found its way into the Japanese press, and on November 29 *Izvestia* noted that the United States was endeavoring to gain Japanese acquiescence to "a joint action by five powers in connection with the Soviet-Chinese conflict." This prompted the following editorial:

The activities of the forces hostile to the U.S.S.R. will be carried as far as possible. Undoubtedly pressure will be exercised on Mukden to induce it once more to withdraw its proposals. The imperialistic press continues to allude to the possibility of a collective appeal of the Powers to the U.S.S.R. and China enjoining them to make peace. This action would of course have for its aim the support and consolidation of the position of the Chinese raiders and the camouflaging of a new attempt at getting hold of the Chinese Eastern Railroad.

And three days later *Izvestia* quoted a Tass telegram from Shanghai to the effect that Nanking officials

are endeavoring either to draw the powers into the conflict or else to break down the negotiations between Mukden and Moscow and to take them into their own hands with a view to frustrating an agreement. It may be surmised that this time also Mukden will administer a defeat to Nanking.

The publication of the Stimson declaration and the Soviet reply in the Russian press of December 4 precipitated a stinging barrage aimed principally at Washington, although France and Great Britain were also contemned for their association with the United States. In contrast, the abstention of Japan was praised. Further fuel was added to Soviet indignation by the provocative speech of Maxim Litvinov on December 4. The substance of the address was an unknowing commentary on the costliness of nonrecognition, for it revealed a fundamental ignorance of Washington's attitude toward the Sino-Soviet conflict, an ignorance which clearly stemmed from the absence of Soviet representation in the United States. Moreover, the Litvinov speech indirectly illustrated the effect on Soviet national pride of Western mistrust and American aloofness. The address was shot through with Moscow's belief that the

Chinese seizure of the C.E.R., as well as its earlier anti-Russian acts, had the tacit support and encouragement of Washington and the European powers.

Without encouragement from the Capitalist Powers China would never have risked attacking the Chinese Eastern Railroad . . . the capitalist States shared the indirect responsibility for the conflict . . . since their anti-Soviet policy always gave promise of their encouragement in any venture directed against the Soviet Government . . . at a time when we are engaged in negotiating a peaceful settlement of the dispute with Mukden, the Peking Government, either on their own initiative or at foreign instigation, are making fresh efforts to obtain the help of the Imperialist Powers and the League of Nations to prevent a peaceful and speedy end to the conflict . . . Fifty-five States have signed the Kellogg Pact, and only three of them, authorized by nobody, have considered themselves chosen for the role of protectors of the Pact. In this capacity they had first of all to rub a sponge across their memory in order to forget temporarily the fact that their troops are stationed in Peking, Tientsin, Shanghai . . . and the American Government has even forgotten that our Soviet Government, which is only twelve years old, is so insignificant a thing that the American Government has not considered itself called upon to recognize it. The American Government says in its statement that it views the trend of events with alarm. But, in so far as we know, there are no representatives of the American Government with us in the U.S.S.R., who might watch from our side what is taking place along the Soviet-Manchurian frontier, while we, who also have no representatives in America, are likewise deprived of the possibility of informing the American Government promptly regarding the events in which it is interested . . . the well-known enemy of the Soviets, Wu Chao-Chu, is a frequent caller at the Washington Department of State and he probably is the principal source of the information at Mr. Stimson's disposal; but does Mr. Stimson not realize that such information cannot be sufficiently full and accurate, and that it is rather onesided, to say the least . . . What results may be expected from the démarche of the Powers? I think, none whatsoever . . .

While Litvinov was speaking to the Central Executive Committee of the U.S.S.R., Secretary Stimson issued a statement to the press in answer to the formal Soviet memorandum of December 3

"Between co-signatories of the Pact of Paris," he noted, it could "never be rightly thought unfriendly that one nation calls to the attention of another its obligations or the dangers to peace which from time to time arise." The American message to Russia and China was motivated not by unfriendly considerations, but by American regard for the Paris Pact. Furthermore, Stimson averred that the publicity given the Manchurian dispute by the American-inspired note had been successful, for, he alleged, it was a tangible force in promoting the Sino-Soviet negotiations.

The Washington statement was immediately attacked by Moscow; according to the Soviet press there was still no satisfactory explanation for the reasons which had motivated the United States to take action "just at the present moment and not at the time when the Mukden and Nanking Governments created a distinct danger to peace in the Far East by seizing the Chinese Eastern Railroad." And once again the nonrecognition policy of the State Department was assailed: the fact that Washington, through its own choosing, had no means of learning the Soviet side of the dispute with China should have "suggested" to the American Government "the need of particular reserve and of abstention from intervention" in the conflict between two states "one of which has no relations with America." [13] "We are compelled to say once more," *Izvestia* editorialized on December 8, that the United States "had either clearly insufficient and incorrect information in its possession when it attempted to interfere" or it "resolved on such interference, while in possession of knowledge of the direct agreement between" Mukden and Moscow. Furthermore, "public opinion" had nothing to do with the Sino-Soviet negotiations: "everyone is excellently aware that . . . agreement was reached in spite of that 'public opinion' which Stimson had in mind." In essence, the guiding factors in the Washington note were declared to be, on the one hand, the American hope "of gaining control of the C.E.R.," and, on the other, the desire "to sow discord between the Soviet Union and other States." [14]

[13] *Izvestia*, December 6, 1929.
[14] Enclosures in Coleman to Stimson, December 12, 9, and 23, 1929 (861.77 C.E./752, 742, 745).

In summary, the Russian case against the Stimson statement was reducible to two specific charges. First, interference was unwarranted either on behalf of the Kellogg-Briand Pact, or on the ground of an "imminent danger of war"; and second, the American action was unfriendly to Russia, having allegedly been taken to advance China's interests as against those of the Soviet Union. The extent to which these charges were justified is still subject to controversy, but certain qualifying factors emerge from a study of the available documents.

Interpreted literally, the Treaty for the Renunciation of War consigned to none of its signatories the guardianship of its provisions, nor did it suggest any means for implementing its terms in the event of their infraction. Strictly speaking, therefore, the Soviet Government was legally entitled to protest against the American-inspired statement of December 2. From Washington's point of view, however, the right of consultation was inherent in the Pact, and the moral obligation of the member states to call the attention of disputing powers to its articles was as strong as any legal commitment. In the words of the American co-author of the agreement:

Where all the nations have joined in a Treaty not to go to war but to settle their disputes by pacific means, why isn't it the business of the United States to do everything it could to prevent the violation of a Treaty which it and the other nations had signed? . . . The time is passed when war is of interest only to the belligerents—it is now of interest to all the world.[15]

It should be stressed further that the State Department took meticulous care to give the impression of friendly suasion rather than pressure; of advice rather than interference. The December declaration was purposely labeled a "statement" in preference to a "note"; it was unsigned and did not request an answer. In short, American and Russian statesmen alike were aware that the Pact of Paris had no sanctions attached, but whereas the Soviet Government

[15] March 28, 1930. From *Frank B. Kellogg: A Biography*, by David Bryn-Jones, p. 255. Copyright, 1937, by David Bryn-Jones. Courtesy of G. P. Putnam's Sons.

read into the treaty an individual national-honor system, Washington regarded itself and all signatory states as moral trustees of international peace through the medium of the Anti-War Agreement.

The Russian interpretation could not be divorced from the circumstances in which it was conceived, however. That the Soviet Union—still the unaccepted Bear of the East—should be the first nation against which the Kellogg Pact was invoked, and that the United States—the one major power which had refused to recognize Russia—should presume to focus world attention on the Sino-Soviet controversy, contributed an emotional element to the whole issue which inevitably beclouded it. In other words, Russia was striking out not simply against the illegality of the December statement in terms of the Kellogg-Briand Treaty, but equally against American nonrecognition and the *cordon sanitaire* mentality which isolation by the West had imposed upon it.

But there was a further cause for Soviet resentment: the Kremlin was already engaged in direct negotiations with Mukden and was convinced that any grave likelihood of war had vanished when Stimson appeared on the scene. In other words, to the Russians the American démarche was anticlimactic and represented the exploitation of the Kellogg Pact in the interests of American imperialism. The question raised by this charge was put by *Izvestia*: Did the United States, or did it not, know of the Mukden-Moscow negotiations when it released its December statement?

There can be no reasonable doubt but that the State Department was cognizant of the Sino-Soviet conversations. As previously noted, both Japan and Germany had explained their abstention from the American declaration on the ground that negotiations between the conflicting powers were already in progress. Moreover, reports from American Foreign Service officers confirming these *pourparlers* were received at the Department on at least four separate occasions between the end of November and December 2. At the same time, Washington was aware that Russia had intensified its military pressure against the Chinese in mid-November; and that the Nanking Government, through November 30, had not been a party to the Mukden-Moscow preliminary discussions, so that its attitude remained undeclared. Whether or not Stimson should have known that the possibility of war was remote, he was convinced that the situation was still fraught with danger.

It is, of course, conceivable that the Secretary of State was aided in reaching this conclusion by a personal desire to carry through a project which had been evolving for at least a week. Furthermore, although he may have realized that Sino-Soviet negotiations had been initiated, Stimson could easily have believed that the December 2 statement would hasten a final settlement even though it aroused Soviet resentment—a contingency which he had anticipated.

The second main argument in the Russian case against the December statement was more easily answered, and had Moscow been in diplomatic communication with the United States it could not fairly have raised the question in the first place. For although the hostile reaction of the American Government to Soviet influence in Peking and Canton in the early 1920's might have led Russia to assume American complicity with China in the 1929 dispute, the diplomatic records leave no shadow of doubt as to Washington's attitude. The very fact that the State Department had been developing its plan for a world-wide appeal from the time of Marshal Chang's earliest bid for negotiations with Moscow disproved the Soviet insinuation that the December declaration was precipitately drafted to promote Mukden's bargaining position in the Sino-Soviet conversations: Stimson's action had paralleled, not complemented, the action of Chang Hsueh-liang. Moreover, the unilateral repudiation of treaties by the Chinese Government was regarded as a greater threat to American Asiatic interests than the existent Russian "sphere" in the Far East, and as an infringement of legal Russian rights; this created a tense political situation in which peace and the Kellogg Pact were in jeopardy. Accordingly the Soviet Union had one of its strongest—albeit unappreciated—supporters on Pennsylvania Avenue.

The initial settlement of the Sino-Soviet dispute by the Khabarovsk Protocol of December 22, 1929,[16] was attained without

[16] This was a preliminary settlement, although it virtually restored the conditions existent prior to the dispute. In May 1930 a Chinese delegation (repre-

benefit of further advice from the United States. The controversy and its pacific negotiations had afforded no concrete proof of the viability of the Anti-War Treaty. Notwithstanding the sanguine pronouncement of Secretary Stimson that "we may have had considerable real effect upon the situation and the subsequent settlement," it is difficult to credit the December statement (and the Kellogg Pact) with more than a negative—and a purely relative—influence. The success of Russian military operations in November had forced Marshal Chang to approach Moscow; but Moscow, absorbed in domestic problems, needed no international publicity to restrain it from war. So that Washington's attitude and the December declaration, if productive of any results, merely accentuated China's predicament and illustrated the necessity of accepting the Soviet terms. Furthermore, the diplomacy attending the Russo-Chinese conflict confirmed the basic fallacy of an international peace pact which was without machinery for its operation and sanctions for its enforcement. And as time was soon to demonstrate, the strength of the Pact was flexible, varying in direct ratio to the weakness of the state or states against which it was invoked. In 1929 neither of the parties to the dispute was prepared for war, and judgment on the treaty was suspended; in 1931 a different condition prevailed, and judgment, accordingly, was rendered.

The Sino-Soviet controversy provided another lesson more immediately relevant to the purposes of this study, by demonstrating at the expense of untold bitterness the exorbitant cost of non-recognition. According to the London *Times*, the tactless obloquies of the Russians so incensed the more disciplined minds in Washington that recognition was delayed for several years. The accuracy of this hypothesis must perforce remain open to question, but there can be no doubt that Russian resentment over what it considered wanton American intrusion, and American resentment over what it considered unwarranted Russian language, deepened

---

senting Mukden and Nanking) went to Moscow, but delays and interruptions ensued with the result that when the Japanese invaded Manchuria, in September 1931, Russia and China were still without mutual diplomatic representation.

the mutual antagonism of both countries and minimized for a time the desire of each to exchange representatives. But of even more basic significance was the almost certain knowledge that had normal relations prevailed between the United States and the U.S.S.R. at the time of the Sino-Soviet dispute, there would have been little justification for the misunderstanding of American motives, or for the war of words which ensued.

But this is conjecture, where conclusions are in order. In the early 1920's when Soviet communism was throwing to the winds Russian imperial claims in China (and, by implication, the claims of all other "China powers"), the United States had just cause, in the vocabulary of diplomatic parlance, to combine its anathema to bolshevism with its traditional policy of preventing the ascendancy in China of any one nation. Correspondingly, Washington's fear of communism and its desire to uphold the Asiatic balance of power worked consonantly in the attempt to frustrate Soviet ambitions. By 1929, however, not only was Russian influence practically nonexistent in the Chinese ruling sphere, but legal Russian rights, negotiated freely by China in 1924, had been openly violated. It mattered not that originally Washington had reacted unfavorably to the Sino-Soviet agreements of that year. There was never the slightest question in American minds as to the guilt of the Chinese in 1929 or as to the necessity of upholding the Soviet claims; for quite apart from its devotion to abstract justice, America's Far Eastern interests were potentially threatened by the Mukden coup. But while Moscow was regarded, for the purposes of this dispute, as an orthodox Western power to whose protection the United States automatically rushed, America continued to isolate the Soviets diplomatically.

The simultaneous adherence to two such contradictory policies was reminiscent of the American attitude during the period of Siberian intervention, with one notable difference. In the years immediately after the Bolshevik Revolution it was possible to hope that the Communist reign would be short-lived, and therefore the protection of Russian sovereignty in Siberia was undertaken potentially on behalf of some future, non-Bolshevik government. In 1929, however, no such hope could be entertained. Moreover, the perverse logic which dictated the American course boomeranged in terms of the actual results.

For in the pattern of Far Eastern political relationships the Japanese policy of silence (far more in keeping with American nonrecognition than the vocal interference of the State Department) won unreserved Soviet commendation, whereas the Washington-sponsored intrusion was thoroughly misunderstood, unappreciated, and resented by the Russian Government. The Sino-Soviet dispute was settled without war and with proper deference paid to Russian interests—the two goals of American policy. But the decade of the twenties, vanishing into the abyss of world economic depression and incipient military aggression, left a residue of American-Soviet antagonism which could only bring aid and comfort to the biding expansionists of Japan.

| The Manchurian "Incident" and American Recognition of Russia

On September 18, 1931, an explosion on the South Manchurian Railroad shattered the nocturnal stillness and rent the fabric of peace. Quickly, and with machine efficiency, Japanese armies descended like locusts to impose order—the "new order"—on the Far East. Once again Manchuria, ancient "cradle of conflict," rocked with the blast of cannon and bowed to the might of the conqueror; but this time it could no longer absorb the tumult, and the echoes therefrom ricocheted to distant places: to Moscow and Washington, to London and Paris and Geneva, to Rome and Berlin. The spark, left to smolder while the nations held council to determine the culprit, spread westward, appearing now in the African desert, now in the Rhineland, Madrid, Austria, Czechoslovakia; and the powers, confused by the traitors among them, unable to render a verdict, watched as the world caught fire, and buried peace in the ashes.

The resurgence of a militant Japanese imperialism ten years after the Washington Conference, sprang from a composite of domestic and external conditions which matured at the turn of the decade. If any one factor were basic in explaining the Manchurian "incident" it was the moral and financial bankruptcy of a world of potential plenty; militarism flourished in the dry rot of economic stagnation; and even as it waxed strong, the enervating winds of depression hushed the feeble protests of stricken nations. Within Japan the endless duel for power between the army and the peacemakers completed a cycle, and the latter—the fruits of economic internationalism gone sour in their hands—relinquished the reins of statecraft to the men of autarchy. They alone could cope with the strangling barriers to world trade by conquering a world of their own and fashioning a self-sufficient economy therein. But if the economic atmosphere were ripe for imperialism, so too was the climate of politics. First, there was China, its nominal unification a poor substitute for genuine unity, its government corrupt, its natural riches fabulous. Second, there was Russia, the unknown quantity but withal the clumsy Bear, striving to hollow its log before winter, snapping now at China, now at Japan, and preferring appeasement to battle in 1931. Third, there was America, distant protagonist of moral suasion, facile with words, reluctant with deeds, democratic skirts lifted high to avoid ideological contamination by the Bear. Fourth, there was Europe, the Armageddon of the ages, too enmeshed in its own contradictions to squander its manpower in Asia; host to the League of Nations but unpracticed in the machinery of peace. It was a time for aggression—and there was no one to prevent it.

Although the explosions on the Japanese-owned South Manchuria Railroad were not, as Tokyo had charged, the work of Chinese soldiers, the mimetic Nipponese found in the "incident" ample justification, and in the history of China ample precedent, for the swift occupation which followed. But at that point, all analogies with the past abruptly ceased. In 1895 Russia had led France and Germany in an effective protest against the war lords of Japan; in 1921 America had presided at a world conference which pressured the Mikado's Government into disgorging a part of its booty and separated Tokyo from its British ally. But in 1931 Russia was suspect among the nations, an outcast at Geneva; and the United States, potentially ready to go farther than the League members in the verbal chastisement of Japan, was unwilling either to apply sanctions or to seek Russian leverage to right the balance of power in Asia.

The Manchurian conflict, apart from its international repercussions and its effect on the Far East throughout the ensuing fourteen years, shed further light on the American-Soviet chronicle. In the first place, among the factors which contributed to the Japanese action in 1931 must be listed the foreknowledge of American-Russian antagonism, appreciably augmented by the Sino-Soviet dispute of 1929. Secondly, the Manchurian crisis initially widened the rift between Moscow and Washington, for each distrusted the other's attitude toward the Japanese invasion. Later, however, the menace to Russia and America alike of a Japanese-dominated Asia helped temporarily to assuage the ideological warfare of the United States and the U.S.S.R., lending some slight impetus to the forces which dictated recognition. But it should be noted that American-Soviet relations between 1931 and November 1933 were only a tiny side show in the vast panorama of Asiatic conflict; had they been anything more, the Sino-Japanese controversy might have had a different dénouement.

The initial attitude of the Soviet Union toward the undeclared war in Manchuria, one of appeasement, was attributable in large measure to three causes: the drive for industrial modernization, which absorbed the energies of the government at home; a sense of military inadequacy (later augmented by the rise of Hitler); a deep distrust of Western and American policy toward Japan, which afforded no hope for support should the Soviet become involved in the Far Eastern struggle. But at the same time Soviet appeasement was sufficiently tempered with strong—albeit sporadic—verbal outbursts and defensive military tactics to confuse China, Japan, and the Western powers alternately regarding the ultimate direction which Russia would take. So that although the immediate reaction of Moscow to the Manchurian "incident" was neither sympathetic to China nor indicative of any intention to protect Russia's Manchurian interests, the Japanese were loath to gamble too heavily on Soviet aloofness in the autumn of 1931, and reports from Manchuria illustrated the fairly marked deference shown Russia by Tokyo. Furthermore, although the Kremlin very early announced its policy of noninterference, based on its "respect for the sovereign rights and the independence of other states," China and world capitals professed for a time to accept the rumor of a Russo-Japanese agreement, whereby Moscow would sell Tokyo a portion of the Chinese Eastern Railroad in return for financial aid and compensation in North Manchuria.[1] It was the result of

[1] *For. Rel.*, 1931, Vol. III, pp. 38, 42. The British Government regarded the rumor as unfounded. The Danish Minister to China informed the American Legation that while there was probably no definite agreement between

this rumor, combined with skepticism regarding the strength of the League of Nations and the dire need to find external aid, which impelled the Chinese to resume diplomatic relations with the Soviet Government on December 12, 1932.

A month earlier Ambassador Grew had cabled his conviction that Moscow's main objective was "to avoid external complications at almost any cost, until such time as the second Five-Year Plan is completed." [2] Superficially this statement could not be reconciled with Moscow's willingness to restore formal relations with China at the end of the year, for in so doing the Kremlin was courting Japanese disfavor. Tokyo at once interpreted the Sino-Soviet move as proof of Russian support for China in the Manchurian conflict, and a Foreign Office spokesman expressed "grave concern for the welfare of the Far East, in view of the probability of the penetration of Communism into China." The Soviets, according to Japan, had "now apparently taken sides" in the controversy; and the restoration of Russo-Chinese relations was "another instance of the Soviet method of doing unpleasant things." [3]

Actually, Moscow's precipitate acceptance of the Chinese bid for relations represented another tack in Soviet policy, whereby appeasement was modified when expediency dictated. Moreover, this latest move emphasized the growing uneasiness with which Russia viewed the spreading Japanese occupation with its potential danger to Siberia and the C.E.R., and the failure to reach a *modus vivendi* with Tokyo. Litvinov had suggested a Russo-Japanese non-aggression treaty in December 1931, but his proposal had been utterly ignored by Japan in the ensuing year. Two months after the suggestion had been made, the Soviet Government again appeased Tokyo by allowing Japanese troops to use the eastern branch of the C.E.R., nominally to safeguard the lives and property of

---

Russia and Japan, "there is at least an understanding that neither will take action prejudicial to the other's interests in Manchuria." Perkins to Stimson, December 11, 1931 (793.94/3163); and on December 23 the American Embassy at Tokyo reported: "Although still watchful and suspicious of each other Japan and Soviet Russia seem to have come to some form of understanding." Neville to Stimson, December 5, 1931 (793.94/3269).

[2] Grew to Stimson, November 5, 1932 (761.94/580).

[3] Same to same, December 16, 1932 (761.93/1497).

Japanese nationals. Simultaneously, however, the psychological necessity of balancing weakness with strength was not lost upon the Russian leaders. Thus *Pravda* (December 24, 1931) issued an emphatic denial in answer to speculation regarding a sale of the southern end of the Chinese Eastern to Japan. Furthermore, the tenor of government comment in Moscow throughout the spring of 1932 revealed a sympathy for the Chinese people and a determination to strengthen Soviet defenses, particularly in the Far East. But by establishing diplomatic relations with China at the end of the year the Soviet Union had no more intention of involving itself in the Sino-Japanese military conflict than had the Western powers.

The attitude of the powers toward the Manchurian controversy contained none of the obfuscation characteristic of Russian policy; in sharp contrast, open appeasement by Europe, seconded by the ineffectual American doctrine of nonrecognition, spurred the Japanese forward in the belief, confirmed by time, that the chief obstacles to the conquest of Manchuria (and later China) resulted from Tokyo's own limitations in view of the immensity of the struggle.

Quite aside from the "Munich mentality" which already pervaded Europe, and the "continental mentality" which had resettled over the United States after the First World War, there can be little doubt that an early reason for the Western world's unwillingness to censure Japan too severely was universal mistrust of Soviet Russia. Certain authors have advanced the dogmatic thesis that the twin fears of communism and of Russia constituted a major factor in the impotence of the League of Nations and in the appeasement policy of League members and the United States vis-à-vis the Manchurian affair. While this perhaps states the issue too arbitrarily, it is beyond cavil that this fear exerted some influence, especially in view of the attitude of the Western powers, notably Britain and America, toward Moscow in 1931.

Although the British Nationalist Government maintained diplomatic relations with Russia, the explosive nature of Soviet propaganda throughout England's colonial possessions and in Southern China in the 1920's automatically forced the imperial British to prefer the limited imperialism of Japan to the boundless communism of Russia. On the other hand, the United States had exerted diplomatic pressure between 1920 and 1929 to counter Soviet influence in China, and one of the first reactions of the State Department to the September 18, 1931, "incident" was apprehension lest Moscow come to the aid of China in its extremity.

> I pointed out to [the Japanese Ambassador] . . . that possibly another reason for [withdrawing from Manchuria] . . . might be that it was necessarily within the range of possibilities—if not probabilities —that the Russians might take the attitude that they were friends of China and would help put out the Japanese; that, if anything of the sort happened, it would infinitely complicate the situation.[4]

And in November the American consul general at Harbin had reported "alarming" rumors concerning "Soviet Russian support" for Chinese troops in North Manchuria.

The American attitude, as well as that of Great Britain and the League, could have been explained on the ground that encouragement of Russian aid to China might have precipitated a general conflagration in the Far East, whereas if the dispute were restricted to the original parties it might be localized and extinguished; but this rationalization did not suffice once the Japanese had extended their occupation and it became evident that they had no intention of leaving. Moreover, so far as the Soviet Government was concerned, the Lytton Report was in itself proof of the degree to which the West was saturated with its fear of communism and its corresponding mistrust of Russia.[5]

[4] Memorandum by Under-Secretary Castle of a Conversation with the Japanese Ambassador (Debuchi), September 25, 1931, *For. Rel., op. cit.*, pp. 68–69.

[5] The Report summarized Russo-Japanese relations between 1917 and 1931 in part as follows: "The Russian Revolution of 1917, followed by the declarations of the Soviet Government of July 25, 1919, and of October 27, 1920 . . . and . . . by the Sino-Soviet agreements of . . . 1924 . . . shattered the basis of Russo-Japanese understanding and cooperation in Manchuria. This fundamental reversal of policy radically changed the relations of the three powers in the Far East. . . . The attitude of the Soviet Government gave a strong impetus to China's nationalistic aspirations. As the Soviet Government and the Third International had adopted a policy opposed to all imperialistic powers which maintained relations with China on the basis of the existing treaties, it

The knowledge that the United States, a nonmember of the League, was invited to the Geneva council table to consider the Sino-Japanese war, while Russia was ignored; the fact that in 1932 the Western campaign against Soviet trade continued unabated; and the recognition that Europe and America were reluctant to use any of the instruments of peace to preserve it in the Far East, convinced the Soviet leaders that the democratic, bourgeois world was not only willing to condone Japanese aggression at the expense of China, but was impelled somewhat by its hostility toward Russia. In view of the alacrity with which Moscow and Nanking had been reminded of their obligations under the Kellogg Pact, the Russians found cause for resentment at Washington's initial reluctance to apply the Pact to Japan. The wedge of suspicion between Russia and the West thus widened in the early stages of the Sino-Japanese conflict, and Tokyo—stressing the menace of communism to the Lytton Commission, to the interested nations whenever opportunity presented, and to the world at the time of the reestablishment of Sino-Soviet relations—sought to drive the wedge further, thereby profiting in the pursuit of its imperial loot.

The success attending the division of East and West was most marked in the autumn and winter months of 1931–1932, which were psychologically critical in predisposing world policy toward the dispute thereafter. During this time the full measure of Japanese ambition had not yet been assayed, and accordingly the steps

---

seemed probable that they would support China in the struggle for the recovery of sovereign rights. This development revived all the old anxieties and suspicions of Japan toward her Russian neighbor. This country, with which she had once been at war, had, during the years which followed that war, become a friend and ally. Now this relationship was changed, and the possibility of a danger from across the North Manchurian border again became a matter of concern to Japan. The likelihood of an alliance between the Communist doctrines in the North and the anti-Japanese propaganda of the Kuomintang in the South made the desire to impose between the two a Manchuria which would be free from both increasingly felt in Japan. Japanese misgivings have been still further increased in the last few years by the predominant influence acquired by the U.S.S.R. in Outer Mongolia and the growth of Communism in China." To the Soviet Union this meant that the Lytton Commission had accepted at full value the Japanese description of the "red menace." League of Nations, *Appeal by the Chinese Government—Report of the Commission of Inquiry* (The Lytton Report), 1932, pp. 36–37.

to be taken against Tokyo were determined in considerable part by factors other than the eventually consuming knowledge of Japan's exhaustless pretensions. The purblind desire of Europe and America to avert conflict in Asia, the financial burden of sanctions at a time of economic chaos, and the forebodings regarding Russian communism were influences toward softening the resistance of the West to Tokyo's scheme of conquest. For Russia, too, anxiety to avoid war and doubt as to the Japanese program contributed to the diversion of Soviet remarks from the Nipponese marauder to the Anglo-Saxon hypocrite. The eagerness of the Kremlin to find fault with the dilatory Western powers was illustrated by an article in *Izvestia* (September 21, 1931) commenting on the vain protests of Washington and Geneva over the Manchurian "incident," and on the official American statement that it "did not find anything contrary to the Kellogg Pact in the actions of the Japanese troops which had occupied Manchuria." The impression was thus given "that Japan's action was well prepared in the sense of getting the agreement of the other imperialist powers." A sharper thrust was made by V. M. Molotov several weeks later at a meeting of the Moscow Soviet on the fourteenth anniversary of the Bolshevik Revolution, when he contrasted the Soviet position with that of the League in respect to the Sino-Japanese conflict. Russia's policy was strictly "unconditional opposition" to military intervention by any state. Conversely, the Western powers (in collusion with Japan) were seeking to divide China, and Tokyo was raising the "red menace" as pretext for its military occupation.

But the primary target of Soviet vituperation in the early months of the dispute was the United States. Moscow had originally expected that the Kellogg Pact sponsor would assume a different attitude, and the explanation for America's forbearance, according to *Izvestia*, could only be found in hostility toward Russia. It was postulated by the Russian press that American industrial and banking circles desired war in the Far East; that the penetration into China of the Japanese troops constituted

in the opinion of the American imperialists an important link in the chain by which one wants to encircle Soviet Union and provoke it into an armed conflict with its neighbors. With this object . . . they are attempting to instigate Japan into a collision with the Soviet Union and thus involve the latter in the Manchurian controversy.[6]

This maligning and misleading propaganda sprang from cynical Russian disillusionment over American policy. Stimson had expressed a positive determination to cooperate with the League of Nations and had assigned Prentiss Gilbert to attend Council meetings through October 24, 1931; but the effect of Gilbert's presence had been slight. Japan and the League had both recognized that the American Government was unlikely to apply either military or economic sanctions at that time; and this inevitably encouraged the Japanese, sapped the already flagging powers of resistance of the League, and thereby contributed to the Soviet conviction of American duplicity. To Russia the intermittent diplomatic protests of the United States to Japan in November and December 1931 and again in 1932, the doctrine of nonrecognition, and the frequent reminders to Tokyo of its obligation as a signatory of the Washington Nine-Power Treaty and the Kellogg-Briand Pact were intended to salve the American conscience rather than to serve as deterrents to the Japanese.[7]

But despite calumnies and opprobriums the U.S.S.R. carried on a clandestine courtship of the United States almost from the outset of the Manchurian invasion. "Appeasement," "capitalism," "hypocrisy," and the other nouns used synonymously with the American Government might depict Soviet scorn, but they could not determine Soviet policy. The men in the Kremlin might despise democratic ideology, but they could not ignore Washington's potential strength as a Pacific power. With these hard facts before them, and with the proximity of Japan to prod them, the Soviet leaders viewed American recognition as an element in the Russian security pattern, and thus as a battle to be won.

[6] *The Finnish Liberal*, Helsingfors, November 25, 1931, enclosure in Brodie (American Legation, Helsingfors) to Stimson, November 28, 1931 (761.94/450).

[7] It should be noted, however, that the American policy, and the acceptance by the League of Nations Assembly of the Lytton Report on February 24, 1933, did precipitate the Japanese withdrawal from the League.

Among the early reports testifying to this policy were accounts of interviews between the American chargé at Kovno, Lithuania, and the Soviet Minister, Karsky. Karsky's remarks assumed added significance, inasmuch as the State Department identified them with a point of view current in Moscow for many years. Moreover, Russian opinion as to Japan's strategic advantage over the United States may easily have influenced Moscow's policy of Japanese appeasement in later years. Toward the end of 1931 Karsky voiced Russia's interest in the United States and Soviet disappointment over Washington's opposition to the establishment of diplomatic relations. Recognition, he averred, would facilitate cooperation in the Far East mutually advantageous to both countries. To the Communists it was apparent that Japanese success in Manchuria would be followed by conquest of the Philippines, and that in a war with America Japan would emerge victorious since military operations would take place so far away from a tenable United States naval base. Moreover, Russian officials expressed the conviction that war between Japan and America would be unavoidable, unless Washington formed some sort of protective alliance with the U.S.S.R. in the Far East. These sentiments were patently motivated by self-interest, but their prescience was tragically and almost fatally revealed a decade later.

At the end of February 1932, Russian Minister Karsky reiterated his belief

that the most salutary thing that could happen in the Far East right now was for Russia and the United States to join in a common pressure upon Japan, if necessary breaking that country as between the two arms of a nut cracker.[8]

In March 1932 the Soviet press played up a statement in *The New Republic,* urging American-Russian cooperation, and gave special emphasis to the sentence that America "could take no more effective action to prevent the spread of war" in the Far East than by "giving Russia every legitimate aid in strengthening her powers of resistance." To the Foreign Minister of Turkey the Russians

[8] Fullerton to Stimson, February 26, 1932 (760N.oo/23).

confided in May that "peace would not finally be secured in the Pacific until the United States recognized the Soviet government." [9] A different route to the same objective was illustrated in Moscow's repeated contention that "had normal relations existed between [the U.S.S.R. and the United States] . . . the Japanese would not have dared to do what they have recently done in Manchuria." [10] In the words of Litvinov, there was little doubt but that the "commencement of the present troubles in the Far East" was traceable to the fact that "not all States situated on the shores of the Pacific Ocean have been maintaining diplomatic relations with one another." Ostensibly this statement was made to explain the restoration of Sino-Soviet relations, but its implied reference to the breach between Russia and America was manifest.

The Soviet Union was geographically more susceptible to Japanese attack than the United States, regardless of Karsky's allusions to the Philippine Islands, and this propelled Moscow's lead in seeking American recognition. Moreover, nonrecognition was solely Washington's policy, unshared by Russia, which further explained the Soviet initiative. But American obduracy had its points of vulnerability. Among these, apart from the eventually decisive economic factors, was the balance of power in Asia; and Russian iteration, combined with Japanese diplomacy and military strategy, supplied additional arguments to the proponents of recognition. As late as December 1932 the State Department continued to parry all inquiries concerning the likelihood of American recognition of Russia with negative rejoinders, but the Department's files for that year reveal the growing American alarm over the Manchurian affair and the corresponding solicitude over the menace to Russia in the spread of Japanese aggression. For example, in January 1932 the American Minister to China stated that the Japanese General Staff regarded the Manchurian affair as an opportunity to extend Japan's strategic boundaries further west "in preparation for the clash with Soviet Russia which they consider inevitable."

This belief was emphasized by the Soviet Minister to Lithuania,

[9] Sherrill (Ankara) to Stimson, May 14, 1932 (861.01/1759).
[10] Memorandum by E. L. Packer of a Conversation with Mr. Boris Skvirsky of the Soviet Union Information Bureau, September 10, 1932 (761.94/575).

who was apprehensive over the aggressive attitude of Japan, noting that Vladivostok was so far from supply bases in Russia "as to imperil the Soviet Government's hold upon this remote territory in the event the Japanese decided to step over into it from Manchuria." [11] In the light of these reports the following excerpt from a Department memorandum on the Manchurian situation had a peculiar significance:

. . . in relation to the underlying principles of the Nine-Power Treaty, Russia may be assumed to be more in sympathy with those principles as a guide to policy than can Japan. For any real solution of the Manchurian problem, Russian rights and interests must be given consideration; and it would be worth the effort of the other powers to gain the adherence of Russia to the theories and plans of the powers as expressed in the Nine-Power Treaty and the various resolutions of the League of Nations, rather than have Russia either stand as an outsider or align herself more and more with the theories and objectives of Japan.[12]

This was indeed a remarkable statement! The Nine-Power Treaty was a product of the Washington Conference, from which the United States had mercilessly excluded the Soviet Government. But ten years later the ultimate failure of American "diplomacy by conference" to check Japanese imperialism was demonstrated; at the same time the stability of the Communist Government had been proved. As a result, Washington began once more to think in the terms of 1905: to conceive of a Far Eastern balance vis-à-vis Japan which would draw Russia to the American side.

Apparently American concern over a Russo-Japanese conflict and the consequent possibility of a Soviet-American rapprochement were not unheeded in Tokyo, for in the spring of 1932 the Japanese Ambassador took pains to impress upon Secretary Stimson that his government was determined to avoid hostilities with the Soviets. Rumors to the contrary, Debuchi asserted, were spread "by the Russians because they wished" to secure American recognition. Following the reestablishment of normal relations between Mos-

[11] Fullerton to Stimson, February 26, 1932 (760N.00/23).
[12] Memorandum, Division of Far Eastern Affairs, March 11, 1932 (793.94/4946).

cow and the Chiang Kai-shek Government in December 1932,
Japan made a further attempt to forestall the reorientation of
American policy, this time employing a sophistry quickly pierced
by Stanley Hornbeck. Debuchi told him that the new Sino-Soviet
agreement caused Japan "to look more than ever to the United
States for friendship and cordial relations." Hornbeck later said
that Debuchi desired to foster the belief that Japan was no longer
suspicious of or hostile to the United States, that "conditions in
Russia" were "extremely bad," and that it would "be profitable
to the United States to adopt an attitude favorable to Japan." [13]

Early in 1933 Senator Johnson stated: "Some move in the direction of normal relationships with Russia at this time would do far
more to remove perils from the Far East . . . than any other single
act." And by the following July, Ambassador Grew noted that relations between Russia and Japan were somewhat similar to those
which had prevailed in Manchuria before the Japanese occupation.
If the latter "foresee an eventual clash as inevitable," the Ambassador cabled,

it is quite possible that they may intend to strike before Soviet Russia
gets stronger—and the time element is all in favor of [Russia] . . .
Therefore, while I do not consider war imminent, I do believe that the
situation is potentially dangerous and bears careful watching.[14]

In view of these exchanges and reports it was apparent that Russia, Japan, the Western European countries, and Washington perceived, in the Manchurian conflict and in the potential danger to
the Soviet Union of Japanese military invasion, a serious menace to
American interests in the Far East. The Soviet Government had
repeatedly emphasized this threat, sensitive to its own isolation and
eager to obtain American recognition. Tokyo had consistently minimized its ambitions in Manchuria and China in general and toward
Russia in particular, hoping to lull American anxiety and postpone
an American rapprochement with the U.S.S.R. Europe had pre-

[13] Memorandum of a Conversation between Mr. Stanley Hornbeck and Mr.
Debuchi, December 29, 1932 (711.94/758).
[14] Reprinted from Joseph C. Grew, *Ten Years in Japan*, p. 95, by permission
of Simon and Schuster, Publishers. Copyright, 1944, by Joseph C. Grew.

dicted American recognition, to counter the ascendancy of Japan; and Washington had made no effort to belittle its concern.

Therefore President Roosevelt's invitation to the Soviet Union to attend the World Economic Conference at London (an obvious prelude to recognition), and his subsequent invitation to President Kalinin to dispatch an envoy to Washington ("to end the present abnormal relations" between the two countries), were greeted then and in later years as proof of the "important element" constituted by the Far Eastern situation in precipitating recognition. The reply of Kalinin to the Roosevelt communication seemed obliquely to substantiate this assertion. The absence of diplomatic relations had rendered more difficult "the process of consolidating world peace," the Soviet official declared, and had "encouraged the forces tending to disturb that peace." But the precise degree to which the Asiatic crisis entered into the American decision must perforce remain untabulated, for in the Roosevelt-Litvinov conversations at the White House "there were no stenographers present and no reports made, and thus, so far as the conferences are concerned, there will be a bare outline and not a full picture exposed to the eye of the future historian." [15]

In view of correlative data and the perspective of history, however, it seems clear that the undeclared Sino-Japanese war exerted only a secondary influence on the reversal of Washington's policy toward Moscow. In other words, by 1933 the United States was convinced, on other than political grounds, of the fatuity of its nonrecognition policy, and there is every reason to believe that the decision to abandon it was made with only minor reference to the Far Eastern situation.

But for Russia the case was otherwise. As previously noted, Soviet officials, prior to recognition, had been meticulous to impress the United States with the connection between Japanese imperialism and Soviet-American relations. During the Washington conferences of October–November 1933, Litvinov made a statement very conceivably intended as a warning to Japan, and therefore further

[15] R. Walton Moore, "Recognition of Soviet Government of Russia" (Radio address, November 22, 1933), *Press Releases*, November 25, 1933, No. 529, pp. 287–288.

illustrative of the significance Russia attached to the Far East in negotiations with the State Department. In a note to President Roosevelt on November 16, the Soviet representative declared:

Following our conversations and following my examination of certain documents of the years 1918 to 1921 relating to the attitude of the American expedition toward the expedition into Siberia, the operations there of foreign military forces and the inviolability of the territory of the Union of Soviet Socialist Republics, the Government of the U.S.S.R. agrees that it will waive any and all claims of whatsoever character arising out of activities of military forces of the United States in Siberia or assistance to military forces in Siberia subsequent to January 1, 1918 . . .

Litvinov's phrase "certain documents" in all probability referred to information given him that America's Siberian policy was dictated mainly by the desire to delimit Japanese expansion in Siberia, and to uphold Russian territorial sovereignty. His motive in using the phrase was revealed in his next words: "the attitude of the American expedition toward . . . the inviolability of the territory of the Union of Soviet Socialist Republics." Here was a studied anachronism: Not only was there no legal U.S.S.R. at that time, but the United States had invariably distinguished between the "Soviet Government" and the "Russian state." In protecting the Asiatic possessions of the latter in 1918–1922, it was certainly not desired that they revert to Soviet control, but that they be held in trust for a future, democratic, Russian government. Apparently Litvinov's free translation was meant to strengthen the Soviet position in Asia by legitimizing its claim of possession.

But this was not all. The August 3, 1918, American note on intervention had announced Washington's determination to safeguard the territorial *integrity* of Russia; to the Soviet diplomat fifteen years later "integrity" became "inviolability." As Professor M. W. Graham pointed out a year later,[16] this substitution of words was deeply purposeful. Military occupation of Siberia was consonant with the upholding of Russia's territorial *integrity*; con-

[16] M. W. Graham, "Russian-American Relations, 1917–1933: An Interpretation," *American Political Science Review*, June 1934, pp. 408–409.

versely, it would be a breach of the principle of territorial *inviolability*. By thus amending the words of the 1918 American note the Soviet Government disingenuously advised Japan of American solicitude for Russia's territorial sovereignty in the Far East. The value ascribed by the Kremlin to Washington's willingness to be thus misquoted was tacitly indicated by the Soviet waiver of all claims against the American Siberian forces.

The United States and Russia established diplomatic relations on November 16, 1933; four days later Ambassador Grew wrote that the appointment of Troyanovsky as Soviet Ambassador to Washington was "an excellent selection. The fact that they picked their principal Japanese expert . . . is regarded here [in Tokyo] as intensely significant." [17] The choice was equally noteworthy as a striking indication of the degree to which the Far Eastern crisis had been instrumental in the *Russian* campaign to win American recognition.

Substantial portions of the American citizenry had never forgiven Russia the "crime" of Communist ideology. Therefore it was hardly conceivable that the status of Far Eastern politics in 1933 would itself have sufficed to justify formal recognition of the Soviet Union. Moreover, America's historical interest in the Asiatic balance of power and the open-door was passive (except for the Siberian intervention), resting on purely verbal diplomacy, and prior to 1941 the recurring struggles in the Far East were not conceived as threats to America's national security. Obversely, there is ample evidence to suggest that American recognition of Russia was primarily the consequence of economic and financial considerations. Pressure groups, representing a commercially starved business world, found that "trade was thicker than bolshevism," and the number of American firms willing and eager to do business with Stalin raised a commanding voice in the halls of Congress and among Administration counselors. The catastrophic decline in American exports to Russia between 1930 and 1933 provided an unanswerable argument for formalized trade relations.

Further factors in prompting recognition were the emphasis by Stalin, after 1928, on "socialism in one country" with its con-

[17] Grew, *op. cit.*, p. 107.

comitant "strategic retreat" from world revolution; the enthusiastic reports of American and European travelers regarding the Soviet experiment and various manifestations of Soviet culture; the psychological break with the long record of diplomatic aloofness heralded by the Democratic victory at the polls in 1932; and, in the light of all these influences, the increasing anomaly of nonrecognition.

The existence of a condition on the Continent of Asia which threatened alike the historic principles of United States' Far Eastern policy and the national security of Soviet Russia obviously sharpened the desire of each to establish normal diplomatic contact with the other, and facilitated the resolution of outstanding problems between the countries. However, notwithstanding some writers who assert that recognition "thwarted" Japanese designs against Asiatic Russia, it in no wise halted the Japanese march through China in ensuing years; nor was it followed by an era of good feeling between Moscow and Washington. Had the immediate aim of the Roosevelt Administration been to check Japanese expansion, a visible tightening of joint American-Soviet diplomacy toward Tokyo would have been logical. Conversely, after the first Locarno-like exultation had passed, the two governments proceeded along solitary paths, and although each desired the neutralization of Japanese imperialism, the State Department would engage in no entangling alliances with the Soviet regime.

In short, recognition was only obliquely an instrument of American Far Eastern policy. Its prime purpose, in a time of strangling depression, was the increment of American trade. Indeed, the dictates of commerce during the thirties quite overshadowed the competitive demands of a balance of power policy in Asia and elsewhere. Correspondingly, while State Department officials continued to protest against Japanese aggression (recognition of the Soviet Union had been one manifestation of this protest), American traders supplied the aggressor with the tools of conquest. When, at long last, the folly of this policy had become manifest, the balance of power was irreparably destroyed. Belated American efforts to reconstruct it precipitated the Japanese attack on Pearl Harbor.

PART THREE

CHAPTER XIII

The Fruits of Recognition

Viewed in perspective, American recognition of Soviet Russia proved to be a statement of fact rather than a harbinger of policy. Because this was so, any strategic gains which the Russians hoped to achieve thereby were stillborn. Consequently, in the "gathering storm" of the thirties American-Soviet relations were virtually peripheral, and had little to do with the deepening crises in Europe and Asia.

In the sixteen years prior to 1933 the doctrine of nonrecognition, compounded of fear, indignation, and isolation, had become increasingly anomalous. By the latter date Washington's diplomatic aloofness toward Moscow lacked justification on any grounds. Politically, economically, and psychologically it was considered costly and of no tangible benefit; the Communist regime was an established government recognized by every other major power, and it was manifest that the American attitude was totally unrealistic.

All these factors entered into the decision of the Roosevelt Administration to end the abnormal conditions between Washington and Moscow. But recognition of the Soviet Union in November 1933 was peculiarly unrewarding to both countries. In large part this was due to the *ex post facto* character of the American action; but of equal importance were the tenacious American traditions of political isolation and economic chauvinism, which precluded a positive, venturesome foreign policy. On the Soviet side, too, there were barriers to a closer understanding; but it is difficult to believe that in the period under review they were as determinative as those in the United States.

It has already been noted that in America the greatest pressure for recognition was economic. Accordingly trade negotiations were

267

undertaken immediately, and in July 1935 a commercial treaty was concluded. While this marked a definite advance over earlier conditions, the relatively small amount of goods which Russia contracted to purchase ($30,000,000) was disappointing to business groups. By 1937 Soviet imports from the United States had more than doubled ($64,224,000 in 1937–1938), but they declined sharply in the following twelve months ($50,255,000 in 1938–1939), the last fiscal year before war broke out. In this same period (1937–1939) American importers purchased goods from the Soviet Union averaging $23,000,000 annually.

If American businessmen were discouraged over the minor fruits of Soviet trade, the Roosevelt Government was equally distressed over the failure to implement various phases of recognition. At the top of the list was the issue of debts, which had nagged successive American administrations since 1918. Preliminary accord regarding the cancellation of respective claims reduced the American figure from $588,000,000 to $150,000,000; and in the light of Russia's offer to pay $100,000,000 a satisfactory compromise seemed imminent. But at that point negotiations foundered. Moscow predicated a final solution on Washington's willingness to extend a further loan, declaring this to be in line with the Washington conferences of 1933 which led to recognition. However, the Johnson Act tied the hands of the United States until Russia honored its legal debts. Additional attempts to resolve the stalemate were unavailing; in 1935 the State Department roundly reproved the Soviet Government for its purported "violation" of the Roosevelt-Litvinov conversations by closing the American consulate in Moscow and reducing the Embassy staff.

A final subject in the 1933 recognition agreement which caused subsequent American-Soviet friction concerned Communist propaganda. In the summer of 1935 the Communist International held its seventh session, at which a report was made on the progress of propaganda in the United States. This immediately precipitated a strong protest by Ambassador Bullitt over the alleged Soviet failure to live up to its antipropaganda pledge in 1933. In sharp rebuttal Moscow distinguished between the Comintern and the Soviet Government, disclaiming any responsibility for the activities of the

Comintern. Small credence was placed by Washington in the theoretical separation of that body from the Russian Government; and, as more recent history has disclosed, the international Communist agency, through whatever name it has operated, has reflected with astonishing accuracy the views of Moscow. Nevertheless, in 1935 the Comintern's discussion of propaganda in America was, if anything, a confession of the weakness of the Party in the United States, and even conservatives failed to share Secretary Hull's alarm.

Conditions within Russia in the mid-thirties further alienated American popular interest in the "great socialist experiment." By this time the first "literature of disillusion" was beginning to appear on American bookshelves, as once-enchanted observers recoiled from the ruthless methods of a single-minded totalitarianism. Moreover, the famous Moscow trials and what to Western eyes was the indiscriminate slaughter of hundreds of "innocents" provided a revolting and unforgivable demonstration of dictator-justice.

Throughout these years American isolationist sentiment waxed in proportion as the European international crisis deepened. United States sympathy for the victims of foreign aggression, and the early efforts of the Roosevelt Administration to bolster anti-Fascist elements in Europe, were crushed under the deadweight of nationalist tradition, which conceived of American security in the hopelessly antiquated framework of the nineteenth century. Oblivious of the interdependence of the twentieth century world, blind to the drastically altered position of the United States as a great power, and to the responsibilities attendant on that position, the proponents of isolationism hastily elaborated a barricade of neutrality legislation to protect them from the lawless aggressions of Germany and Italy. The sublime unreality of this attitude was of the same coin as that which had dictated nonrecognition of the Soviet Union in the years after 1917. Both policies were unrelievedly negative, and both failed to achieve their objectives. Moreover, among the subscribers to the neutrality policy were many who had never reconciled themselves to the Soviet Government, and who, in the frank hope that the Axis might be prevailed upon to turn eastward against the Stalinist regime, were willing to abide and even to support Hitler and Mussolini.

Unhappily, these American elements had numerous counterparts in the democracies of Western Europe, men of the Hoare-Laval, Daladier-Chamberlain ilk who, while less sanguine of the possibility of isolation, basked in the chimera of appeasement. They too were congenitally distrustful of the Soviet regime with its horrendous attack on the middle and upper classes. To them the state capitalism of the Nazis was preferable to the state socialism of the Communists, and peace at almost any price was preferable to another war.

The anti-Communist attitude of France, Britain, and America was lucidly revealed during the Spanish Civil War; Anglo-French appeasement, and apprehension over Soviet communism, were repeatedly manifested in the League of Nations; and the unfeigned popular rejoicing in Britain, France, and America which greeted the Munich "triumph" needed no explication.

In the light of these attitudes and events it was patently ludicrous to anticipate cordial relations between Moscow and Washington. By no act or word did the United States lend comfort to the Russians in their repeated attempts to erect a viable system of collective security in Europe. Nor were the Anglo-French powers sincerely desirous of a close-knit alliance with the Communists. Notwithstanding these facts, Moscow's subsequent Non-Aggression Treaty with Germany (August 23, 1939)—which was logically precipitated by the cool noncooperativeness of the Western democracies—called forth from them a mélange of surprise, invective, and anger. By a curious twist of reasoning Stalin's consorting with Hitler was damned as wholly opportunistic and amoral by the very persons who had applauded the crass betrayal of Czechoslovakia by Neville Chamberlain. Was it perchance because they blamed the Russian leader for failing to heed the expensive lesson of Munich? Or was it because the *modus vivendi* between the Soviet Union and the Third Reich abruptly dispelled any lingering hope that Hitler and Stalin would destroy each other while the West remained safely on the side lines? Whatever the reason, it was not idealistic.

The formal outbreak of the Second World War in September 1939 was followed by the quick occupation of Latvia, Esthonia, and Lithuania by Soviet troops, the participation of Russia in the rape of Poland, and the Russo-Finnish War. These events completed the alienation of America from Russia. Indeed, had popular opinion—or even the opinion of numerous congressmen and senators—prevailed during the ensuing hysterical weeks, diplomatic relations very conceivably would have been severed. News of the Soviet invasion of Finland prompted spontaneous condemnation of the Russians. "My country will no longer grasp the bloody hands of Stalin," declared Senator King of Utah. Representative John W. McCormick of Massachusetts proposed an amendment to the State Department Supply Bill in February 1940, which would have omitted the salary of the American Ambassador to Russia; the amendment lost by three votes. In New York, Fiorello LaGuardia told a luncheon of 1,200 persons that civilization was on the side of Finland; that Finland was on the side of God. The American-Russian Chamber of Commerce announced on February 8 that it was closing its Moscow office. In the House of Representatives, John Dingell of Michigan unceremoniously dispatched both Hitler and Stalin to the nether regions; the Finns, he declared, were "fighting to stop anti-Christ and the hosts of hell led by Beelzebub." Republican politicians solemnly averred that Russia should never have been recognized by the United States—as if this might have altered the subsequent course of history.

The President and the State Department lagged perceptibly behind public and Congressional opinion through the Finnish War, although both were strongly opposed to the Soviet policy. A moral embargo imposed on Russia on December 2, 1939, was gradually extended to include aerial equipment, certain minerals, etc., and was maintained until January 1941. On July 15, 1940, several months after the conclusion of the Russo-Finnish struggle, President Roosevelt issued an executive order sequestering the property and credits of the Baltic States (Latvia, Lithuania, Esthonia) in the United States to prevent their expropriation by Moscow. A week later Acting Secretary of State Welles issued a statement condemning the admission of the three Baltic countries into the Soviet Union. And in the spring of 1940 the American Ambassador to Russia (Laurence Steinhardt) left Moscow for four months. In August, Foreign Minister Molotov bitterly castigated American policy toward Russia, accusing Washington of illegal action in regard to Baltic properties in this country.

Yet notwithstanding the fact that American-Soviet relations had reached a new low in the spring and summer of 1940, the door was never finally locked. The fall of France and the air blitz on England so thoroughly alarmed the American Government that it dared not cut all its bridges to Russia. Moreover, the Soviet Union was already suspicious of Germany, and the two powers were beginning to fall out over their respective spoils in Eastern Europe.

On August 6 a one-year extension of the American-Russian trade agreement was approved and Ambassador Steinhardt returned to Moscow; and on January 21, 1941, the American moral embargo on airplane shipments to Russia was withdrawn. Welles and Soviet Ambassador Oumansky in a series of eighteen conversations painstakingly explored the possible bases for closer relations in the winter and spring of 1940–1941. The American diplomat was convinced, after Hitler's failure to win the Battle of Britain, that the Nazi forces would gamble on an eastern drive. The poor showing of Soviet troops in the Finnish War, and the knowledge that a German victory over Russia would enhance America's insecurity, automatically shed a new light on Washington's attitude toward Moscow. American ships began to ply the Pacific waters to Vladivostok with wheat, petroleum, and mineral products.

Suddenly, in April 1941, the devious strands of American-Soviet collaboration were snapped with the announcement of the Russo-Japanese Neutrality Pact.[1] In view of the growing impasse between Japan and the United States, the Soviet action was regarded by the American public as a direct slap, and as ultimate proof that Moscow, despite the folly of its policy, was irretrievably committed to the cause of the Axis powers. However, official Washington reserved judgment. On April 14 the State Department opined that the Pact's significance "could be overestimated. The agreement would seem to be descriptive of a situation which has in effect existed between the two countries for some time past. It therefore comes as no surprise . . ."

[1] See Appendix D.

Two months later Hitler launched his attack on Russia. Following the lead of British Prime Minister Churchill, the United States Government, despite its mistrust of the Soviet dictatorship, declared that "any defense against Hitlerism" would "redound to the benefit of our own defense and security." This did not mean a twenty-four hour reversal of American sentiment, however. Antagonism against Russia had been too deep and too general for a precipitate about-face by the government. Moreover, the consensus of opinion in the Western democracies was that the Russians could not hold out for more than a few months.

But as the weeks passed the Soviet forces demonstrated their staying power, while at the same time the United States was drawn inexorably into the vortex of war. Under these rapidly changing conditions in the autumn of 1941, statements of friendship for Russia and promises of aid to Russia seemed less apocryphal.

In October, a joint British-American mission to Moscow arranged for mutual aid in the prosecution of the war and the American Government agreed to extend lend-lease assistance to the Soviets—a decision which had been postponed earlier because of administration and congressional fear of domestic political repercussions. Moreover, in a statement on the Moscow Conference, American representative Averell Harriman noted: "It is the determination of the three Governments to establish, after the final destruction of Nazi tyranny, a peace which will give all countries an opportunity to live in security on their own territory without knowing either fear or want." This expression of common purpose and common dedication was, significantly, the most striking illustration of American-Russian friendship in the eight years subsequent to recognition. Just as significantly, it found its motivation not in abstract principles or traditions of amity, but in the very present threat of a common enemy.

In the decade preceding Pearl Harbor, Japan progressively monopolized the Far Eastern spotlight. In proportion as she did so, the United States shifted its role from a major protagonist to one less ambitious. Washington continued to speak its piece, but left the action to others; with the result that after a few years its static lines no longer fitted the swift-moving plot, and the American Government was rudely shoved from the stage.

In contrast to Washington, and in part because of the latter's abstention from Far Eastern politics, Moscow spoke softly and carried a big stick in its approach toward Japan—a policy eminently more pragmatic than that adhered to by the Western Republic. Although the United States and the Soviet Union were opposed to Japanese aggrandizement, they made no conspicuous effort to join forces. Throughout the entire tragic decade American-Soviet relations in the Far East were for the most part dormant—a fact of no small significance to the Japanese, and of inestimable cost to Washington, Moscow, and every peace-loving nation of the world.

The Manchurian "incident" of 1931 had been for the Japanese a highly successful trial balloon. It had revealed the weakness of China, the impotence of the League, and the passivity of the United States in the face of calculated aggression.

The first of these "revelations" was perhaps not too surprising, in view of China's traditional inability to protect itself against imperialistic foreign states. Yet to the Japanese it was auspicial, for the Nationalist Government of Chiang Kai-shek, which bid fair to establish a strong regime over and against the debilitating rivalries of hostile war lords, had been from the outset an unwelcome portent in the eyes of Tokyo. Therefore confirmation of China's continuing vulnerability was a source of satisfaction and an incentive to further aggression.

The impotence of the League could less easily have been predicted. The obvious handicap under which it labored because of the absence of the United States and the U.S.S.R. from its membership had been partially offset by the successes achieved in its handling of minor disputes in the twenties. Moreover, the international atmosphere was peculiarly tuned to the language of cooperation; conferences for arms limitation, the Locarno Pact, the (Anti-War) Pact of Paris, stood as milestones leading the way from the pathological diplomacy of war to the enlightened diplomacy of peace. Opinion the world over was revolted by the barbarities of brute force and dubious of their capacity to achieve good.

The combination of these factors undoubtedly gave pause to the

Japanese aggressor; but, as events proved, it was not enough to stem the rising tide of the Second World War. In the first place, the anathema toward force remained purely negative. Ships were sunk, armies dispersed; but the very real problems dividing nations—the problems which historically had stimulated armaments—were left unresolved except as feckless platitudes could resolve them. So that when, as with Japan, the "have-not" states employed might to achieve their objectives, the verbal proponents of pacifism lacked the imagination, the spiritual strength, and the resources to cope with the situation. In the second place, the Japanese were given an unexpected ally in the depression of 1929, which they used shamelessly and to striking advantage in the years ahead. On the one hand, they argued with conviction that their atavistic aggrandizement was from economic necessity, that the high tariffs imposed by the Western world, the relentless pressure of population within the overcrowded Japanese islands, and the scarcity of raw materials impelled military and political expansion on the continent of Asia. On the other hand, the unprecedented economic collapse made the members of the League extremely loath to assume the financial burden of sanctions against Japan or to incur the huge expenses contingent on rearmament.

American passivity in the face of Japan's invasion confirmed the Japanese in their imperialistic intent, even as it provided the League of Nations with additional justification for inaction. In 1931–1932, as again in 1935 (Italy versus Ethiopia), the Geneva powers held a dim view of sanctions without full American participation and support. But the United States was the recipient of one-third of Japan's foreign trade, a factor of possibly telling significance, given the rending agony of depression. Furthermore, the American isolationist mood was not to be shaken by an "incident" or even by a war in the Pacific. Acting in perfect consistency with its age-old China policy, Washington was brave with words; and on January 7, 1932, it made a strong protest to both Japan and China, declaring that it would not recognize any infringement of "the treaty rights of the United States or its citizens in China, including those which relate to the sovereignty, the independence, or the territorial and administrative integrity of the Republic of China." Nonrecognition was also extended to violations of the open-door policy and of the Kellogg-Briand Pact. But both the League members and Japan perceived the shallowness of American concern, and acted accordingly.

In the spring of 1933 the Japanese Kwantung Army came to a halt in North China. By this time Manchuria had been amputated and, under Japanese auspices, had achieved the dubious status of an "independent" nation, renamed Manchukuo. The cessation of Japanese military activity was not intended as a prelude to peace in the Far East. The need to digest the territory already conquered, to consolidate and strengthen military forces for future advances, and to assess once again the possible reactions of the West (Japan had left the League of Nations two months previously) influenced Tokyo in concluding a temporary truce in Hopei Province.

The Far Eastern policy of Soviet Russia combined caution with firmness at this time. As we have seen in Chapter XII, Moscow alternately approached China and Japan between 1931 and 1933, and although its over-all attitude was seemingly one of resignation to Tokyo's incursions into Manchuria, Russia's geographical propinquity placed definite limits on its appeasement policy. The problem before Japan, therefore, was to determine how far it could safely proceed without precipitating a conflict with the Soviet Union. Relatively speaking, Japan possessed nearly all the advantages and few disadvantages in a potential struggle with Russia. Its armies were concentrated *en masse* on the continent and, equally important, were within easy supplying distance of the home islands. Conversely, the Soviet Government was constructing Siberian defenses, and the battle of logistics had yet to be won. Tokyo could not call on other governments for supplementary strength; but the European nations and the United States through the limitation of their armaments had elevated Japan to a dominating position as a Pacific sea power, and this more than compensated for a lack of foreign allies.

Under these circumstances it was in Moscow's interest to prepare its own defenses and simultaneously to seek Western friends, before the Asiatic balance of power was thrown irreparably out of joint. The Russian pursuit of both these goals was in part responsible for the Japanese cease-fire order in May 1933.

Six months later the Roosevelt Administration entered into diplomatic relations with the U.S.S.R. We do not know whether the Soviet Government, as a consequence of the Roosevelt-Litvinov conversations, anticipated informal cooperation with Washington in the Far East; but at least Moscow trusted that American recognition would be an added deterrent to further Japanese imperialism.

This sanguine hope was shared by the American Ambassador at Tokyo, who confided in his diary on February 8, 1934: "our recognition of the Soviet Union has injected into the situation a restraining influence, probably of greater effect than any other single integral." [2] In the light of later history, Mr. Grew's notation seems strangely naïve; but this is only because his government failed to grasp the opportunity he perceived to check the Japanese. Psychologically, the early months of 1934 were crucial in Far Eastern international politics. Japan's forces in North China were still quiescent; Tokyo's appetite was unsated, but an impressive stand by the West might well have diminished it. The League of Nations, together with the United States and Great Britain, were providing aid and credits to expedite Chinese recovery. The Soviet Union, which was concluding nonaggression pacts in the West and, in September 1934, was to join the League, had at length gained entrance at least to the anteroom of the family of nations.

In other words, a tentative anti-Japanese entente was not an impossible daydream at this time. Moreover, those isolationists in the United States who had argued for an unequivocal American withdrawal from the Far East after the Manchurian "incident" had apparently lost their case. Japanese insolence, and the traditional American Asiatic policy, guaranteed the continuing interest of Washington. Idealistic motives—innate American sympathy with the "underdog," opposition to military aggression, respect for treaty commitments, and support of the rights of all peoples to independence and self-determination—and the more materialistic considerations of economic interest (which could best be preserved through the open-door and a balance of power) served in 1934

[2] Grew, *op cit.*, p. 120.

as in previous years to fix American attention on the Far East.

Viewed in this context, Ambassador Grew's words take on deeper significance. The United States and the Soviet Union had established diplomatic relations at a conspicuous moment; and had the opportunity been fully exploited the subsequent history of the Far East might have been other than the dark tragedy it was.

Perhaps the decisive date in this period of Asiatic diplomacy was April 18, 1934, when the Japanese Foreign Office threw down the glove in the form of the "Amau statement." This informed the Western powers in no uncertain terms of Tokyo's "Monroe Doctrine" for the Far East, and laid the claim to Japan's supreme and exclusive right in matters affecting China. By way of implementation, Nippon closed Manchukuo and North China to Anglo-American business interests. The ineffectualness of American protests, however vigorous, was attested by Grew at the end of the year. In his diary on December 27 he described the aim of the Japanese army and navy "to obtain trade control and eventually predominant political influence in China, the Philippines, the Straits Settlements, Siam and the Dutch East Indies, the Maritime Provinces and Vladivostok, one step at a time, as in Korea and Manchuria, pausing intermittently to consolidate and then continuing." Given these "dreams of empire," "we would be reprehensibly somnolent if we were to trust to the security of treaty restraints or international comity to safeguard our own interests or, indeed, our own property." [3]

These remarks were noted during the preliminary naval conversations at London, which looked toward the termination of the 1930 London Treaty, in 1936. The insistence of Japan on naval equality with Britain and the United States was resisted by the latter powers, whereupon Japan gave the required two years' notice to terminate the existing naval ratios. This precipitated new discussions with the West, as the United States prepared to rebuild its navy in competition with Tokyo.

Notwithstanding the strong protests emanating from Washington in 1933–1934, the Amau statement provoked no concrete action from the West, and in January 1935 the Nipponese Kwantung

[3] *Ibid.*, p. 147.

Army again embarked on military conquest throughout North China.

During the remainder of the thirties repetitive American denunciations in no wise altered Japan's China policy. American isolationism was at its zenith in 1937–1938 and opinion polls revealed that to the majority of the population the Far East was too remote to warrant our interest, much less our interference. The full-scale war (undeclared) launched by the Japanese in China in 1937 evoked shockingly little concern from the American public, and even the sinking of the *Panay* in December, with the egregious Japanese violation of American rights and property, stimulated a comparatively mild popular reaction in the United States. Meantime in the autumn of 1937 the Brussels Conference of the Nine-Power Pact signatories and Soviet Russia failed signally in the effort to initiate a collective front in Asia.

In October and December 1938, Washington dispatched its two strongest notes to Tokyo, charging the Nipponese marauder with flagrant infractions of the open-door and of American rights in China. By this time Japan had begun to press France and Britain, taking advantage of their weakness as reflected in the Munich accord. The high-handed treatment accorded Anglo-French nationals by the Japanese in China; the audacity of Japan's obvious intention to take over Hong Kong and Indo-China; the continuing pillage and destruction in China itself—all exerted a moderating influence on American isolationism. But diplomatic protests alone, however strongly couched, were impotent. Both Tokyo and Washington were aware at the end of 1938 that the United States Government had reached a turning point. Henceforth either it would have to implement its oft reiterated diplomatic position, or retreat. The Japanese gambled on the latter, and proceeded with their imperial timetable, moving south in China and Indo-China.

Although the Export-Import Bank advanced a fresh credit of $25,000,000 to China in December 1938 and strong groups in America began a vigorous campaign to blacklist Japan by imposing an embargo on war materials, a Gallup poll in June 1939 revealed that, despite a sizable majority of American opinion favorable to economic measures against Japan, only 6 per cent supported the use of force. Figures published at this time indicated that Japan was impressively dependent on the United States for the essentials of modern war: 90 per cent of Japan's scrap iron, 66 per cent of its petroleum, 45 per cent of its lead, and more than 55 per cent of its strategic war materials came from America. But in the summer of 1939 the State Department contented itself with notifying Tokyo that the 1911 commercial treaty between the two countries would terminate in six months. Not until twelve months later, to the day, did Washington take the first steps toward an economic embargo against Japan. By that time the Second World War was nearly a year old in Europe, France had fallen, and Britain was reeling under Goering's sky attack. By that time, too, the Roosevelt Administration was keenly aware of the global nature of the war, and of its ultimate responsibility therein. A staunch refusal to retreat in the face of increasing Japanese provocations, and the moderate but continuing American naval rearmament, made a showdown with Tokyo only a question of months.

Significantly, America's participation in the Second World War was precipitated by its *Far Eastern* policy. To the die-hard isolationists, this fact comprised unanswerable vindication of their thesis: had the United States remained a Continental power, involvement in the War would have been superfluous. But to other observers the moral of Pearl Harbor lay in a different direction. They held that the responsibility for our struggle against Japan lay not in American interests in the Far East *per se*, but in the shortsightedness and naïveté of American diplomacy. This incompetence was the product of diverse influences and, because they were complex, their analysis did not automatically insure their resolution.

The proponents of this theory noted that Americans by and large were like the boy who, at sixteen, still wore knee pants and curls in order to escape his growing responsibilities, and counted upon his elders to protect him against the petty vicissitudes of life. There had been a time in the youth of America when its idealistic pronouncements regarding the open-door and the territorial integrity of China had reflected British interests equally, and the elder cousin's naval prowess furnished an impressive backdrop for the American statements. But that was in the nineteenth century.

For thirty-five years Anglo-Saxon power had been slowly retrenching, and in proportion the thalassic might of Japan had extended over an ever-widening radius in Eastern Asia. Unwilling to shake themselves free of the delusion of their moral invincibility—indeed, unwilling even to acknowledge their former dependence on benevolent British power—the majority of Americans continued to proclaim their Far Eastern formulae without the slightest intention of injecting therein the ballast of military and naval support. Paradoxically, it was equally unthinkable to them that they should withdraw from Asia or take concrete measures to protect their foreign interests. Obviously, in the event of determined aggression by another nation the United States would have no recourse but to fall back, albeit protestingly, until a point was reached beyond which it refused to go. At that point, with the advantage strongly on the side of the aggressor, conflict would ensue.

The unreality of this brand of paper diplomacy, combined with an historic American aversion to foreign commitments, precluded the implementation of our Far Eastern policy by alliances with other interested states. American isolationists denounced the alliance system as un-American and dangerous, declaring that it would drag the United States into "foreign" wars. Apparently the suggestion that we might draw other powers into "American" wars was unworthy of consideration.

In this frame of reference, it is at once apparent why Washington pursued a unilateral and an unsuccessful policy in its efforts to maintain some semblance of a balance of power in the Far East. From the outset of the Manchurian crisis Great Britain lagged behind the State Department when the latter inveighed against Japan; for the British understood that the Americans spoke without the authority of force and that, in so speaking, they were inviting trouble instead of compliance. Apart from England and France, both of which were unwilling to challenge Tokyo in the thirties, Soviet Russia was the only conceivable power in sympathy with the basic American position. But Russia, too, knew the impotence of words and was unmoved by them. On the other hand, from Washington's point of view the Soviet Government was the least desirable "friend."

It will be remembered that the hysterical fear of communism had never wholly vanished from certain powerful circles in America; and, as the decade wore on, the influence of these groups (including conservative business interests and the Catholic Church) was increasingly felt. The House Committee on un-American activities, under the chairmanship of Martin Dies, was a focus and a breeding ground for anti-Communist activities. Its uncritical and adolescent excesses, its star chamber and un-American proceedings, and its lugubrious ballyhoo served only to blind American citizens to the far graver menace of fascism and to confirm them in the strange wisdom of isolation.

Notwithstanding this ideological bias toward communism, American Far Eastern diplomacy was the product essentially of the American nationalist tradition. The Communist fear, accordingly, reinforced but in no vital sense determined the United States policy. Therefore, the Soviet support of the Chinese Communists, although viewed with suspicion in Washington, in no wise prevented the consolidation of a joint Soviet-American front against Japan. At the same time, the repeated Japanese harangues against Communist infiltration in China, the consistent Japanese efforts to turn Chiang Kai-shek against the Chinese "Reds," and even the conclusion by Tokyo and Berlin of the Anti-Comintern Pact (November 25, 1936), were dictated basically by non-Communist motives. The Japanese regarded Moscow in the thirties as the same potential obstacle to the fulfillment of their imperialist designs as in the years 1895–1904, and 1907–1917. The Nipponese objective, therefore, was to minify, if not to neutralize, the threat from the north by effectively isolating the Russian Bear.

The Soviet response to the ominous international picture in the Far East was more realistic than that of any other power. Given the growing menace of nazism in Europe, the undeviating ambition of Japan in Asia, the dangerously weak condition of China, the innocuous diplomacy of the United States, and the absence of any substantial Russian ally, the Soviet Government was hardly in an enviable position. Yet it succeeded in safeguarding its own Asiatic territory and in diverting the Japanese to the south. Simultaneously it substantially bolstered China's powers of resistance. The fact that

Russia's policy was conducted at the expense of British, French, and American Far Eastern interests was a tribute to Moscow's ability to look to its own well-being in a mad world. It was smart politics.

In compounding a formula for national security, Russia tempered appeasement with steel and in so doing garnered the slow respect of the Japanese. Thus, Moscow's sale of the Chinese Eastern Railroad to Japan in 1935, despite a strong Chinese protest against this alleged violation of the 1924 Sino-Soviet Treaty, was manifestly a Soviet gesture of appeasement. It was modified, however, by the conclusion of a Russian–Outer Mongolian gentleman's agreement (1934) in which each country pledged to aid the other in the event of aggression by a third power; in March 1936 this agreement was extended in a pact providing for the stationing, respectively, of Soviet and Mongolian troops in each other's territory. Although this was an impressive factor in preventing a Mongolian-Manchukuo border dispute from erupting into active hostility, the Chiang Kai-shek Government protested the Soviet pact, again on the ground of the 1924 Russo-Chinese Treaty, Article V of which stated that no "foreign state may conclude with [Outer Mongolia] . . . any treaties or agreements."

The Chinese reaction was not unexpected, in view of the unregenerate hatred of Chiang for the Soviet rulers. Indeed, he had more than once indicated his preference—if a choice were inevitable—as between the Japanese imperialists and the Russian Communists; and his seeming concentration on crushing the Chinese Soviet forces, to the neglect of consolidating his country to ward off the Nipponese, had facilitated Japan's task even as it had won for him the widening hostility of his own people. However, after the Sian "incident" (December 1936), when Chiang's kidnapers pleaded with him for a united front, the civil war was temporarily halted. The Chinese "Reds," whether or not at the behest of Moscow, cooperated effectively with the Kuomintang until the signing of the Russo-Japanese Neutrality Pact in 1941.

Meantime Japan had joined the Berlin Axis, hoping thereby to insure at least the negative acquiescence of Russia in its continuing depredations in China. In reply the Soviets further strengthened their fortifications along the Manchurian-Mongolian border and increased their shipments of military supplies to China. In July 1937 the Japanese determined to end the China "incident" by launching a full-scale attack. The following month Russia concluded a Non-Aggression Pact with Chiang Kai-shek's government. Despite notable successes, Japan was still far from ultimate victory over China the following summer, when the first of several undeclared wars broke out against the Russians along the northern frontiers. Surprised by the unexpected striking power of the Soviet military machine, the Japanese sustained significant defeats which effectively deterred them from further adventures in that direction. If additional arguments were needed to turn Tokyo from the north, they were supplied in August 1939 by the Nazi-Soviet Non-Aggression Pact and, in the summer of 1940, by the success of the German blitzkrieg in Europe.

By the agreement of 1939 Russia was momentarily exempted from the implications of the Anti-Comintern Pact. The Nazi triumph over France and Western Europe effectively wiped out the resistance of those powers to Japanese incursions into Southeast Asia. The United States was the only conceivable enemy left, but the Japanese apparently felt that any potential American resistance could be dispelled, first by Tokyo's full membership in the Rome-Berlin Axis in October 1940, and second by the conclusion of the Russo-Japanese Neutrality Pact the following April.

For the Soviet, the pact with Japan was intended primarily to guarantee the Siberian hinterland if Russia should become involved in the European struggle. For the Japanese, it was viewed as a similar assurance against a Russian attack should Tokyo go to war with the Western powers. The confidence of each signatory in the Pact was ironically witnessed by the large number of Russian and Japanese forces retained on the Siberian-Manchurian border.

American condemnation of the Soviet-Japanese agreement was as naïve as the American policy of the preceding decade. In response the Kremlin contended that Washington's economic assistance to Tokyo had vastly facilitated the Japanese war against China, a point which could not easily bear refuting. Notwithstanding these exchanges, Japan was feared equally by both countries; in 1941 as in 1914 she had wrecked the balance of power, and thereby threatened the Far Eastern interests of Russia and the United States. Consequently the Nazi onslaught against the Soviet Union in June 1941, together with the worsening relations of Tokyo and Washington, ultimately worked to facilitate a Russo-American rapprochement. In July, Washington evinced deep concern over rumors that Japan was preparing to attack Russia.[4] Simultaneously American ships stepped up their crossings to Siberia, the petroleum which had formerly been destined for Japan went to Russia, and Tokyo's protests over what it termed American-Soviet "encirclement" of Japan were unavailing. It has been suggested, and is worth considering, that among the reasons for the Japanese attack on Pearl Harbor was the belief that an American-Russian understanding was imminent.

In retrospect, recognition of the U.S.S.R. by Washington in 1933 had been a barren gesture. Neither in Europe nor in Asia, neither in economic terms nor in political terms, had it borne fruit worthy of note. In the Far East recognition had provided an opportunity to reorient American-Soviet relations, to tighten resistance to Japan, and very possibly to thwart the establishment of the "Greater East Asia Co-Prosperity Sphere." Under the accepted rules of the balance of power game, that was the orthodox move. The Russians knew this from experience, the Americans from observation. This is not to predict that peace would have been guaranteed had such an alignment been established, for the balance of power policy has historically emptied itself in war. But it is to suggest, rather, that given the "rules" of the game, and the avowed American policy of preserving an equilibrium in the Far East, it was the logical step to expect. Failure to rebuild a more durable balance through an American-Soviet understanding must rest mainly with the United States, for the diplomacy of the period and the exigencies of the situation afford ample proof that the Russians were desirous of an accord. The crudities of Soviet manners, and the cruelties of the Soviet system did indeed repel Americans, but in the thirties at least they were a lesser evil than unchecked, rampaging Japanese aggression.

The proof of the postulate lies in its subsequent history. In the

[4] *For. Rel.*, Japan, 1931–1941, Vol. II, pp. 502–503.

war against Japan after December 1941, America and Russia became increasingly "friendly" and eventually were allies. One of their primary purposes in defeating the Axis nations was to reestablish a *balance of power* in Europe and Asia. Had steps been taken toward this end a decade earlier, they would have been infinitely less costly and they might, temporarily, have succeeded. But by 1941 only a cataclysmic, soul-shaking, inhuman blood orgy could turn the tide of aggression, and not even that could restore the balance of power.

CHAPTER XIV

The Fruits of War

The Second World War was the most damning indictment ever made against Western civilization. It claimed the lives of twenty-five million persons, cost well over a trillion dollars, and cast into oblivion the archaic framework of the prewar world. At the same time, it solved few of the problems which had precipitated it, and left in its wake a residue of bitterness, hatred, frustration, and fear which ill equipped men for the arduous task of building a new and better world.

As we move on in the postwar period, increasingly the victims of a Third World War psychosis, the trend of international politics during and since the war becomes at once more recognizable and more alarming. We are awakening from the dreams we took refuge in during the dark days of conflict, when the realities of brutal, barbarous struggle shocked and repelled us and the vision of a united world haunted the hearts and minds of millions of men. Today, as American-Soviet relations dip from one low to another and passions mount, we are indulging in another kind of wishful thinking; we are looking to our defenses—military, political, economic—and seeking security through a formula of armaments, alliances, good will, and a new balance of power. Incongruously, the dream of the family of nations still persists side by side with the competing dream of national sovereign security. Paradoxically, both are the fruits of war; but they cannot ripen simultaneously, and as more and more attention is focused on security the fruit of one world withers perceptibly on the vine.

To trace the devious strands of world politics which comprise the pattern of current international relations is a many-sided task, only part of which can be attempted here. Yet it is suggested that

287

the history of American-Soviet relations in the Far East during
the war and postwar years provides a central clue to an analysis
of the crisis of our time.

The disillusionment which has swept America since the war, and
which exerts such an enervating influence on the efforts at peace-
making, stems in largest part from the steady deterioration in
American-Soviet amity. Recalling the ecstatic eulogies heaped upon
our Russian ally by Americans of all political and social walks
during the war years, and the coals of wrath now so freely showered
on the "Red menace," one is confronted with a most dramatic
illustration of the inconstancy of international friendship. The
build-up of American-Soviet cordiality during the war was motivated by naïveté, idealism, and expediency, and the main initiative
and enthusiasm were American, not Russian. It will be recalled
that frequent American complaints charged that the Soviet Government withheld from its people the amount of lend-lease material
supplied by the United States to Russia, that American and Allied
victories against Germany were given too little attention in the
Soviet press, that the Russians were unwilling to pool their military
secrets with those of their Allies or to make available air bases on
Soviet territory for Allied bombing missions.

In contrast, Britain and the United States were generous in their
praise of Russia. On the unofficial level, despite a minority who
either reserved judgment or questioned the future plans of the
U.S.S.R., a spate of books and articles lauded all things Soviet,
and explained to an avid public how the long tradition of
American-Russian friendship made the wartime alliance of the two
powers the natural culmination of an historical process. Americans
discovered that Soviet citizens, too, came of a pioneering stock,
and that the peoples of both countries had a natural affinity toward
one another. The Russian Bear was also praised, although with
more restraint, by official circles in Washington. Thus Acting Secretary of State Dean Acheson, in November 1944, could note that
"the destiny of our friendship" with Russia was to build an international organization "to keep the world's peace . . . We will
not fail in this solemn trust." Likewise, he could speak of "the
splendid attitude displayed" at the Dumbarton Oaks conversa-

tions "by those fine public servants, Ambassador Gromyko and Lord Halifax." Thus too could Secretary of State Hull envisage a postwar international organization (after the Four-Power Declaration at Moscow, October 1943) to obviate the need for "spheres of influence, for alliances, for balance of power," which had characterized international relations "in the unhappy past."

These remarks, and others of similar content, could be reproduced at length. However, it is only fair to add that the sanguine expectations of Messrs. Hull and Acheson were often qualified by an acknowledgment that grave problems and American-Soviet differences had yet to be resolved. The unquestioning confidence of preceding months was gradually replaced by the cautious optimism of Franklin D. Roosevelt, as revealed in his Message to Congress on January 6, 1945: "The nearer we come to vanquishing our enemies the more we inevitably become conscious of differences among the victors"; "Nations like individuals do not always see alike or think alike, and international cooperation and progress are not helped by any nation assuming that it has a monopoly of wisdom or of virtue"; "We cannot deny that power is a factor in world politics . . . But in a democratic world . . . power must be linked with responsibility . . ." Moreover, a less idealistic group of career men in the State Department (who balked at the "Trust Russia" school) never succumbed to the friendship fever of their colleagues, and were gradually eased from positions of influence or remained as a minority opinion until the postwar course of American-Russian relations had vindicated their viewpoint. Nevertheless, it can be asserted fairly that at the end of the war the prevailing mood of the American public was one of ardent friendship for the Soviet peoples and admiration for their leaders, and that the American Government reflected this sentiment in its initial postwar foreign policy.

Several factors contributed to the rapid division of East and West into semi-hostile camps after V-E Day. Those who, on the one hand, quickly adduced proof of Russia's guilt or, on the other, rushed to the defense of the Soviet Union and charged the West with perfidy overlooked a tremendously significant fact—namely, that American-Soviet friendship, constructed mainly of no sterner stuff than expedience, had been shaped in the matrix of war. Once the struggle had ended, the disparate elements in the East-West alliance fell apart. This should have surprised no one conversant with the rudiments of international power politics, for as long as the nations continued to act within an anarchic political system the war itself guaranteed the postwar rivalry of the victors.

It is true that the mantle of power rested uneasily on the shoulders of the two inexperienced super-states, and that the clumsiness with which each exercised its new role inevitably generated friction.

It is true that the naïveté of the United States and the suspicious nature of the Soviet Union invited difficulty and trouble at every stage of negotiations. Washington ventured forth into the postwar era with the faith of a tyro; and Moscow, indoctrinated with the belief that the Western democracies were "soft" and decadent, wrongly mistook generosity for appeasement and strove to displace American influence in Europe and Asia. When, in consternation over Soviet opportunism, Washington changed its compliance to stiff resistance, the Russians claimed to see the fulfillment of Marxist-Leninist-Stalinist prophecy regarding the aggressive ("fascist") nature of imperialist-capitalist states, and the chasm between the United States and the U.S.S.R. was further widened.

It is likewise true that the ideological gulf separating communism and democracy has accentuated the points of conflict between the two governments, although in view of their wartime cooperation it seems more plausible to credit ideology with an accessory role in the present strained relations.

But when all these points have been taken into consideration, they remain subsidiary to the compelling condition of world anarchy, within which the power struggle between contending nations is eternally reenacted. Seen in this larger context, the only ways in which the present conflict between Russia and the United States differs from international rivalries of other days are in the names of the contenders and the stakes involved. Dwarfing all previous struggles, the Second World War encompassed the entire planet, wreaked fiendish devastation over vast areas, and willed a bankrupt globe to the "victors." Two nations alone emerged from the holocaust with active or potential strength sufficient to warrant the classification of first-rate powers. The war had not only undermined the power fundament throughout the world, but it had wiped out the complex balance by eliminating, for the time at least, Britain, France, Germany, Italy, and Japan as vital power factors. And so it was that the United States and the Soviet Union, which prior to yesterday had had practically no overlapping foreign interests, suddenly found themselves face to face and treading on each other's toes in two continents—Europe and Asia. The disintegration of German and Japanese military prowess left an irresistible vacuum. China, the immediate heir to Asiatic power, was too hopelessly entangled in its own political contradictions, too ravaged by years of unremitting conflict to grasp its inheritance; England and France, worn haggard by the global struggle, no longer possessed the physical strength or the financial resources to play determinate roles in Europe or Asia; and the United Nations, a fledgling organization, was not yet of sufficient stature to stand against the biting winds of anarchy. Consequently the Soviet and American governments were drawn inexorably into the power vacuums, with none to slow their pace, to question their deed, or to soften their impact.

Since the war American-Soviet relations in the Far East, as well as in Europe, have been almost unrelievedly negative and continually more depressing. Each country has been engaged in a search for national security in which its protagonist has appeared as the villain. Unwilling to merge their drives for security in a common front within the world organization, each is faced with an inevitable and perilous dilemma; under existing circumstances Russia and the United States are each other's only potential enemies, and therefore their respective concepts of "national security" are exclusive and incompatible: America's "security" spells insecurity to the Russian leaders, and vice versa.

With this grave picture in mind one can examine perhaps most realistically the record of American-Russian postwar relations in Asia. The Far Eastern drama is composed of three acts, each progressing simultaneously on separate stages, and each influencing the course of the others. In Japan, China, and Korea the fruits of war are still being harvested, and they are, with few exceptions, bitter indeed.

The war against Japan extended over three years, eight months, during the last two days of which the Soviet Union joined forces with the Western nations and China. Despite the initial comment of *Pravda*, labeling the Japanese attack on Pearl Harbor "treacherous" and naming Japan the aggressor, the Russian Government maintained a scrupulous neutrality, thereby fulfilling the letter of its Pact with Japan and simultaneously serving its own national interests, which militated decisively against a two-front war. The logic in the Soviet position was thoroughly understood by the United States Government, as distinguished from various sections of American public opinion which failed to appreciate the strategy of the situation and even suggested that Russia was aiding the Nipponese. But Russo-Japanese relations had been strained too long to permit cooperation between the Far Eastern rivals; moreover, Russia had nothing to gain and everything to lose by a Japanese victory. Not only would American defeat have terminated the vital flow of military supplies from the United States to the Soviet Union, thus jeopardizing Russia's position in the European war, but Japanese military success would clearly threaten Russian rights and interests in Eastern Asia.

In other words, regardless of the different official status of Moscow and Washington toward Tokyo from December 7, 1941, until August 9, 1945, Japan was equally the enemy of both. However, in any accurate appraisal of the Soviet eleventh-hour entry into the Japanese war, this factor of a common Japanese foe comprises only one element in Russian reasoning and, indeed, by August 1945 it was an element definitely of secondary importance. A major cause behind the Soviet declaration of war was Moscow's fear of the United States. Moreover, a reciprocal American suspicion of Russian Far Eastern motives made the State Department uneasy concerning Moscow's eagerness to join the Asiatic struggle. This paradox is easily explained by a brief consideration of changing power relationships during the war years.

As long as the Japanese were victorious and effectively challenging the Western powers throughout Asia, Russia and the United States had a mutual interest in Tokyo's defeat which determined and dominated their relations with each other. Furthermore, while this condition persisted, Far Eastern international politics were following a familiar course so far as Washington and Moscow were concerned, for the three-cornered rivalry of Russia, America, and Japan, with Japan at the apex of the triangle and the other two states on the defensive, had been a traditional feature of the Asiatic pattern throughout most of the preceding half-century. The only difference was one of degree; Japan had at length overreached itself, and a chronic diplomatic situation now had ruptured into an angry war.

Toward the end of 1944 there was no doubt in Soviet minds that Japan's defeat was assured and that Tokyo could not afford to embroil itself with the U.S.S.R. At the same time, the advancing second front in Western Europe, together with Russian victories over Hitler's armies in the East, signified almost certain triumph in the German theater. To the men in the Kremlin this auspicious situation was the signal for a shift in strategy both in Europe and in Asia. In the Far East, the eventual collapse of Japan would spell the supremacy of American influence unless positive Soviet action were taken while the war still continued. In short, to the Russians (as, indeed, to their Allies) the United Nations were held together by the threat of declared enemies; once these were overcome it was logical to anticipate new rivalries among the victors. Thus, as the Nipponese slowly succumbed to the gathering might of the United States, the figure of Uncle Sam gradually replaced the Son of Heaven in Soviet Far Eastern calculations. Concretely, Moscow began thinking of entering the Japanese war in order to assure participation in the peace settlements and the protection of Russia's Asiatic interests.

The American reaction to the prospective power situation following a United States victory over Japan was probably not too dissimilar from that of the U.S.S.R., but one important point bears stressing. Washington was carrying the brunt of the struggle against Tokyo, and the immediate advantages of Soviet co-belligerency, in terms of shortening the conflict, thereby saving thousands of American lives and millions of dollars, had a far more telling effect on American strategists than did the potential political disadvantages which might eventuate in the postwar period, as a result of wartime Russian military cooperation. This reasoning was buttressed by military intelligence reports which grossly overestimated Japanese strength and powers of resistance in Manchuria.[1]

Consequently, at the Yalta Conference in February 1945 American energies were expended in an effort to secure Soviet participation in the Asiatic conflict. As the initiative was clearly American, the bargaining advantage fell to the Soviets. In return for Stalin's promise to enter the war against Japan within two or three months of the surrender of Germany, Churchill and Roosevelt met Russia's demands on so broad a scale as to guarantee an active postwar role for the Soviet Union in Asia and, by the same token, to augment the likelihood of Soviet-American (and British) rivalry there. This phase of the Yalta negotiations, which remained secret for several months after the death of President Roosevelt, proposed to reward Russia for its future cooperation at the expense not only of Japan, but of China as well. Thus, Japan would be forced to divest itself of southern Sakhalin Island, the Kuriles, and Manchuria. The first two areas were pledged to the Soviet Union. Nominally, Chinese sovereignty was reasserted over Manchuria, but the three leaders at Yalta recognized Russia's "preeminent interests" in Dairen (which was to be internationalized under Chinese control) and in the Chinese Eastern and South Manchurian railroads. Moreover, the two railroads would be "jointly operated" by a Sino-Soviet company. It was further agreed that the Tsarist lease of Port Arthur as a naval base would be "restored." And finally, the status quo in Outer Mongolia was to be preserved. With an ironic gesture the Big Three acknowledged that the concurrence of Generalissimo Chiang Kai-shek was required for the implementation of the points affecting China (and the American President was given the task of obtaining it); but in the next breath they

[1] D. N. Rowe, "American Policy Toward China," *Annals of the American Academy of Political and Social Science*, January 1948, p. 139.

affirmed that the Soviet claims "shall be unquestionably fulfilled after Japan has been defeated"—which left little latitude for debate by the Chinese Government.[2]

This secret Yalta Agreement illustrated vividly the fact that in power politics honor and morality are the eternal victims of expedience and rationalization. Apart from President Roosevelt's acquiescence in Soviet demands which manifestly compromised America's Chinese Ally, the Chief Executive and his State Department advisers apparently were not troubled by the prospect that Stalin, at their behest, might be forced to violate an international commitment (the Soviet-Japanese Neutrality Pact) by entering the Far Eastern war. The American attitude was allegedly justified on the ground that Russian participation in the war would hasten its dénouement. Certainly this was a goal worth pursuing, but its cost in terms of American principles of international conduct was exorbitant.

Moreover, a cruel retribution lay in store for the United States. On April 5, 1945, Soviet Russia notified Japan of its intention to denounce the Russo-Japanese Neutrality Pact, effective one year later. In July 1945 at the Potsdam Conference, following the capitulation of Germany, the Russians informed Secretary of State Byrnes of their desire to enter the Asiatic struggle. Instead of exulting over the avidity of the Soviets to redeem their Yalta pledge, the American officials were frankly embarrassed. It was now clear to them that Japan shortly would be forced to its knees; the successful New Mexico experiments with the atomic bomb had wholly altered the Far Eastern picture, so that Russian aid was regarded as superfluous. Of far greater significance, Russian cooperation was not wanted, for it could only mean Communist infiltration and entrenchment throughout that part of Asia covered by the Yalta understanding. The United States had no desire to see Moscow in so potentially powerful a position, particularly as the collapse of Japan would leave Washington alone to challenge future Soviet pretensions in the Far East.

In the eyes of the Politbureau, apprehension over postwar Ameri-

[2] See Appendix E.

can influence in Asia accounted in large part for Russia's eagerness to fulfill the Yalta formula. The impending defeat of Japan threatened to uproot the power fundament in the Far East, and both the United States and the U.S.S.R., for decades suspicious of or actually hostile to the Nipponese, now uneasily confronted each other across the Japanese abyss.

Faced with Soviet determination to enter the war, and unwilling to repudiate the Yalta Agreement, President Truman and his aides sought to make the best of a bad bargain. At least they were able to satisfy the prickings of their own consciences as to the prospective Soviet violation of the Russo-Japanese Neutrality Pact. "We did not believe," wrote Secretary Byrnes, "the United States Government should be placed in the position of asking another government to violate its agreement without good and sufficient reason." [3] Such a reason being absent in the actual military situation, Secretary Byrnes and Ben Cohen, a veteran Roosevelt adviser, proceeded to find one in the Moscow Declaration of October 30, 1943, and in Articles 106 and 103 of the United Nations Charter. In Paragraph 5 of the Moscow Declaration, Russia, Britain, China, and the United States agreed to "consult with one another . . . with a view to joint action in behalf of the community of nations." Article 106 of the Charter stated that the four states would continue to act conjointly in conformity with the Moscow Agreement until ratification of the Charter. And Article 103 stated that "in the event of a conflict between the obligations" of the U.N. members and their obligations "under any other international agreement, their obligations under the present Charter shall prevail." On the basis of these three clauses, President Truman notified Stalin that, although the Soviet Union had not even ratified the Charter at this time, "it would be proper" for Russia "to indicate its willingness to consult and cooperate with other great powers now at war with Japan with a view to joint action on behalf of the community of nations to maintain peace and security." [4]

The Soviet Government, at whose express request the Truman

[3] James F. Byrnes, *Speaking Frankly* (New York: Harper and Brothers, 1947), p. 207.
[4] *Department of State Bulletin,* August 12, 1945, p. 207.

letter had been formulated, quickly responded with a declaration of war on Japan.[5] On August 8, Molotov handed a statement to the Japanese Ambassador at Moscow which referred to the Allied proposal that the Soviet Government participate in the war, and declared that Russia, "true to its obligation as an Ally," had accepted the proposal in the conviction that only through fighting Japan could peace be brought nearer. The state of war was made effective August 9. On August 6 the first atomic bomb had blasted Hiroshima; two days later the second bomb fell on Nagasaki. On August 9 (August 10 Tokyo time) the Soviet Ambassador in Japan presented Foreign Minister Togo with the Russian declaration of war; in return the Japanese statesman handed the Soviet envoy a copy of the message just dispatched to the United States (by Switzerland) with Japan's offer to surrender. The Russians had come in just under the line, and had won certainly the greatest single political victory of the entire war—the victory of Yalta.

In his report to the nation on the Potsdam Conference (August 9) President Truman took this defeat in good grace. "The Soviet Union," he averred, "before she had been informed of our new weapon, agreed to enter the war in the Pacific. We gladly welcomed into this struggle . . . our gallant and victorious ally . . ." While this sentiment undoubtedly aided the cause of American friendship for Russia, it did not reflect the opinion of Mr. Truman's Secretary of State or of his advisers. It is at least a good probability that the statement was made more for the record than from the facts of the situation. The same may also be said of the assertion by Secretary Byrnes that, despite our major burden in crushing Japan, "we had always regarded the war as one against the Axis, and *we intended that the occupation of Japan should be an Allied responsibility*." [6] The subsequent history of American policy toward Japan and the attitude of General MacArthur and of State Department political officers toward the Allied Council in Tokyo and the Far Eastern Commission clearly refute all statements of American interest in inter-Allied cooperation vis-à-vis Japan. In short, although the United States has given every indication that it intends

[5] See Appendix F.
[6] Byrnes, *op. cit.*, p. 213. Italics mine.

to fulfill the onerous obligations contracted at Yalta, it has reso-
lutely sought to forestall additional Soviet encroachments in Eastern Asia. For their part, the Russians entertain an equally lively
determination to check the spread of American influence in the
Orient. And so in the ruthless game of international power-
politics the die has again been cast; the United States and the
Soviet Union vie for position while the nations of the Far East
look on opportunistically, cynically, and disappointedly. Hope has
become a leaven on short rations.

The Truman Administration had decided before V-J Day that
the occupation of Japan would be mainly an American show. The
history of condominiums, the early difficulties and frictions pursuant to the establishment of four-power rule in Berlin, and the revo-
lutionized power status in the Far East led to this decision. Moreover, American strength had been of conclusive importance in
winning the Japanese war, and the War, Navy, and State Departments agreed that the occupation should be preeminently an American responsibility. The appointment of General MacArthur as Supreme Commander of all occupation forces made it doubly certain
that the voice of the United States would dominate.

Those United Nations which had been at war with Japan consented initially to Washington's asserted leadership. The Instrument of Surrender, signed September 2, 1945, alluded to "the Supreme Commander for the Allied Powers," as did the United States
Initial Post-Surrender Policy for Japan (August 29, 1945). In Part II,
Section 1, it explicitly noted: "Although every effort will be made,
by consultation and by constitution of appropriate advisory bodies,
to establish policies for the conduct of the occupation and the control of Japan which will satisfy the principal Allied Powers, in the
event of any differences of opinion among them, the policies of the
United States will govern."

In view of these provisions, the American proposal for a Far Eastern Advisory Commission—submitted on August 22 to the governments of Australia, Canada, China, France, the Netherlands, New
Zealand, the U.S.S.R., the United Kingdom, and the Philippine
Islands—could best be regarded as a sop to the Allies, and as a calculated move to obviate unwanted United Nations suggestions for

a more effectual inter-Allied program. Oddly enough, Moscow (and China) immediately accepted the American proposal, while Great Britain objected on the ground that the Commission's powers would be purely advisory. The British position was reinforced by the ardent desire of Australia and New Zealand for more responsible roles in the formation of Allied policy toward Japan.

Although the Far Eastern question was not on the agenda of the London Conference of Foreign Ministers in September 1945, Secretary Byrnes met with Secretary Bevin in an effort to gain his adherence to the Washington proposal. The American statesman agreed that at the forthcoming Far Eastern Advisory Commission's first meeting the United States would support the suggestions that the commission be permitted to meet both in Tokyo and in Washington, and that India be invited to participate. On this basis the British Government approved the American proposal. Almost simultaneously, however, Molotov began to attack the American occupation policy and to demand, in place of the Far Eastern Advisory Commission, an Allied Control Council for Japan. Secretary Byrnes, who was unprepared for such a discussion, mustered sufficient votes to exclude the subject of a control council from the London agenda; but throughout the Conference, Foreign Minister Molotov kept harping on it, and complaining of the way in which General Mac-Arthur was carrying out the surrender terms. According to the Soviet diplomat, his government feared that United States policy would facilitate a revival of Japanese military strength and aggression. It was allegedly for this reason that Russia revoked its sanction for the Advisory Commission, demanding in its stead more active participation by Britain, China, and the Soviet Government in the formation and implementation of policy toward Japan. The same viewpoint was reiterated by Premier Stalin to Ambassador Averell Harriman on October 25, after the Soviet representative in Tokyo had been recalled, ostensibly because he was neither informed nor consulted by MacArthur. Stalin asserted that Russia was not being accorded consideration in the occupation of Japan commensurate with its great-power status. In support of this charge he listed several grievances, expressing doubt that the Washington meeting of the Far Eastern Advisory Commission could resolve the difficulties. Accordingly, the American envoy was told that Russia would not be present at the meeting, but that if the United States desired to reach an understanding with Moscow, this could best be accomplished through bilateral talks.

The Washington Conference of the Far Eastern Advisory Commission was doomed from the outset. In the first place, Russia's boycott cast the shadow of Allied disunity over the proceedings and undermined considerably the prestige of the Commission. Secondly, the hesitations and criticisms of other interested powers, mostly unpublicized at London—where blame for obstructionism had been focused on the Soviet whipping boy—emerged at Washington and further discredited the American concept of inter-Allied policy formation. Consequently, in November and December extended Allied negotiations sought a compromise arrangement which would be mutually satisfactory. This was finally agreed upon, with Russian concurrence, at the Moscow meeting of Foreign Ministers during the latter part of December.

In theory, the results of the Moscow Conference were favorable to the critics of America's role in Tokyo; in practice, the United States emerged with its ultimate authority unimpaired. In other words, the provision by the Foreign Ministers for a Far Eastern Commission in Washington (to replace the abortive Advisory Commission) and for an Allied Council in Tokyo was chiefly a gesture to save Allied face.[7] The fact was that General MacArthur was in firm and unyielding control of operations in Japan and the other governments involved were powerless to alter the situation.

To the Far Eastern Commission, consisting of the United States, the nine governments listed in Washington's initial proposal of August 22, 1945, and India, were assigned the task of formulating the policies and principles of governing the Japanese occupation, and the responsibility for the fulfillment of the surrender terms. Within this broad framework the following qualifying factors were of decisive significance: The Commission could in no way interfere with the existing chain of command from the American Government to General MacArthur; the United States was em-

[7] The Moscow Conference decisions on the formation of the Far Eastern Commission and the Allied Council are given in Appendices H and I.

powered to issue interim directives to the Supreme Commander when urgent questions arose for which it had formulated no policy; and although these directives would be subject to review by the F.E.C., the veto power (granted to Great Britain, China, Russia, and the United States) protected the American program at all times. By this same veto power, no basic policy could be voted without American concurrence.

In actual operation, the Commission has been considered a moderate success. The veto right has not been exercised; under the expert and sensitive guidance of the chairman, General Frank McCoy, a maximum of international accord has been achieved; and compromise among conflicting viewpoints has been earnestly striven for by the various delegations. Whether such unusual harmony would obtain if the Commission's meetings were public, or if the Big Four possessed equal powers and no handicap were given the United States, is another question.

The career of the group sitting in Tokyo has been far more stormy, though equally ineffectual in so far as its influence on American policy has been concerned. Indeed, the Allied Council has belied its name: it has not performed the usual functions of a council, and its unhappy sessions have made the word "Allied" a *non sequitur*.

The Council, authorized only to advise and consult with the Supreme Commander for the Allied Powers (or "S.C.A.P.," as MacArthur's headquarters quickly became known), was placed under the chairmanship of the Supreme Commander or his deputy. At its first session in April 1946 it was enlightened as to the role assigned it by S.C.A.P.; "good will, mutual understanding, and broad tolerance" were expected, and advice was to be rendered only upon request. The subsequent turbulent history of the body has been eloquently depicted in Richard E. Lauterbach's provocative book, *Danger from the East*. He writes that with the aid of the Soviet delegate (General Kuzma Derevyanko) MacArthur's deputy, George Atcheson, Jr., "turned the Council into a forum for Soviet-American ideological battles, name-calling, and mutual recrimination. The result has been to demonstrate how, in an area where the United States is in control, we can hamstring an allied group more neatly and more effectively than the Russians and with less unfavorable publicity." [8]

By a combination of parliamentary stratagems Atcheson succeeded in placing the Allied Council in a ridiculous and farcical position. The net result was wholly deplorable. In the first place, his tactics embarrassed, angered, and alienated not only the Soviet envoy, but the British and Chinese as well. William McMahon Ball (representing jointly Britain, Australia, New Zealand, and India) and the Chinese delegate frequently were moved to protest the high-handed by-passing of the Council by General MacArthur. In answer Atcheson accused his British and Chinese colleagues of being pro-Russian. Secondly, the endless bickering within the Council was hardly calculated to raise Japanese esteem of the Allies. And finally, because of his uncompromising obstinacy in defending his concepts of American occupation policy and in attacking his critics, Atcheson ineluctably reached the point where he began to uphold the status quo in Japan.

Permeating the entire picture of the Japanese occupation, and of far deeper ultimate significance than what happens at any particular time, is the bitter and basic rivalry between the United States and Russia. Indeed, it is this antagonism that increasingly determines the attitudes of the American Government and General MacArthur—to such an extent that the future status of Japan (like that of Germany in Europe) has ceased to be an end of Allied policy, but is more nearly a means to an end in the Far Eastern power struggle. Consequently, the goal of the occupation, as conceived prior to V-J Day, has been subtly transmuted, even though lip service is still accorded to the original purpose. In sum, it appears that Japan has been viewed by responsible American officials not as a potential future enemy, but as a potential future ally. An awareness of this trend is vital in any explanation or evaluation of the American occupation policy.

In the first place, it explains why friction between the United States and Soviet Russia on the Allied Council is inevitable and why, as each month passes, that friction heightens their suspicion of

[8] Richard E. Lauterbach, *Danger from the East* (New York: Harper and Brothers, 1947), p. 152.

each other; this in turn augments the anti-Soviet bias of S.C.A.P., which then pursues policies destined to create more friction between the Russian and American representatives on the Council. Tragically, this vicious spiral must repeat itself without surcease so long as the prevailing concept of the occupation persists.

In the second place, it goes far to explain the paternalism of MacArthur, and his growing tolerance of parties and reforms in Japan which have fallen conspicuously short of being "democratic." As in so many other areas of the world, American fear of communism has translated itself into support of reactionary right-wing groups which, in Japan as elsewhere, have been quick to profit by the world-wide political rivalry of America and Russia. The first elections in postwar Japan, in April 1946, were a Conservative landslide, and so were the general elections a year later. The Yoshida Government went through the motions of democracy; but behind the façade, Japan's economic trusts (the *Zaibatsu*) retained most of their strength, prewar nationalist political figures operated silently and efficiently, and the government slyly exploited MacArthur's Russophobia by giving loud support to the Truman Doctrine, by playing up the menace of communism, and by resisting undesired domestic reforms on the grounds that they would redound to Communist advantage.

Thirdly, it helps to account for Allied disagreement over reparations and the question of the extent to which Japan should be deindustrialized. This subject has aroused the anxiety of Australia, New Zealand, the Philippines, and China to a degree equal to that of the Soviet Union, for they feel that if Japan were revived as an anti-Communist bastion it would soon repeat its aggressive program throughout Asia and would gain a decisive advantage in the trade of the Pacific. The Chinese in particular have expressed alarm and resentment over American policy in Japan; yet the collapse of the Nationalist Government has been a vital factor in the shaping of that policy.

And finally, the basic disagreement between Russia and America over the future role of Japan in Far Eastern world politics is responsible for the failure, since July 1947, to convene a Japanese peace conference. At that time State Department officials met with representatives of all the countries which were members of the Far Eastern Commission and laid before them American proposals on a peace treaty conference. According to the American suggestion, the gathering would include delegates from the Far Eastern Commission states, and decisions would be reached by a two-thirds majority. By the end of the month the U.S.S.R. had responded with a counter-proposal to the effect that the Council of Foreign Ministers should consider the peace treaty problems in the first instance, and that the principle of unanimity in voting should be adhered to. In reply, the State Department held that the Council of Foreign Ministers at no time had been accorded any authority in regard to this question. The primary interest of the eleven powers represented on the F.E.C. had been recognized by their inclusion in that body and, therefore, all eleven should be included in the peace conference discussions.

The Chinese Government, which occupied an unenviable position between the Eagle and the Bear, sought a compromise whereby eleven-nation representation would be granted, but decisions by a two-thirds majority would have to include the affirmative vote of Britain, China, Russia, and the United States. This suggestion, which was vastly more compatible with the Soviet than with the American approach, was not followed through by the other powers. An American statement on May 19, 1948, confessed that it had "been impossible to resolve the conflict" between the American, Russian, and Chinese proposals. There has since been occasional talk of the advisability of a separate peace treaty between Japan and the F.E.C. powers with the exception of Russia. But the Chinese attitude at any such conference would be unpredictable and conceivably embarrassing for Washington; moreover, it is still felt that such a solution might prove more dangerous in the long run than the continuance of a technical state of war between Japan and the Allies.

Since V-J Day Soviet press organs have carried a running attack on American methods and objectives in Japan, the essence of which has been to picture the MacArthur program as basically anti-Russian. This Soviet theme may be rationalized as Communist propaganda, but its undeviating persistence over a three-year period also suggests a genuine alarm over developments in Japan. Soviet writers have referred at length to American articles which picture a future Japan as an American ally against Russia, and because of their sensitivity to such ideas they are more aware of this trend in our thinking than most of our own people.

The gathering momentum of this trend is deducible from even a cursory survey of American periodicals. Among the more representative articles the following deserve notice: "The United States and the Pacific Islands," by Admiral Thomas C. Hart (retired), in the January 1948, *Annals of the American Academy of Political and Social Science;* "Our New Friends, the Japanese," by Bonner Fellers, in the February 1948, *Nation's Business;* "Japan and the Pacific Problem," by Admiral William V. Pratt (retired), in *Newsweek,* June 7, 1948. In the words of Admiral Pratt:

It would be a sad commentary on us should we now lose our position of leadership in Japan only to see it pass into the hands of the Soviets. . . . Are there any other reasons why we need the steadfast friendship of Japan? Yes, decidedly; what might be called geopolitical reasons. Where can there be found such a racially pure, virile, and determined people as in Japan? Not in China . . . Not in Korea. Not in India . . . And there is the added value of Japan's strategic position. With Japan a strong and a steadfast friend the entire Pacific problem takes on a different character from what it would if the Soviet Union controlled Japan. The hope for peace in the Pacific is greatly increased.[9]

There is something dangerously misleading in this conception of Japan as a potential ally. Surely it is naïve to assume that the Nipponese, who have cherished dreams of empire for decades, and who came so perilously close to realizing them, will suddenly change character and rest content to play the role of American spearhead in the Pacific. As has been noted, there is already evidence of a resurgent nationalism, nurtured by conservative, chauvinist-militarist elements. Their objective is a strong Japan, sufficiently powerful to bargain with *either* the United States *or* Russia (as in former days) in order to recapture their influence and leadership

[9] Adm. William V. Pratt, U.S.N., Ret., "Japan and the Pacific Problem," *Newsweek,* June 7, 1948, p. 32.

in Asia. Unless this aspiration is thoroughly comprehended, our policy toward Tokyo may backfire: we may create in the Far East not a trustworthy friend, but a Frankenstein monster.

The American occupation has not been without its happier aspects. In the course of the third year of S.C.A.P.'s operations its positive achievements began to emerge, and these have been summed up by a former S.C.A.P. official as the precipitation of a "moderate middle-class revolution, designed to create a stable system of capitalistic democracy." [10] Such reforms as the distribution of land ownership, recognition of trade unionism and minimum rights for labor, health measures, and the beginnings of a broader educational franchise constitute notable efforts. But even as credit is given, ultimate judgment must be reserved until these and other reforms have been tested on the hard rock of time.

It should be noted here that the shortcomings of the American occupation spring from a complex of factors, so that while in many instances the direction of policy has taken its cue from the status of Soviet-American relations, it has also reflected other influences and forces. Among these might be mentioned the absence of adequately trained and informed personnel to administer an Oriental country with alien customs and mores, the Herculean size of the task undertaken, the unfortunate American penchant to "get things done" speedily, the superficiality of many of the paper reforms, the insulation of S.C.A.P. from constructive criticisms through its self-assured Commander and his sycophantic staff, and the tendency to isolate the Japanese problem from its world context.

Nevertheless, American-Soviet rivalry in the Far East has provided the general framework within which our occupation policy has been enacted, and regardless of our success in overcoming particular weaknesses in S.C.A.P.'s operation, the problem posed by Japan will remain fundamentally unresolved so long as American-Russian hostility persists. This is not to place the onus for such a situation on the United States to the exclusion of the Soviet Government. It is too frequently forgotten that in June 1946 the State Department circulated the draft of a four-power treaty, which pro-

[10] W. I. Ladejinsky, "Trial Balance in Japan," *Foreign Affairs*, October, 1948, p. 115.

posed the cooperation of Britain, China, Russia, and America over a twenty-five-year period to guarantee Japanese demilitarization. For a year no official responses regarding this proposal were published, and thereafter the psychological moment in which it might have been effected had passed. It is also too often overlooked that many earnest critics of our Japanese policy, both within and outside the Truman Administration, have sought genuinely for a viable compromise with the Soviets and have deplored the Atcheson-type attitude of American officials in Tokyo. And, because so many Soviet outbursts against S.C.A.P. have been justified in varying degrees, it is dangerously easy to underestimate the goals of Soviet policy. For there is no reason to believe that, if the Japanese occupation were a Russian show, Japan would not become (for a time at least) a Soviet satellite—an island in the outer defenses of the U.S.S.R. in its power struggle against the United States.

The Japanese dilemma is one manifestation of the over-all problem of great-power relationships in the postwar world. Not even an understanding of the ambitious designs of the Nipponese supplies an answer to the problem. To the degree that Japan is kept weak, it will provide a breeding ground for communism and an inexhaustible drain on American resources; to the degree that it is allowed to retrieve its former power status it will be increasingly difficult for America to control its actions. Reeducation is at best a long-run proposition; its ultimate success will be hypothetical so long as Japan's geographic location is politically so precarious. In summary, the existence of a non-aggressive, peaceful Japan can be guaranteed only if it is to the joint interest of the Soviet Union and the United States. Thus, the Japanese problem remains one of the unpalatable fruits of war; every conceivable attempt to remedy the situation must fall short until a remedy is found for the explosive anarchy in which the nations dwell.

In the rosters of international conferences during the war and postwar years China has been listed among the great powers. Its government is a permanent member of the Security Council of the United Nations; it is honored as one of the Big Four in Far

Eastern conclaves; the right of veto is accorded it. Yet China, far from being a first-class nation today, is an amorphous entity, the victim of a disintegrating civil war on the one hand, and of an American-Soviet diplomatic duel on the other. It does not follow that China will become the pawn of either Russia or the United States, for it is too large, too unpredictable, and too steeped in its own traditions ever to be assigned such a role. But at the same time China was and is capable of being exploited both by Moscow and by Washington, and while this condition persists there is little hope for a strong and unified national government.

Observers of American policy toward China since 1945 have witnessed a dichotomy of purpose which has redounded to the disadvantage of both China and the United States, and to the sole benefit of Russia. The explanation of our seemingly fickle and vacillating attitude, whereby we have alternately condoned and condemned Soviet Far Eastern interests, and pressured and appeased Generalissimo Chiang Kai-shek, once again lies beyond the periphery of our relations with the government immediately concerned and in the broader picture of our world-wide power rivalry with the Soviet Union.

At Yalta in February 1945, when the American Government coveted Soviet assistance in the Japanese war, President Roosevelt compromised a cardinal principle of American Far Eastern policy—respect for the territorial integrity of China. By recognizing the status quo in Outer Mongolia, the President admitted Soviet sovereignty over it (which China had never done); by agreeing to the internationalization of Dairen and the safeguarding of Russia's "preeminent interests" in that city, to a Soviet lease of Port Arthur as a naval base, and to joint Sino-Soviet operation of the South Manchurian and Chinese Eastern railroads, Roosevelt, Churchill, and Stalin effectively undermined China's "full sovereignty in Manchuria," which they had meticulously recognized. The Yalta Agreement was also an implied violation of the Cairo Declaration of December 1943, which stated that Manchuria would be restored to the Republic of China.

American pressure on the Nationalist Government in June 1945 brought about the dispatching of Chinese emissaries to Moscow to

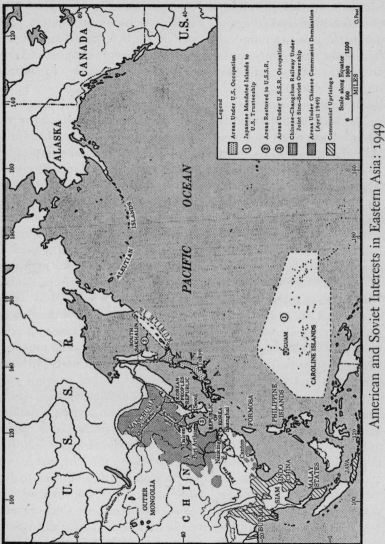

Legend

Areas Under U.S. Occupation

① Japanese Mandated Islands to U.S. Trusteeship

② Areas Restored to U.S.S.R.

③ Areas Under U.S.S.R. Occupation

Chinese–Changchun Railway Under Joint Sino-Soviet Ownership

Areas Under Chinese Communist Domination (April 1949)

Communist Uprisings

Scale along Equator

0   500   1000   1500
MILES

O. Peel

American and Soviet Interests in Eastern Asia: 1949

negotiate a treaty in fulfillment of the Yalta bargain. This treaty of "friendship and alliance," finally concluded on August 14,[11] amounted to a stunning Soviet victory, for by giving Russia access to a warm water port and by recognizing Soviet interests in Manchuria, the balance of power in the Far East was shifted sharply in favor of Moscow.

This was only one effect of the Yalta Agreement.

The Soviet declaration of war on Japan, made in payment of the Crimea bargain, was followed by the invasion of North Manchuria by Soviet forces. The subsequent transfer of all movable industrial equipment to Soviet territory as war booty, and the delivery of Manchuria to Chinese Communist troops, were mighty blows to the Nationalist Government, both economically and politically. American protests in 1946 over Russian activities regarded as "contrary to the principle of the Open Door" and prejudicial to future American trade relations with Manchuria were practically ineffectual and morally curious in view of America's behavior at Yalta. Meanwhile the United States had found it necessary to send sizable Marine forces to North China immediately after V-J Day as a protective measure in the face of Russia's proximity. Thus the American Government, which, through its pressure on China as a consequence of Yalta, had sanctioned the Soviet invasion of Manchuria, was confronted with the unhappy results of its liberality with another nation's territory.

The final withdrawal of Soviet troops from Manchuria (May 3, 1946) in no way affected the situation in Dairen and Port Arthur, nor did it ameliorate conditions in Manchuria proper. The American Government has vainly sought to argue the Russians into fulfilling the original plan for Dairen, whereby the city was to be governed by China as an international port. But according to the Sino-Soviet Treaty, pending the termination of the state of war with Japan (that is, until a peace treaty has been concluded), Dairen falls under the regime of the naval base at Port Arthur, and Russia has therefore rejected every American request on this subject. Moreover, joint Sino-Soviet operation of the Chinese Eastern and

11 See Appendix G.

South Manchurian railroads has produced sharp friction and has been wholly unsatisfactory.

After the war Manchuria became the scene of devastating civil strife between Chinese Nationalist forces and the Chinese Communists, under whose control it had fallen by autumn, 1948. Here again the bifurcation of American policy added to the hopeless confusion; and here, too, our attitudes and activities were illustrative of our larger concern over relations with the U.S.S.R.

In the late summer and early autumn of 1944, before the Soviet Union had come to be regarded with overt suspicion, the Stilwell-Gauss plea for a unified China educed a sympathetic response from Washington. Pressure was put on Chiang Kai-shek to subordinate his struggle against the Chinese Communist Party in the interests of the war effort. By the end of the year, however, Stilwell had been shamefully recalled and Gauss had resigned in protest over the policy of Special Emissary Patrick J. Hurley, whose frank appeasement of the Generalissimo had precipitated the Stilwell ouster and ended all hope of a *modus vivendi* with the Chinese Communists. Hurley's policy stemmed in part from his ignorance of Oriental psychology; it was not possible to promise American support for the Kuomintang and simultaneously to expect continued Nationalist cooperation with Yenan. The support should have come only as a result of the cooperation. But Hurley was also motivated by a Russophobia, and he could not accept criticism of his methods by American on-the-spot observers, including veteran Foreign Service officials.

Hurley was appointed to succeed Ambassador Gauss, and remained as the United States Ambassador to China until November 27, 1945, when he resigned in a cyclonic fury of indignation over Washington's less than wholehearted support of Chiang Kai-shek.

The appointment of General George C. Marshall as special envoy to China was a carefully calculated move by the Truman Administration which, had it succeeded, would have atoned for Yalta and Yalta's aftermath. But, ironically, the Crimea Conference had in a sense undermined in advance the Marshall mission of ten months later. It was the thankless, exhausting, and impossible task of America's wartime Chief of Staff to effect a viable compromise between the Kuomintang and the Communist Party, to broaden the representative basis of China's government. How was this assignment affected by the secret agreement at Yalta?

In the first place, the fact that the Nationalist Government had been forced to enter into a compromising treaty with Russia, at the insistence of the United States, dealt a striking blow to the prestige of the Kuomintang, thereby weakening its bargaining position vis-à-vis other political factions in China; this redounded psychologically to the advantage of the Chinese Communists, who, thanks to their Russian comrades, inherited an enviable position in Manchuria as they relieved the gradually departing Soviet troops. And finally, their position was further strengthened by the proximity of the Russians in Dairen and Port Arthur. All these factors made them less amenable than they might otherwise have been to a working partnership with the government of Chiang Kai-shek.

It was the fervent hope of the State Department to bring about an end to the Chinese civil war. In part, a strong element of idealism prompted this effort; in part, it was shrewd politics. A China in chaos meant a China peculiarly receptive to Communist ideology; and given the propinquity of Soviet controlled areas in the north, the spectre of communism was terrifyingly real. On the other hand, a China united would gradually be able to stand alone; presumably it would be a China friendly to the United States and an important—perhaps even a crucial—factor in the Asiatic balance of power. In view of worsening American-Russian relations in November–December 1945, the Marshall mission was a highly strategic gamble.

In spite of the unstinting, heartbreaking dedication of General Marshall to his job over a twelve-month period, his mission failed. Among a score of reasons given for the failure, the following may be noted here: First, many responsible American officials and Congressional representatives never understood the inner nature of the Chinese struggle, or the fact that compromise and cooperation between political groups representing diametrically opposed philosophies of government were impossible. Too many trite analogies were drawn between the two-party system in America, or multiparty systems in Western European democracies, and the situation in China; and it was not realized that agreement on the purpose of government, characteristic of the democratic state, was absent from the Chinese political scene. The battle was over ends, not means, and ultimately neither side was willing to forgo its separate goals.

Second, lack of comprehension in the United States regarding the Chinese picture gave American policy an uncertainty, hesitation, and inconsistency which fatally weakened Marshall's efforts. Between January and March 1946, the General had accomplished a near miracle. Cease-fire and truce agreements that had been secured throughout China were extended to Manchuria; both Communists and Nationalists had signified their faith in Marshall. But on March 11 he flew to Washington and did not return until April 18. In the meantime the American Government, despite Marshall's objective neutrality, continued to aid the Kuomintang. American planes flew whole Nationalist armies into Communist-held areas; some $200 million of lend-lease supplies were delivered to Chiang; another $800 million of surplus war materials went to the Gimo. It looked very much as if apprehensive American officials, tied to the Kuomintang from habit and from fear of communism, were playing both ends against the middle; they may have wished the Marshall mission well, but in the event of its failure they wanted to guarantee the further resistance of Chiang Kai-shek.

A third reason for the collapse of the Nationalist-Communist negotiations is found in developments during March and April. Marshall's absence removed the pressure for compromise, and extremists in both camps took advantage of the situation to promote their respective causes. Sympathy in the United States for the Nationalists, and evidences of aid being extended them, punctured the faith of Communist leaders and stiffened Kuomintang resistance. Indeed, Marshall had no sooner departed than the Kuomintang Central Executive Committee vetoed the most significant results of the All-Party Political Consultative Conference (P.C.C.) which had convened two months earlier. Thus in one move the Communist-inspired resolutions of the P.C.C.—including the principle of cabinet government, and provisions for a broad ruling coalition and for provincial constitutions—were voided, and by the time Marshall returned too much ground had been lost. Despite a face-saving effort to continue the Communist-Nationalist discussions, it was only a question of months before their final rupture.

One further cause for the breakdown of negotiations in China was inherent in the situation described. Chiang understood the implications of American-Soviet rivalry and recognized his peculiar position in that struggle. He knew, for instance, that the Truman Administration regarded a strong China as an asset in the American security system and that, in a crisis, the State Department would likely feel impelled to support the Nationalist regime as against the Yenan group. Thus the Nationalist leader was fully cognizant of the implications behind the Marshall mission. He assumed that the latter's failure would not mean the end of American aid to Kuomintang China and that, conversely, it would spell further assistance in the fight against the Communists. He believed that his own dictatorial hold on the Chinese Government would be tightened in such a contingency.

On December 18, 1946, President Truman issued a statement on American policy toward China which, in view of conditions in that unhappy country, had an ambiguous ring. General approval was voiced for the purposes which had motivated the Marshall mission; a broader base for China's National Government was urged. But simultaneously no doubt was left of American support for the existent regime, in the light of which the American pledge of aid to "the Chinese people" in bringing about peace could have referred only to the Chiang Government.

On January 7, 1947, General Marshall left China. With him went the last American effort to mediate in the civil war, and with him, too, went the remnants of peace in China.

The next American mission to Nanking was headed by Lieutenant General Albert Wedemeyer. His report in the summer of 1947 was suppressed because of the European crisis, for the State Department's strategy was to give Europe precedence in the world-wide struggle against communism. The Wedemeyer analysis of the situation (made public two years later in the Government's White Paper) favored the Nationalists, although Wedemeyer's proposed five-year aid program was made contingent on drastic domestic reforms. The General's attitude toward the Chinese "Reds" was perhaps revealed by his alleged statement before the Senate Appropriations Committee on Marshall aid for China: "It does not matter whether Chiang is a benevolent despot . . . or a republican or a democrat. The fact is, the man has fought Communism all his life."

As relations with Russia became progressively more exacerbated in Europe and Asia, American thinking in regard to China adjusted itself to the over-all pattern of anti-Communist strategy. The primary purpose and justification of aid to China stemmed from the fear of communism. Republicans—some genuinely disturbed, many out for political profit—scored the Administration for neglecting China in the Marshall Plan estimates, and forced the President to request a $300 million appropriation for Chiang's government in 1948. William C. Bullitt, who in his lifetime has descended the scale from ecstatic rhapsody over the Soviet experiment to vitriolic denunciation, urged an American loan to China of one and one-third billion dollars in order to eliminate the Chinese Soviets and bring about internal reforms. Admiral Thomas C. Hart (retired), addressing a Navy Week dinner in October 1947, alleged that the Russians were well along in the establishment of Manchuria as a Communist state. Early in 1948 General MacArthur made a plea for greater aid to China in America's global planning. And in March, General Chennault asserted that "the bulk of the United States military effort should be used in defeating the Communist armies in China," for only thus could a Soviet-dominated Asia be averted.

Meantime it was reported that between the end of the Japanese War and June 1947 the United States had underwritten the Nationalist Government to the tune of more than two billion dollars. As of March 31, 1948, a total of over five thousand Army, Navy, and Marine personnel was still stationed in China. And the American Military Advisory Group in China (M.A.G.I.C.), consisting of approximately a thousand officers and men, was performing a distinct service to the Chiang regime.

But despite all these manifestations of aid the Nationalists steadily lost ground to the Communists after mid-summer 1948. And as the inevitability of Nanking's ultimate collapse appeared increasingly certain, the United States slowly shifted its emphasis in the Far East. Not even the desperate Chinese gesture of a personal visit to Washington by Madame Chiang in December 1948 succeeded in staying American support for the Kuomintang. Indeed, even as China's "first lady" conversed with high Washington officials, Economic Cooperation Administrator Paul G. Hoffman, on a round-the-world junket, blasted Nationalist hopes. In a statement in Shanghai on December 16 Hoffman indicated that future aid to China might hinge on the formation of a coalition government (presumably a resurrection of the compromise solution sought by General Marshall in 1946, only this time with the balance of power in Communist hands). At the same time, funds earmarked for the tottering Nanking Government were held in Washington pending the fate of the Kuomintang cause.

In view of American-Soviet rivalry in the Far East, and of State Department and Treasury support of Chiang Kai-shek over the past two years, it would seem singularly inconsistent, on the surface at least, to envisage American economic aid to a Chinese government dominated by Chiang's (and America's) foe. For notwithstanding a possible acquiescence by the Communists in a coalition regime, there is no reason to believe that "coalition" would amount to more than window-dressing. Yet perhaps the inconsistency is less striking when placed against the alternative of stopping all assistance to China. Manifestly this would throw the Communists, who will need foreign aid from some source, straight into Soviet arms. Conversely, American monetary help might conceivably encourage the Chinese Communists in a course more independent of Moscow. From the writings and speeches of the Chinese "Red" leaders, their ultimate Marxist leanings are unquestionable, but they are also cognizant of the need for China to go through a stage of controlled capitalism and managed industrialization as a prelude to a socialist state. Thus, while an American aid program to a Chinese Communist-dominated government would be given and received for palpably different reasons, it would serve American interests inasmuch as it deflected Chinese policy away from the

Soviet Union; in the short run, it might give Washington a much needed breathing space.

Viewed in perspective, American policy toward China between August 1945 and January 1949 has been a pendulum, swinging confusingly between two antithetical goals. It has attempted to strengthen the National Government; it has sought to achieve political recognition by Chiang of the Chinese Communists; it has declared that it would not intervene in the Chinese civil strife; it has extended monetary, military, and moral aid to the Kuomintang; it has turned a deaf ear to the plea of the "Missimo."

But these drastic fluctuations in the American policy, however deplorable, were anything but capricious. As already noted, our attitude toward China has been dictated by considerations extending far beyond China itself. Changing relations with the Soviet Union and the global nature of American-Russian hostility not only have motivated shifts in American policy toward China, but have necessitated a system of priorities for Marshall Plan aid. The fact that Europe had precedence in aid over China, despite the potential ally Washington had in the Generalissimo, was indicative of the primacy accorded to the West in State Department strategy. More recently, it illustrated the hopelessness with which Washington regarded the Nationalist position.

The Soviet reaction to the Truman policy has been predictable and consistent. It should be observed that Russia agreed to recognize only the Nationalist Government in the Sino-Soviet Treaty of August 1945, and that no concrete proof has yet been adduced for the charges of material Soviet aid to the Chinese Communists in Manchuria and North China. But this of course in no wise has affected Russian sympathy for the Yenan Government; for a strong Kuomintang Government, friendly to America, clearly would have been inimical to Soviet ambitions in Asia.

The Russian press has roundly accused the United States of seeking to reduce China to the status of a satellite. Such factors as the continued presence of American troops in North China long after the withdrawal of the last Soviet forces from Manchuria, the "equal" trade treaty between Washington and Nanking in November 1946 (with its one-sided advantages for the United

States), the economic and military aid rendered the Kuomintang since V-J Day—all have drawn unreserved Soviet condemnation in the purported "interest" of China.

The consensus of American reporters and objective students has been that American support for the Nationalist Government was grounded primarily in the latter's anti-communism, and only secondarily in our respect for a duly recognized regime or our belief that American economic interests might be more adequately protected by that government. Moreover, the history of the Kuomintang and the practices of the Gimo brought small comfort to those who would have liked to believe that, under our promptings, Chiang's government might gradually have become more democratic. In essence, our aid to Nanking was conceived of as aid to a future ally in a potential American-Soviet conflict. As in so many other parts of the world, our China policy rested on our concepts of military strategy. These concepts, formulated by the military men who were so dominant in the American diplomatic corps after the war, quite ignored the underlying economic, social, and political problems germane to the situation in China. They were concepts meet, perhaps, in a time of war, but of themselves wholly insufficient to cope with the postwar situation. For in the longer period a willingness to sacrifice America's ideals from hysterical fear of Russia would have been tantamount to a sacrifice of the best in the American way of life for a short-lived military advantage. In China, as in Japan and many European countries, the blind support of a government (no matter how reactionary and unpopular), simply because it might be used in the struggle against communism, would have assured us only of the enmity of the freedom-starved masses; it would have provided only grist to the propaganda mills of the Chinese (and Russian) Communists; it would have issued at last only in failure.

The fruits of war, so stunted and so distorted in Japan and China, have proven equally disappointing in the peninsula of Korea. As early as December 1943 the Allies represented at the Cairo Conference had declared that the Hermit Kingdom, for thirty-five years a subject country in the Japanese Empire, would become "free and independent." At Teheran in November 1943 Stalin and Roosevelt had informally agreed that, after a period of international control, Korea's independence would be recognized. At Yalta the two heads of state had reaffirmed their intention to seek the establishment of a sovereign Korean government, with a trusteeship in the immediate postwar future if this seemed expedient. And finally at Potsdam the powers again agreed that Korea was to become a sovereign state.

Despite these solemn pledges, it was fatuous to believe that an independent Korea could exist as more than a hapless pawn, in view of the power-revolution precipitated by the war in Asia. Had China emerged as a first-class state, the subsequent history of Korea might well have been different. But given the unrelieved juxtaposition of America and Russia, there was hardly an alternative to what transpired.

When it had been determined at Yalta that the Soviet Union would participate in the Far Eastern war, American and Russian military staff officers drew up plans whereby northern Korea was assigned as a Soviet theater of operations and southern Korea as an American sector. In July 1945 at Potsdam the Joint Chiefs of Staff agreed that the 38th Parallel would divide the two zones. This decision was ostensibly made (probably in good faith by the Americans at least) purely as a military measure. It was expected (again by the Americans, on the basis of prior understandings with the Soviets) that both Russian and American occupation forces would speedily give way (within six to twelve months) to a civilian (Allied) trusteeship of perhaps five years' duration. Thereafter, Korea was to blossom into statehood. These optimistic expectations overlooked the fundamental nature of the Asiatic power situation and Korea's unique role therein. They further overlooked the relation of Soviet Russia to Korea.

Ever since Russia emerged as a Far Eastern power (after the mid-nineteenth century) it has evinced a lively interest in the peninsula because of the latter's proximity to Siberia (the territories are contiguous in the northeastern corner of Korea, not far south of Vladivostok), because of Korea's wealth in resources, and because of its strategic political and military location. But it was the Japanese who profited in the first instance by China's inability to retain control over its suzerainty, and the Russo-Japanese War in 1904–1905 adequately confirmed Japan's claim to the peninsula. However, Korea's location guaranteed the continued interest of third powers in its fate, and there can be small doubt that it has been on the Soviet Far Eastern agenda for many years. In a real sense the Russians regard Korea as the Poland of the East; and its role over the past half-century qualifies it for that distinction. The countries which have vied for control of Korea (like Poland) have conceived of its independence mainly as a means of preventing it from falling under hostile aegis. As with Poland, Russia has viewed the fate of Korea as inexorably affecting its own security. Consequently, the Koreans, like the Poles, have had a history of frustrated nationalism, and have lived at the sufferance of powerful neighbors.

Thus the stage was set for trouble in Korea well before V-J Day. In view of these factors the Soviet-American understanding regarding the division of the territory for occupation purposes complicated, but did not create the problems which have since characterized the situation. In brief, each of the two Allies, in its exclusive search for a favorable power alignment in Asia, has been determined that a future Korea shall be "friendly" and "democratic," as those words are understood in Moscow and Washington respectively. The inevitable result, after three years of diplomatic dueling, has been the creation of two Korean governments, one oriented toward Russia and the other toward the United States. That this is no solution of the underlying problem is clearly appreciated by all concerned. The duel is not over; it has merely assumed a new guise.

As long as the nations are committed to the perpetuation of the sovereign-state system it is quixotic to expect the great powers to forgo extension of their security spheres. Indeed, the United States has more than once admitted the justice of Russia's demand that the states bordering the Soviet Union shall be "friendly," even though it has not approved Soviet methods of obtaining this assurance. Viewed from Russian eyes, Korea fits the category of a border state; at the same time Moscow finds it difficult to account for sustained American interest in the peninsula, for by no stretch of the imagination can Korea be considered integral to America's continental security. The Soviet leaders are disturbed, therefore, at the American lack of *realpolitik* in dealing with the problem of Korea. In fact, they are strongly convinced that American interest in the Hermit nation, far from being either defensive or idealistic, is offensive and potentially of an aggressive nature. This makes the Russians more than ever determined that Korea shall be friendly to the U.S.S.R. Their determination, not too difficult to appreciate by Americans who try to picture Washington's attitude if the situation were reversed, is further stiffened by the direction of American policy in Japan and China.

For its part the United States is faced with a tougher task in rationalizing its objectives in Korea than is the Soviet Union. For the record, our primary objective has been to implement our war-time pledges respecting Korean independence. We were in Korea to protect the southern zone from the northern (Soviet-occupied) zone, again in the assumed interest of the Korean people. But when one examines American-Soviet relations in their broader context, and the American occupation history in South Korea, our real objectives emerge from those we profess. On the one hand, the Korean masses have by no means unanimously shared the opinion that the United States has advanced their genuine interests. On the other hand, in the light of the trend in our world-wide relations with Russia, Korea—like Japan and China—is not an end but a means in American foreign policy. It is one thing to admit and applaud our idealistic goals, but it is quite another to superimpose them on the political and strategic motives which have in the main determined our attitude toward Korea.

Within this wider framework of American and Russian policy throughout Eastern Asia the confused and disorderly events in Korea fall into a rather simple pattern: Soviet officials rejected American proposals, United States spokesmen rejected Russian proposals, and a majority of the Korean populace apparently rejected the whole purpose of the occupation.

On August 2, 1945, an estimated Soviet army of 200,000 men marched into North Korea. Notwithstanding their initial blundering, the Communists soon proceeded in methodical fashion to build a People's Republic. Many thousands of Koreans exiled in Siberia in years past, who had become fervent Soviet citizens, returned to their native land under Russian auspices, where they constituted a middleman bureaucracy through which the Russians unostentatiously operated. Soviet occupation policy thereafter was to erect a strong, well armed, viable government, analogous to Russia's satellites in the West. The fact that large numbers of Koreans fled to the American zone (estimates reached over one million refugees) was impressive testimony of the widespread dissatisfaction of a sizable minority over Soviet methods. At the same time it is noteworthy that the Russian occupation, in its early stages at least, allied itself with the liberal forces who were in revolution against the economic and political status quo, and that Russian reforms redounded to the advantage of the Korean masses and those who had resisted the Japanese.

In contrast, the American occupation force from the beginning sought out the conservatives, as these were the only Koreans who were familiar with the government because of their relatively favored position under Japanese rule. More than that, Lieutenant General John R. Hodge, Commander of the United States forces in Korea, announced that "to prevent chaos" he would retain Japanese officials on a temporary basis. The political blind spot which accounted for this major *faux pas* unfortunately typified American occupation policy for many months, for neither the State Department, the Army, nor the Navy had personnel trained in Korean affairs. Filled with the best intentions, General Hodge brought to his new job small political understanding and he was given advisers who were generally ill briefed. Even so essential a matter as knowledge of the Korean language was absent from the American contingent, and this further increased the dependence of the occupying authorities on Korean collaborationists and former Japanese administrators. Consequently, as against Soviet policy in the north, Hodge found himself working with the conservatives, advocates of the status quo, and against the democratic and liberal elements.

Soviet forces had entered Korea even before Russia had declared war on Japan. The American occupation army did not land until three weeks after the Japanese surrender. In the crucial interim period South Korea had organized itself politically through the establishment of People's Committees. These groups sent 600 delegates to a national convention in Seoul where a People's Republic was proclaimed, representative of all political factions including the Korean Communists. Its platform was exceedingly liberal and democratic, and this garnered wide popular support. But Hodge had no authority to recognize an indigenous Korean government; moreover, as soon as it was noted that the Soviet Military Government had recognized the local agencies of the People's Republic in the north, Hodge instinctively began opposing their southern counterparts. His next step was to appoint an eleven-man Advisory Council under the chairmanship of a conservative, collaborationist landlord. This further alienated the disillusioned and bitter Korean liberals, who wondered if their liberation amounted to more than the substitution of one overlordship for another.

The subsequent history of A.M.G. followed the by now familiar theme; the United States supported the Syngman Rhee rightist elements and pressured them into excluding the Communist minority from the Provisional Government in South Korea. It urged the conservatives to sponsor liberal reforms, but the fact that they *were* conservative (and anti-Soviet) was vastly more important to Washington than the nature or degree of their democratic proclivities.

In the Soviet zone, on the other hand, a forced socialist economy emerged, the converse in philosophy, methods, and aims of the American-sponsored regime. The Russians isolated and suppressed factions which they accused of Fascist (that is, Western capitalistic) leanings. And because of the monolithic, totalitarian type government which they evolved through their Korean stooges, they succeeded in their purpose far more conspicuously than the Americans in theirs. The "National Government" in the north, under the Premiership of Moscow-trained Kim Il Sung, was "friendly" to the U.S.S.R.—so much so that in September 1948 the Soviet Government announced its intention of withdrawing all Russian troops from Korea by the end of the year. But the United States, despite sponsorship of the Rhee Government, was uncertain of Rhee's staying-power should the American props be withdrawn.

Accordingly, Washington perceived in the Soviet declaration with regard to the evacuation of foreign troops from Korea an ulterior motive, and hastened to implement its arms program so that, when it should withdraw, the government of South Korea might defend itself.

In the opinion of many objective Koreans neither the American nor the Soviet Government succeeded, regardless of the "friendliness" of the two Korean regimes toward their respective benefactors. For Korea remains today a divided country. The fruits of Allied victory taste sour.

The establishment of military governments in the Russian and American zones belied the original intention of the Americans that the splitting of Korea and the presence of occupation forces should be only an interim, emergency measure. And because it was obvious that neither side was going to pull out in the immediate future, and that some action had to be taken in regard to the wartime pledges to the Koreans, the whole subject was placed on the agenda of the Moscow Foreign Ministers' Conference in December 1945. The resulting agreement [12] provided for an American-Soviet Joint Commission to assist in the formation of a provisional Korean government, composed of democratic organizations, and to work with that government for "the development of democratic self-government and the establishment of the national independence of Korea." The Joint Commission was to submit its proposals to the United States, the U.S.S.R., the United Kingdom, and China, which would then work out "an agreement concerning a four-power trusteeship of Korea for a period up to five years."

The immediate response of all Korean parties in the American zone, except the leaders of the left-wing People's Republic, was a sharp protest over the trusteeship feature of the Moscow Agreement, for "trusteeship" was the word Japan had used prior to its annexation of Korea. According to A.M.G., the abstention of the People's Republic leadership from this nearly unanimous protest was traceable to orders from Moscow. In North Korea "trusteeship" was translated "guardianship," and the Soviet-sponsored

[12] See Appendix J.

parties expressed their approval. After a cable from Secretary Byrnes intimating that the American-Soviet Joint Commission might be able to obviate the need for a trusteeship, the South Korean dissidents were somewhat mollified, and on January 8, 1946, all the parties in the American zone signed a statement approving the Moscow formula. However, in the light of later events the preliminary denunciation of the Moscow decision was more significant, for it threw a monkey-wrench into the Joint Commission with fatal consequences.

The Commission convened in preliminary session at Seoul on January 16, 1946. Three weeks later it adjourned, having achieved practically nothing except an agreement to meet again after separate consideration of the matters discussed. The 38th Parallel, which so effectively cut Korea in two, was perhaps mainly responsible for the failure of this first meeting. The Americans wanted to consider ways and means of minifying the barriers to communication and exchange between north and south, but Colonel General Shtikov averred that these matters did not fall within the purview of the conference.

On March 20 the two parties again convened, this time for a six-week session which was characterized by friction, snags, and stalemates. Reflecting the generally worsened relations between the two powers resulting from the Iranian crisis then before the United Nations, the Joint Commission finally adjourned *sine die* on May 8. The most provocative issue was introduced by Shtikov at the opening meeting. "We do not intend," he stated, "to deal with any Korean parties or individuals who have opposed the decisions of the three Foreign Ministers in Moscow." This of course would have disqualified practically every political faction in South Korea except the extreme left-enders. American opposition to the Soviet proposal led to a Russian compromise: the U.S.S.R. agreed that Korean parties which would now consent to trusteeship—regardless of former opposition—would be eligible to discuss ways of establishing a provisional government. After more deliberation, this compromise was finally drafted in an American-Soviet three-paragraph declaration. Entitled Communiqué Number Five, it had to be signed by every Korean "democratic party" and social organization which wished the privilege of consulting with the Joint Commission. The text, published on April 17, read:

We————declare that we will uphold the aims of the Moscow Decision on Korea as stated in Paragraph 1 of this decision, namely:
The re-establishment of Korea as an independent state, the creation of conditions for developing the country on democratic principles, and the earliest possible liquidation of the disastrous results of the protracted Japanese domination in Korea.

Further, we will abide by the decisions of the Joint Commission in its fulfillment of Paragraph 2 of the Moscow Decision in the formation of a Provisional Korean Democratic Government; Further, we will cooperate with the Joint Commission in the working out by it with the participation of the Provisional Korean Democratic Government, of proposals concerning measures foreseen by Paragraph 3 of the Moscow Decision.[13]

But having reached agreement, the Americans and Russians were unable to resolve fundamental differences over each other's interpretation of what constituted "democratic" parties. To the Soviets, the list of organizations in the United States zone consisted predominantly of "reactionary" groups, and Shtikov accused the Americans of boycotting mass workers' and peasants' organizations. In denying the Russian charges, A.M.G. simultaneously pointed out that the Soviet list included no conservative groups.

Further difficulty arose from Hodge's statement to the conservative factions in South Korea who from the outset were opposed to Communiqué Number Five. Their principal grievance stemmed from the Soviet admonition that the Joint Commission might decide in favor of continued trusteeship for Korea, and that in signing the Communiqué the Korean parties would have to acquiesce in any such decision. In response, Hodge told them: "Signing the declaration for consultation with the Joint Commission does not indicate that the political party or social organization favors trusteeship, or that the organization commits itself to support of trusteeship." This evoked a torrent of criticism from the Soviets, who accused Hodge of distorting "the substance of the Moscow de-

[13] *Department of State Bulletin*, January 26, 1947, p. 173.

cision" and of sabotaging the April 17 Commission decision. The Russians feared that in signing Communiqué Number Five the South Korea conservatives had no intention of cooperating with the Commission after a government was formed. And because the concept of a legal opposition was incomprehensible to the Russians, particularly as it would consist, in their opinion, of American puppets, there was no hope for further progress at that point. The United States delegation was equally obstinate in its criticisms of the Soviet position. It therefore needed only the startling eleventh-hour suggestion of General Archibald V. Arnold (Hodge's Military Governor), that the division at the 38th Parallel be abolished, to blast the Commission wide open and end the session.

But a refusal to meet in no sense ended the Korean impasse, and over the summer both Moscow and Washington made repeated references to the problem, with the result that it became the subject of diplomatic communications between Hodge and General Chistiakov, Soviet commander in North Korea. The commander finally answered one of Hodge's letters on October 26, and offered to continue the negotiations of the Joint Commission, but on Soviet terms. Further exchanges in November and December indicated that both sides were willing to make adjustments, but no actual steps were taken to resume the parleys. In the spring of 1947 the diplomatic correspondence was shifted to the foreign minister level. On April 8 Secretary of State Marshall requested Molotov to set a time and place for the resumption of talks. Molotov replied on April 20, suggesting that the Commission meet a month later, and blaming the United States for the previous rupture of negotiations. On May 2 Marshall again communicated with the Soviet Foreign Minister in an effort to define the terms of operation of the Commission. At this point the Americans were on the offensive and had the upper hand, because a three-year program of American aid to Korea was being drafted. It is therefore plausible to suggest that the Soviets were unwilling to court blame for a refusal to meet in conference. At any rate, on May 7 Molotov agreed that the terms of reference as laid down by Hodge in a communication to General Chistiakov (December 24, 1946) would be satisfactory. In line with these terms, the Joint Commission reconvened on May

21 with the understanding that it would consult only with Korean parties and social organizations declaring their intention of upholding the Moscow decision, and that the Commission could exclude from further consultations only those parties or individuals which fomented active opposition to either of the two powers, the Commission, and/or the Moscow accord. Moreover, the exclusion of such groups could be effected only by mutual American-Soviet agreement.

In the course of the next three weeks 39 parties and 396 social organizations registered for consultation with the Joint Commission. Of these, 36 parties and 361 organizations were from South Korea; 45 per cent represented rightest elements; 8 per cent, moderate rightists. Of the 3 parties and 35 organizations from the north, all were Communist-dominated. In view of these statistics the way was paved for a renewed deadlock in the Commission over the worn question of whether Korean political and social groups could be excluded from consultations without a hearing, on the grounds of their previous opinions and statements. The Soviets not only insisted on an affirmative answer, but held out for their own definition of what constituted a "social" organization. The American delegation understandably charged that the Russian viewpoint violated all the previous agreements on the Korean question, and refused to take any but a standard dictionary definition of "social." Thus the Joint Commission, which had had such a stormy career, was again destined to frustration. Throughout the dull summer days the two delegations continued to meet, the Russians at length giving in to the American contention. But further disagreement arose when the Soviets proposed to call various South Korean parties before the Commission for questioning; and by the terms of its operation, the Commission could not proceed as long as both states were not in accord.

As hope dwindled that the American-Soviet Joint Commission would resolve any of the basic problems before it, Secretary Marshall and Foreign Minister Molotov once again entered into negotiations. In a lengthy communication on August 26, the State Department, after reviewing events of the preceding three months, submitted an outline of several proposals designed to achieve the aims of the Moscow Agreement and suggested that the four Pacific powers (Britain, China, the U.S.S.R., and the United States) meet in Washington on September 8 to consider it. The proposals included: the holding of early elections in both zones to choose wholly representative provisional legislatures; the appointment by the zonal legislatures of representatives to a national provisional legislature at Seoul for establishing aid to Korea; the presence of U.N. observers while these steps were being executed; the maintenance of an informal liaison between the United Nations and the Korean groups until an independent Korean state should be established; the conclusion of an agreement between the Korean Government and the four powers regarding a date for evacuation of the occupation forces.

At the same time the American Government proposed that the Commission draft a joint report indicating the reasons for its inability to function. Molotov agreed to this last suggestion, but sharply scolded Secretary Marshall for his "unilateral acts . . . such as the dispatch of an invitation to the Governments of Great Britain and China to take part in the discussion" of the Korean problem. Russia regarded this proposal as "inexpedient" "in as much as the Joint Commission is still far from exhausting all its possibilities for working out agreed recommendations, which is entirely possible." Molotov similarly rejected the American proposals for a provisional Korean government on the ground that they "cannot fail to entail the further division of Korea" through their projected setting up of separate provisional legislative assemblies in the two zones.

Meanwhile, notwithstanding Russia's acquiescence, the Joint Commission was unable even to agree on a report as to why it had been unable to agree. According to the official summary of the fifty-ninth meeting of the Commission in September 1947, the American Chief Commissioner proposed

that the full report of each delegation be transmitted to the two governments concerned with a covering letter signed by the two Chief Commissioners stating that neither side agreed fully with the contents of the other's report. The Soviet Delegation declined this proposal. The Chief Commissioner of the American Delegation then proposed that the sections of the two reports dealing with the positions of the two delegations be extracted from the full reports and transmitted to the governments concerned with a covering letter of the nature indicated above. This proposal the Soviet Delegation also declined and gave no reason for refusing to forward both statements except that this would not constitute a "joint" report . . . The Chief Commissioner of the American Delegation proposed, as the only other alternative, that each delegation report to its government that no agreement could be reached on a joint report. The Chief Commissioner of the Soviet Delegation accepted this proposal.[14]

It was in the light of this absurd and hopeless situation—the bankruptcy of the Joint Commission, the Soviet refusal to consult with China and Britain, and the seemingly exaggerated Russian obstructionism—that the United States decided to place the Korean problem in the lap of the United Nations. On September 17 the State Department informed Foreign Minister Molotov of this decision and on the same day Secretary Marshall, in his opening address before the second regular session of the General Assembly, drew attention to the situation in Korea and asked that the problem of Korean independence be included on the Assembly's agenda. This evoked an acrid rejoinder from Soviet delegate Andrei Vyshinsky. "Having arbitrarily outlined the situation in such a way that the futility of the work of the Joint Soviet Union-American Commission on Korea is attributed to the Soviet Union, Mr. Marshall makes a proposal which is in direct violation of the Moscow Agreement on Korea reached by the Foreign Ministers in December 1945."

Although the Soviet delegation held that Korea fell outside the competence of the United Nations, a majority voted for its inclusion on the Assembly agenda. The Russians counterattacked with the proposal, first made on September 26 in the Joint Commission, that Soviet and American troops be withdrawn simultaneously and the trusteeship system dropped. Following the rejection of this proposal by the American representative on the Commission, Gromyko submitted it, on October 28, to the General Assembly's First Committee, which had been charged with con-

14 *Ibid.*, September 28, 1947, p. 625.

sideration of the problem, and coupled it with the Soviet program for the establishment of a Korean National Government. Gromyko also proposed that "elected representatives of Korea, excluding persons maintained by the foreign military authorities, should be heard by the Committee and by the General Assembly."

The result of the U.N. discussions was a decisive blow to the Soviet position. On November 14 the Assembly voted 43–0, with six (Soviet bloc) abstentions, in favor of a revised American resolution establishing a United Nations Temporary Commission on Korea. The Soviet resolution in regard to the evacuation of all foreign troops from Korea was defeated (34–7, with 16 abstentions). The Soviet bloc then announced that it would boycott the U.N. Commission.

The General Assembly, in its resolution, named as commission members Australia, Canada, China, El Salvador, France, India, the Philippine Republic, Syria, and the Ukrainian S.S.R. The Ukrainian Government at once signified its refusal to participate. The resolution further recommended that United States-supervised elections be held in Korea "not later than March 31, 1948, on the basis of adult suffrage and by secret ballot to choose representatives with whom the Commission may consult regarding the prompt attainment of the freedom and independence of the Korean people and which representatives, constituting a National Assembly, may establish a national government of Korea." Moreover, the resolution proposed the convocation of the National Assembly and formation of a National Government "as soon as possible" after the election; suggested that "immediately upon the establishment of a National Government," the U.N. Commission, in consultation with it, should arrange with Russia and America for the withdrawal of their armed forces from Korea "if possible within 90 days"; and called upon all United Nations members "to refrain from interfering in the affairs of the Korean people during the interim period preparatory to the establishment of Korean independence . . ."

Thwarted by the Assembly action, the U.S.S.R. determined to block implementation of the resolution and so to demonstrate a favorite Soviet principle, namely, that without Big Power unanimity the United Nations was impotent. First, Russia reiterated its contention that the Korean problem fell outside U.N. jurisdiction; it was a matter solely of American-Soviet concern. The Ukrainian abstention from participating in the U.N. Korean Commission emphasized this thesis. Second, when the Commission, under the chairmanship of Dr. K. P. S. Menon of India, reached Seoul, the Russians made clear their refusal not only to recognize it, but to receive it in the northern zone, even for a courtesy call on the Soviet Commander. Simultaneously, under Russian directions blueprints were drawn for a puppet regime in North Korea, and the formation of a Korean Army was expedited.

After weeks of debate over the legal snarl resulting from the Soviet boycott, over whether elections could be held in a single zone of Korea in the light of the General Assembly resolution, over whether the "Little [Interim] Assembly" should be consulted in view of Russia's conviction that that body was "unconstitutional," the U.N. Korean Commission voted in early March, and at the recommendation of the Interim Assembly, to conduct elections in South Korea in May. Among Korean leaders this decision had been urged by Syngman Rhee, but opposed by a second rightist leader, Kim Koo, and by the leader of the centrist parties, Kimm Kiusic.

In the two-month interval between the U.N. Commission's announcement regarding a separate election in South Korea and election day, the Soviet occupying authorities hurried their plans for a North Korean government. In a move calculated to split the South Korean parties the Russian-controlled radio at Pyongyang invited leaders of all political coloring in the south to attend a conference April 14. The invitation singled out especially those in Seoul who had registered opposition to the United Nations Commission's election plans. Dr. Syngman Rhee rejected the offer outright. Americans in South Korea expressed concern over the new Soviet strategy, but voiced no objection to Russia's inviting any Koreans who wished to attend the conference.

The elections in the American zone on May 10 resulted in an overwhelming victory for the rightists and a personal triumph for Dr. Rhee. A.M.G. was quietly jubilant over this "vindication" of American-supported conservatives, although it is significant that General Hodge had tried, after the first year of the American occupation, to broaden Korean political thinking by seeking a compromise between rightist and centrist parties. Moreover, it was secretly hoped that Syngman Rhee's arch conservatism would be somewhat modified as a result of his active participation in the Korean Government.

A 200-member National Assembly was set up in Seoul following the elections, and 100 seats were conspicuously left open for North Korea pending the holding of free elections there under U.N. auspices.

The Koreans south of the 38th Parallel were in a better position to operate their own government in the summer of 1948 than they had been at any time under the American occupation. As a consequence of many months of learning the hard way, A.M.G. had appreciably increased its understanding of Korean problems, and it improved its approach to Korean politics after 1946. In the autumn of that year elections were held to an Interim Legislative Assembly, which was also to contain 45 appointive seats and to operate within the framework and under the ultimate authority of the Military Government. Hodge sought to atone for the startling victory of the reactionaries by filling the appointive seats with center and left-center politicians. Although this infuriated Dr. Rhee, the Interim Assembly convened in December 1946 and continued to function in ensuing months. Among the more significant measures credited to it were a child-labor law (effective June 1, 1947) and a liberal election law (passed June 27, 1947). Progress in Korean lawmaking was supplemented by still other A.M.G. moves. A Bureau of Justice, consisting entirely of Koreans and operating nominally as a branch of Military Government, was given almost full responsibility for the administration of justice in the southern zone. Educational facilities were extended so that many more young people had an opportunity for schooling than ever before. On May 17, 1947, A.M.G. announced that, effective at once, the Korean legislative, administrative, and judicial organs were to be redesignated the Provisional Government of South Korea. In July 1947 private international trade was begun and the United States increased its shipments to Korea of needed foods, fertilizers, equipment, etc.

Notwithstanding these advances, the Republic of Korea, which came into legal being under the Presidency of Syngman Rhee in mid-August 1948, faced a rocky future. The country was still hopelessly divided; it was still a focal point of American-Soviet conflict. In the north a Soviet-sponsored, Communist, People's Democratic Republic challenged the authority and validity of the South Korean government. A huge North Korean Army, Communist trained, allegedly awaited the opportunity to invade the American zone and overthrow its rightist authorities. A series of Communist-inspired revolts broke out in South Korea in the autumn of 1948, and were quelled only with difficulty.

Both regimes sent representatives to the third session of the United Nations General Assembly, in September 1948. For a time it appeared that the Assembly would sidestep the issue, postponing it for consideration at the session scheduled for April 1949. But in the last crowded days an American-Chinese-Australian resolution to recognize the South Korean Republic, continue the U.N. Korean Commission, and withdraw eventually all American and Soviet occupation forces passed the Assembly's Political Committee by a 41–6 vote. Soviet spokesmen denounced the American position, accusing the United States of sponsoring a reactionary clique, and labeling the Rhee government an American puppet. Simultaneously Moscow sought to embarrass Washington by announcing plans for the withdrawal of all Soviet forces from North Korea.[15] But at Paris a Soviet proposal, based on the allegation that the U.N. Korean Commission was illegal, and asking for its dissolution, received a smashing 42–6 defeat. And Russian efforts to prevent by filibustering a final vote on the American resolution in the Assembly succeeded only in delaying Assembly adjournment for a period of hours. Passage of the resolution assured President Rhee that the moral force of the vast majority of world states stood behind his

[15] On December 30, 1948, the U.S.S.R. issued a statement that the last Soviet troops had left the Northern zone. Three and a half months later, on April 18, 1949, President Rhee announced that discussions were under way between representatives of the Republic of Korea and the United States, regarding "the establishment of a date in the course of several months for the withdrawal from Korea of United States troops."

government, and that the United Nations had recognized it as the only legal spokesman for all Korea.[16]

To this extent the new Republic had gained a strong psychological victory, and a probable breathing space. Yet the very fact that Korea had become a United Nations problem was symbolic of its true position. More than three years after V-J Day the Hermit Kingdom was still the tragic victim of the fruits of war. Its fate lay not in its own hands, for the stream of Korea's destiny was powerless against the forcing tide of American-Soviet rivalry.

[16] Notwithstanding this recognition, the Republic of Korea was barred from U.N. membership by a Soviet veto in the Security Council in April 1949.

CHAPTER XV

The Fruits of Anarchy

The story of American-Russian relations in the Far East is conspicuously lacking in inspiration, ingenuity, or vision. It has followed a pattern familiar in the annals of politics; deviations have been relatively minor and unimportant. The significance of the record, therefore, lies not in its uniqueness, but in the proof it gives of the inability of the sovereign state system to promote international security. The United States and the U.S.S.R. are rivals today in every part of the world. So long as they adhere to the anachronism of national sovereignty, their rivalry must continue. So long as their rivalry persists, peace must remain a phantom. For state sovereignty shorn of its sophistry is simply international anarchy. Anarchy in turn connotes an absence of law. And law, the scabbard in which might reposes, is the basic prerequisite for an orderly society. Without it, the sword of might is unchained, naked, and double-edged.

The theory of the balance of power is an unworthy substitute for law. Its advocates propound it as if they had discovered something intricate and wonderful. In reality, all they have discovered is an ephemeral *modus vivendi*. In fact, the balance of power is the only device left to nations for their protection in an anarchic world. Yet in the end it does not serve even that limited purpose, for the doctrine is mutually exclusive as between nations. If we in America condone and apply it, we have no just ground for objecting if Russia does likewise. If we are agreed that the United States must have a certain degree of power—in terms of allies, armaments, and bases, in the pursuit of a viable balance—we cannot question Russia's right to follow a similar course. Yet manifestly it is impossible for both states, simultaneously, to create balance of power conditions in which each will feel "safe." The only conceivable enemy of the Soviet Union today is America; our only conceivable foe is Russia. The men in the Kremlin regard every step we take to implement our power position as a potential threat to Russia. The State Department views with alarm every forward march of the Soviets. Thus a balance of power policy is not a static condition which can be attained and held, but a dynamic, ceaseless process of maneuvering—a continual cold war. Moreover, the route of the balance of power has led traditionally through dark forests, ending in an ammunition dump. And war has never solved the basic issues at stake. One power or set of powers has been defeated, but from the ashes other powers have risen, cloaked with national interests and a resolve to redress the power balance. Nowhere has this been better illustrated than in the history of the past fifteen years, a history which has demonstrated the tragic truth that the balance of power is a hungry master, driving the nations which subscribe to it to war and to destruction, and then creating new victims for a new struggle.

In defeating Japan and Germany, the United States and its allies did not end the conflict for power; it simply shifted to other centers. Nor can we say that the war was for moral ends—granted the treachery of our enemies. England and France fought for Poland not out of morality or sentiment, but largely because Poland was the mathematical spot on the map of Europe which foredoomed the balance of power if it, too, fell to Hitler. America fought Japan—not out of moral indignation—but mainly because at long last the United States Government refused to allow Japan to annex any more of the Far East, with its implications for American balance of power interests there.

As we pursue our foreign policy today, striving in Asia and in Europe to swing the balance in our favor, we repeatedly affirm our pacific intentions and express wonder that Moscow can misconstrue our deeds, whether they consist of a Marshall Plan, a visit of cruisers to eastern Mediterranean ports, a North Atlantic Treaty, or measures adopted in China, Japan, Korea. Naturally we are convinced of our innocence. That is the fatal charm in balance of power operations, for every other nation is convinced of its innocence too. And whether at any particular point in history one state has a greater degree of rightness on its side is, in one sense, almost immaterial; for states which are committed to anarchy have ruled out universal norms and disinterested, higher judgments. In their place they have elevated the concepts of national interest and national security—the only standards in international politics. Any resemblance between them and more universal standards of justice is frequently coincidental.

In other words, in a world shattered by anarchy, self-preservation is the highest goal of the nation; and the balance of power is the crude instrument designed to promote that goal. But the fruits of anarchy are self-defeating in this era. Self-preservation is no longer sufficient, for we have at last reached the point in our material and scientific progress where survival must be a community project.

The only answer to anarchy is government of the whole. This has been attested by an impressive number of "world citizens"; but, unhappily, we have developed an unhealthy attitude toward it. We have been taken off guard by the daring nature of the proposal, and so have commenced backsliding. Our emphasis has come to be that a world state is not practical today, that it had best be postponed to an indeterminate future.

But if "realism" prohibits the establishment of a world government, does it forbid experimenting with the idea? The American people, in contrast to the Russians, have it in their power to commit their country to an international order in which law shall govern nations. Therefore, a positive current policy for us might perhaps include, among others, these two points: First, a sharp remembrance at all times of the true character of the game of balance of power—which should make us more tolerant of other countries, victims of this game even as we are, and should make us less convinced of our own moral rectitude. Second, a determination to see the United Nations evolve into a world government within this century. This means supporting American foreign policy in Asia and in Europe only as it can be reconciled with world interests (and not with our nationalistic conception of world interests). It means supporting the Marshall Plan in terms of Marshall's original statement—as a plan aimed not at any country or doctrine, but at hunger, privation, fear, and chaos. It means urging our government to reconcile its diplomacy with the stated aims of the United Nations, and to operate increasingly under the aegis of that organization instead of seeking refuge in provocative military pacts. It means viewing ourselves as world citizens—even as we are American citizens living in separate American states.

This is not a simple creed to follow. Like all idealistic causes, it has only a small minority actively preaching it today. Yet the great majority of the earth's peoples are overwhelmingly desirous of peace, and there exists a tremendous, untapped reservoir of support for a world government if this is attempted strongly, creatively, selflessly. We ought perhaps to remember that the balance of power, which has never prevented war over the long run, is neither realistic nor viable in the present age. We ought perhaps to remember also that we have never earnestly sought to win peace by eliminating the obstacles to it, by destroying the virus of war. Man has conquered space and time, and he has conquered the physical world, not by violating the laws of nature and natural science, but by discovering them and working within their inexorable logic. Man can also conquer war—the greatest disease in today's world—but not by perpetuating anarchy, nor by violating the fundamental truth of his common brotherhood.

Peace demands a moral foundation as strong as the foundations we lay in the physical world to conquer the hidden secrets of nature. This is the day of building—not of worshiping at the altars of tired nationalisms. The promise of tomorrow is yet held prisoner at the shrine of yesterday. It is time to release it.

DECLARATION OF THE COUNCIL OF PEOPLE'S COMMISSARIES TO THE CHINESE PEOPLE AND THE GOVERNMENTS OF SOUTH AND NORTH CHINA [1]

On this day when the Soviet Army, having defeated the army of the counter-revolutionary despot, Kolchak, supported by foreign bayonets and foreign gold, is making a triumphant entry into Siberia, where it is marching to unite with the revolutionary people of Siberia, the Council of People's Commissaries sends the following brotherly message to all the peoples of China:

It is not in order to commit acts of violence, to enslave or conquer that Soviet Russia and the Soviet Red Army are now, after a struggle of two years and unprecedented efforts, marching over Ural to the East. Every Siberia peasant and worker knows this by this time. We carry to the peoples their emancipation from the yoke of foreign bayonets and foreign gold, which are strangling the oppressed peoples of the East and—foremost among them—the people of China. It is not only to our toiling classes that we are bringing help, but also to the people of China and we once again recall to it what we had told it since the first days of the Great October Revolution of 1917, but what had possibly been concealed from it by a corrupt American-European-Japanese press.

Immediately after seizing the power in October, 1917, the Workers' and Peasants' Government made an appeal to the peoples of the world, proposing to them to establish a real lasting peace.

[1] J. B. Condliffe, ed., *Problems of the Pacific: Proceedings of the Second Conference of the Institute of Pacific Relations, Honolulu, Hawaii, July 15 to 29, 1927* (Chicago: The University of Chicago Press, 1928), Section 6, "Documents Relating to the Chinese Question," Compiled by Mingchien Joshua Bau, pp. 266–268.

This peace should have been based on the renunciation of all seizures of alien land, of bringing by force of alien nationalities into the fold of another people, and of all contributions. Every people, great or small, whenever it lives and whether it had hitherto had independent life— or had been included against its own will into the make-up of another State—must enjoy full liberty in its inner life, and no Government must keep it by force within its boundaries.

Then the Workers' Peasants' Government declared null and void all the secret treaties signed with Japan, China, and the former Allies —treaties through which, by violence and bribery, the Tsar's Government, together with its allies, had fettered the nations of the East and, especially, the people of China, to the interests of Russian capitalists, Russian landlords, and Russian generals. The Soviet Government had already then proposed to the Chinese Government to enter into negotiations on the cancellation of the treaty of 1896, the Peking Protocol of 1901, and all the agreements with Japan from 1901 to 1916, and the handing over to the Chinese people of all that had been taken away from it by the Tsar's Government either on its own account or in common accord with the Japanese and the Allies. Negotiations on this question were proceeding till March, 1918, but the Allies jumped unexpectedly at the throat of the Peking Government, showering gold upon the Peking mandarins and the Chinese press and forced the Chinese Government to give up all relations with the Russian Workers' and Peasants' Government. Without waiting for the Chinese Eastern Railway being turned over to the Chinese people, Japan and the Allies seized this line themselves, made an irruption into Siberia, and even compelled the Chinese troops to lend them a hand in this criminal and unprecedented brigandage, while the people of China, the Chinese workers and peasants, could not even know the truth why this onslaught was made on Manchuria and Siberia by the American, European, and Japanese depredators.

Today we are calling again to the Chinese people and wish to open their eyes.

The Soviet Government has renounced all the conquests made by the Tsarist Government, which had taken away from China, Manchuria, and other parts of the country. Let the peoples themselves who live in these areas decide within the limits of which state they want to remain and which country they wish to make their home.

[The Soviet Government returns to the Chinese people without indemnification the Chinese-Eastern Railway, and all forests, mines,

gold, and other concessions seized by Russian generals, merchants, and capitalists under the regime of the Tsar, Kerensky, and the bandits Horvat, Semenov, and Kolchak.[2]]

The Soviet Government forsakes its share of the Boxer Indemnity, and this it is obliged to repeat for the third time because, according to information having reached us, in spite of our renunciation, this portion of the indemnity is still being raised by the Allies with a view to satisfying the fancies of the former Tsarist ambassador to Peking and former Tsarist consuls in China. All of these Tsar's lackeys have long since lost their powers, but they nevertheless remain where they were and continue, with the help of Japan and the Allies, to deceive the Chinese people. The people of China must know this and must drive them out of the country as cheats and deceivers.

The Soviet Government annuls all special privileges, all the factories of the Russian merchants on Chinese soil. No Russian official, priest, or missionary shall interfere in Chinese affairs, and if he is guilty of a criminal offense, he shall be tried in all justice in local courts. There must be no other power, no other courts but the power and courts of the Chinese people.

Besides these main points, the Soviet Government is ready to come to an agreement with Chinese people, in the persons of its duly authorized representatives, also on all other questions, and thus once for all do away with acts of violence and injustice committed on China by former Russian Governments in common with Japan and the Allies.

The Soviet Government is fully aware that the Allies and Japan will do all in their power so that this time again the voice of the Russian workers and peasants might not reach the Chinese people, telling it that in order to give back the Chinese people all that has been seized from them, it is necessary first to do away with brigands installed in Manchuria and Siberia. Therefore, its message to the Chinese people the Soviet Government sends with its Red Army, which

[2] This italicized paragraph did not appear in the official Soviet version of the note. It was included, however, in copies of the declaration published in the press (both foreign and domestic) throughout China, Manchuria, and Siberia. *The China Year Book* (1924–5) reprinted the text of the declaration, including the paragraph in question, giving as its source the original French text as translated by the Chinese Foreign Ministry (pp. 868–70). The paragraph as quoted here is taken from *Soviet Russia* (Official Organ of the Russian Soviet Government Bureau), June 5, 1920, p. 568. Interestingly, the source given by this magazine was not the Soviet Government but rather "a Vladivostok newspaper, 'The Far-Eastern Review,'" of March 18, 1920.

is going over Ural to the east to help the Siberian peasants and workers in their fight for liberation from bandit Kolchak and his ally, Japan.

If the people of China wish to become free, like the Russian people, and be spared the lot prepared for them by the Allies at Versailles, which would make of China a second Korea or a second India, let it understand that its only ally and brother in its struggle for national freedom are the Russian workers and peasants and their Red Army.

The Soviet Government makes a proposal to the people of China, in the person of its Government, to enter without delay into official relations with us and send its representatives to meet our army.

[*Signed*] L. KARAKHAN
Acting People's Commissary for Foreign Affairs
Moscow, July 25, 1919

* * *

TO THE MINISTRY OF FOREIGN AFFAIRS OF THE CHINESE REPUBLIC: [3]

More than a year ago, on July 25, 1919, the People's Commissariat of Foreign Affairs of the Russian Socialist Federative Soviet Republic issued a declaration to the Chinese people and the governments of North and South China, wherein the Russian Government, renouncing all the former Tsarist treaties concluded with China, and returning to the Chinese people all that had been seized from it by force and robbed by the Tsar's Government and the Russian bourgeoisie, proposed to the Chinese Government to enter upon official negotiations with a view to establishing friendly relations.

We have now had information conveyed to us to the effect that this declaration has been received by the Chinese Government, and that the various layers and organizations of the people of China are voicing their sincere desire that the Chinese Government should start negotiations with us with a view to establishing friendly relations between China and Russia.

The Government of the Chinese Republic has delegated to Moscow a Military and Diplomatic Mission, headed by General Chang Sulin; we welcome most gladly the arrival of the Chinese Mission to Moscow, hoping that through direct negotiations with your Repre-

[3] Condliffe, *op. cit.*, pp. 268–270.

sentatives we shall establish a mutual understanding of the common interests uniting China and Russia. We are satisfied that there do not exist any such questions between the Russian and Chinese peoples as could not be solved to the common advantage of both of them. We are aware that the enemies of the Russian and Chinese peoples are trying hard to prevent our friendship and our closer rapprochement, for they understand that the friendship of two great peoples and their reciprocal help will so much strengthen China that no foreigners will then be able to put such fetters on and rob the Chinese people as is being done today.

Unfortunately, however, there is something standing in the way of an early establishment of friendly relations between China and Russia. Your mission, which could perfectly well ascertain our sincere and friendly attitude toward China, has not up till now received the proper instructions which could empower it to enter upon the path of settling formal friendly relations between the two peoples.

Whereas, it expresses its regret at the rapprochement being delayed, and important political and commercial interests of both States failing to materialize, the People's Commissariat of Foreign Affairs, prompted by its desire to be helpful and to speed up the establishment of friendship between the two peoples, declares that it will unswervingly abide by those principles which were laid down in the Declaration of the Russian Soviet Government of July 25, 1919, basing on them the friendly agreement between China and Russia.

In development of the principles contained in that Declaration, the People's Commissariat of Foreign Affairs deems necessary, for the benefit of both Republics, to propose to the Ministry of Foreign Affairs of the Chinese Republic the following main points of agreement:

Article I

The Government of the Russian Socialist Federative Soviet Republic declares null and void all the treaties concluded with China by the former governments of Russia, renounces all seizures of Chinese territory and all Russian concessions in China, and restores to China, without any compensation and for ever, all that had been predatorily seized from her by the Tsar's Government and the Russian bourgeoisie.

Article II

The Governments of both Republics shall take all the necessary measures for immediately establishing regular trade and economic relations. A special treaty to this effect shall be subsequently concluded on the principle of the clause of the most favored nation, applying to both contracting parties.

Article III

The Chinese Government pledges itself: (1) not to proffer any aid to Russian counter-revolutionary individuals, groups or organizations, nor to allow their activities in Chinese territory; (2) to disarm, intern and hand over to the Government of the Russian Socialist Federative Soviet Republic all the detachments and organizations to be found in Chinese territory at the time of the signing of this Treaty, which are fighting against the R.S.F.S.R. or States allied with her, and to give over to the Government of the R.S.F.S.R. all their arms, supplies and property; (3) the Government of the Russian Socialist Federative Soviet Republic takes upon itself the same obligations with regard to persons or organizations carrying on a rebel struggle against the Republic of China.

Article IV

All the Russian citizens residing in China shall be subject to all the laws and regulations acting in the territory of the Chinese Republic and shall not enjoy any rights of extraterritoriality. The Chinese citizens residing in Russia shall be subject to all the laws and regulations acting in the territory of the Russian Socialist Federative Soviet Republic.

Article V

The Government of the Chinese Republic pledges itself, immediately upon the signing of the present treaty, to sever connections with persons styling themselves as diplomatic and consular representatives of the Russian State without having any powers from the Government of the Russian Socialist Federative Soviet Republic, and to deport such persons from China. To hand over to the Russian State, in the person of the Government of the Russian Socialist Federative Soviet Republic, the buildings of the Embassy and consulates and other property and archives of the same, situated in Chinese territory and belonging to Russia.

Article VI

The Government of the Russian Socialist Federative Soviet Republic renounces any compensation paid out by China as indemnity for the Boxer rising, provided that under no circumstances shall the Government of the Chinese Republic pay any money out of this indemnity to the former Russian consuls or to any other persons or Russian organizations putting up illegal claims thereto.

Article VII

Following immediately upon the signing of the present Treaty there shall be mutually established diplomatic and consular representatives of the Republic of China and the Russian Socialist Federative Soviet Republic.

Article VIII

The Russian and the Chinese Governments agree to sign a special treaty on the way of working the Chinese Eastern Railway with regard to the needs of the Russian Socialist Federative Soviet Republic, and in the conclusion of the treaty there shall take part, besides China and Russia, also the Far Eastern Republic.

The above points of agreement the People's Commissariat of Foreign Affairs advances as the main clauses, which can be discussed in a friendly way with your representatives and amendments made which the Chinese Government shall deem necessary for common benefit.

The relation between the two great peoples are not exhausted by the agreement as stated above, and representatives of both States will have to settle subsequently trade, frontier, railway, customs and other questions, embodying them in special treaties.

All measures will be taken on our part with a view to establishing closest and sincere friendship between both parties, and we hope that on the part of the Chinese Government there will also be made an equally sincere and prompt proposition, thus making it possible to proceed at an earliest date to the conclusion of a friendly treaty.

[*Signed*] L. KARAKHAN
Acting People's Commissary for Foreign Affairs
Moscow, September 27, 1920

AGREEMENT ON GENERAL PRINCIPLES FOR THE SETTLEMENT OF THE QUESTIONS BETWEEN THE UNION OF SOVIET SOCIALIST REPUBLICS AND THE REPUBLIC OF CHINA, MAY 31, 1924 [1]

The Union of Soviet Socialist Republics and the Republic of China desiring to reestablish normal relations with each other, have agreed to conclude an agreement on general principles for the settlement of the questions between the two countries, and have to that end named as their Plenipotentiaries, that is to say—

The Government of the Union of Soviet Socialist Republics: Lev Mikhailovitch Karakhan,

His Excellency the President of the Republic of China: V. Kyuin Wellington Koo,

Who, having communicated to each other their respective full powers, found to be in good and due form, have agreed upon the following Articles:

Article I. Immediately upon the signing of the present Agreement, the normal diplomatic and consular relations between the two Contracting Parties shall be reestablished.

The Government of the Republic of China agrees to take the necessary steps to transfer to the Government of the Union of Soviet Socialist Republics the Legation and Consular buildings formerly belonging to the Tsarist Government.

Article II. The Governments of the two Contracting Parties agree to hold, within one month after signing the present Agreement, a Conference which shall conclude and carry out detailed arrangements

[1] *Russian Review* (Russian Information Bureau, Washington, D.C.), October 15, 1925, pp. 416–419.

relative to the questions in accordance with the principles as provided in the following Articles.

Such detailed arrangements shall be completed as soon as possible and, in any case, not later than six months from the date of the opening of the Conference as provided in the preceding paragraph.

Article III. The Governments of the two Contracting Parties agree to annul at the Conference as provided in the preceding Article, all Conventions, Treaties, Agreements, Protocols, Contracts, etc., concluded between the Government of China and the Tsarist Government and to replace them with new treaties, agreements, etc., on the basis of equality, reciprocity and justice, as well as the spirit of the Declarations of the Soviet Government of the years of 1919 and 1920.

Article IV. The Government of the Union of Soviet Socialist Republics, in accordance with its policy and Declarations of 1919 and 1920, declares that all Treaties, Agreements, etc., concluded between the former Tsarist Government and any third party or parties affecting the sovereign rights or interests of China, are null and void.

The Governments of both Contracting Parties declare that in future neither Government will conclude any treaties or agreements which prejudice the sovereign rights or interests of either of the Contracting Parties.

Article V. The Government of the Union of Soviet Socialist Republics recognizes that Outer Mongolia is an integral part of the Republic of China and respects China's sovereignty therein.

The Government of the Union of Soviet Socialist Republics declares that as soon as the questions for the withdrawal of all the troops of the Union of Soviet Socialist Republics from Outer Mongolia,— namely, as to the time limit of the withdrawal of such troops and the measures to be adopted in the interests of the safety of the frontiers —are agreed upon on the Conference as provided in Article II of the present Agreement, it will effect the complete withdrawal of all the troops of the Union of Soviet Socialist Republics from Outer Mongolia.

Article VI. The Governments of the two Contracting Parties mutually pledge themselves not to permit within their respective territories the existence and (or) activities of any organizations, or groups whose aim is to struggle by acts of violence against the Governments of either Contracting Party.

The Governments of the two Contracting Parties further pledge themselves not to engage in propaganda directed against the political and social systems of either Contracting Party.

Article VII. The Governments of the two Contracting Parties agree to redemarcate their national boundaries at the Conference as provided in Article II of the present Agreement, and pending such redemarcation, to maintain the present boundaries.

Article VIII. The Governments of the two Contracting Parties agree to regulate at the aforementioned Conference the questions relating to the navigation of rivers, lakes, and other bodies of water which are common to their respective frontiers, on the basis of equality and reciprocity.

Article IX. The Governments of the two Contracting Parties agree to settle at the aforementioned Conference the question of the Chinese Eastern Railway in conformity with the principles as hereinafter provided:

1. The Governments of the two Contracting Parties declare that the Chinese Eastern Railway is a purely commercial enterprise.

The Governments of the two Contracting Parties mutually declare that with the exception of matters pertaining to the business operations which are under the direct control of the Chinese Eastern Railway, all other matters affecting the rights of the National and the Local Governments of the Republic of China—such as judicial matters, matters relating to civil administration, military administration, police, municipal government, taxation and landed property (with the exception of lands required by the said Railway)—shall be administered by the Chinese Authorities.

2. The Government of the Union of Soviet Socialist Republics agrees to the redemption by the Government of the Republic of China, with Chinese capital, of the Chinese Eastern Railway, as well as all appurtenant properties and the transfer to China of all shares and bonds of the said Railway.

3. The Governments of the two Contracting Parties shall settle at the Conference as provided in Article II of the present Agreement the amount and conditions governing the redemption as well as the procedure for the transfer of the Chinese Eastern Railway.

4. The Government of the Union of Soviet Socialist Republics agrees to be responsible for the entire claims of the shareholders, bondholders and creditors of the Chinese Eastern Railway incurred prior to the Revolution of March 9, 1917.

5. The Governments of the two Contracting Parties mutually agree that the future of the Chinese Eastern Railway shall be determined by the Union of Soviet Socialist Republics and the Republic of China, to the exclusion of any third party or parties.

6. The Governments of the two Contracting Parties agree to draw up an arrangement for the provisional management of the Chinese Eastern Railway pending the settlement of the questions as provided under Sec. 3 of the present article.

7. Until the various questions relating to the Chinese Eastern Railway are settled at the Conference as provided in Article II of the present Agreement, the rights of the two Governments arising out of the Contract of August 27 (September 8), 1896, for the Construction and Operation of the Chinese Eastern Railway, which do not conflict with the present Agreement and the Agreement for the Provisional Management of the said Railway and which do not prejudice China's rights of sovereignty, shall be maintained.

Article X. The Government of the Union of Soviet Socialist Republics agrees to renounce the special rights and privileges relating to all Concessions in any part of China acquired by the Tsarist Government under various Conventions, Treaties, Agreements, etc.

Article XI. The Government of the Union of Soviet Socialist Republics agrees to renounce the Russian portion of the Boxer indemnity.

Article XII. The Government of the Union of Soviet Socialist Republics agrees to relinquish the rights of extraterritoriality and consular jurisdiction.

Article XIII. The Governments of the two Contracting Parties agree to draw up simultaneously with the conclusion of a Commercial Treaty at the Conference as provided in Article II of the present Agreement, a Customs Tariff for the two Contracting Parties in accordance with the principles of equality and reciprocity.

Article XIV. The Governments of the two Contracting Parties agree to discuss at the aforementioned Conference the questions relating to the claims for the compensation of losses.

Article XV. The present Agreement shall come into effect from the date of signature.

In witness whereof, the respective Plenipotentiaries have signed the present Agreement in duplicate in the English language and have affixed thereto their seals.

Done at the City of Peking this Thirty-first Day of May, One

Thousand Nine Hundred and Twenty-Four, which is the Thirty-first day of the Fifth Month of the Thirteenth Year of the Republic of China.

L. M. KARAKHAN   V. K. WELLINGTON KOO
  (*Seal*)   (*Seal*)

DECLARATION

The Government of the Union of Soviet Socialist Republics and the Government of the Republic of China declare that immediately after the signing of the Agreement on General Principles between the Union of Soviet Socialist Republics and the Republic of China of May 31, 1924, they will reciprocally hand over to each other all the real estate and movable property owned by the former Tsarist Government and China, and found in their respective territories. For this purpose each Government will furnish the other with a list of the property to be so transferred.

In faith whereof, the respective Plenipotentiaries of the Governments of the two Contracting Parties have signed the present Declaration in duplicate in the English language and have affixed thereto their seals.

Done at the City of Peking this Thirty-First Day of May, One Thousand Nine Hundred and Twenty-Four, which is the Thirty-First Day of the Fifth Month of the Thirteenth Year of the Republic of China.

Seals.   L. KARAKHAN
                                 V. K. WELLINGTON KOO

DECLARATION

The Government of the Union of Soviet Socialist Republics and the Government of the Republic of China hereby declare that it is understood that with regard to the buildings and landed property of the Russian Orthodox Mission belonging as it does to the Government of the Union of Soviet Socialist Republics the question of transfer or other suitable disposal of the same will be jointly determined at the Conference provided in Article II of the Agreement on General Principles between the Union of Soviet Socialist Republics and the Republic of China of May 31, 1924, in accordance with the internal laws and regulations existing in China regarding property-holding in the inland. As regards the buildings and property of the Russian Orthodox Mission belonging as it does to the Government of the Union of Soviet Socialist Republics at Peking and Patachu, the Chinese Government will take steps to immediately transfer same as soon as the Government of the Union of Soviet Socialist Republics will designate a Chinese person or organization, in accordance with the laws and regulations existing in China regarding property-holding in the inland.

Meanwhile the Government of the Republic of China will at once take measures with a view to guarding all the said buildings and property and clearing them from all persons now living there.

It is further understood that this expression of understanding has the same force and validity as a general declaration embodies in the said Agreement on General Principles.

In faith whereof, the respective Plenipotentiaries of the Governments of the two Contracting Parties have signed the present Declaration in duplicate in the English language and have affixed thereto their seals.

Done at the City of Peking this Thirty-First Day of May, One Thousand Nine Hundred and Twenty-Four, which is the Thirty-First Day of the Fifth Month of the Thirteenth Year of the Republic of China.

Seals. L. KARAKHAN
V. K. WELLINGTON KOO

DECLARATION

The Government of the Union of Soviet Socialist Republics and the Government of the Republic of China jointly declare that it is understood that with reference to Article IV of the Agreement on General Principles between the Union of Soviet Socialist Republics and the Republic of China of May 31, 1924, the Government of the Republic of China will not and does not recognize as valid any treaty, agreement, etc., concluded between Russia since the Tsarist regime and any third party or parties, affecting the sovereign rights and interests of the Republic of China. It is further understood that this expression of understanding has the same force and validity as a general declaration embodied in the said Agreement on General Principles.

In faith whereof, the respective Plenipotentiaries of the Governments of the two Contracting Parties have signed the present Declaration in duplicate in the English language and have affixed thereto their seals.

Done at the City of Peking this Thirty-First Day of May, One Thousand Nine Hundred and Twenty-Four, which is the Thirty-First Day of the Fifth Month of the Thirteenth Year of the Republic of China.

Seals.   L. KARAKHAN
                       V. K. WELLINGTON KOO

DECLARATION

The Government of the Union of Soviet Socialist Republics and the Government of the Republic of China jointly declare that it is understood that the Government of the Republic of China will not transfer either in part or in whole to any third Power or any foreign organization the special rights and privileges renounced by the Government of the Union of Soviet Socialist Republics in Article X of the Agreement on General Principles between the Union of Soviet Socialist Republics and the Republic of China of May 31, 1924. It is further understood that this expression of understanding has the same force and validity as a general declaration embodied in the said Agreement on General Principles.

In faith whereof, etc.

Seals.   L. KARAKHAN
                       V. K. WELLINGTON KOO

DECLARATION

The Government of the Union of Soviet Socialist Republics and the Government of the Republic of China jointly declare that it is understood that with reference to Article XI of the Agreement on General Principles between the Union of Soviet Socialist Republics and the Republic of China of May 31, 1924:

1. The Russian share of the Boxer Indemnity which the Government of the Union of Soviet Socialist Republics renounces, will after the satisfaction of all prior obligations secured thereon be entirely ap-

propriated to create a fund for the promotion of education among the Chinese people.

2. A special Commission will be established to administer and allocate the said fund. This Commission will consist of three persons two of whom will be appointed by the Government of the Republic of China and one by the Government of the Union of Soviet Socialist Republics. Decisions of the said Commission will be taken by unanimous vote.

3. The said fund will be deposited as it accrues from time to time in a Bank to be designated by the said Commission.

It is further understood that this expression of understanding has the same force and validity as a general declaration embodied in the said Agreement of the two Contracting Parties on General Principles.

In faith whereof, etc.

Seals.   L. KARAKHAN
                           V. K. WELLINGTON KOO

DECLARATION

The Government of the Union of Soviet Socialist Republics and the Government of the Republic of China agree that they will establish equitable provisions at the Conference as provided in Article II of the Agreement on General Principles between the Union of Soviet Socialist Republics and the Republic of China of May 31, 1924, for the regulation of the situation created for the citizens of the Government of the Union of Soviet Socialist Republics by the relinquishment of the rights of extraterritoriality and consular jurisdiction under Article XII of the aforementioned Agreement, it being understood, however, that the nationals of the Government of the Union of Soviet Socialist Republics shall be entirely amenable to Chinese jurisdiction.

In faith whereof, etc.

Seals.   L. KARAKHAN
                           V. K. WELLINGTON KOO

DECLARATION

The Government of the Union of Soviet Socialist Republics and the Government of the Republic of China, having signed the Agreement on General Principles between the Union of Soviet Socialist Republics and the Republic of China of May 31, 1924, hereby agree, in explanation of Article V of the Agreement for the Provisional Management of the Chinese Eastern Railway of the same date, which provides for the principle of equal representation in the filling of posts by citizens of the Union of Soviet Socialist Republics and those of the Republic of China, that the application of this principle is not to be understood to mean that the present employees of Russian nationality shall be dismissed for the sole purpose of enforcing the said principle. It is further understood that access to all posts is equally open to citizens of both Contracting Parties, that no special preference shall be shown to either nationality, and that the posts shall be filled in accordance with the ability and technical as well as educational qualifications of the applicants.

In faith whereof, etc.

Seals.   L. KARAKHAN
                                                    V. K. WELLINGTON KOO

NOTE OF WELLINGTON KOO TO KARAKHAN

Peking, May 31, 1924.

Dear Mr. Karakhan:

On behalf of my Government, I have the honor to declare that, an agreement on General Principles for the settlement of the Questions between the Republic of China and the Union of Soviet Socialist Republics having been signed between us today, the Government of the Republic of China will, in the interests of friendship between the Republic of China and the Union of Soviet Socialist Republics, discontinue the services of all the subjects of the former Russian Empire now employed in the Chinese army and police force, as they constitute by their presence or activities a menace to the safety of the Union of Soviet Socialist Republics. If you will furnish my Government with a list of such persons, the authorities concerned will be instructed to adopt the necessary action.

I have the honor to remain,

                                        Yours faithfully,
                                        V. K. WELLINGTON KOO

NOTE OF KARAKHAN TO WELLINGTON KOO

Peking, May 31, 1924.

Dear Dr. Koo:

I have the honor to acknowledge the receipt of the following Note from you under this date:

[A repetition of Wellington Koo's note follows.]

In reply, I beg to state, on behalf of my Government, that I have taken note of the same and that I agree to the propositions as contained therein.

I have the honor to be,

Very truly yours,

L. M. KARAKHAN

AGREEMENT FOR THE PROVISIONAL MANAGEMENT OF THE CHINESE EASTERN RAILWAY, MAY 31, 1924 [2]

The Union of Soviet Socialist Republics and the Republic of China mutually recognizing that, inasmuch as the Chinese Eastern Railway was built with capital furnished by the Russian Government and constructed entirely within Chinese territory, the said railway is a purely commercial enterprise and that, excepting for matters appertaining to its own business operations, all other matters which affect the rights of the Chinese National and Local Governments shall be administered by the Chinese Authorities, have agreed to conclude an Agreement for the Provisional Management of the Railway with a view of carrying on jointly the management of the said Railway until its final settlement at the Conference as provided in Article II of the Agreement on General Principles for the Settlement of the Questions between the Union of Soviet Socialist Republics and the Republic of China of May 31, 1924, and have to that end named as their Plenipotentiaries, that is to say:

The Government of the Union of Soviet Socialist Republics: LEV MIKHAILOVITCH KARAKHAN.

His Excellency the President of the Republic of China: V. KYUIN WELLINGTON KOO.

[2] *Russian Review* (Russian Information Bureau, Washington, D.C.), November 1, 1925, pp. 439–440.

Who having communicated to each other their respective full powers found to be in good and due form, have agreed upon the following Articles:

Article I. The Railway shall establish, for discussion and decision of all matters relative to the Chinese Eastern Railway, a Board of Directors to be composed of ten persons, of whom five shall be appointed by the Government of the Union of Soviet Socialist Republics and five by the Government of China.

The Government of the Republic of China shall appoint one of the Chinese Directors as President of the Board of Directors, who shall be Director-General.

The Government of the Union of Soviet Socialist Republics shall appoint one of the Russian Directors as Vice-President of the Board of Directors, who shall also be the Assistant Director General.

Seven persons shall constitute a quorum, and all decisions of the Board of Directors shall have the consent of not less than six persons before they can be carried out.

The Director-General and Assistant Director-General shall jointly manage the affairs of the Board of Directors, and they shall both sign all the documents of the Board.

In the absence of either the Director-General or the Assistant Director-General, their respective Governments may appoint another Director to officiate as the Director-General or the Assistant Director-General (in case of the Director-General, by one of the Chinese Directors, and in that of the Assistant Director-General, by one of the Russian Directors).

Article II. The Railway shall establish a Board of Auditors to be composed of five persons, namely, three Russian Auditors, who shall be appointed by the Government of the Union of Soviet Socialist Republics, and two Chinese Auditors, who shall be appointed by the Government of the Republic of China.

The Chairman of the Board of Auditors shall be elected from among the Chinese Auditors.

Article III. The Railway shall have a manager, who shall be a national of the Union of Soviet Socialist Republics, and two Assistant Managers, one to be a national of the Union of Soviet Socialist Republics and the other to be a national of the Republic of China.

The said officers shall be appointed by the Board of Directors and such appointments shall be confirmed by their respective Governments.

The rights and duties of the Manager and Assistant Managers shall be defined by the Board of Directors.

Article IV. The Chiefs and Assistant Chiefs of the various Departments of the Railway shall be appointed by the Board of Directors.

If the Chief of Department is a national of the Union of Soviet Socialist Republics, the Assistant Chief of the Department shall be a national of the Republic of China, and if the Chief of Department is a national of the Republic of China, the Assistant Chief of Department shall be a national of the Union of Soviet Socialist Republics.

Article V. The employment of persons in the various departments of the railway shall be in accordance with the principle of equal representation between the nationals of the Union of Soviet Socialist Republics and those of the Republic of China.

Article VI. With the exception of the estimates and budgets, as provided in Article VII, of the present agreement, all other matters, on which the Board of Directors cannot reach an agreement shall be referred for settlement to the Governments of the Contracting Parties.

Article VII. The Board of Directors shall present the estimates and budgets of the Railway to a joint meeting of the Board of Directors and the Board of Auditors for consideration and approval.

Article VIII. All the net profits of the Railway shall be held by the Board of Directors and shall not be used pending a final settlement of the question of the present Railway.

Article IX. The Board of Directors shall revise as soon as possible the statutes of the Chinese Eastern Railway Company, approved on December 4, 1896, by the Tsarist Government, in accordance with the present Agreement and the Agreement on General Principles for the Settlement of the Questions between the Union of Soviet Socialist Republics and the Republic of China of May 31, 1924, and, in any case, not later than six months from the date of the constitution of the Board of Directors.

Pending their revision, the aforesaid statutes, insofar as they do not conflict with the present Agreement on General Principles for the Settlement of the Questions between the Union of Soviet Socialist Republics and the Republic of China, and do not prejudice the rights of sovereignty of the Republic of China, shall continue to be observed.

Article X. The present Agreement shall cease to have effect as soon as the question of the Chinese Eastern Railway is finally settled at the Conference as provided in Article II of the Agreement on General Principles for the Settlement of the Questions between the Union of Soviet Socialist Republics 'and the Republic of China of May 31, 1924.

Article XI. The present Agreement shall come into effect from the date of signature.

In witness whereof, the respective Plenipotentiaries have signed the present agreement in duplicate in the English language and have affixed thereto their seals.

Done at the city of Peking this Thirty-First Day of May, One Thousand Nine Hundred and Twenty-Four, which is the Thirty-First Day of the Fifth Month of the Thirteenth Year of the Republic of China.

L. KARAKHAN

V. K. WELLINGTON KOO

AGREEMENT BETWEEN THE GOVERNMENT OF THE AUTONOMOUS THREE EASTERN PROVINCES OF THE REPUBLIC OF CHINA AND THE GOVERNMENT OF THE UNION OF SOVIET SOCIALIST REPUBLICS, MUKDEN, SEPTEMBER 20, 1924 [3]

The Government of the Autonomous Three Eastern Provinces of the Republic of China and the Government of the Union of Soviet Socialist Republics, desiring to promote the friendly relations and regulate the questions affecting the interests of both Parties, have agreed to conclude an Agreement between the two Parties, and to that end named as their Plenipotentiaries, that is to say:

The Government of the Autonomous Three Eastern Provinces of the Republic of China:

Cheng Tsian, Lui Yung-huan and Chung Shih-ming

The Government of the Union of Soviet Socialist Republics:

Nikolai Kirillovich Kouznetzov

Who, having communicated to each other their respective full powers, found to be in good and due form, have agreed upon the following Articles:

Article I. The Chinese Eastern Railway

The Governments of the two Contracting Parties agree to settle the question of the Chinese Eastern Railway as hereinafter provided:

[3] C. Walter Young, *The International Relations of Manchuria* (Chicago: The University of Chicago Press, 1929), pp. 295-300.

(1) The Governments of the two Contracting Parties declare that the Chinese Eastern Railway is a purely commercial enterprise.

The Governments of the two Contracting Parties mutually declare that, with the exception of matters pertaining to the business operations which are under the direct control of the Chinese Eastern Railway, all other matters affecting the rights of the National and the Local Governments of the Republic of China, such as judicial matters, matters relating to civil administration, military administration, police, municipal government, taxation and landed property (with the exception of lands required by the Chinese Eastern Railway for itself) shall be administered by the Chinese Authorities.

(2) The time-limit as provided in the Article XII of the Contract for the Construction and Operation of the Chinese Eastern Railway of August 27th/September 8th, 1896, shall be reduced from eighty to sixty years, at the expiration of which the Government of China shall enter gratis into possession of the said Railway and its appurtenant properties.

Upon the consent of both Contracting Parties, the question of a further reduction of the said time-limit, that is, sixty years, may be discussed.

From the date of signing the present Agreement, the Union of Soviet Socialist Republics agrees that China has the right to redeem the Chinese Eastern Railway. At the time of redemption, the two Contracting Parties shall determine what the Chinese Eastern Railway had actually cost, and it shall be redeemed by China with Chinese capital at a fair price.

(3) The Government of the Union of Soviet Socialist Republics agrees in a Commission to be organized by the two Contracting Parties to settle the questions of the obligations of the Chinese Eastern Railway Company in accordance with Section 4 of Article IX of the Agreement on General Principles for the Settlement of the Questions between the Republic of China and the Union of Soviet Socialist Republics signed on May 31st, at Peking.

(4) The Governments of the two Contracting Parties mutually agree that the future of the Chinese Eastern Railway shall be determined by China and the Union of Soviet Socialist Republics to the exclusion of any third party or parties.

(5) The Contract for the Construction and Operation of the Chinese Eastern Railway of August 27th/September 8th, 1896, shall be completely revised, in accordance with the terms specified in this

Agreement, by a Commission of the two Contracting Parties in four months from the date of signing the present Agreement. Pending the revision, the rights of the two Governments arising out of this Contract, which do not conflict with the present Agreement and which do not prejudice China's right of sovereignty, shall be maintained.

(6) The Railway shall establish, for discussion and decision of all matters relating to the Chinese Eastern Railway, a Board of Directors to be composed of ten persons, of whom five shall be appointed by China and five by the Union of Soviet Socialist Republics.

China shall appoint one of the Chinese Directors as President of the Board of Directors, who shall be ex-officio the Director-General.

The Union of Soviet Socialist Republics shall appoint one of the Russian Directors as Vice-President of the Board of Directors, who shall be ex-officio the Assistant Director-General.

Seven persons shall constitute a quorum, and all decisions of the Board of Directors shall have the consent of not less than six persons before they can be carried out.

The Director-General and the Assistant Director-General shall jointly manage the affairs of the Board of Directors, and they shall jointly sign all the documents of the Board.

In the absence of either the Director-General or the Assistant Director-General, their respective Governments may appoint another Director to officiate as the Director-General or the Assistant Director-General (in the case of the Director-General, by one of the Chinese Directors, and in that of the Assistant Director-General, by one of the Russian Directors).

(7) The Railway shall establish a Board of Auditors to be composed of five persons, namely, two Chinese Auditors, who shall be appointed by China, and three Russian Auditors, who shall be appointed by the Union of Soviet Socialist Republics.

The Chairman of the Board of Auditors shall be elected from among the Chinese Auditors.

(8) The Railway shall have a Manager, who shall be a national of the Union of Soviet Socialist Republics, and two Assistant-Managers, one to be a national of the Republic of China, and the other to be a national of the Union of Soviet Socialist Republics.

The said officers shall be appointed by the Board of Directors, and such appointments shall be confirmed by their respective Governments.

The rights and duties of the Manager and the Assistant Managers shall be defined by the Board of Directors.

(9) The Chiefs and the Assistant Chiefs of the various departments of the Railway shall be appointed by the Board of Directors.

If the Chief of a department is a national of the Republic of China, the Assistant Chief of that department shall be a national of the Union of Soviet Socialist Republics, and if the Chief of a department is a national of the Union of Soviet Socialist Republics, the Assistant Chief of that department shall be a national of the Republic of China.

(10) The employment of persons in the various departments of the Railway shall be in accordance with the principal of equal representation between the nationals of the Republic of China and those of the Union of Soviet Socialist Republics.

(NOTE:—In carrying out the principle of equal representation, the normal course of life and activities of the Railway shall in no case be interrupted or injured, that is to say, the employment of the people of both nationalities shall be in accordance with the experience, personal qualifications and fitness of the applicants.)

(11) With the exception of the estimates and budgets as provided in Section 12 of Article I of the present Agreement, all other matters on which the Board of Directors cannot reach an agreement, shall be referred to the Governments of the Contracting Parties for a just and amicable settlement.

(12) The Board of Directors shall present the estimates and budgets of the Railway to a joint meeting of the Board of Directors and the Board of Auditors for consideration and approval.

(13) All the net profits of the Railway shall be held by the Board of Directors and shall not be used pending a final settlement, in a joint Commission, of the question of its distribution between the two Contracting Parties.

(14) The Board of Directors shall make a complete revision, as soon as possible, of the Statutes of the Chinese Eastern Railway Company approved on December 4th, 1896, by the Tsarist Government in accordance with the present Agreement and not later than four months from the date of constitution of the Board of Directors.

Pending their revision, the aforesaid Statutes, insofar as they do not conflict with the present Agreement and do not prejudice the rights of sovereignty of the Republic of China, shall continue to be observed.

(15) As soon as the conditions of the redemption by China of the Chinese Eastern Railway are settled by both Contracting Parties, or as soon as the Railway reverts to China upon the expiration of the time-limit as stipulated in Section 2 of Article I of the present Agreement,

all parts of this Agreement concerning the same shall cease to have effect.

Article II. Navigation

The Governments of the two Contracting Parties agree to settle, on the basis of equality, reciprocity and the respect of each other's sovereignty, the question relating to the navigation of all kinds of their vessels on those parts of the rivers, lakes, and other bodies of water, which are common to their respective borders, the details of this question to be regulated in a Commission of the two Contracting Parties within two months from the date of signing the present Agreement.

In view of the extensive freight and passenger interests of China on the lower Amur River into the sea, and the extensive freight and passenger interests of the Union of Soviet Socialist Republics on the River Sungari up to and including Harbin, both Contracting Parties agree, on the basis of equality and reciprocity, to take up the question of securing the said interests in the said Commission.

Article III. Boundaries

The Governments of the two Contracting Parties agree to redemarcate their boundaries through a Commission to be organized by both Parties, and, pending such redemarcation, to maintain the present boundaries.

Article IV. Tariff and Trade Agreement

The Governments of the two Contracting Parties agree to draw up a Customs Tariff and conclude a Commercial Treaty in a Commission to be organized by the said Parties on the basis of equality and reciprocity.

Article V. Propaganda

The Governments of the two Contracting Parties mutually pledge themselves not to permit within their respective territories the existence and/or activities of any organization or groups whose aim is to struggle by acts of violence against the Government of either Contracting Party.

The Governments of the two Contracting Parties further pledge themselves not to engage in propaganda directed against the political and social systems of either Contracting Party.

Article VI. Commissions

The Commissions as provided in the Articles of this Agreement shall commence their work within one month from the date of signing this Agreement, and shall complete their work as soon as possible and not later than six months. This does not apply to those Commissions, whose time-limits have been specified in the respective Articles of this Agreement.

Article VII

The present Agreement shall come into effect from the date of signature.

In witness whereof, the respective Plenipotentiaries have signed the present Agreement in duplicate in the Chinese, Russian and English languages, and have affixed thereto their seals.

In case of dispute, the English text shall be accepted as the standard.

Done at the City of Mukden this Twentieth Day of the Ninth Month of the Thirteenth Year of the Republic of China, which is the Twentieth Day of September, One Thousand Nine Hundred and Twenty-Four.

Signed:

CHENG TSIAN	[Seal]
LUI YUNG-HUAN	[Seal]
CHUNG SHIH-MING	[Seal]
KOUZNETZOV	[Seal]

THE SOVIET-JAPANESE CONVENTION OF JANUARY 20, 1925 [1]

REGARDING THE BASIC PRINCIPLES OF INTERRELATIONS BETWEEN THE UNION OF SOVIET SOCIALIST REPUBLICS AND JAPAN

The Union of Soviet Socialist Republics and Japan, desiring to firmly establish mutual good-neighborly relations and economic cooperation, decided to conclude a convention regarding the basic principles of such relations and have for this purpose appointed their representatives, namely:

The Central Executive Committee of the Union of Soviet Socialist Republics appointed: Lev Mikhailovich Karakhan, Ambassador to China.

His Majesty, the Emperor of Japan appointed:

Kenkiti Yoshizawa, Envoy Extraordinary and Minister Plenipotentiary in China, Djushia, Chevalier, First Class Order of "Holy Treasure," who upon presenting to each other their respective credentials, these being found in proper and correct form, agreed upon the following:

Article I. The high contracting parties agree that with the coming into force of the present convention diplomatic and consular relations are established between them.

Article II. The Union of Soviet Socialist Republics agrees that the Treaty concluded in Portsmouth in September 5, 1905, remains in full force.

It is agreed that all treaties, conventions and agreements outside of the above mentioned Portsmouth treaty entered into between Japan and Russia up to November 7, 1917, will be revised at the conference

[1] *Russian Review*, April 1, 1925, pp. 146–149.

which is to take place subsequently between the governments of the contracting parties, and that they may be changed or cancelled as will be called for by the changed circumstances.

Article III. The governments of the high contracting parties agree that with the coming into effect of the present convention they will take up the revision of the fishing treaty of 1907 taking into consideration those changes which might have taken place in the general conditions since the said fishing treaty was concluded.

Until such a revised treaty is concluded the government of the Union of Soviet Socialist Republics will adhere to the practice established in 1924 in regard to the leasing of fisheries to Japanese subjects.

Article IV. The governments of the high contracting parties agree that with the coming into effect of the present convention they will take up the matter of concluding a treaty regarding trade and shipping in accordance with the principles set forth below and that until such a treaty is concluded the general relations between the two countries will be regulated by these principles:

1. Citizens and subjects of each of the high contracting parties, in accordance with the laws of each country, will have the right of (a) full freedom of entry, movement and stay in the territory of the other party, and (b) constant full protection of the safety of life and property.

2. In accordance with the laws of the country, each of the high contracting parties, gives on its territory, to citizens or subjects of the other party, to the widest possible extent and on conditions of reciprocity, the right of private ownership, as well as freedom to engage in trade, shipping, mining and other peaceful occupations.

3. Without prejudice to the right of each contracting party to regulate by its own laws the system of international trade in that country, it is understood that neither of the contracting parties will apply against the other party in particular any prohibitive measures, limitations or taxation, which might act as obstacles to the development of economic or other intercourse between the two countries; and both countries propose to grant to the trade, shipping and industry of each country, insofar as possible, the privileges of the most favored country.

The governments of the high contracting parties further agree from time to time, as circumstances may demand, to enter into negotiations to conclude special agreements regarding trade and shipping for the purpose of regulating and cementing the economic relations between the two countries.

Article V. The high contracting parties solemnly confirm their desire and intention to live in peace and amity with each other, conscientiously to respect the undisputed right of each State to arrange its own life within the limits of its own jurisdiction at its own desire, to refrain and restrain all persons in their governmental service, as well as all organizations receiving any financial support from them, from any open or secret action, which may in any way whatsoever threaten the peace or safety of any part of the territory of the Union of Soviet Socialist Republics or of Japan.

It is further agreed that neither of the high contracting parties will permit on the territory under its jurisdiction the presence of:

(a) Organizations or groups claiming to be the government of any part of the territory of the other party, or

(b) Foreign subjects or citizens, in regard to whom it has been established that they actually carry on political work for these organizations or groups.

Article VI. In the interests of the development of economic relations between the two countries, and taking into consideration the needs of Japan with respect to natural resources, the Government of the Union of Soviet Socialist Republics is ready to grant to Japanese subjects, companies and associations concessions for the exploitation of mineral, timber and other natural resources in all parts of the territory of the Union of Soviet Socialist Republics.

Article VII. The present convention is subject to ratification. Such ratification by each of the high contracting parties should be notified as soon as possible through the diplomatic representatives in Peking to the government of the other party, and from the date of the last of such notifications this convention comes into full force.

The formal exchange of ratifications will take place in Peking within the shortest possible time.

In testimony whereof the respective representatives have signed the present convention in duplicate, in English, and have affixed their seals thereto.

Drawn up in Peking, this twentieth day of January, in the year one thousand nine hundred and twenty five.

(*Signed*) L. KARAKHAN
(*Signed*) K. YOSHIZAWA

Protocol (A)

The Union of Soviet Socialist Republics and Japan, upon signing this date the convention regarding the basic principles of interrelations between them, found it desirable to regulate certain questions in connection with the above convention and through their respective representatives have agreed upon the following stipulations:

Article I. Each of the high contracting parties binds itself to turn over to the other party the immovable and movable property belonging to the embassy and consulates of that party and actually situated on the territory of the first party.

In the event that it be found that the land occupied by the former Russian government in Tokio is situated in such a way as to interfere with the plans for laying out the city of Tokio or for serving the public needs, the government of the Union of Soviet Socialist Republics will be ready to consider the proposals, which may be made by the Japanese government with the view to eliminating such difficulties.

The Government of the Union of Soviet Socialist Republics will give to the Japanese government all reasonable facilities in the choice of suitable sites and buildings for a Japanese embassy and consulates to be established on the territory of the Union of Soviet Socialist Republics.

Article II. It is agreed that all questions regarding debts to the government or subjects of Japan in connection with State loans or treasury bonds issued by the former Russian governments, namely the imperial Russian government and its successor—the Provisional government—are left for decision at subsequent negotiations between the Government of the Union of Soviet Socialist Republics and the Japanese government.

It is intended that in regulating these questions the government or subjects of Japan, all conditions being equal, will not be placed in a less favorable position than that which the Government of the Union of Soviet Socialist Republics will concede to the government or citizens of any other country on the same questions.

It is also agreed that all questions relating to claims of the government of one party against the government of the other party, or of citizens of one party to the government of the other, are left to be regulated at the subsequent negotiations between the Government of the Union of Soviet Socialist Republics and the Japanese government.

Article III. In view of the fact that the climatic conditions in Northern Sakhalin prevent immediate transportation home of the Japanese troops now stationed there, these troops will be completely evacuated from the said region by May 15, 1925.

This evacuation must commence just as soon as climatic conditions permit, and in each and all of the districts in Northern Sakhalin thus evacuated by Japanese troops will immediately afterwards be restored full sovereignty of corresponding authorities of the Union of Soviet Socialist Republics.

Details regarding the transfer of administration and winding up the occupation will be arranged in Alexandrovsk between the commander of the Japanese army of occupation and representatives of the Union of Soviet Socialist Republics.

Article IV. The high contracting parties mutually declare that at the present time there exists no treaty or agreement regarding military alliance, or any other secret agreement concluded by either of them with any third party, which might constitute a violation of or threat to the sovereignty, territorial rights or national safety of the other contracting party.

Article V. The present protocol will be considered ratified with the ratification of the convention regarding the basic principles of the interrelations between the Union of Soviet Socialist Republics and Japan as signed this date.

In witness whereof the respective representatives have signed the present protocol in duplicate, in English, and affixed their seals thereto.

Drawn up in Peking, this twentieth day of January in the year One thousand nine hundred twenty five.

(*Signed*) L. Karakhan
(*Signed*) K. Yoshizawa

Protocol (B)

The high contracting parties have agreed upon the following basic stipulations for concession agreements to be concluded during the period of five months from the day of complete evacuation of Northern Sakhalin by Japanese troops, as provided in Article III of Protocol (A), signed this date by representatives of the Union of Soviet Socialist Republics and of Japan.

1. The government of the Union of Soviet Socialist Republics agrees to give to Japanese concerns recommended by the Japanese government concessions for the exploitation of 50 per cent of the area of every oilfield in Northern Sakhalin, mentioned in the memorandum presented to the representative of the Union of Soviet Socialist Republics on August 29, 1924. In order to ascertain the area which is to be leased to Japanese concerns for such exploitation, each of the mentioned oilfields is to be divided into checkerboard squares, from 15 to 40 dessiatins each, the Japanese being given such a number of these squares as will

represent 50 per cent of the entire area; it being understood that the squares thus to be leased to the Japanese, should not as a rule be adjacent, but should include all wells which are now being drilled or worked by the Japanese. As regards the remaining unleased oil lands mentioned in the same memorandum, it is agreed that should the government of the Union of Soviet Socialist Republics decide to offer these lands, in full or in part, on concessions to foreigners, Japanese concerns will enjoy equal chances in regard to such concessions.

2. The government of the Union of Soviet Socialist Republics will grant to Japanese concerns recommended by the Japanese government the right, for a period from five to ten years, of carrying on exploration work on the oil-fields along the eastern shore of Northern Sakhalin over an area of one thousand square versts, which must be allotted within a year from the date of the conclusion of concession agreements, and if, as a result of such exploration work by the Japanese, oil should be located, a concession for the exploitation of 50 per cent of the oil-field area thus established will be granted to the Japanese.

3. The government of the Union of Soviet Socialist Republics agrees to grant to Japanese concerns recommended by the Japanese government concessions for the exploitation of coal deposits on the western shore of Northern Sakhalin over a definite area, which is to be established by concession contracts. The government of the Union of Soviet Socialist Republics further agrees to grant to such Japanese concerns concessions for coal mining in the Dui district over an area to be established in the concession contracts. As regards coalfields situated outside the definite area mentioned in the previous two sentences, it is also agreed that should the government of the Union of Soviet Socialist Republics decide to offer them on concession to foreigners, Japanese concerns will be given equal rights in regard to such concessions.

4. The period of the concessions for the exploitation of oil and coal fields, as set forth in the previous paragraphs, is to be established for 40 to 50 years.

5. As payment for the above mentioned concessions Japanese concessionnaires will turn over annually to the Government of the Union of Soviet Socialist Republics—in the coalfields, from 5 to 8 per cent of the gross output; in the oil-fields, from 5 to 15 per cent of the gross output. It is proposed that in the event of striking oil gushers, the payment may be increased to 45 per cent of the gross production.

The percentage of production thus to revert as payment will be finally determined in the concession contracts, it being subject to change in accordance with the scale of annual production by a method to be established in the above mentioned contracts.

6. The said Japanese concerns shall have the right to cut timber necessary for the needs of the enterprise, and to erect various structures to facilitate communication and transportation of materials and products. The details in connection therewith will be stipulated in the concession contracts.

7. In view of the above mentioned rental and taking into consideration the unfavorable conditions, in which the enterprises will be placed owing to the geographical position and other general conditions in the said regions, it is agreed that there will be a duty-free import and export of all articles, materials and products necessary for such enterprises or produced in the latter, and that the enterprises will not be subject to such taxation or limitations as would actually make profitable exploitation impossible.

8. The government of the Union of Soviet Socialist Republics will provide for the said enterprises all reasonable protection and facilities.

9. The details in connection with the aforementioned articles will be stipulated in the concession contracts.

The present protocol is to be considered ratified with the ratification of the convention regarding the basic principles of interrelations between the Union of Soviet Socialist Republics and Japan as signed this date.

In witness whereof the respective representatives have signed the present protocol in duplicate, in English, and have affixed thereto their seals.

Drawn up in Peking, this twentieth day of January in the year One thousand nine hundred and twenty-five.

(*Signed*) L. KARAKHAN
(*Signed*) K. YOSHIZAWA

Upon signing this day the convention regarding the basic principles of interrelations between the Union of Soviet Socialist Republics and Japan, the undersigned representative of the Union of Soviet Socialist Republics has the honor to declare that the recognition by his government of the validity of the Portsmouth treaty of September 5, 1905, in no way signifies that the government of the Union shares with the former Tsarist government the political responsibility for the conclusion of the said treaty.

Peking, January 20, 1925.

(*Signed*) L. KARAKHAN

NEUTRALITY PACT BETWEEN THE U.S.S.R. AND JAPAN, APRIL 13, 1941 [1]

The Presidium of the Supreme Soviet of the U.S.S.R. and His Majesty the Emperor of Japan, guided by a desire to strengthen peaceful and friendly relations between the two countries, decided to conclude a pact on neutrality, for the purpose of which they appointed their representatives:

For the Presidium of the Supreme Soviet of the U.S.S.R., Viacheslav M. Molotov, Chairman of the Council of People's Commissars and People's Commissar for Foreign Affairs.

For His Majesty the Emperor of Japan, Yosuke Matsuoka, Minister of Foreign Affairs, Jusanmin, Cavalier of the Order of the Sacred Treasure, first class; and Yoshitsugu Tatekawa, Ambassador Extraordinary and Plenipotentiary in the U.S.S.R. Lieutenant General, Jusanmin, Cavalier of the Order of the Rising Sun, first class, and the Order of the Golden Kite, fourth class—who, after the exchange of their credentials, which were found in due and proper form agreed on the following:

Article 1. Both contracting parties undertake to maintain peaceful and friendly relations between them and mutually respect the territorial integrity and inviolability of the other contracting party.

Article 2. Should one of the contracting parties become the object of hostilities on the part of one or several third powers, the other contracting party will observe neutrality throughout the duration of the conflict.

Article 3. The present pact comes into force from the day of its ratification by both contracting parties and remains valid for five years. In case neither of the contracting parties denounces the pact one year

[1] *Tass*, April 13, 1941.

before expiration of the term, it will be considered automatically prolonged for the next five years.

Article 4. The present pact is subject to ratification as soon as possible. Instruments of ratification shall be exchanged in Tokyo also as soon as possible.

In confirmation whereof the above-named representatives signed the present pact in two copies, drawn up in the Russian and Japanese languages, and affixed thereto their seals.

Done in Moscow, April 13, 1941, which corresponds to the 13th day of the fourth month of the 16th year of Showa.

Signed by MOLOTOV, YOSUKE MATSUOKA,
YOSHITSUGU TATEKAWA.

Declaration

In conformity with the spirit of the neutrality pact concluded April 13, 1941, between the U.S.S.R. and Japan, the governments of the U.S.S.R. and Japan in the interests of insuring peaceful and friendly relations between the two countries, solemnly declare that the U.S.S.R. pledges to respect the territorial integrity and inviolability of Manchoukuo, and Japan pledges to respect the territorial integrity and inviolability of the Mongolian People's Republic.

Moscow, April 13, 1941, signed on behalf of the government of the U.S.S.R. by MOLOTOV; on behalf of the government of Japan by YOSUKE MATSUOKA and YOSHITSUGU TATEKAWA.

THE YALTA AGREEMENT REGARDING JAPAN,
FEBRUARY 11, 1945

The leaders of the three Great Powers—the Soviet Union, the United States of America and Great Britain—have agreed that in two or three months after Germany has surrendered and the war in Europe has terminated the Soviet Union shall enter into the war against Japan on the side of the Allies on condition that:

1. The status quo in Outer-Mongolia (The Mongolian People's Republic) shall be preserved;

2. The former rights of Russia violated by the treacherous attack of Japan in 1904 shall be restored, viz:

(a) the southern part of Sakhalin as well as all the islands adjacent to it shall be returned to the Soviet Union,

(b) the commercial port of Dairen shall be internationalized, the preeminent interests of the Soviet Union in this port being safeguarded and the lease of Port Arthur as a naval base of the USSR restored,

(c) the Chinese-Eastern Railroad and the South-Manchurian Railroad which provides an outlet to Dairen shall be jointly operated by the establishment of a joint Soviet-Chinese Company, it being understood that the preeminent interests of the Soviet Union shall be safeguarded and that China shall retain full sovereignty in Manchuria;

3. The Kuril islands shall be handed over to the Soviet Union.

It is understood, that the agreement concerning Outer-Mongolia and the ports and railroads referred to above will require concurrence of Generalissimo Chiang Kai-shek. The President will take measures in order to obtain this concurrence on advice from Marshal Stalin.

The Heads of the three Great Powers have agreed that these claims of the Soviet Union shall be unquestionably fulfilled after Japan has been defeated.

For its part the Soviet Union expresses its readiness to conclude with the National Government of China a pact of friendship and alliance between the USSR and China in order to render assistance to China with its armed forces for the purpose of liberating China from the Japanese yoke.

February 11, 1945

J. STALIN
FRANKLIN D. ROOSEVELT
WINSTON S. CHURCHILL

U.S.S.R. DECLARATION OF WAR ON JAPAN, AUGUST 8, 1945

After the defeat and capitulation of Hitlerite Germany, Japan remained the only great power which still stands for the continuation of the war.

The demand of the three powers, the United States, Great Britain and China, of July 26 for the unconditional surrender of the Japanese armed forces was rejected by Japan. Thus the proposal made by the Japanese Government to the Soviet Union for mediation in the Far East has lost all foundation.

Taking into account the refusal of Japan to capitulate, the Allies approached the Soviet Government with a proposal to join the war against Japanese aggression and thus shorten the duration of the war, reduce the number of casualties and contribute toward the most speedy restoration of peace.

True to its obligation as an Ally, the Soviet Government has accepted the proposal of the Allies and has joined in the declaration of the Allied powers of July 26.

The Soviet Government considers that this policy is the only means able to bring peace nearer, to free the people from further sacrifice and suffering and to give the Japanese people the opportunity of avoiding the danger of destruction suffered by Germany after her refusal to accept unconditional surrender.

In view of the above, the Soviet Government declares that from tomorrow, that is from August 9, the Soviet Union will consider herself in a state of war against Japan.

TREATY OF FRIENDSHIP AND ALLIANCE BETWEEN THE U.S.S.R. AND THE CHINESE REPUBLIC, AUGUST 14, 1945 [1]

The Presidium of the Supreme Council of the Union of Soviet Socialist Republics and the President of the National Government of the Chinese Republic,

desiring to strengthen the friendly relations existing between the Soviet Union and the Chinese Republic by means of an alliance of good neighborliness following military cooperation,

having decided to render each other assistance in the struggle against aggression on the part of enemies of the United Nations in this world war and cooperation in the war against Japan until its unconditional surrender,

expressing unswerving desire to cooperate in upholding peace and security for the good of the peoples of both countries and all freedom-loving nations,

acting in accordance with the principles affirmed in the common Declaration of the United Nations on the First of January, 1942, the Declaration of the Four Powers signed in Moscow on October 30, 1943, and in formation of the International Organization of the United Nations,

have decided to conclude with this aim the present treaty and have appointed as their plenipotentiaries:

The Presidium of the Supreme Council of the Union of Soviet Socialist Republics: Vyacheslav Mikhailovich Molotov, People's Commissar for Foreign Affairs of the Soviet Union;

The President of the National Government of the Chinese Republic: Wang Shih-chieh, Minister for Foreign Affairs of the Chinese Republic.

[1] *The New York Times,* August 27, 1945, p. 5.

These, after the exchange of their credentials in complete and due form, have agreed as below:

Article I

The high contracting parties have agreed together with the United Nations to wage war against Japan until final victory. The high contracting parties have promised to give each other all indispensable military and other assistance and support in this war.

Article II

The high contracting parties have pledged themselves not to enter into separate negotiations with Japan and not to conclude a peace agreement or armistice without mutual agreement with either the present Japanese Government or with any other Government or organ in power in Japan which will not clearly repudiate all aggressive intentions.

Article III

The high contracting powers have pledged themselves after the conclusion of the war against Japan to undertake mutually all existing measures in order to make it impossible to repeat the aggression and breach of peace by Japan. If one of the high contracting powers finds herself involved in military operations against Japan as a result of the aggression and breach of peace by Japan, the other high contracting party will give military and other assistance and support with the means at its disposal. This article remains in force until such time as, following the demand of the two high contracting parties, the responsibility shall be laid on the Organization of the United Nations for the prevention of further aggression on the part of Japan.

Article IV

Each of the high contracting parties pledges itself not to conclude any alliance whatsoever and not to take part in any coalition whatsoever directed against the other contracting party.

Article V

The high contracting parties, taking into consideration the interests of security and economic development of both parties, agree to work together in close and friendly cooperation after the conclusion of peace and to act according to the principles of mutual respect for their sovereignty and territorial entity and noninterference in the internal affairs of both contracting parties.

Article VI

The high contracting parties agree to give each other all possible economic assistance in the post-war period with a view to lightening and speeding up the national rehabilitation of both countries in order to make their contribution to the prosperity of the world.

Article VII

Nothing in this treaty should be interpreted in a way which would prejudice the rights and duties of both high contracting parties as members of the Organization of the United Nations.

Article VIII

The above treaty shall be ratified within the shortest possible time. The exchange of ratification documents will take place in Chungking as soon as possible.

The treaty comes into force immediately upon ratification and remains in force for a period of thirty years. Unless one of the high contracting parties should make one year before expiration of the treaty a declaration of its desire to denounce the agreement, the agreement will remain valid for an unlimited period. Each of the high contracting parties can terminate this agreement by giving one year's notice to the other high contracting party.

In confirmation of the above the plenipotentiaries have signed and sealed this treaty.

Drawn up in Moscow on the 14th of August 1945 which corresponds to the 14th day of August of the thirty-fourth year of the Chinese Republic, in two copies, each in the Russian and Chinese languages, both texts being equally valid.

As plenipotentiary of the Presidium of the Supreme Council of the Union of Soviet Socialist Republics

MOLOTOV

As plenipotentiary of the National Government of the Chinese Republic

WANG SHIH-CHIEH

AGREEMENT BETWEEN THE UNION OF SOVIET SOCIALIST REPUBLICS AND THE CHINESE REPUBLIC ON THE CHANGCHUN RAILWAY

AUGUST 14, 1945

The Presidium of the Supreme Council of the Union of Soviet Socialist Republics and the President of the National Government of the Chinese Republic, desiring to strengthen friendly relations and economic ties between the two countries on a basis of full equality and rights and interests of both parties, have agreed as to the following:

Article I

After expulsion of the Japanese armed forces from the Three Eastern Provinces of China the main trunk lines of the Chinese Eastern Railway and the South Manchuria Railway leading from the station of Manchuria (Manchouli) to the station of Pogranichnaya and from Harbin to Dalny (Dairen) and Port Arthur shall be joined into one railway system under the name of the Chinese Changchun Railway. This railway system will become the joint property of the Soviet Union and the Chinese Republic and will be jointly exploited by them. Only that land and those branch lines will be the joint property and will be jointly exploited which have been constructed by the Chinese Eastern Railway line in the period of Russian and joint Soviet and Chinese administration as well as the South Manchuria Railway during the period of Russian administration, which are intended for the direct requirements of these railways as well as subsidiary undertakings servicing these railways and constructed in the periods of time mentioned above.

All other railways and subsidiary undertakings will be the full property of the Chinese Government. The joint exploitation of the abovementioned railways will be carried out by one single administration under Chinese sovereignty as a purely commercial transport undertaking.

Article II

The contracting parties agree that the rights of common property of the above railway line belong to both parties equally and must not be transferred by either in full or in part.

Article III

The contracting parties with the aim of joint exploitation of the above railway, agree to set up a Sino-Soviet company of the Chinese Changchun Railway Company. An administration of ten members is being constituted for this company, five of them being appointed by the Chinese and five by the Russians. The administration will have its seat in the town of Changchun.

Article IV

The Chinese Government out of the members of the administration of the Chinese citizens appoints a chairman of administration and assistant chairman of administration.

The Soviet Government out of the Soviet citizens members of the administration appoints a deputy chairman of administration and a deputy assistant chairman of administration.

In decisions concerning administration, the chairman's vote counts as two. The legal quorum of administration is seven people.

All important questions which the administration agrees to defer must be handed over to the decision of the Governments of the contracting parties for just and friendly solution.

Article V

A commission of revision will be attached to the administration consisting of six members, of which three are appointed by the Chinese Government and three by the Soviet Government. The president of the revision committee will be elected from among the Soviet members. The deputy chairman will be elected from among the Chinese members. The chairman's vote counts as two. The quorum of the commission is five members.

Article VI

For current matters the administration will appoint a managing director of the Chinese Changchun Railway from among the Soviet members and a deputy managing director from among the Chinese members.

Article VII

The revision commission will appoint a chief controller and his deputy. The chief controller will be appointed from among the Chinese citizens and the deputy chief controller from among the Soviet citizens.

Article VIII

The directors and deputy directors of services and departments of the railway as well as station masters of the more important stations are to be appointed by the administration. The managing director has the right to suggest candidates for these posts. Single members of the administration can also suggest candidates, following the consent of the managing director of the railway.

Should the chief of a service or department be a Chinese citizen, the deputy chief must be a Soviet citizen. Should the chief of a service or department be a Soviet citizen, his deputy must be a Chinese citizen. Chiefs of services and departments will be appointed from among Soviet and Chinese citizens on a 50-50 basis.

Article IX

The Chinese Government has the responsibility of guarding the railway. For the guarding of the railway premises, equipment and other installations and in order that goods in transit should not be liable to destruction or loss or theft the Chinese Government will set up and control a railway police force. The railway police must at the same time maintain normal order on the railway. As to the duties of the police in carrying out the requirements of this article, these will be drawn up by the Chinese Government after consultation with the Soviet Government.

Article X

Only in a period of war against Japan can the railway be used for the transport of Soviet troops. The Soviet Government has the right to transport on this railway by transit without customs inspection military equipment in sealed carriages guarded by the railway police force, and the Soviet Union will not have its own armed escort.

Article XI

Goods transported on the railway by transit from one Soviet station to another and also from Soviet territory to the port of Dalny (Dairen) and Port Arthur or *vice versa* will not be subject to customs or any other duties by Chinese authorities. Such goods on arrival in Chinese territory are liable to customs examination.

Article XII

The Chinese Government pledges to supply the railway with coal according to a special agreement.

Article XIII

The railway line is subject to taxes in the same way as other Chinese State railways.

Article XIV

The contracting parties have agreed to supply the Chinese Changchun Railway administration with working capital in sums agreed upon in the Statutes of the Railway. Profits and loss from the exploitation of the line shall be divided between the two parties.

Article XV

The contracting parties within one month from the signing of the above agreement will appoint three representatives each, who, in Changchun, will work out a statute on the joint exploitation of the road. This statute must be drawn up within two months and will then be submitted to confirmation by both Governments.

Article XVI

The property which will go over to joint possession of the Union of Soviet Socialist Republics and the Chinese Republic and will be liable to joint exploitation according to Article I of the present agreement must be defined by a commission which must consist of three representatives of each Government.

This commission must be set up in Changchun within one month of the signature of the present agreement. This commission must end its work within three months of the beginning of joint exploitation of the railway and present its findings for confirmation by both Governments.

Article XVII

The present agreement has been concluded for a period of thirty years. After expiration of this period the Chinese Changchun Railway with all its property will revert to the full possession of the Chinese Government at free cost.

Article XVIII

The present agreement comes into force from the day of ratification.

Drawn up in Moscow the 14th of August, 1945, which corresponds to the 14th of August of the thirty-fourth year of the Chinese Republic, in two copies, each in the Russian and Chinese languages, both texts being equally valid.

MOLOTOV, for the Soviet Union;
WANG SHIH-CHIEH, for the Chinese Republic.

SOVIET-CHINESE AGREEMENT ON PORT ARTHUR

August 14, 1945

Both contracting parties, in accordance with the Soviet-Chinese Treaty of Friendship and Alliance, and as a supplementary section to it, have agreed upon the following:

1. With the aim of strengthening the security of China and the U.S.S.R. and the preventing of aggression again by Japan, the Government of the Chinese Republic agrees to joint utilization by both of the contracting parties of Port Arthur as a naval base.

2. The exact frontiers of the area of the naval base noted in the point above are defined in the description and map appended.

3. The contracting parties have agreed to turn Port Arthur into a purely naval base at the disposal of the battleships and merchant ships of China and the U.S.S.R. alone. A Chinese-Soviet military commission will be established on questions of the joint use of the above-named naval base. It is to consist of two Chinese and three Soviet representatives. The chairman of the commission is appointed by the Soviet side and the vice chairman by the Chinese side.

4. The defense of the above-noted naval base is given the Government of the U.S.S.R. by the Chinese Government. The Government of the U.S.S.R., with the aim of the defense of the naval base, establishes the necessary equipment, and the cost is borne by the Government of the U.S.S.R.

5. Civil administration in the given area belongs to China, and in making appointments for responsible leading posts the Chinese Government shall take into account the interests of the U.S.S.R. in the given area. The civil administration in the town of Port Arthur is appointed and dismissed by the Chinese Government by agreement with the Soviet military command.

Suggestions which the Soviet military command in this area makes to the Chinese civil administration with the aim of securing defense will be carried out by the Chinese administration. In disputable cases the question will be put for examination and decision by a Chinese-Soviet military commission.

6. The government of the U.S.S.R. has a right to maintain in the area noted in Point 2 its Army, Naval and Air Forces and determine their location.

7. The Soviet Government has also the task of establishing the maintenance of lighthouses, signals and other equipment necessary for the security of navigation in the given area.

8. When the agreement comes to an end all the equipment and public property put up by the U.S.S.R. in the given area is handed over without compensation and becomes the property of the Chinese Government.

9. The period of the present agreement is for thirty years. The agreement comes into force from the day of its ratification. The plenipotentiaries signed the above agreement and put their seals upon it.

Done in Moscow August 14, 1945, which is equivalent to August 14 of the thirty-fourth year of the Chinese Republic.

In two copies each in the Russian and Chinese languages and both texts have equal validity.

On behalf of the Presidium of the Supreme Soviet of the Union of Soviet Socialist Republics, MOLOTOV;

On behalf of the President of the National Government of the Chinese Republic, WANG SHIH-CHIEH.

SOVIET-CHINESE AGREEMENT ON PORT DAIREN

August 14, 1945

In view of the fact that the Treaty of Friendship and Alliance has been concluded between the Union of Soviet Socialist Republics and the Chinese Republic, also of the fact that the Union of Soviet Socialist Republics has guaranteed respect for Chinese sovereignty of the Three Eastern Provinces as an inseparable part of China, in order to insure the interests of the Union of Soviet Socialist Republics in Dairen as an import and export port of commodities, the Chinese Republic hereby expresses its consent:

1. to proclaim Dairen a free port open to trade and shipping of all countries;

2. to set aside for leasing to the U.S.S.R. piers and warehouses in the said free port on the basis of separate agreement.

3. Administration in Dairen will be exercised by China.

The chief of the port shall be appointed from among Soviet citizens by the manager of the Chinese Changchun Railway by agreement with the Mayor of the town of Dairen. The assistant chief of the port shall be appointed in the above way from among Chinese citizens.

During peacetime Dairen shall not be included in the sphere of operations of regulations on the naval base contained in the agreement on Port Arthur of August 14, 1945, and will become subject to the military regime established in the port only in event of war with Japan. Goods coming from abroad to this free port and transported over the Chinese Changchun Railway directly to the U.S.S.R., also goods coming from the U.S.S.R. over the above railways through the free port for export, or materials and equipment for the port installation coming from the U.S.S.R. are exempted from customs duties.

The above goods must be transmitted in sealed cars. Chinese import duties shall be levied on goods entering China through the free port. Goods exported from other parts of China to the free port are subject to export duties during the period while such continued to be levied in China.

The present agreement has been concluded for a term of thirty years. The present agreement comes into force as from the day of its ratification.

In testimony of which plenipotentiaries signed the present agreement and have fixed their seals thereto.

Done in Moscow August 14, 1945, which corresponds to August 14 of the thirty-fourth year of the Chinese Republic. In two copies each in Russian and Chinese languages, both texts having equal force.

Signed on the authorization of the Supreme Soviet of the U.S.S.R., MOLOTOV;

On the authorization of the Presidium of the National Government of the Chinese Republic, WANG SHIH-CHIEH.

SOVIET-CHINESE AGREEMENT ON THE THREE EASTERN PROVINCES

August 14, 1945

Agreement on relations between the Soviet commander-in-chief and the Chinese administration after the entry of Soviet troops into the territory of the Three Eastern Provinces of China in connection with the present joint war against Japan:

Relations between the Soviet commander-in-chief and the Chinese administration should correspond to the spirit of friendship and allied relations existing between the two countries.

Agreed on the following:

1. After the entry of Soviet troops as a result of hostilities into the territory of the Three Eastern Provinces of China, supreme authority and responsibility in the zone of hostilities in all questions relating to the prosecution of the war for the period necessary for operations shall rest with the commander-in-chief of the Soviet armed forces.

2. Representatives of the National Government of the Chinese Republic and the personnel shall be appointed for the restored territories who shall: (a) establish and direct in accordance with Chinese laws the administration on the territory cleared of the enemy; (b) render assistance in establishing cooperation in the restored territories between the Chinese armed forces both regular and irregular and the Soviet armed forces; (c) insure active collaboration between the Chinese administration and the Soviet commander-in-chief and in particular issue instructions to local organs to this effect being guided by the requirements and wishes of the Soviet commander-in-chief.

3. To insure contact between the Soviet commander-in-chief and the representatives of the National Government of the Chinese Republic a Chinese military mission will be appointed with the headquarters of the Soviet commander-in-chief.

4. In the zones under the supreme authority of the Soviet commander-in-chief the administration of the National Government of the Chinese Republic for the restored territory shall maintain contact with the Soviet commander-in-chief, through the representative of the National Government of the Chinese Republic.

5. As soon as any part of the restored territory ceases to be a zone of direct hostilities the National Government of the Chinese Republic shall assume full authority as regards civilian affairs and shall render the Soviet commander-in-chief every assistance and support through its civil and military organ.

6. All persons belonging to the Soviet armed forces on Chinese territory shall be under the jurisdiction of the Soviet commander-in-chief. All Chinese nationals, both civilian and military, shall be under Chinese jurisdiction. This jurisdiction shall also extend to the civilian population on Chinese territory, even in the event of crimes and offenses

against the Soviet armed forces, with the exception of crimes and offenses committed in the zone of hostilities which are subject to jurisdiction of the Soviet commander-in-chief. In disputable cases questions shall be decided in agreement between the Soviet commander-in-chief and the representative of the National Government of the Chinese Republic.

7. A separate agreement shall be concluded concerning financial questions involved in the entry of Soviet troops to the territory of the Three Eastern Provinces of China.

8. The present agreement comes into force immediately upon ratification of the Treaty of Friendship and Alliance between the U.S.S.R. and China signed on this date. Done in Moscow on August 14, 1945, which corresponds to August 14 of the thirty-fourth year of the Chinese Republic.

In two copies, each in Russian and Chinese languages, both the texts having equal force.

For the Presidium of the Supreme Council of the U.S.S.R., MOLOTOV; *For the President of the National Government of the Chinese Republic*, WANG SHIH-CHIEH.

EXCHANGE OF NOTES REGARDING SOVIET AID TO THE CENTRAL GOVERNMENT OF CHINA AND CHINESE SOVEREIGNTY OVER MANCHURIA AND SINKIANG

August 14, 1945

Honorable Mr. Minister, in connection with the signing on this date of the Treaty of Friendship and Alliance between China and the U.S.S.R. I have the honor of placing on record that the following provisions are understood by both contracting parties in the following way:

1. In accordance with the spirit of the above treaty and for the implementation of its general ideas and purposes the Soviet Government is ready to render China moral support and assistance with military equipment and other material resources, this support and assistance given fully to the National Government as the Central Government of China.

2. In the course of negotiations on the ports of Dairen and Port Arthur, also on the joint operation of the Chinese Changchun Railway, the Soviet Government regarded the Three Eastern Provinces

as part of China and again confirmed its respect for China's full sovereignty over the Three Eastern Provinces and recognition of their territorial and administrative integrity.

3. As to latest events in Sinkiang, the Soviet Government confirms that, as stated in Article V of the Treaty of Friendship and Alliance, it has no intention to interfere with China's internal affairs. In the event that you, Mr. Minister, confirm your agreement with such understanding of the above points, the present note and your answer to it shall constitute a part of the above Treaty of Friendship and Alliance. Accept, Mr. Minister, the assurances of my very high respect.

Molotov

In his note of reply Minister of Foreign Affairs of China Wang Shih-chieh declared his complete agreement with such understanding of the above stated points.

EXCHANGE OF NOTES REGARDING OUTER MONGOLIA

August 14, 1945

Mr. People's Commissar:

In view of the desire for independence repeatedly expressed by the people of Outer Mongolia, the Chinese Government declares that after Japan's defeat, if a plebiscite of the people of Outer Mongolia confirms this desire, the Chinese Government will recognize the independence of Outer Mongolia in her existing boundaries.

The above statement will be binding after the ratification of the Treaty of Friendship and Alliance signed by the Chinese Republic and the U.S.S.R. on August 14, 1945.

I beg you, Mr. People's Commissar, to accept the assurances of my very high respect.

Wang Shih-chieh

The note from People's Commissar of Foreign Affairs of the U.S.S.R. Molotov to Minister of Foreign Affairs of the Chinese Republic Wang Shih-chieh.

Mr. Minister:

Hereby I confirm receipt of your note in which you state that "in view of the desire for independence repeatedly expressed by the people

of Outer Mongolia the Chinese Government declares after Japan's
defeat, if a plebiscite of peoples of Outer Mongolia confirms this desire, the Chinese Government will recognize the independence of Outer
Mongolia in her existing boundaries. The above statement will be binding after the ratification of the Treaty of Friendship and Alliance signed
by the Chinese Republic and the U.S.S.R. on August 14, 1945."

The Soviet Government, with satisfaction, has taken note of the
above note of the Government of the Chinese Republic and declares
on its part that it will respect the state of independence and territorial
integrity of the Mongolian Peoples Republic. I beg you, Mr. Minister,
to accept the assurances of my very high respect.

MOLOTOV

COMMUNIQUE ON THE MOSCOW CONFERENCE OF THE THREE FOREIGN MINISTERS
DECEMBER 27, 1945

ESTABLISHMENT OF THE FAR EASTERN COMMISSION

Agreement was reached, with the concurrence of China, for the establishment of a Far Eastern Commission to take the place of the Far Eastern Advisory Commission. The Terms of Reference for the Far Eastern Commission are as follows:

I. Establishment of the Commission

A Far Eastern Commission is hereby established composed of the representatives of the Union of Soviet Socialist Republics, United Kingdom, United States, China, France, the Netherlands, Canada, Australia, New Zealand, India, and the Philippine Commonwealth.

II. Functions

A. The functions of the Far Eastern Commission shall be:

1. To formulate the policies, principles, and standards in conformity with which the fulfillment by Japan of its obligations under the Terms of Surrender may be accomplished.

2. To review, on the request of any member, any directive issued to the Supreme Commander for the Allied Powers or any action taken by the Supreme Commander involving policy decisions within the jurisdiction of the Commission.

3. To consider such other matters as may be assigned to it by agreement among the participating Governments reached in accordance with the voting procedure provided for in Article V-2 hereunder.

B. The Commission shall not make recommendations with regard to the conduct of military operations nor with regard to territorial adjustments.

C. The Commission in its activities will proceed from the fact that there has been formed an Allied Council for Japan and will respect existing control machinery in Japan, including the chain of command from the United States Government to the Supreme Commander and the Supreme Commander's command of occupation forces.

III. *Functions of the United States Government*

1. The United States Government shall prepare directives in accordance with policy decisions of the Commission and shall transmit them to the Supreme Commander through the appropriate United States Government agency. The Supreme Commander shall be charged with the implementation of the directives which express the policy decisions of the Commission.

2. If the Commission decides that any directive or action reviewed in accordance with Article II-A-2 should be modified, its decision shall be regarded as a policy decision.

3. The United States Government may issue interim directives to the Supreme Commander pending action by the Commission whenever urgent matters arise not covered by policies already formulated by the Commission; provided that any directives dealing with fundamental changes in the Japanese constitutional structure or in the regime of control, or dealing with a change in the Japanese Government as a whole will be issued only following consultation and following the attainment of agreement in the Far Eastern Commission.

4. All directives issued shall be filed with the Commission.

IV. *Other Methods of Consultation*

The establishment of the Commission shall not preclude the use of other methods of consultation on Far Eastern issues by the participating Governments.

V. *Composition*

1. The Far Eastern Commission shall consist of one representative of each of the States party to this agreement. The membership of the Commission may be increased by agreement among the participating Powers as conditions warrant by the addition of representatives of other United Nations in the Far East or having territories therein. The Commission shall provide for full and adequate consultations, as oc-

casion may require, with representatives of the United Nations not members of the Commission in regard to matters before the Commission which are of particular concern to such nations.

2. The Commission may take action by less than unanimous vote provided that action shall have the concurrence of at least a majority of all the representatives including the representatives of the four following Powers: United States, United Kingdom, Union of Soviet Socialist Republics and China.

VI. *Location and Organization*

1. The Far Eastern Commission shall have its headquarters in Washington. It may meet at other places as occasion requires, including Tokyo, if and when it deems it desirable to do so. It may make such arrangements through the Chairman as may be practicable for consultation with the Supreme Commander for the Allied Powers.

2. Each representative on the Commission may be accompanied by an appropriate staff comprising both civilian and military representation.

3. The Commission shall organize its secretariat, appoint such committees as may be deemed advisable, and otherwise perfect its organization and procedure.

VII. *Termination*

The Far Eastern Commission shall cease to function when a decision to that effect is taken by the concurrence of at least a majority of all the representatives including the representatives of the four following Powers: United States, United Kingdom, Union of Soviet Socialist Republics and China. Prior to the termination of its functions the Commission shall transfer to any interim or permanent security organization of which the participating governments are members those functions which may appropriately be transferred.

It was agreed that the Government of the United States on behalf of the four Powers should present the Terms of Reference to the other Governments specified in Article I and invite them to participate in the Commission on the revised basis.

COMMUNIQUE ON THE MOSCOW CONFERENCE OF THE THREE FOREIGN MINISTERS DECEMBER 27, 1945

ESTABLISHMENT OF THE ALLIED COUNCIL

The following agreement was . . . reached, with the concurrence of China, for the establishment of an Allied Council for Japan:

1. There shall be established an Allied Council with its seat in Tokyo under the chairmanship of the Supreme Commander for the Allied Powers (or his Deputy) for the purpose of consulting with and advising the Supreme Commander in regard to the implementation of the Terms of Surrender, the occupation and control of Japan, and of directives supplementary thereto; and for the purpose of exercising the control authority herein granted.

2. The membership of the Allied Council shall consist of the Supreme Commander (or his Deputy) who shall be Chairman and United States member; a Union of Soviet Socialist Republics member; a Chinese member; and a member representing jointly the United Kingdom, Australia, New Zealand, and India.

3. Each member shall be entitled to have an appropriate staff consisting of military and civilian advisers.

4. The Allied Council shall meet not less often than once every two weeks.

5. The Supreme Commander shall issue all orders for the implementation of the Terms of Surrender, the occupation and control of Japan, and directives supplementary thereto. In all cases action will be carried out under and through the Supreme Commander who is the sole executive authority for the Allied Powers in Japan. He will consult and advise with the Council in advance of the issuance of

orders on matters of substance, the exigencies of the situation permitting. His decisions upon these matters shall be controlling.

6. If, regarding the implementation of policy decisions of the Far Eastern Commission on questions concerning a change in the regime of control, fundamental changes in the Japanese constitutional structure, and a change in the Japanese Government as a whole, a member of the Council disagrees with the Supreme Commander (or his Deputy), the Supreme Commander will withhold the issuance of orders on these questions pending agreement thereon in the Far Eastern Commission.

7. In cases of necessity the Supreme Commander may take decisions concerning the change of individual Ministers of the Japanese Government, or concerning the filling of vacancies created by the resignation of individual cabinet members, after appropriate preliminary consultation with the representatives of the other Allied Powers on the Allied Council.

COMMUNIQUE ON THE MOSCOW CONFERENCE OF THE THREE FOREIGN MINISTERS
DECEMBER 28, 1945

EXCERPT PERTAINING TO KOREA

1. With a view to the re-establishment of Korea as an independent state, the creation of conditions for developing the country on democratic principles and the earliest possible liquidation of the disastrous results of the protracted Japanese domination in Korea, there shall be set up a provisional Korean democratic government which shall take all the necessary steps for developing the industry, transport and agriculture of Korea and the national culture of the Korean people.

2. In order to assist the formation of a provisional Korean government and with a view to the preliminary elaboration of the appropriate measures, there shall be established a joint commission consisting of representatives of the United States command in Southern Korea and the Soviet command in Northern Korea.

In preparing their proposals the commission shall consult with the Korean democratic parties and social organizations.

The recommendations worked out by the commission shall be presented for the consideration of the governments of the Union of Soviet Socialist Republics, China, the United Kingdom and the United States prior to final decision by the two governments represented on the joint commission.

3. It shall be the task of the joint commission, with the participation of the provisional Korean democratic government and of the Korean democratic organizations, to work out measures also for helping and assisting (trusteeship) the political, economic and social progress

of the Korean people, the development of democratic self-government and the establishment of the national independence of Korea.

The proposals of the joint commission shall be submitted, following consultation with the provisional Korean government for the joint consideration of the governments of the United States, Union of Soviet Socialist Republics, United Kingdom and China for the working out of an agreement concerning a four-power trusteeship of Korea for a period up to five years.

4. For the consideration of urgent problems affecting both Southern and Northern Korea and for the elaboration of measures establishing permanent coordination in administration-economic matters between the United States command in Southern Korea and the Soviet command in Northern Korea, a conference of the representatives of the United States and Soviet commands in Korea shall be convened within a period of two weeks.

BIBLIOGRAPHY

MANUSCRIPT SOURCES

OFFICIAL PAPERS (National Archives):
United States Department of State Archives, 1914–1932.

PRIVATE PAPERS (Division of Manuscripts, Library of Congress):

Ray Stannard Baker.
Tasker H. Bliss.
William Jennings Bryan.
Robert Lansing.

Breckinridge Long.
William Boyce Thompson.
Henry White.
Woodrow Wilson.

PUBLISHED SOURCES

OFFICIAL DOCUMENTS, TREATIES, ETC.:

Barbusse, Henri, *The Soviet Union and Peace: The Most Important of the Documents Issued by the Government of the U.S.S.R. Concerning Peace and Disarmament from 1917 to 1929*. Martin Lawrence, Ltd.: London, 1929.

British and Foreign State Papers, Vol. XI. London, 1841–1939.

Bunyan, James, *Intervention, Civil War, and Communism in Russia, April-December 1918*. Johns Hopkins Press: Baltimore, 1936.

Carnegie Endowment for International Peace, *Korea, Treaties and Agreements*. Division of International Law, Pamphlet No. 43: Washington, 1921.

———, *Shantung: Treaties and Agreements*. Division of International Law, Pamphlet No. 42: Washington, 1921.

———, *The Sino-Japanese Negotiations of 1915*. Division of International Law, Pamphlet No. 45: Washington, 1921.

———, *Treaties and Agreements with and Concerning China: 1919–*

1929. Division of International Law, Pamphlet No. 50: Washington, 1929.

Chicherin, George, *Two Years of Foreign Policy; the Relations of the RSFSR with Foreign Nations, from November 7, 1917, to November 7, 1919*. The Russian Soviet Government Bureau: New York, 1920.

Cumming, C. K., and Pettit, Walter W., comp. and ed., *Russian-American Relations, March, 1917–March, 1920, Documents and Papers*. Harcourt, Brace and Howe (for the League of Free Nations Association): New York, 1920.

Laloy, Emile, *Les documents secrets des archives du ministère des affaires étrangères de Russie, publiés par les Bolcheviks*. Paris, 1919.

Laserson, Max M., ed., "The Development of Soviet Foreign Policy in Europe, 1917–1942; A Selection of Documents." *International Conciliation*, No. 386. Carnegie Endowment for International Peace: New York, January, 1943.

League of Nations, *Appeal by the Chinese Government—Report of the Commission of Inquiry*. Series of League of Nations Publications: VII. Political 1932. VII. 12. Geneva, October 1, 1932.

————, *Treaty Series*, Vol. XXXIV, No. 866; Vol. XXXVII, No. 955. Published by the League of Nations: Geneva.

MacMurray, John V. A., ed., *Treaties and Agreements with and Concerning China, 1894–1919*, 2 vols. Carnegie Endowment for International Peace, Division of International Law: Washington, 1919.

Malloy, W. M., *Treaties, Conventions, International Acts, Protocols and Agreements Between the United States of America and Other Powers* (1776–1909), 2 vols. G.P.O.: Washington, 1910.

Richardson, J. D., *Messages and Papers of the Presidents*, Vol. 2. Prepared under the direction of the Joint Committee on Printing, of the House and Senate, Pursuant to an Act of the 52d Congress of the United States. Published by the Bureau of National Literature: Washington, 1913.

Union of Soviet Socialist Republics: Commissariat of Foreign Affairs, *Soviet-American Relations, 1918–1933*. (In Russian) Moscow, 1934.

United States Documents and Publications:
The Abrogation of the Russian Treaty, 62d Congress, 2d Session,

House Committee on Foreign Affairs, Report No. 179. G.P.O.: Washington, 1911.

American State Papers, Vols. III, V ("Foreign Relations."). Gales and Seaton: Washington, 1832ff.

America's Message to the Russian People, Addresses by members of the Special Diplomatic Mission of the United States to Russia in the year 1917. G.P.O.: Washington, 1918.

Conference on the Limitation of Armament, Washington, November 12, 1921–February 6, 1922. G.P.O.: Washington, 1922.

The Congressional Globe, Vol. XXX, 33d Congress, 2d Session. John C. Rives, ed.: Washington, 1855.

The Congressional Record, 1918–1920. G.P.O.: Washington.

Department of State Bulletin, 1940–1948. G.P.O.: Washington.

Establishment of Diplomatic Relations with the Union of Soviet Socialist Republics, Department of State, Publication No. 528, Eastern European Series No. 1. G.P.O.: Washington, 1933.

Exchange of Notes Between the United States and Japan, Canceling the Lansing-Ishii Agreement of November 2, 1917, Signed April 14, 1923, Treaty Series No. 667. G.P.O.: Washington, 1923.

Korea 1945–1948, Department of State Publication 3305, Far Eastern Series 28, October 1948.

Message from the President of the United States, Transmitting Report of William W. Rockhill, Late Commissioner to China, with Accompanying Documents, 57th Congress, 1st Session, Senate Document No. 67. G.P.O.: Washington, 1902.

Papers Relating to Foreign Affairs, 1862. (This series subsequently called *Papers Relating to the Foreign Relations of the United States*.) G.P.O.: Washington, 1862.

Papers Relating to the Foreign Relations of the United States, 1862–1932. G.P.O.: Washington.
  "The Lansing Papers, 1914–1920," 2 vols.
  "1918, Russia," 3 vols.
  "1919, Russia," 1 vol.
  "The Paris Peace Conference," Vols. 1–4, 7, 11.
  "Japan, 1931–1941," 2 vols.

Proceedings of the Alaskan Boundary Tribunal, Vol. II, 58th Congress, 2d Session, Senate Document No. 162. G.P.O.: Washington, 1904.

Russian Account of the Official Mission to Russia of Hon. G. V.

Fox, *in 1866.* (Translated for the Department of State by Buynitzky.) G.P.O.: Washington, 1867.

Wheeler-Bennett, John W., *Documents on International Affairs—1929.* Oxford University Press: London, 1930.

Woodhead, H. G. W., ed., *The China Year Book: 1924–5, 1929–30.* University of Chicago Press: Chicago, 1925, 1930.

BIOGRAPHIES, MEMOIRS, ETC.:

Adams, Charles Francis, ed., *The Memoirs of John Quincy Adams,* Vol. IV. J. B. Lippincott and Co.: Philadelphia, 1874–1877.

Adams, H., ed., *The Writings of Albert Gallatin,* Vol. I. J. B. Lippincott and Co.: Philadelphia, 1879.

Baker, G. E., ed., *The Works of William H. Seward,* Vol. III. Redfield Company: New York, 1853–1884.

Baker, Ray Stannard, *Woodrow Wilson: Life and Letters,* Vol. VIII. Doubleday, Page and Co.: New York, 1939.

Bryn-Jones, David, *Frank B. Kellogg.* G. P. Putnam's Sons: New York, 1937.

Buchanan, Sir George, *My Mission to Russia and Other Diplomatic Memoirs,* Vol. II. Little, Brown, and Co.: Boston, 1923.

Byrnes, James F., *Speaking Frankly.* Harper and Brothers: New York, 1947.

Croly, Herbert, *Willard Straight.* The Macmillan Company: New York, 1925.

Dennett, Tyler, *John Hay.* Dodd, Mead & Co.: New York, 1933.

———, *Roosevelt and the Russo-Japanese War.* Doubleday, Page and Co.: New York, 1925.

Dugdale, Blanche E. C., *Arthur James Balfour,* Vol. II. Hutchinson & Co., Ltd.: London, 1936.

Francis, David R., *Russia from the American Embassy, April, 1916–November, 1918.* Charles Scribner's Sons: New York, 1922.

Graves, William S., *America's Siberian Adventure, 1918–1920.* Jonathan Cape and Harrison Smith: New York, 1931.

Grew, Joseph C., *Ten Years in Japan.* Simon and Schuster, Inc.: New York, 1944.

Hard, William, *Raymond Robins' Own Story.* Harper and Brothers: New York, 1920.

Ishii, Viscount Kikujiro, *Diplomatic Commentaries.* (Trans. and ed. William R. Langdon.) Johns Hopkins Press: Baltimore, 1936.

Izvolski, Alexander, *Recollections of a Foreign Minister* (Memoirs of

Alexander Izvolski). (Trans. Louis Seeger.) Doubleday, Page and Co.: Garden City, N.Y., and Toronto, 1921.

Jefferson, Thomas, *Writings*, Vol. XI (Library Edition). Thomas Jefferson Memorial Association of the United States: Washington, 1903.

Kennan, George, *E. H. Harriman*, Vol. II. Houghton Mifflin Company: New York, 1922.

Lane, Franklin K., *The Letters of Franklin K. Lane, Personal and Political*. (Ed. Annie W. Lane and Louise Herrick Wall.) Houghton Mifflin Company: New York and Boston, 1922.

Lansing, Robert, *War Memoirs*. The Bobbs-Merrill Company: Indianapolis, 1935.

Lloyd George, David, *Memoirs of the Peace Conference*, Vol. I. Yale University Press: New Haven, 1939.

Lockhart, R. H. Bruce, *Memoirs of a British Agent*. G. P. Putnam's Sons: New York, 1932.

March, Peyton C., *The Nation at War*. Doubleday, Doran & Co.: New York, 1932.

Moore, John Bassett, ed., *The Works of James Buchanan*, Vol. II. J. B. Lippincott and Co.: Philadelphia, 1908–1910.

Nabokov, C., *The Ordeal of a Diplomat*. Duckworth and Company: London, 1921.

Noulens, Joseph, *Mon ambassade en Russie sovietique, 1917–1919*, Vol. II. Plôn: Paris, 1933.

Palmer, Frederick, *Bliss, Peacemaker*. Dodd, Mead & Co.: New York, 1934.

———, *Newton D. Baker*, Vol. II. Dodd, Mead & Co.: New York, 1931.

Pooley, A. M., ed., *The Secret Memoirs of Count Tadasu Hayashi*. E. Nash: London, 1915.

Pringle, Henry F., *Theodore Roosevelt*. Harcourt, Brace and Company: New York, 1931.

Reinsch, Paul S., *An American Diplomat in China*. Doubleday, Page and Co.: New York, 1922.

Roosevelt, Theodore, *An Autobiography*. Charles Scribner's Sons: New York, 1929.

Rosen, Baron, *Forty Years of Diplomacy*, Vol. I. Alfred A. Knopf: New York, 1922.

Sazonov, Serge, *Fateful Years, 1909–1916*. Frederick A. Stokes Co.: New York, 1928.

Seymour, Charles, ed., *The Intimate Papers of Colonel House*, Vol. III. Houghton Mifflin Company: Boston, 1928.

Thayer, William R., *Life and Letters of John Hay*, Vol. II. Houghton Mifflin Company: Boston, 1915.

White, T. H., ed., *The Stilwell Papers*. William Sloane Associates, Inc.: New York, 1948.

Yarmolinsky, Abraham, ed. and trans., *The Memoirs of Count Witte*. Doubleday, Page and Co.: Garden City, N.Y., and Toronto, 1921.

BOOKS, SPECIAL STUDIES, ARTICLES:

Ackerman, Carl W., *Trailing the Bolsheviki*. Charles Scribner's Sons: New York, 1919.

Adamov, E. A., "Russia and the United States at the Time of the Civil War." *Journal of Modern History*, Vol. II, 1930, pp. 586–602.

Adams, Ephraim D., *Great Britain and the American Civil War*, Vol. II. Longmans, Green & Co.: London, 1925.

American Foundation, Committee on Russian-American Relations, *The United States and the Soviet Union*. A Report on the Controlling Factors in the Relations Between the United States and the Soviet Union. New York, 1933.

Andrews, Clarence L., "Russian Plans for American Dominion." *Washington Historical Quarterly*, Vol. XVIII, pp. 83–92.

Bailey, Thomas A., *A Diplomatic History of the American People*. F. S. Crofts & Co.: New York, 1941.

———, "Why the United States Purchased Alaska." *Pacific Historical Review*, Vol. III, March, 1934, pp. 39–50.

Bakhmetev, Boris, "The Issue in Manchuria." *The Slavonic Review*, Vol. III, No. 23, December, 1929, pp. 305–314.

Barnes, Joseph, ed., *Empire in the East*. Doubleday, Doran & Co.: New York, 1934.

Barrows, David P., "Japan as our Ally in Siberia." *Asia*, Vol. XIX, September, 1919, pp. 727–731.

Bau, Mingchien J., *The Foreign Relations of China*. Rev. and enl. ed.; Fleming H. Revell Company: New York, 1922.

Bemis, Samuel Flagg, *A Diplomatic History of the United States*. Henry Holt & Co.: New York, 1936.

———, ed., *American Secretaries of State and Their Diplomacy*, Vol. X. Alfred A. Knopf: New York, 1929.

Bemis, Samuel Flagg, *The Diplomacy of the American Revolution*. D. Appleton–Century Co., Inc.: New York, 1935.

Bemis, Samuel F., and Griffin, Grace G., eds., *Guide to the Diplomatic History of the United States, 1775–1921*. G.P.O.: Washington, 1935.

Benns, F. Lee, *Europe Since 1914*. 6th ed.; F. S. Crofts & Co.: New York, 1945.

Beresford, Lord Charles, *The Break-up of China: With an Account of Its Present Commerce, Currency, Waterways, Armies, Railways, Politics, and Future Prospects*. Harper and Brothers: New York & London, 1899.

Biggerstaff, Knight, *The Far East and the United States*. Cornell University Curriculum Series in World History, No. 2. Cornell University Press: Ithaca, 1943.

Blakeslee, George H., *The Recent Foreign Policy of the U.S.A.* The Abingdon Press: New York, 1925.

Bland, J. O. P., *Recent Events and Present Policies in China*. William Heinemann: London, 1912.

Brebner, J. B., "Canada, the Anglo-Japanese Alliance and the Washington Conference." *Political Science Quarterly*, Vol. L, March, 1935.

Buell, Raymond L., *The Washington Conference*. D. Appleton and Company: New York, 1922.

Bullitt, William Christian, *The Bullitt Mission to Russia*. B. W. Huebsch: New York, 1919.

Callahan, James M., *Russo-American Relations During the American Civil War*. West Virginia University Studies in American History, Series 1, No. 1. West Virginia University Press: Morgantown, 1908.

Carnegie Endowment for International Peace, "Diplomatic Relations between the United States and Japan, 1908–1924." *International Conciliation*, No. 211. New York, 1925.

Carter, Gwendolyn W., *The British Commonwealth and International Security; The Role of the Dominions, 1919–1939*. The Ryerson Press: Toronto, 1947.

Chamberlin, William Henry, *The Russian Revolution*, Vol. II. The Macmillan Company: New York, 1935.

Churchill, Winston L. S., *The World Crisis—1918–1928. The Aftermath*. Charles Scribner's Sons: New York, 1929.

Clyde, Paul Hibbert, *International Rivalries in Manchuria, 1689–1922.* The Ohio State University Press: Columbus, 1926.

———, *United States Policy toward China: Diplomatic and Public Documents, 1839–1939.* Duke University Press: Durham, 1940.

Coates, W. P. and Z. K., *A History of Anglo-Soviet Relations.* Lawrence and Wishart: London, 1943.

Cocks, F. Seymour, ed., *The Secret Treaties and Understandings.* 2d. ed.; Union of Democratic Control: London, 1918.

Condliffe, J. B., ed., *Problems of the Pacific, 1927.* University of Chicago Press: Chicago, 1928.

Cooper, Russell M., *American Consultation in World Affairs.* The Macmillan Company: New York, 1934.

"Correspondence of the Russian Ministers in Washington, 1818–1825, I." *American Historical Review,* Vol. XVIII, 1913, pp. 309–345.

Council on Foreign Relations, *Survey of American Foreign Relations, 1930.* Yale University Press: New Haven, 1930.

Cresson, W. P., *The Holy Alliance. The European Background of the Monroe Doctrine.* Oxford University Press: New York, 1922.

Dallin, David J., *The Big Three. The United States, Britain, Russia.* Yale University Press: New Haven, 1945.

———, *Russia and Postwar Europe.* Yale University Press: New Haven, 1943.

———, *Soviet Russia and the Far East.* Yale University Press: New Haven, 1948.

———, *Soviet Russia's Foreign Policy, 1939–1942.* Yale University Press: New Haven, 1942.

Davies, Raymond A., and Steiger, Andrew J., *Soviet Asia, Democracy's First Line of Defense.* The Dial Press: New York, 1942.

Davis, Jerome, "One Hundred and Fifty Years of American-Russian Relations, 1777–1927." *Annals of the American Academy of Political and Social Science,* Vol. CXXXII, July, 1927.

Dennett, Tyler, *Americans in Eastern Asia.* The Macmillan Company: New York, 1922.

———, "The Open Door." In Barnes, Joseph, ed., *Empire in the East.* Doubleday, Doran & Co.: New York, 1934.

———, "The Open Door Policy as Intervention." *Annals of the American Academy of Political and Social Science,* Vol. CXXXVIII, September, 1933, pp. 78–83.

Dennett, Tyler, "Seward's Far Eastern Policy." *American Historical Review*, Vol. XXVIII, No. 1, October, 1922, pp. 45–62.

Dennis, A. L. P., *Adventures in American Diplomacy, 1896–1906.* E. P. Dutton & Co., Inc.: New York, 1928.

————, *The Foreign Policies of Soviet Russia.* E. P. Dutton & Co., Inc.: New York, 1924.

Dulles, Foster Rhea, *America in the Pacific: A Century of Expansion.* 2d ed.; Houghton Mifflin Company: New York and Boston, 1938.

————, *Forty Years of American-Japanese Relations.* D. Appleton–Century Co., Inc.: New York, 1937.

————, *The Road to Teheran.* Princeton University Press: Princeton, 1944.

Eyre, James E., Jr., "Russia and the American Acquisition of the Philippine Islands." *Mississippi Valley Historical Review*, Vol. XXVIII, 1942.

Fairbank, John King, *The United States and China.* Harvard University Press: Cambridge, 1948.

Far Eastern Republic, *Japanese Intervention in the Russian Far East.* Special Delegation of the Far Eastern Republic to the U.S.A. G.P.O.: Washington, 1922.

Fay, Sidney B., *Origins of the World War*, Vol. I. The Macmillan Company: New York, 1935.

Field, F. V., *American Participation in the China Consortiums.* University of Chicago Press: Chicago, 1931.

Fischer, Louis, *The Soviets in World Affairs*, 2 vols. Jonathan Cape: London, 1930.

Foster, John W.: *A Century of American Diplomacy.* Houghton Mifflin Company: New York, 1900.

————, *American Diplomacy in the Orient.* New ed.; Houghton Mifflin Company: New York and Boston, 1926.

Fox, William T., *The Super Powers.* Harcourt, Brace and Company: New York, 1944.

Golder, Frank A., "The American Civil War Through the Eyes of a Russian Diplomat." *American Historical Review*, Vol. XXVI, 1921, pp. 454–463.

————, "Catherine II and the American Revolution." *American Historical Review*, Vol. XXI, October, 1915.

————, "The Purchase of Alaska." *American Historical Review*, Vol. XXV, April, 1920, pp. 411–425.

———, "Russian American Relations during the Crimean War." *American Historical Review*, Vol. XXXI, 1926.

———, "The Russian Fleet and the Civil War." *American Historical Review*, Vol. XX, 1915.

———, "The Russian Offer of Mediation in the War of 1812." *Political Science Quarterly*, Vol. XXXI, No. 3, September, 1916.

Grace, W. F., "Russia and the Times in 1863 and 1873." *Cambridge Historical Journal*, Vol. I, No. 1, 1925, pp. 95–102.

Graham, Malbone W., "Russian-American Relations, 1917–33: An Interpretation." *American Political Science Review*, Vol. XXVIII, No. 3, June, 1934, pp. 387–409.

Griswold, A. Whitney, *The Far Eastern Policy of the United States*. Harcourt, Brace and Company: New York, 1938.

Haines, C. Grove, and Hoffman, Ross J. S., *The Origins and Background of the Second World War*. Oxford University Press: New York, 1943.

Hershey, Amos, *The International Law and Diplomacy of the Russo-Japanese War*. The Macmillan Company: New York, 1906.

Hildt, J. C., *Early Diplomatic Negotiations of the United States with Russia*. Johns Hopkins University Studies in Historical and Political Science, Vol. 24. Johns Hopkins Press: Baltimore, 1906.

Hishida, S., *Japan Among the Great Powers*. Longmans, Green & Co.: New York, London, Toronto, 1940.

Hornbeck, Stanley K., "American Policy and the Chinese-Russian Dispute." Address, Institute of Politics, Department of State, August 29, 1929. Reprinted in *Chinese Social and Political Science Review*, Vol. XIV, No. 1, Shanghai, January, 1930, pp. 41-60.

Hsu Shuhsi, "The Manchurian Question." In Condliffe, J. B., ed., *Problems of the Pacific*, 1929. University of Chicago Press: Chicago, 1930.

Hudson, G. F., *The Far East in World Politics*. 2d ed.; Oxford University Press: London, 1939.

Ichihashi, Yamato, *The Washington Conference and After*. Stanford University Press: Stanford, 1928.

Jaffe, Philip, *New Frontiers in Asia*. Alfred A. Knopf: New York, 1945.

Johnson, Willis Fletcher, *America's Foreign Relations*, Vol. I. The Century Co.: New York, 1916.

Joseph, Philip, *Foreign Diplomacy in China, 1894–1900*. G. Allen & Unwin Ltd.: London, 1928.

Chinese Social and Political Science Review, Vol. XVI, 1932–1933.

Pollard, Robert T., *China's Foreign Relations, 1917–1931*. The Macmillan Company: New York, 1933.

Pooley, A. M., *Japan's Foreign Policies*. G. Allen & Unwin Ltd.: London, 1920.

Pratt, Admiral William V. (U.S.N., Ret.), "Japan and the Pacific Problem." *Newsweek*, June 7, 1948, p. 32.

Price, E. B., *The Russo-Japanese Treaties of 1907–1916 Concerning Manchuria and Mongolia*. Johns Hopkins Press: Baltimore, 1933.

Quigley, H. Scott, "The Threat of War Between the Soviet Union and China." "II. The Struggle to Control the Chinese Eastern Railway." *Current History*, Vol. XXX, No. 6, September, 1929, pp. 1100–1110.

Quigley, H. Scott, and Blakeslee, George H., *The Far East*. World Peace Foundation: Boston, 1938.

Reinsch, Paul S., *World Politics at the End of the 19th Century as Influenced by the Oriental Situation*. The Macmillan Company: New York, 1900.

Rhodes, H. Winston, *Russia, the Coming Power in the Pacific*. Progressive Publishing Society: Wellington, New Zealand, 1945.

Robertson, William S., "Russia and the Emancipation of Spanish America." *Hispanic American Historical Review*, Vol. XXIV, 1941.

Romanov, Boris A., *Russia in Manchuria, 1892–1906*. (In Russian) Leningrad Asiatic Institute: Leningrad, 1928.

Savvin, V. P., *Relations between Tsarist Russia and the U.S.S.R. and China*. (In Russian) Moscow, 1930.

Schuman, Frederick L., *American Policy Toward Russia Since 1917*. International Publishers: New York, 1928.

———, *Soviet Politics at Home and Abroad*. Alfred A. Knopf: New York, 1946.

Shippee, L. B., "Oregon and the Diplomacy of 1821–1827." *Oregon Historical Society Quarterly*, Vol. XIX, 1918.

Simpson, Bertram Lenox (Pseud. B. L. Putnam-Weale), *The Coming Struggle in Eastern Asia*. Macmillan and Co., Ltd.: London, 1908.

Sorokin, Pitirim A., *Russia and the United States*. E. P. Dutton & Co., Inc.: New York, 1944.

Spargo, John, *Russia as an American Problem*. Harper and Brothers: New York, 1920.

Spector, Ivar, "Soviet Foreign Policy in the Pacific." In Mossé, Robert, ed., *Soviet Far East and Pacific Northwest*. University of Washington Press: Seattle, 1944.

Stalin, Joseph, *Leninism*, Vol. II. G. Allen & Unwin Ltd.: London, 1933.

Steiger, G. Nye, *A History of the Far East*. Ginn & Co.: New York, 1936.

Stewart, George, *The White Armies of Russia*. The Macmillan Company: New York, 1933.

Strakhovsky, Leonid, *Intervention at Archangel*. Princeton University Press: Princeton, 1944.

———, *The Origins of American Intervention in North Russia* (1918). Princeton University Press: Princeton, 1937.

Straus, O. S., "The United States and Russia: Their Historical Relations." *North American Review*. August, 1905.

Takeuchi, Tatsuji, *War and Diplomacy in the Japanese Empire*. Doubleday, Doran & Co.: Garden City, N.Y., 1935.

Tatum, E. H., Jr., *The United States and Europe, 1815–23*. University of California Press: Berkeley, 1936.

Thomas, B. P., *Russo-American Relations, 1815–1867*. Johns Hopkins University Studies in Historical and Political Science, Vol. 48, No. 2. Johns Hopkins Press: Baltimore, 1930.

Toynbee, Arnold J., ed., *Survey of International Affairs—1929; 1932*. Oxford University Press: New York, 1930, 1933.

Treat, Payson J., *Diplomatic Relations Between the United States and Japan, 1853–1895*, 2 vols. Stanford University Press: Stanford, 1932.

———, *Diplomatic Relations Between the United States and Japan, 1895–1905*. Stanford University Press: Stanford, 1938.

———, *The Far East*. Harper and Brothers: New York, 1935.

———, *Japan and the United States, 1853–1921*. Houghton Mifflin Company: New York and Boston, 1921.

Trotsky, Leon, *The History of the Russian Revolution*, Vol. I. Simon and Schuster, Inc.: New York, 1937.

Varneck, E., and Fisher, H. H., eds., *The Testimony of Kolchak*. Stanford University Press: Stanford, 1935.

Vernadsky, George, *Political and Diplomatic History of Russia*. Little, Brown and Co.: Boston, 1936.

Vinacke, Harold M., *A History of the Far East in Modern Times*. 2d. rev. ed.; F. S. Crofts & Co.: New York, 1936.

Wallace, Henry A. (and Steiger, Andrew J., collaborator), *Soviet Asia Mission*. Reynal and Hitchcock: New York, 1946.

Wang, C. C., "The Dispute between Russia and China." *Nineteenth Century and After*, Vol. CVII, No. 636, February, 1930, pp. 167–178.

Ward, A. S., and Gooch, G. P., eds., *The Cambridge History of British Foreign Policy, 1783–1919*, Vol. I. Cambridge University Press: Cambridge, 1922–1923.

Weigh, Ken S., *Russo-Chinese Diplomacy*. The Commercial Press, Ltd.: Shanghai, 1928.

White, T. H., and Jacoby, A., *Thunder Out of China*. William Sloane Associates, Inc.: New York, 1946.

Willoughby, Westel W., *Foreign Rights and Interests in China*, Vol. I. Johns Hopkins Press: Baltimore, 1927.

———, "The Sino-Japanese Controversy and the League of Nations." *American Journal of International Law*, Supplement, Vol. XXVII, 1933.

Wilton, Robert, "The Rush for Siberia: Causes of the Present Crisis in the Pacific." *Fortnightly Review*, Vol. CXVI, November, 1921, pp. 782–805.

Wood, G. Z., *The Twenty-One Demands: Japan versus China*. Fleming H. Revell Company: New York, 1921.

Woodhead, H. G. S., Arnold, J., and Norton, Henry K., *Occidental Interpretations of the Far Eastern Problem*. University of Chicago Press: Chicago, 1926.

Yakhontoff, Victor A., *Russia and the Soviet Union in the Far East*. Coward-McCann: New York, 1931.

Young, C. Walter, *The International Relations of Manchuria*. University of Chicago Press: Chicago, 1929.

———, *Japan's Special Position in Manchuria; Its Assertion, Legal Interpretation, and Present Meaning*. Johns Hopkins Press: Baltimore, 1931.

Zabriskie, Edward H., *American-Russian Rivalry in the Far East. A Study in Diplomacy and Power Politics, 1895–1914*. University of Pennsylvania Press: Philadelphia, 1946.

Ziff, William B., *Two Worlds. A Realistic Approach to the Problem of Keeping the Peace*. Harper and Brothers: New York, 1946.

PERIODICALS AND NEWSPAPERS:

Amerasia.
American Historical Review.
American Journal of International
Law.
American Political Science
Review.
Annals of the American Academy
of Political and Social Science.
Cambridge Historical Journal.
China Year Book.
Chinese Social and Political
Science Review.
Christian Science Monitor.
Economist.
Far Eastern Survey.
Foreign Affairs.
International Affairs.
International Conciliation.
International Organization.
Izvestia.
Journal of Modern History.

Mississippi Valley Historical
Review.
Nation.
Nation's Business.
New Republic.
New Times.
New York Times.
Newsweek.
Nineteenth Century and After.
North American Review.
Oregon Historical Society
Quarterly.
Pacific Historical Review.
Political Science Quarterly.
Pravda.
Russian Review.
Slavonic Review.
Soviet Press Translations.
Soviet Russia.
Soviet Russia Today.
Virginia Quarterly Review.
Washington Historical Quarterly.
Yale Review.

INDEX

Acheson, Dean, 288, 289
Adams, John Quincy, 7 ff.
Aigun, Treaty of (1858), 18
Alaska, sale of, 12-13
Alexander I, Tsar of Russia, 3, 6, 7, 8 ff.
Alexander II, Tsar of Russia, 12
All-Party Political Consultative Conference (P.C.C.), 313
Allied Council for Japan, 297, 299-303 *passim*; establishment of, by Moscow Conference (1945), 394-395
American Civil War, 10 ff.
American Military Advisory Group in China (M.A.G.I.C.), 315
American-Russian Treaty for the Advancement of General Peace (1915), 35
American-Russian Treaty of Commerce and Navigation (1832), 10, 14
Amur Republic, 152, 153
Amur River, 17, 18, 65, 147
Anglo-Japanese Alliance (1902), 20, 21, 31, 163-166 *passim*, 171, 179 n., 184
Anti-Comintern Pact (1936), 282, 284
Arnold, Archibald V., 327
Atcheson, George, Jr., 301, 302
Australia, 298, 299, 302, 303, 331, 334
Austria, 7, 184, 247

Baker, Newton D., 114 n.; attitude toward Siberian intervention,
    * Cited.

76 n., 84, 117 n., 131 n., 132 n.
Baker, Ray Stannard, c.* 82 n.
Bakhmetev, Boris, 48-49, 104, 112, 118, 133, 160, 170, 171 n., 192, 193, 199
Baku Conference, 191
Balance of power, xii, xiii, 8, 20, 22, 24, 29, 31, 36, 47, 89, 133, 137, 140, 146, 162, 165, 180, 188, 190, 245, 248, 257, 258, 262, 263, 276, 277, 281, 284-289 *passim*, 310, 312, 336 ff.
Balfour, Arthur James, 53; and Siberian intervention, 59-60, 67
Ball, William McMahon, 302
Barbusse, H., c. 100 n., c. 102 n.
Bau, Mingchien J., c. 340 n.
Bell, Edward, 148, 157, 159 n., 212 n.
Benson, Admiral William S., 77
Berton, Samuel R., 48 n.
Bevin, Ernest, 299
Bliss, General Tasker H., 70-71
Bolshevism, 51, 85, 98, 101, 102, 104 n., 107, 111, 118, 138, 143, 153, 159 n., 197, 245, 262. See also Communism
Borah, William E., 137
Borodin, Michael, 196
Boxer Rebellion, 20, 208
Brest-Litovsk, Treaty of, 49, 59, 60 ff., 65
Briand, Aristide, 227
Brodie, Edward E., 255 n.
Brodovsky, S., 229 n.
Brooklyn, U.S.S., 66
Brukhanov, 227 n.

Brunow, Baron, 11
Brussels Conference (1937), 279
Bryan, William Jennings, 32-35 *passim*
Bryn-Jones, David, c. 241 n.
Bullitt, William C., 268, 315; and Siberian intervention, 57; mission to Russia (1918), 101
Byrnes, James F., 295-299 *passim*, 325

Cairo Conference (1943), 318
Cairo Declaration (1943), 308
Caldwell, John K., 104 n., 107, 150, 157, 175, 176
Canada, 164 n., 298, 331
Castle, William R., Jr., 225, 252 n.
Cecil, Lord Robert, 53, 53 n.
Central powers, 40, 50, 58, 59, 62, 65, 66, 81, 97, 116
Chamberlain, Neville, 270
Chang Hsueh-liang, 229, 232, 234, 243, 244
Chang Tso-lin, 131, 203, 212, 220, 229
Changchun Conference, 181, 182, 183
Changchun Railway, Sino-Soviet Agreement (1945) on, 380-384
Cheliabinsk, affair at, 73
Chennault, Claire, 315
Chiang Kai-shek, 220, 232, 274, 282, 283, 294, 308, 311-317 *passim*
Chiang Kai-shek, Mme., 316, 317
Chicherin, Georges, 64, 74, 99, 100, 168 n., 186, 199, 202, 213
China, and Twenty-one Demands, 33; internal disunity of, 33-34; entrance into World War I, 41; and Chinese Eastern Railroad, 79, 128, 160, 172, 174, 200-209 *passim*, 220, 221; and Inter-Allied operation of Siberian railroads, 128; and Washington Conference, 172, 173, 176, 203, 209 n.; severs relations with Soviet Union, 218; restores relations with Soviet Union, 250, 258; and Allied occupation of Japan, 302, 303, 304. *See also*

Japan, Intervention in Siberia, Manchuria, Mongolia, Russia
Chinese Eastern Railroad, 19, 64 n., 79, 83, 114, 119, 120, 121, 124, 126, 128, 131, 132, 139, 143, 153, 158, 160, 161, 162, 171, 173 n., 178, 200, 201, 202, 206 ff., 216, 217, 220, 221, 227, 229, 233, 236, 238 ff., 249, 250, 283, 294, 308, 310; Sino-Soviet Agreement (1924) on, 207 ff., 215, 221, 223-224, 227, 356-363. *See also* Changchun Railway, China, Japan, Sino-Soviet dispute, Soviet Union, U.S.A.
Chinese Eastern Railroad Corporation, 19, 173
Chistiakov, General, 327
Chita Republic, 152, 153, 154
Churchill, Winston S., 101, 273, 294, 308
Clemenceau, Georges, 52, 59, 101
Cocks, F. Seymour, c. 41 n.
Cohen, B., 296
Colby, Bainbridge, 144, 148-153 *passim*, 159 n.
Coleman, Frederick W. B., 186 n., 227 n., 240
Communism, 51, 59-64 *passim*, 85, 97, 105, 118, 137, 143, 146, 183, 188 ff., 194, 196, 222, 245, 250 ff., 270, 282, 290, 303, 307, 312 ff., 318. *See also* Bolshevism
Communist International (Comintern), 169, 190, 196, 215, 268, 269
Communist Party, Chinese, 196, 311, 312; Russian, 145, 214, 227 n.
Condliffe, J. B., c. 340 n., c. 343 n.
Congress, U.S., and Crimean War, 10; abrogation of Commercial Treaty of 1832, 14; and Siberian intervention, 87, 115, 135-136, 137; House of Representatives, 271; House Committee on Un-American Activities, 282; Senate Appropriations Committee on Marshall Aid for China, 315
Congress of Vienna, 7, 16
Constantine, Grand Duke, 12

Convention of 1824 (American-Russian), 10
Coolidge, Calvin, 187, 199, 210
Crane, Charles R., 48 n.
Crane, Richard, 154, 156, 193
Crimean War, 10, 12
Curzon, Lord, 164
Czechoslovakia, 247, 270; troops in Siberia, 51, 72-86 *passim*, 89, 91 ff., 99, 103, 113, 118, 119, 135, 138, 150, 154, 178, 209 n.; and Inter-Allied operation of Siberian railroads, 127 n.

Dairen, 19, 294, 308, 310, 312; Conference at, 150 n., 156, 157, 175, 176, 181; Sino-Soviet Agreement (1945) on, 385-386
Daladier, Edouard, 270
Daniels, Josephus, 75, 82 n.
Daschkoff, André, 7
Davis, John W., 165 n.
Davis, Major W. J., 155
Debuchi, Katsuji, 216, 252 n., 258, 259
Declaration of London (1915), 35
Dennis, A. L. P., c. 36 n., c. 71 n., c. 153 n., c. 179 n.
Derevyanko, Kuzma, 301
Dies, Martin, 282
Dingell, John, 271
Dugdale, Blanche E. C., c. 53 n.
Dulles, Foster Rhea, c. 76 n.
Dumbarton Oaks Conference (1944), 288
Duncan, James, 48 n.
Duranty, Walter, c. 226 n.

Egypt, 159 n.
El Salvador, 331
Eliot, Charles, *apologia* of Japanese imperialism in Asia, 159 n.
Emerson, Colonel, 48, 69, 119, 122
Esthonia, 270, 271
Ethiopia, 275
Export-Import Bank, 279

Far Eastern Advisory Commission, 298, 299, 300

Far Eastern Commission, 297, 300, 301, 304; establishment of, by Moscow Conference (1945), 391-393
Far Eastern Republic, 145, 150-160 *passim*, 168, 170, 176, 183, 184, 197, 201, 202, 205; and U.S.A., 154 ff., 181; and Washington Conference, 169, 170, 175, 176, 179
Fascism, 282
Fellers, Bonner, 305
Field, F. V., c. 28 n.
Finland, 61 n., 101, 271
Fischer, Louis, 229 n.
Five-Year Plan, 227, 250
Four-Power Pacific Treaty (1922), 171, 179 n.
Fourteen Points, 99; Point Six of, 99 n.
Fox, Gustavus, 13 n.
France, 11, 16, 18, 20 n., 25, 27, 28, 41, 49, 73, 84, 91, 100, 121, 146, 163, 166 n., 167, 170, 171, 193, 237 n., 248, 270, 272, 279, 280, 281, 291, 298, 331, 337; and Siberian intervention, 51-86 *passim*, 90 ff.; relations with Kolchak Government, 105, 107; attitude toward General Graves, 108; and Inter-Allied operation of Siberian railroads, 123, 127 n., 160; and Chinese Eastern Railroad, 206, 207; and Sino-Soviet dispute, 225, 228, 235
Francis, David R., 37-41 *passim*, 49, 53, 61, 67, 73, c. 74 n., 76, 98 n.; attitude toward Siberian intervention, 56, 62; and communism, 98
Frazier, Arthur H., 70 n.
Fullerton, H. S., 256 n., 258 n.

Gauss, Clarence E., 311
Germany, 16, 20 n., 28, 39, 40, 41, 48-57 *passim*, 60 ff., 67, 70 ff., 84, 94, 163, 184, 228, 229, 231, 234, 235, 236, 242, 248, 269 ff., 284, 288, 291 ff., 302, 337. *See also* Third Reich
Glennon, James H., 48 n.

Goering, Hermann, 279
Golder, Frank A., 11, c. 12 n.
Gorchakov, Alexander M., 12
Goto, Baron, 70, 121-126 *passim*, 217
Graham, M. W., 261, c. 261 n.
Graves, General William S., c. 66 n., c. 85 n., 87, 90, 93, c. 109 n., 113-117 *passim*, 159; and Siberian intervention, 89, 107 ff., 116, 117; departure from Siberia, 139
Grew, Joseph C., 250, 259, c. 259 n., 262, c. 262 n., 277, c. 277 n., 278, c. 278 n.
Griswold, A. Whitney, c. 34 n., c. 79 n.
Gromyko, Andrei, 289, 330, 331

Halifax, Lord, 289
Hanson, George Charles, 197, 206 n., 211, 212 n., 216, 217
Hara, 118, 129, 176
Harding, Warren G., 164, 199; Administration of, 144, 145, 163
Harriman, E. H., 25, 26
Harriman, W. Averell, 273, 299
Harris, E. L., 92, 104, 107, 108, 117, 120
Harris, Major General P. C., 110 n.
Harrison, Leland, 218
Hart, Admiral Thomas C., 305, 315
Harvey, George, 164 n.
Hay, John, 20 n., 21
Hildt, J. C., c. 7 n.
Hitchcock, Gilbert M., 100
Hitler, A., 249, 269, 270, 272, 273, 337
Hoare, Sir Samuel, 270
Hodge, Lieutenant General John R., 322, 323, 326, 327, 332, 333
Hoffman, Paul G., 316
Holy Alliance, 7 ff.
Hornbeck, Stanley, 259
Horvat, D. L., 64, 65, 121; Siberian government of, 78; agreement with China regarding Chinese Eastern Railroad, 79
House, Colonel Edward M., 53, 55, 58 n., 60 n., 78 n.; and Siberian intervention, 57, 72
Howard, Sir Esme, 230
Hughes, Charles Evans, 146, 149, 152, 156, 157 n., 164-184 *passim*, 199, 202-213 *passim*
Hull, Cordell, 269, 289
Hungerford, R. S., 98 n.
Hurley, Major General Patrick J., 311

Ichihashi, Yamato, c. 166 n., c. 177 n.
India, 299, 300, 302, 305, 331, 332
Indo-China, 279
Inter-Allied Treaties, 1915, 40, 49; 1917, 41, 43, 49, 162, 184
Intervention in North Russia, 85 n., 90, 91, 98, 99
Intervention in Siberia, 47-141; U.S.A. and, 47, 50-98 *passim*; Allies and, 50-86 *passim*, 90 ff., 99; reasons given for, 51, 54-55, 65, 67, 74, 80, 97 n., 99, 138, 140; evaluation of American role in, 139 ff.; effect on Siberian people of, 140; effect on Soviet-Western relations of, 140. *See also* China, France, Japan, Soviet Union, United Kingdom, U.S.A.
Ishii, Viscount Kikujiro, 36, c. 36 n., 42, c. 42 n., 43, 67, 78, 81, 83, 105, 127
Isolation, in American foreign policy, 5, 19, 267, 269, 275, 279, 282
Italy, 20 n., 49, 127 n., 146, 167, 184, 193, 228, 234, 235, 236, 269, 275, 291
Izvestia, 145 n., 168, 179 n., 185 n., 186, 195, 197, 207, 210, 228, 238, 240, 242, 254

Japan, 150, 151, 174, 175 ff., 182, 183; emergence as Pacific power, 17; annexation of Korea, 23; gains in World War I, 30 ff., 43, 162-163; entrance into World War I, 31, 43; and Twenty-one Demands, 32 ff., 43; and Lansing-Ishii Agreement, 42-43; and Siberian intervention, 51-86 *passim*, 91, 94 ff., 129, 139, 150, 151, 174, 175 ff., 182, 183; and Chinese Eastern Railroad, 54, 78, 79, 82, 97, 113-114, 123, 124, 130, 131, 135, 136, 144, 151, 152, 158-161 *passim*, 165, 172, 174; relations with Semenov, 105, 106, 111, 130, 152, 176; and Inter-Allied operation of Siberian railroads, 121-135 *passim*, 139; and evacuation of troops from Siberia, 143, 183, 184, 204; and Far Eastern Republic, 152, 153, 165, 166 n., 175, 176, 182; and Dairen Conference, 156-157, 165, 175, 176, 177; and Washington Conference, 165 ff., 176 ff., 181; and Sino-Soviet dispute, 225, 228, 233 ff., 242, 246; and Manchurian "incident," 247, 248, 251, 255, 257, 259, 274, 276, 278; and Sino-Japanese War (1937–1945), 283, 284; results of Allied occupation in, 303. *See also* China, Korea, Russia, Soviet Union

Jefferson, Thomas, 3, 6, 7
Jenkins, Douglas, 60, 198 n.
Joffe, A. A., 185, 196, 197, 198, 205
Johnson, Hiram, 136 n., 259
Johnson, Nelson T., 163 n., 216 n., 230, 231
Johnson Act, 268
Jusserand, J. J., 81 n., 90

Kalinin, M. I., 260
Kalmykov, General, 131
Kamchatka, province of, 153, 186
Karakhan, L. M., 185, 186, 200, 207, 208-213 *passim*, 217, 218, 221, 227, 229
Karsky, M., 256, 257
Kato, Baron, 32, 34
Kawakami, K. K., c. 175 n.
Kellogg, Frank B., 215, 216 n.
Kellogg-Briand Peace Pact, 222-230 *passim*, 234-244 *passim*, 253 ff., 276; reservation *in re*, 236 f. *See also* Pact of Paris

Kerensky, Alexander, 49, 153, 170, 175
Kestler, Pai, 169 n.
Khabarovsk Protocol, 243
Kim Il Sung, 323
Kim Koo, 332
Kimm Kiusic, 332
King, William H., 42, 271
Kinoshita, 124
Knight, Admiral Austin M., 64, 75
Knox, General Sir Alfred, 108-109
Knox neutralization proposals, 26-27
Kolchak, Alexander, 64, 101, 102, 106-110 *passim*, 127, 129, 132, 133, 159 n.; split with Semenov, 68; execution of, 118, 135
Kolchak Government, 105, 110 ff., 114, 115, 130, 159 n.; establishment of, 103; union with Ufa Government, 104; collapse of, 115 ff., 119, 135, 137 n.; and Inter-Allied operation of Siberian railroads, 127. *See also* Omsk Government
Komura Treaty (1905), 22-23
Koo, V. K. Wellington, 82, 96, 173 n., 197
Korea, 17-23 *passim*, 26, 150, 151, 159 n., 169, 175, 176, 217, 278, 291, 305, 318, 319, 320-335, 337; annexation of, by Japan, 23; American-Soviet occupation of, 319-334; Joint American-Soviet Commission in, 324, 325, 326-330; Moscow Conference (1945) and, 324-330; United Nations and, 329 ff., 334-335; Republic of, 334, 335 n.; Moscow Conference Communiqué on, 396-397. *See also* China, Japan, Russia, Soviet Union
Krasnoshchekov, Alexander M., 153, 154, 157
Kuomintang, 196, 214, 215, 218, 253 n., 283, 311 ff., 316 ff. *See also* Nationalist Party
Kurile Islands, 294
Kuropatkin, General A. N., 20
Kwantung Army (Japanese), 276, 278-279

Ladejinsky, W. I., c. 306 n.
LaGuardia, Fiorello H., 271
Lansing, Robert, 37-43 *passim*, 60 n.,
 67, 70 n., 72, 76 n., 90, 98 n., 104,
 109, 111 n., 114 n., 118, 120, 129,
 137, 139, 165 n.; and Siberian intervention, 54-57 *passim*, 67, 68,
 75, 78, 89, 91, 95, 113, 117, 138;
 and communism, 63, 67-68, 98;
 and Kolchak Government, 107,
 117 n., 137 n.
Lansing-Ishii Agreement (1917), 39,
 42-43, 82, 184
Latvia, 270, 271
Lauterbach, Richard E., 301, c.
 301 n.
Laval, Pierre, 270
League of Nations, 112, 133, 151,
 163, 233, 239, 248, 250, 253, 255,
 258, 270, 274, 276, 277; and Manchurian "incident," 248, 251-255
 passim, 258, 274, 275
Lend-Lease, 273, 288, 313
Lenin, V. I., 53, 70, 103, 142,
 150
Lewis, James Hamilton, 85 n.
Li-Lobanov Treaty (1896), 19, 79.
 See also Russo-Chinese Treaty
 (1896)
Limitation of naval armaments, 162-
 166 *passim*, 171, 276
Lincoln, Abraham, Administration
 of, 11
Lithuania, 101, 256, 257, 271
Litvinov, M., 237 n., 238, 239, 250,
 260, 261, 268, 277
Lloyd George, 101, c. 101 n., c.
 102 n.
Locarno Pact, 223, 274
Lockhart, R. H. Bruce, 72, c. 73 n., c.
 76 n.
London Conference (1945), 299
London Naval Treaty (1930), 278
London *Times*, 244
Long, Breckinridge, 82, 95, 137,
 192 n.
von Ludendorff, Erich, 57
Lytton Commission, 253, 253 n.
Lytton Report, 252, 255 n.

MacArthur, General Douglas, 297-
 304 *passim*, 315
McCormick, Cyrus H., 48 n.
McCormick, John W., 271
McCoy, General Frank, 301
Macgowan, David B., 66
MacMurray, John V. A., c. 37 n.,
 79 n., 82, 215, 217, 218, 222, 226,
 229, 233 n.; attitude toward Kolchak Government, 106 n.
MacVeagh, Charles, 216
Maiski, Ivan, c. 153 n.
Malevski, 34
Malloy, W. M., c. 14 n.
Manchu Government, 17, 18, 33
Manchukuo, 276, 278, 283
Manchuria, 17, 20-28 *passim*, 32, 78,
 79, 82, 95, 96, 114, 119, 123 ff.,
 128 ff., 135, 143, 146, 151, 152,
 159 n., 197, 203, 208, 212, 216,
 217, 220-235 *passim*, 239, 240,
 244 n., 247-259 *passim*, 276, 278,
 281, 283, 284, 294, 308-317 *pas-
 sim*; Sino-Soviet Agreement (1945)
 on, 388-389. *See also* China, Chi-
 nese Eastern Railroad, Intervention
 in Siberia, Japan, Russia, Soviet
 Union
March, General Peyton C., 77, c.
 78 n.
Maritime Republic, 152, 153
Marshall, General George C., 316,
 327 ff., 338; mission to China,
 311 ff.
Marshall Plan, 315, 317, 337, 338
Martens, L. A. K., 103 n.
Marxism, 60, 146, 189
Marye, George Thomas, 36
Masaryk, Thomas G., 66
Mayer, F., 213
Menon, K. P. S., 332
Millard, T. F., c. 40 n.
Molotov, V. M., 187, 254, 272, 297,
 299, 327 ff.
Mongolia, 26, 28, 32, 168, 192, 198,
 199 n., 208, 212, 216, 253 n., 283,
 294, 308; Sino-Soviet Agreement
 (1945) on, 389-390. *See also*
 China, Russia, Soviet Union

Monroe, James, 9
Monroe Doctrine, 5, 9
Moore, R. Walton, 260 n.
Morris, Roland S., 68, 78, 79, 82 n., 94, 95, 106, 110, 111 n., 113, 120-130 *passim*, 143, 147; and Siberian intervention, 93, 104, 105, 107 n., 113-117 *passim*, 151, 153 n., 159 n.; critique of American-Japanese relations, 134
Moscow Conference, 1941, 273; 1943, 289, 296; 1945, 300, 324, 325, 330, 389-397
Motono, 42
Mott, John R., 48 n.
Mussolini, B., 269
Myers, 233 n.

Nakajima, General, 69
Napoleon Bonaparte, 7, 16
Nationalist Party (China), 189, 196, 214. *See also* Kuomintang
Nazi-Soviet Non-Aggression Treaty (1939), 270, 284
Nazism, 282
Nerchinsk, Treaty of (1689), 17
Netherlands, 298
Netherlands Indies, 278
Neville, E. L., 225 n., 250 n.
New Zealand, 298, 299, 302, 303
Nicholas II, Tsar of Russia, 21
Nielsen, O. N., 66
Nikolaievsk, 144, 147-150 *passim*; massacre of Japanese subjects in, 147, 153, 157, 177
Nine-Power Treaty (1922), 255, 258, 279
Nishi-Rosen Agreement (1898), 19
North Atlantic Treaty (1949), 337
North Korean People's Republic, 322, 323, 334
North Sakhalin Island, 144, 147 n., 152, 153, 158, 182, 186; Japanese occupation of (1920), 147, 148, 155, 165, 177, 178, 183, 184; evacuation of Japanese troops from, 184-188 *passim*
Norway, 184
Noulens, Joseph, 76, c. 76 n.

Official Gazette (Japan), 143
Oi, General, 150
Omsk Government, 107, 109, 112 ff., 115, 117, 118, 120, 133; election of Kolchak as dictator, 105; pleas for American aid, 106; collapse of, 115 ff., 137-138. *See also* Kolchak Government
Oumansky, Constantine A., 272

Packer, E. L., 257 n.
Pact of Paris, 228, 231-237 *passim*, 240, 241, 274. *See also* Kellogg-Briand Peace Pact
Paikes, 202
Palmer, F., c. 77 n.
Panay, U.S.S., 279
Paris Peace Conference, 87, 89, 114, 163; policy toward Soviet Government, 100 ff., 107; policy toward Kolchak Government, 110 ff., 115
Pearl Harbor, 30, 263, 273, 280, 285, 292
Peking, Treaty of (1860), 18
Perkins, B. A., 250 n.
Perry, Admiral Matthew C., 17
Pershing, General John J., 71
Philippine Islands (and Republic), 19, 23 n., 24, 256, 257, 278, 298, 303, 331
Pichon, Stephen, 59
Pinkney, William, 8
Poland, 12, 101, 271, 320, 337
de Poletica, Pierre, 8
Polk, Frank L., 59 n., 63 n., 81, 82 n., 106, 107, 110, 125, 127, 131, 132 n., 136, 193; attitude toward General Graves, 109
Poole, DeWitt C., 100, 157 n., 205
Poole, General, 91, 92
Popov, Admiral, 12
Port Arthur, 19, 21, 294, 308, 310, 312; Sino-Soviet Agreement (1945) on, 384-385
Portsmouth, Treaty of (1905), 22, 24 ff.
Potsdam Conference (1945), 295, 297, 319

Pratt, Admiral William V., 305, c. 305 n.
Pravda, 145, 168, 251, 292
Prince, J. D., 213 n.
Prinkipo Conference, 101, 110
Prussia, 7

Radek, Karl, 183
Radzutsk, Jan, 226
Reading, Lord, 68, 77 n.
Red Army, 198, 230
Reinsch, Paul S., 31, 32, 66, 69, 75, 128, 131; and Lansing-Ishii Agreement, 42; and Siberian intervention, 56, 74
Rhee, Syngman, 323, 332 ff.
Robins, Raymond, 48 n., 61, 64
Rodgers, Admiral, 107
Roosevelt, Franklin D., 260, 261, 268, 271, 277, 289, 294, 295, 308, 319
Roosevelt, Theodore, 20 n., 181; and Russo-Japanese War, 21-22; and Treaty of Portsmouth, 22; and balance of power, 24
Root, Elihu, 173; head of Special Diplomatic Mission to Russia, 48; and Siberian intervention, 57
Root-Takahira Agreement (1908), 26
Rowe, D. N., c. 294 n.
Rozanov, General, 117
Russell, Charles Edward, 48 n.
Russia, geography of, 5-6; alliance with Napoleon, 7; recognition of U.S.A., 7; visit of fleet to New York and San Francisco, 11-12; attitude of Tsarist Government toward Jews, 14, 22; entente with England, 14; early relations with China, 17-18; and Twenty-one Demands, 34. *See also* China, Chinese Eastern Railroad, Manchuria, Russian Revolution (March 1917), Russian Revolution (November 1917), Russian Provisional Government, Soviet Union
Russian-American Company, 9, 12
Russian Provisional Government, 47 ff., 104, 119, 122, 126, 170, 192, 193, 199, 210; American recognition of, 47; and Siberian intervention, 56, 71, 93; at Paris Peace Conference, 100, 101; and American evacuation of Siberia, 135
Russian Railroad Service Corps, 48, 119, 120, 122
Russian Revolution, March 1917, 41, 47, 50; November 1917, 47 ff., 56, 73, 90, 190, 252 n., 254
Russo-Asiatic Bank, 19, 124, 173-174, 201
Russo-Chinese Bank. *See* Russo-Asiatic Bank
Russo-Chinese Treaty (1896), 128, 201 ff. *See also* Li-Lobanov Treaty
Russo-Finnish War (1939–1940), 271, 272
Russo-Japanese Convention, 1925, 90, 181, 186, 187, 212, 213, 365-371; 1928, 217, 225
Russo-Japanese Fisheries Convention (1928), 217
Russo-Japanese Neutrality Pact (1941), 272, 283, 284, 292, 295, 296, 372-373
Russo-Japanese Treaty, 1907, 25-26, 37 n., 38 n.; 1910, 27, 37 n.; 1912, 27-28, 34; 1916, 35 ff., 37-43 *passim*
Russo-Japanese War (1904–1905), 18, 21, 181, 320; America and, 21 ff.
Rykov, Alexei, 207 n.

Sazonov, Serge, 34-39 *passim*, 133
Schurman, Jacob Gould, 157, 169 n., 172, 197, 202, 203, 204, 206, 234
Scott, Hugh L., 48 n.
Semenov, Gregory, 64, 71, 103, 107, 108, 130 ff., 154, 155, 160, 175; split with Kolchak, 68, 105, 106; support of, by Japan, 105, 106, 111, 152. *See also* Japan
Serebriakov, L., 216
Seward, William H., 11, 13
Seymour, Charles, c. 60 n.
Sharp, William G., 70 n.
Sherrill, Charles H., 257 n.

Shidehara, Baron Kijuro, 111 n., 139, 147, 148 n., 157, 176 ff., 225
Shimonoseki, Treaty of (1895), 17-18
Shtikov, Terentyi, 325, 326
Siam, 278
Siberia, anti-Soviet groups within, 64-65, 68, 97, 98, 129, 137, 140; German and Austrian prisoners in, 51, 66, 71, 73, 77, 81, 99; autonomous governments in, 103, 152, 153
Siberian railroads, Inter-Allied plan for operation of, 120, 123, 126-134 *passim*, 138, 158, 160, 161, 172, 201, 203, 204, 229
Simanovsky, 234-235
Sinclair Corporation, 183
Sinkiang, Sino-Soviet Agreement (1945) on, 388-389
Sino-Japanese Agreements (March, May, 1918), 69, 82, 96, 119, 162
Sino-Japanese War (1894–1895), 17-18
Sino-Japanese War (1937–1945), 279
Sino-Russian Treaty (1902), 20
Sino-Soviet Agreements (1924), 200, 207-212 *passim*, 221, 223-224, 227, 231, 245, 252 n., 283, 347-359, 359-364; Chinese violation of, 221 ff., 230, 231
Sino-Soviet dispute (1929), 129, 220-246 *passim*, 248; America and, 222-246 *passim*; United Kingdom and, 225, 228, 230, 231, 235, 236, 238; France and, 225, 228, 235, 236, 238; Japan and, 225, 228, 233-238 *passim*, 242, 246; Italy and, 228, 234 ff.; Germany and, 228, 231-236 *passim*, 242
Sino-Soviet Non-Aggression Pact (1937), 284
Sino-Soviet Treaty (1945), 310, 312, 317, 377-390
Skvirsky, Boris, 205, 257 n.
Slaughter, Major H. H., 114 n.
Slocum, Lieutenant Colonel S. L. H., 108 n.

Smidovitch, I., 227 n.
Smirnov, 227 n.
Smith, Charles H., 107, 127, 145, 148, 149
Smith, E. N., 98 n.
Soukine, 114; and General Graves, 116-117
South America, 7 ff.
South Manchurian Railroad, 172, 247, 248, 294, 308, 310
South Sakhalin Island, 294
Soviet Union, and Siberian intervention, 60 ff., 98 ff.; and Far Eastern Republic, 152 ff., 169, 184, 261; and Washington Conference, 167 ff., 172 n., 178-179, 181, 202; and Chinese Eastern Railroad, 190, 200-201, 202, 205 ff., 211, 216, 217, 220, 224, 249 ff., 283, 294; Declaration of 1919, 191, 192, 197, 198, 205, 252 n., 340-343; Declaration of 1920, 191, 197, 198, 201, 205, 252 n., 343-346; and Manchurian "incident," 249 ff., 254-262 *passim*, 276, 277; and Sino-Japanese War (1937–1945), 282-283; declaration of war on Japan (1945), 297, 310, 376; and Allied occupation of Japan, 299, 300 ff., 304; policy toward Korea, 319-334, 335 n.
Spain, 9; Spanish-American War, 5; and South American colonies, 7 ff.; Spanish Civil War, 270
Spring-Rice, Sir Cecil, 53 n.
Stalin, J., 214, 221, 262, 270, 271, 295, 296, 299, 308, 319
Steinhardt, Laurence, 271, 272
Stevens, John F., 48, 119, 121 ff., 125 ff., 132 n., 151, 152, 166 n., 176; and Siberian intervention, 56; and railroads in Siberia, 120, 124 ff., 129-131, 135
Stilwell, General Joseph W., 311
Stimson, Henry L., 223-244 *passim*, 250 n., 255, 256 n., 257 n., 258
de Stoeckl, Baron Eduard, 12-13
Sturmer, M., 37 n.
Sun Yat-sen, 33, 189, 196, 214

Supreme Commander for the Allied Powers (S.C.A.P.), 301, 303, 306, 307

Supreme War Council, and Siberian intervention, 55-56, 59, 70

Switzerland, 297

Syria, 331

Taft, William Howard, 26, 181

Taft-Katsura Agreement (1905), 23 n.

Taiping Rebellion, 18

Tanaka, Baron Giiche, 64, 118, 129

Teheran Conference (1943), 319

Terauchi, J., 57, 113

Third International, 191

Third Reich, 270. *See also* Germany

Thomas, B. P., c. 10 n., c. 11 n.

Thomas, Edward B., 182 n.

Thompson, Colonel William Boyd, 48

Thomson, Alfred R., 66

Togo, Shigenori, 297

Trans-Baikal, district of, 106, 152, 153, 217

Trans-Siberian Railroad, 18, 48, 62, 69, 108, 119, 120, 126, 129 ff., 136, 139, 205. *See also* Intervention in Siberia

Treaty of Tilsit, 7

Trotsky, Leon, 49, 62, 97, 142; and Siberian intervention, 71-72; and Czechoslovak troops, 73

Troyanovsky, Alexander, 262

Truman, Harry S., 296 ff., 314, 317

Truman Doctrine, 303

Tuck, S. Pinkney, 199

Tumulty, Joseph P., 110 n.

Turkey, 256

de Tuyll, Baron, 9

Twenty-one Demands, 32 ff.; and Sino-Japanese Agreement (1915), 37, 162

U.S.A., principles of foreign policy, 5; emergence as Pacific power, 19; and open-door doctrine, 5, 16-17, 20, 23, 27, 33, 37, 86, 136, 146, 149, 160 n., 165, 179, 262, 276, 277, 279, 280, 310; and Russo-Japanese

War, 21-22; and most-favored-nation clause, 5, 16-17, 23; and international consortium, 28, 30, 35, 161; and Twenty-one Demands, 32 ff.; and Russo-Japanese Treaty (1916), 35 ff., 39-40; entrance into World War I, 39; and Lansing-Ishii Agreement, 42-43, 47; and Siberian intervention, 47, 50-98 *passim*; and nonrecognition of Soviet Union, 49, 50, 85, 102-103, 144, 146, 183, 199, 200, 210, 223, 238-246 *passim*, 256, 257, 260, 263, 267, 269; sympathy for Czechoslovak troops in Siberia, 74 ff., 77 ff.; *aide-memoire* (July, 1918), 79-80; and Chinese Eastern Railroad, 79, 89, 126, 128, 130, 131, 136, 158, 160, 161, 171, 172, 174, 192, 201-209 *passim*; *aide-memoire* (August 3 1918), 83-84, 87-93 *passim*, 103, 108, 111, 136 n., 154, 261, 262; reasons for withdrawal from Siberia, 89, 131-139 *passim*; public reaction to Siberian intervention, 87, 89, 94, 115, 135, 137; and Kolchak Government, 103, 105 ff., 109 ff., 113 ff., 117, 118, 127; and Inter-Allied operation of Siberian railroads, 120-139 *passim*, 201; and evacuation of Siberia, 139, 142; and Japanese occupation of Sakhalin, 148, 149; and Far Eastern Republic, 155, 157, 158; and protection of Russian interests in China, 191, 193, 201, 222, 223, 243, 245; and Sino-Soviet dispute, 222-246; and Manchurian "incident," 248, 251-259 *passim*, 263, 278; and recognition of Soviet Union, 249, 257-263 *passim*, 267, 268, 277, 278, 285; and Russo-Finnish War, 271-272; and Nazi-Soviet War, 273; and Sino-Japanese War (1937–1945), 279, 280; and Allied occupation of Japan, 297-307; and Chinese Civil War, 308, 311-318; policy toward Korea, 319-334

Uchida, Baron Kosai, 126, 160
Ufa, formation of government at, 104; union with Kolchak Government, 104
Ughet, Serge, 199
Ukrainian Soviet Socialist Republic, 331, 332
Ungern Sternberg, Baron, 198
United Kingdom, 7, 9, 11 ff., 14, 16, 18, 19, 25, 27, 28, 41, 49, 80-81, 121, 137 138, 146, 163, 166 n., 167, 171, 179 n., 184, 196, 214, 215, 237 n., 249 n., 251, 252, 270, 272, 277 ff., 281, 288, 291, 296, 298-307 *passim*, 324, 329, 330, 337; and American-Russian friendship, 5 ff., 10, 14, 29; and open-door doctrine, 23-24; and Twenty-one Demands, 33; and Siberian intervention, 51-86 *passim*, 90 ff.; occupation of Murmansk, 61 n.; relations with Kolchak Government, 105, 107, 109; attitude toward General Graves, 108, 109; and Inter-Allied operation of Siberian railroads, 123, 127 n., 159 n., 160, 161, 172, 204; and American evacuation of Siberia, 133, 135, 159; and Chinese Eastern Railroad, 163, 203; and recognition of Soviet Union, 184; and Sino-Soviet dispute, 225, 228, 235, 236; Battle of Britain, 272
United Nations, 293, 298
United Nations Organization, 291, 307, 325, 329, 338, 339; Charter of, 296; and Korea, 329 ff., 334-335; General Assembly, 330, 331, 334; Korean Commission, 331, 332, 334; Interim Assembly, 332
Ussuri Railroad, 122

V-E Day, 289
V-J Day, 298, 302, 304, 310, 318, 320
Vagts, Alfred, c. 21 n.
Valdai Hills, 6
Van Deman, Lieutenant Colonel Ralph H., 108 n.

Verkneudinsk Republic, 152, 153
Versailles Treaty, 114, 115, 137, 151, 162, 184
Vladivostok Government, 150-155 *passim*
Vyshinsky, A., 330

Wang, C. C., 203
Warren, Charles B., 176, 182 n., 183
Washington Conference (1921–1922), 30, 89, 142, 146, 160-181 *passim*, 184, 203, 212, 214, 216, 247, 258; and Chinese Eastern Railroad, 171 ff., 178, 202-210 *passim*
Wedemeyer, Lieutenant General Albert G., 314, 315
Weigh, Ken S., c. 209 n.
Welles, Sumner, 271, 272
White, John C., 186 n.
Williams, E. T., 37 n.
Wilson, Woodrow, 28, 32, 36, 47, 53, 54, 56, 65, 72, 77 n., 78 n., 81 n., 82 n., 85 n., 99, 110 n., 114, 115, 118, 133, 137, 149, 162, 163, 188; and Lansing-Ishii Agreement, 42; and Siberian intervention, 55, 57-86 *passim*, 91, 92, 95, 100, 136, 140, 141; message to Russian people (March, 1918), 61; and Soviet Union, 85, 101, 102; and Czechoslovak troops in Siberia, 92; and Kolchak Government, 110 ff.
Wiseman, Sir William, 58 n.
World Economic Conference (1933), 260
World War I, 30, 40-41, 50, 53, 68, 97, 162, 163
World War II, 270, 274, 280, 287, 288, 290-298 *passim*, 308, 310
Wu, C. C., 224, 225, 230, 239

Yakhontoff, Victor A., c. 38 n., 221
Yalta Agreement (1945), 294 ff., 298, 308, 310, 311, 312, 374-375
Yalta Conference (1945), 294, 308, 311, 319
Yen, H., 173 n., 203
Yoshida, Shigeru, 303

Young, C. Walter, c. 359 n.
Yourin, Ignatius, 154 ff.
Yuan Shih-kai, 33, 196

Zabriskie, Edward H., c. 21 n., c. 27 n.
Zaibatsu, 303